THE GROWING EDGE

Teaching and Learning through The Bodyworks

Helen H. Johnson

Foreword by Parker J. Palmer

Illustrations by Heather W. Eccleston

Photographs by the author

GEMINI PRESS][•][AMHERST, MASSACHUSETTS

Published by][•][Gemini Press, 506 Pine Street, Amherst MA 01002
Text design by Dede Heath
Typeset in Adobe Sabon and Gill Sans
Printed and bound by Versa Press

Publisher's Cataloging in Publication

Johnson, Helen H.
The growing edge: teaching and learning through the Bodyworks / Helen H. Johnson; foreword by Parker J. Palmer; illustrations by Heather W. Eccleston; photographs by the author.
p. cm.
Includes bibliographical references and index.
LCCN: 96–75348.
ISBN 0–9650964–0–8
1. Early childhood education. 2. Science—Study and teaching (Early childhood) 3. Mind and body in children. I. Title.
LB1139.23.J64 1996 372.3'044
QB196–20150

---

7 50
81C

More praise for the growing edge

(continued from back cover)

"It's a 10! A real life "Magic School Bus" journey, as the children gain a greater awareness of themselves as members of the human race."
–Sandra Elsas, kindergarten teacher, Morton, IL

". . . Makes such sense and feels so true. I see people in great pain who were inadequately supported in the sixth sense. . . . Everyone! Quick! Read this! Time's a wastin'!"**–Jenifer McKenna, psychotherapist**

"In her clear, melodic voice, Sandy captures the spirit of lifelong learning. Through her insightful chronicle of teaching young children about the mystery and beauty of their bodies, she bridges personal and communal respect, mutual responsibility and an awareness that all life is sacred. This joyful book is a must-read for anyone who cares about the well-being of humanity and its interdependent relationship with the earth."**–Robert Olney, elementary science and health teacher, and trustee, Maine Audubon Society**

"I know firsthand the value of Sandy's work. My son's experience with The Bodyworks enriched our whole family. Now I find *The Growing Edge* moving, insightful, and relevant to my practice as a child psychologist."**–Elizabeth Shea Clement, Ph.D., parent, child psychologist**

"Children in my multi-age primary classroom were animated, enthusiastic, and energized throughout our three-month study of The Bodyworks." **–Barbara Yarbrough, primary teacher, Glasgow, KY**

". . . A boon to teachers, parents, and observers of humankind."
–Margaret Wagner, headmistress, Louise S. McGehee School, LA

". . . Helped emphasize hands-on learning, learning over time. It showed my college students everything true for them is true for children."
– Sandy Tucker, instructor in human development, MiraCosta College, CA

"I can't wait to put The Bodyworks into action with girls from six to fifteen as a lead in to Preventing Adolescent Pregnancy (Girls, Inc. curriculum)."**–Romy Amos, executive director, Alameda County Girls' Club, CA**

". . . Written in the vivid, disarming style of a storyteller. I became quite attached to the characters and would love to see a sequel five years from now!"**–Jennifer Sage Smith, Community Outreach Coordinator, C. Everett Koop Institute**

This book is dedicated

to the memory of Elise Logan Eccleston, my firstborn,

who broke me open and made me new,

to Sylvia Duncan Harry Macdonald, my mother,

the creator of "the molecule dance,"

whose love of words and books brimmed over,

and to Mark Peter Johnson, my husband,

who is the lion and the rock in my life.

Contents

Week 3. The Brain 51

Week 4. Digestive Tract, Lungs 82

Acknowledgments

I'm deeply grateful for the wisdom, support, encouragement, and affection of friends and family during the long gestation of this book.

In particular, I thank my colleagues at the Gorse Child Study Center, Mount Holyoke College: Susannah Heard; Patricia Ramsey; Valerie Sawka; Barbara Sweeney; our teaching interns, Pamela Molochko and Heather Wright; and former staff members Marguerite Davol, Susan Jensen, Kim Bressem, and Donna Lucia.

I wish I could mention by name all the wonderful children and their wonderful parents; without them there would be no story.

Friends and family have responded to portions of the manuscript at various stages. I'm grateful to Dee DeGeiso, Jean Harlan, Mary Johnson, Sheila Kelley, Mary Ellen Miller, Johanna Plaut, Tom Plaut, Criss Quigley, Patty Ramsey, Valerie Sawka, Pat Schneider, Jodi Searle, Liz Shea, Edith Sullwold, Kenton Tharp, Diane Westfall, and the amazing women of Pat Schneider's Thursday Writers' Workshop.

Others have offered creative listening and valuable ideas at critical moments. A heartfelt thank-you to Peggy Dutton, Cricket Eccleston, Mary Johnson, Margaret Lobenstine, Nancy Platner, and Barry Wadsworth. Jenny McKenna provided professional perspective in the original crisis.

I bow to the wise women of the Wednesday morning Interbeing sangha, and to Nikki Cobb, who recognized the ripeness.

Paul Langdon, Tim Toffoli, Abby Fox, Teena Johnson-Smith, Kevin Prime, and the staff of the Faculty Resource Center, especially Anjali Sridhar, have graciously shared technical expertise, as have Bill Belmonte, Joshua Carey, and Tibby Wagner.

Many people, including Agostinho Coutinho, Joan Ericson, Chelvanaya Gabriel, Dick Johnson, John Lemly, and Beth Walker, have interrupted their work to help me with mine.

Sandra Elsas introduced *The Growing Edge* to Versa Press. Joan Grenier gave it a home at the Odyssey BookShop.

Pamela Molochko has helped me juggle the roles of teacher and learner.

Mark Johnson has picked up the pieces.

Many Mount Holyoke College students have contributed observations, insights, and energy. I particularly remember Emily Bucy, Jill Farrell, Robin Franklin, Gillian Keller, Kim Murdoch, Caryn O'Toole, Rebecca Piccone, K Soysa, Jenny Wackerle, and Sophie Yohani.

Also, Rhodora Agana, Shelley Bagoley, Angela Barbieri, Clara Beshoar, Carolyn Cartelli, Lisa Osgood Curtin, Adria DeLeonibus, Beth Donahue, Kathleen Driscoll, Margaret Ellis, Elena Fichera, Kate Foley, Deb Frank, Susan Granville, Amy Green, Heather Holbrook, Meredith Huffman, Jennifer Johan, Rachel Joyce, Laura Jukins, Sarah Kidd, Maggie Koong, Natalie LaCroix, Carol Lasquade, Nancy McComish, Colleen McQuillen, Peggy O'Shea, Chinda Peou, Jennifer Putnam, Amy Robbins, Laurie Russell, Faith SanFelice, Cara Testa, Kristin VanDerStucken, Julie Washburn, Kate Weeber, Cary Williams, Amy Wise, Shaad Yans, Maria Zavala, and Regina Zerne.

I've been blessed by teachers who inspired, challenged, and guided me, especially Gail Little and the late Janet Yancey of the Louise S. McGehee School, the late William R. Hogan and Henry Kmen of Tulane University, Peter Elbow of the University of Massachusetts, Pat Schneider of Amherst Writers and Artists, and Edith Sullwold, Ph.D.

Many writers, scientists, and artists have inspired me, their work seeping in so deep I can no longer trace the sources. I owe a great debt to all the anonymous teachers whose shoulders I stand on.

Without Tom Plaut's energy, advice, support, and grant for "Bogglers," *The Growing Edge* would never have been finished. Without Dede Heath's talents, skills, and generosity, it would never have been published. I thank Dede, Tom, and Johanna Plaut more than I can say.

Foreword

Do we in the west fully understand the price we have paid for a culture that elevates intellect and spirit at the expense of the body? In a thousand subtle ways, we are taught to regard the flesh as a downward drag on our lives—lives that might otherwise soar free on the wings of thought and contemplation. Riddled with needs, which must be met, and filled with wants, which can be obsessive, the human body is viewed as little more than a necessary evil: it is the earthly vehicle of our minds and spirits, but it must be disciplined and transcended whenever possible.

Education in the western world has, for the most part, done little more than transmit this anti-body bias in an unbroken string from one generation to the next. Our schools educate the mind, first and foremost; we sometimes educate the will; we occasionally remember to educate the conscience; but rarely if ever do we educate the body—except in those universities where big money can be made for success in the "sports" arena!

Of course, our denial or repression of the body has a shadow side, and in our culture the shadow is clear: the human body itself has become our secret obsession. Pornographic disrespect for the body lurks in every realm of our lives from advertising to male-female relations to religion. Our denial of the flesh masks a powerful and altogether natural fascination with the flesh—but in a culture that regards the body as a thing of the night, that fascination cannot be brought into the day's full light.

As a student of western culture I thought I understood these things. But not until I read Helen Johnson's superb book, *The Growing Edge,* did I understand the depth of the price we pay for our bias against the flesh. Even more important, not until I read this book did I understand that there is a proven and practical way to help the next generation grow up without inflicting on them my own generation's wounded image of the body.

Helen Johnson's book is written on the firm foundation of eight years of experience with "The Bodyworks," a nursery school curriculum that she designed and implemented at the Gorse Child Study Center at Mount Holyoke College. Working with four-year-olds, she has found wondrous ways to introduce them to the workings of their own bodies at an age when their fascination is strong but not yet distorted. How I wish I had experienced such teaching in my preschool years! Such simple knowledge of my body might have saved me much grief, physical and psychological, in later years.

But *The Growing Edge* is not only about a "health and hygiene" curriculum, as it was obtusely named when I was in school. Helen Johnson has found ways to help her students—and an older reader like myself—connect knowledge of their bodies with knowledge of all things human and divine. As Johnson says about the way the children's interests unfold as they grow with this curriculum, ". . . most things surface sooner or later in some form, especially the Biggies: sex, death, poops, 'the other,' and God."

That single sentence makes it clear that Helen Johnson has the wonderful gift of naming these realities and their relationships openly and honestly and with humor. But given the sensitivities that surround the topic, it is also important to note that her approach is not "in your face." Instead, it is premised on the deepest respect for the integrity of the student and the student's family, and for the sacredness of the subjects that the curriculum evokes.

The results of this reverence for students and subject are remarkable and far-reaching—and *The Growing Edge* is full of stories that prove the point. One of my favorite tales is about a preschool youngster named Clint.

At the family dinner table one night, his older brothers told an ugly racist joke based on differences in physical features. As the parents struggled to respond, Clint spoke directly to his brothers: "I don't like it when you talk like that. It's not funny, what people look like."

Clint's mother, telling the story to Helen Johnson the next day, continues:

"So there's this stunned silence, and then he keeps going. Clint says, 'Like some people look different on the outside, but we're all the same on the inside. Everybody's got a food tube and all that stuff. Like when we saw that old guy the other day that only had one arm, and I started to be scared of him, and then I thought he eats food and it goes down and makes poops and pees just like Daddy, just like everybody. . . . Besides, suppose somebody captured you and made you a slave just because you had a different color of skin.' . . . And then he just keeps going, all the way from Africa to slave ships to Harriet Tubman and Rosa Parks and Martin Luther King. . . ."

Here is one of the finest educational success stories I have ever heard. Not only does four-year-old Clint understand some basic facts about how the human body works, but he has understood something more subtle still: that the truths of the human body make us one people, despite our external differences. Clint's experience with "The Bodyworks" curriculum gave him a rare and powerful form of knowledge, knowledge that is, at once, both scientific and spiritual.

Whether one is four or forty or fourscore, what better thing could one know than Clint's claim that ". . . some people look different on the outside, but we're all the same on the inside." We should all aspire to grow as wise and knowing as Clint—and reading *The Growing Edge* will help us and our children do exactly that.

Parker J. Palmer is an award-winning writer, teacher, and activist who earned his Ph.D. with honors in sociology from the University of California at Berkeley. His work spans a wide range of institutions—universities, public schools, community organizations, religious institutions, corporations, and foundations—including faculty positions at Beloit College, Berea College, and Georgetown University. Among his many publications are To Know As We Are Known *and* The Active Life. *Dr. Palmer currently serves as Senior Associate of the American Association of Higher Education, and as Senior Advisor to the Fetzer Institute and director of their "Teacher Formation Program." He is working on a new book,* The Courage to Teach.

I. Orientation

Prologue

The Growing Edge works in four dimensions. First, it's a story. Sixteen four- and five-year-olds and their teachers are engaged in an adventure. Lively anecdotes chronicle their day-by-day discovery of themselves as individuals and as a group.

Second, it's a journal. It records my efforts to observe children, to decipher their behavior, and to shape curriculum in response to their emerging needs.

Third, it's an exploration of the relationship between developmental theory and practice. It's all about process.

Finally, *The Growing Edge* is about an emergent curriculum. The Bodyworks curriculum enables young children to construct life-size three-dimensional working models of their own bodies, outside and inside. It develops in response to the cognitive, emotional, social, and physical needs of individual children at different stages of development.

The book is organized into sections. Orientation (Part I) describes how the project was conceived in response to a specific need, and developed a life of its own. It orients readers to my classroom in the Gorse Child Study Center, the laboratory school of Mount Holyoke College, where The Bodyworks has continued to evolve for eight years. Journal (Part II) contains the anecdotal record of the children's experience with The Bodyworks, followed by my reflections. The Growing Edge (Part III) evaluates The Bodyworks curriculum in terms of prevailing theories of developmental psychology and proposes a paradigm shift. The Bodyworks (Part IV) offers tips for teachers interested in recreating the curriculum, "Bogglers" for adults, a brief bibliography, blueprints for the bodyworks model, illustrations, and photographs.

In my eight years with The Bodyworks, I've come to see that children's relationships to their own bodies are a powerful hidden core curriculum in early childhood. I hope to help other teachers, parents, and therapists become more aware of the questions children are asking through their behavior, more aware of the answers we give them in what we invite and what we discourage.

Gorse Child Study Center is a community of learning and support. Children, parents, college students, and I come to each other, vulnerable, our lives unfinished and our bare faces hanging out. The heart of our relationship is mutual trust, respect, and confidentiality, framed by the one-way mirror of an observation booth.

Anecdotes in *The Growing Edge* have been drawn from my experience with nearly one hundred children and families over eight years. I've created fictional characters who carry the action. These are not case studies; they are the children, families, and college students of my imagination, cross-sections cut from many lives and years glued together. I ask readers not to try to tease out the fragments. It would be grossly misleading to project memories of real people onto my fictional characters.

The sparse detail, episodic form, and colorful names may allow other teachers and parents to glimpse bits of themselves and their children in the Gorse mirror. If a character springs to life, it's because she is Every Child, Parent, Teacher, caught in moments of grace or grief, fully deserving compassion without judgment.

Here are the children who often command the center of attention, and those who hover on the fringe.

Here are the children who already speak with authority, and those who haven't yet found their voices.

Here are the children who give and receive with joy, and those who remain out of reach.

Here are the children carried by the current, and those who swim upstream.

Here are the children who rest comfortably in their families, and those who carry secret burdens.

Here are the children who embrace the unknown, and those who shrink from it.

Here are the children who brim with ideas and plans, and those who wait for a spark to ignite them.

Here are the children who whirl and spin, and those who wonder and dream.

Here are the children who know the world is made for them, and those who fear it is not.

The Growing Edge is more than an opportunity to re-invent The Bodyworks curriculum, for different children, teachers, and environments. Ultimately it's an invitation to rediscover with children the seamless human mystery beneath our surface differences in age, size, gender, ability, class, race, and culture. Let's reveal and celebrate the web of life that binds all species together. The Bodyworks opens a door to what Rachel Carson called "the sense of wonder." At the growing edge, learning and teaching merge.

Bodyworks Begins

Shirelle, age 4, glued loops of twine to represent the brain on a cardboard shaped "head." She threaded the "spinal cord" through macaroni "vertebrae." "Hey," she crowed, "mine is just like Clint's."

I responded, "Yes, your bodies look different on the outside, but inside your spinal cord and nerves look just alike." Shirelle looked around the classroom with her mouth open, turning back with wide eyes: "Just like *everyone else's?*"

At circle, Bo blurted, "Sometimes you could have loosey-goosies."

Zack jumped in, "Sometimes you could get loosey-goosies in your pants. Sometime you could get loosey-goosies on your floor."

I tried to reassure them, "Yes, that can happen to children and grownups too. Diarrhea happens if you're sick or eat too much of some kinds of food or if food is spoiled. But you can't help it if you have diarrhea. People understand if you have an accident."

Shirelle, Bo, Zack and their friends at nursery school were working hard at The Bodyworks. The project began eight years ago, when I woke up in the middle of the night with the answer I'd been seeking for months. I couldn't know then how significant the answer would be, how many ripples it would release in fourteen children, their families and friends, my teaching assistants and me. I didn't anticipate it would touch other teachers, parents, and therapists wrestling with the developmental needs of children in their care.

The Bodyworks began with an opportunity disguised as a problem: a classroom full of anxious four-year-olds. Six days into the school year, one of the children was suddenly hospitalized. Questions were large, answers neither simple nor satisfying. Beneath cognitive issues tossed a sea of emotions.

Few questions actually surfaced in words. They were loud in silent sidelong looks, extraordinary attention paid to ordinary hangnails and nosebleeds; hospital dramas with our set of small jointed toy figures and emergency room props; the choosing of picture books.

Children need simple and direct answers, even when the truth is troubling. What if no one yet wants to ask questions out loud? There are times when children need to turn away from the search for understanding and turn back to simple immersion in experience.

As their teacher I respected this need. At the same time I knew the children would need to circle back to big questions. How could I help strengthen their vitality and their trust in the mysterious workings of life?

Intuitively, I knew that the children's own bodies—the focus of their anxiety—must undo it. I remembered a classic body-image activity. What brilliant teacher first conceived the notion of young children painting their own life-size self-portraits? The project never fails to capture and hold attention through all its stages: outlining oneself on butcher paper, painting in one's hair, features and clothing; cutting out the final two-dimensional "Me." Mystery and wonder shimmer at the edges, along with delight, curiosity, openness to concepts as well as experience.

Could we take this project beyond the surface "Me" to the interior core? I wanted somehow to help each child expand her sense of her own insides, not only bones but flesh and blood and breath, muscle and motion and sensation. We needed a three-dimensional working model of the human body, however schematic. Obviously we couldn't represent the entire human body, but there had to be a way to construct the systems most relevant to a four year old.

I hoped to create enough momentum to carry the children far beyond our classroom hours together. At best, each child would make his own model body. A collective model would not meet deep needs in the same way. I scouted out a number of books and other resources, but an appropriate project still hovered outside my reach.

One day I spontaneously set out a new book. It was full of flaps to open, suitable only for one careful child at a time, so I put it on a table with an adult to oversee its use. Within minutes a group of children had clustered around Claire Smallman and Edwina Riddell's wonderful *Outside-In.*[1] For the next week they patiently took turns "reading," asking questions, studying favorite pages, kibitzing over each others' shoulders. Clearly, this book of anatomy and physiology had unlocked many levels of questions. It beckoned the children to follow anxious curiosity into new terrain.

Not much later I woke up in the middle of the night. In my mind's eye I saw the age-appropriate working model of the essential "insides." It took work to design the details, but the key structural elements were all given: a paper bag "torso" suspended from coat hanger "shoulders", with cardboard "skull" and limbs stapled in place. The bag's front panel was cut away to leave a three-sided container for the heart, lungs, and digestive tract. On the back, the spinal cord ran up to the brain. Arms and legs were jointed. Nerves, arteries and veins, and muscles completed the body systems. What about gender differences?—so crucial a developmental issue for four-year-olds! I added urinary and simplified reproductive organs as well.

Successive problems presented themselves and were resolved step-by-step within the simple basic structure. How to keep materials cheap, preferably familiar, and easily replaceable?

I constructed a prototype, imagining four-year-olds duplicating it. Even a streamlined version took over an hour to make. One of my priorities is that children be involved in every stage of a process, though the finished product may seem compromised from the adult perspective. I want them to know the work is their own and to be able to do it again if they want to, even if they need help along the way.

During activity period I try to stay free to oversee the classroom as a whole. My developmental philosophy prizes the teachable moments that pop up in a carefully shaped space. I couldn't tie myself to a single project, no matter how rich and appropriate, nor could I turn over a formidable curriculum such as The Bodyworks to a rotating staff of student assistants. The very quantity of materials, techniques, and concepts was daunting.

"Fit" was a primary concern. Curriculum should intersect wide-ranging interests and skills, so each child feels at once competent and stimulated. The well-conceived project allows the child who is developmentally youngest to work without anxiety toward mastery of skills while the most mature child ranges freely, elaborating and refining, winging beyond what is given. The teacher must keep close track of each child, pacing, redirecting, supporting her through many transitions and perspective shifts. "Fit" is especially important when subject matter carries heavy emotional and social charge.

Creating the Insides seemed to require a one-to-one adult:child ratio—an impossibility—but intuition urged me to go forward, to make tradeoffs. I broke the project into small bits, carefully sequenced, realizing all children would have to complete each task before anyone progressed to the next. Risking fragmentation and the loss of momentum, I allowed the project to evolve.

The pragmatic decisions about methodology had far-reaching benefits. It took several days for the whole group to complete each "system," because only one or two children at a time worked at The Bodyworks table with a teacher. Color-coding made brain, heart, lung, digestive, urinary, and reproductive tracts distinct. The elapsed time between each child's "turns for The Bodyworks" helped further to set each organ system apart. The children's hands-on experience was reinforced by their observation and conversation with peers and by the shared cumulative insights of the teaching staff—like a wave gathering energy. Parents tracked the process enthusiastically and the children found themselves "teaching" classroom visitors. (Ultimately, one grandfather took the finished product to show his pinochle cronies!) Related materials were available in other areas during activity period, and we talked and sang at circle time, gradually saturating rather than dramatically immersing the group.

Initially I wasn't sure how much information the children might want, or how best to present it. In fact, I wasn't confident of my own grasp of all the systemic details, much less of my student assistants' expertise. I kept the "content" simple, and prepared my staff daily with a few key concepts to be shared informally with the children. We kept reference books handy.

A pattern evolved. A teacher would take a child or two over to the prototype hanging in the doorway, and begin talking about the day's work, launching a swift current of dialogue, gesture, and activity:

"Today we're going to make the brain. Do you know what your brain does? . . . It gets messages and sends messages. . . . Pretend you put your finger on the stove. The nerves in your finger send a message to your brain: Hot, Hot, Hot! Then your brain sends a message back to your finger: Get off the stove! . . . See the string tangled up here? That's like your brain inside your head. Follow the string with your finger. . . . That's called the spinal cord. See how it runs through the big pieces of macaroni? . . . They're bones that protect it. . . . Feel the middle of my back . . . feel all those little bumps. Can you feel your own vertebrae? . . . Let's go over to the table. . . . How do you think you should start? . . . Good idea, you get the scissors. . . ."

This blend of activity, conversation, and "research" wove through each child's construction segment. I've rarely seen children so deeply engaged, so open, so absorbent. It was plain that our project was a perfect fit for this group of four-year-olds; the process seemed nearly organic. The Bodyworks stretched out for almost two months, firing the development of children and adults alike, while traditional interest areas flourished alongside.

If we choose to see children as budding scientists actively exploring themselves and their environment, we can appreciate the preschool classroom as a well-equipped laboratory for experiments with the sense of self. The young child's experience has led her to infer that there is more to her body/self than can be seen. She knows that her heart beats, breath goes in and out, wastes emerge, blood comes through broken skin, boys' and girls' bodies look different. She wants to understand why these things happen, how she—her "self"—happens.

In building a model of her Insides, a child delightedly expands her sense of her own body's power: the power to transform food into energy, then into waste, to pump blood through a web of tiny tubes, to fill and empty her lungs, to send and receive messages, to throw away dead skin and grow new, to keep a place for a baby perhaps to grow, to open and close passageways, to mend broken bone and torn muscle. Her sense of connectedness between her infant self, her child self, and her adult self deepens. As the child's sense of her own inner physical self enlarges, so does her sense of belonging among others who share the same wondrous powers. Her awareness is strengthened by her glimpse of the common "insides" beneath unique "outsides." Surface differences—size, age, ability, race, gender—dwindle in significance.

The Bodyworks met the children where they were—physically, intellectually, socially, emotionally—and helped them move joyfully along the spiral of self-knowledge. The project grew out of specific and unusual needs, but it struck chords resonating in all young children.

It was a magic moment when we attached the life-size self-portraits hanging to the Insides. In making models of their bodies, the children had shaped a new and lifegiving sense of the self. It had been very hard work. It was worth it. They could hardly wait to take their bodyworks home.

That was the first year. The Bodyworks affirmed the validity of the problem-solving approach to early childhood education—teachers and children on a voyage of mutual discovery. The news traveled quickly. Teachers, parents, and therapists urged me to put together a "cookbook" to share the curriculum. I realized that it would take more than an outline to prepare others to adapt The Bodyworks to their own settings. In creating the project, I had done a great deal of thinking which was crucial to using The Bodyworks appropriately.

It's not simply a matter of gathering up a few paper bags and jumping in, as one young teacher discovered the hard way. Visiting our school, she discovered The Bodyworks in progress. She checked a body book out of the library, assembled a box of odds and ends, improvised a model of her own, and took it all to her daycare group of older 3s, young 4s, and an occasional 5-year-old. Within days the children were busily cutting and gluing; the parents were curious; the questions were flying thick and fast; and she was in way over her head.

She hadn't considered how materials suggest functions. Her Styrofoam "noodles" resembled illustrations of the cerebellum, but they didn't embody the concept of "roads" for brain messages to travel on through the body. She hadn't sequenced stages of construction, so the children were confusing parts of different systems. She hadn't anticipated challenges related to "poops" and "babies," or figured out how to respond appropriately to children at such different stages in development or to parents' concerns. Frantic, she called me. Together we planned how she could bring the project to a speedy close, and I promised her the first draft of *The Growing Edge.*

The Context

Eight years later, what does the success of The Bodyworks tell us about learning and teaching? What can I offer others who would like to meet children at the growing edge?

The Bodyworks curriculum changes every year because it's "developmental." It begins as a teacher initiative, then goes forward in response to emergent learning. There's no way to anticipate and plan what will come up, or how, or when. Most things surface sooner or later in some form, especially the Biggies: sex, death, poops, "the other," and God.

Each teacher, each child, each setting is unique. I can introduce you to The Bodyworks and demonstrate it as an organism evolving from day to day. Ultimately you will have to find the growing edge with the children you teach. I offer you my experience in journal form. It's not intended as a model. Consider it the report of an advance scout. Use it to project yourself into the territory.

As you read, imagine yourself, your children. Try on my responses, invent your own. Mine are not necessarily the best responses, simply what I was able to offer to a particular child on a particular day. Today or tomorrow I might respond differently. Surely you will. Use my journal as a workbook, a private role play to help you discover your own strengths, anxieties, growing edges, the gaps in your own information.

I carry a small spiral notebook in my pocket. The children are used to seeing me scribbling in it. Sometimes I record a conversation while participating in it. Rarely do they ask about my notes. When they do, I explain I'm very interested in each child in the class, and I'm trying to learn to be a better teacher. Like a scientist, I look and listen carefully, and record what I notice.

Whether or not they ask, the children seem to like this kind of attention. It makes them feel important. They know that I respect their privacy, and—like all children—they subtly or blatantly "hide" things from me. (Shh, *she*'s coming!) But in general, they don't want to hide—our deepest wish as people is to be found, to be known and cherished. They are glad I find them—either they connect the notebook with the process or they view it as a harmless idiosyncrasy!

I've culled six years of notes, compressing, disguising, and reattributing material to protect the identities of individuals. Though each child, each year, probably had this intensity and range of experience, I would not have been able in any single year to document The Bodyworks so fully and teach it at the same time.

A few details will help orient you to my classroom at the Gorse Child Study Center, Mount Holyoke College, in South Hadley, Massachusetts.

Ours is a nursery-school program, two-and-a-half hours a day, five days a week, September to May. Our schedule depends on the weather, the day's special events, and everyone's energy. There's always some time outdoors, an extended activity period, snack, and circle time. At the end of our morning, children go home, next door to daycare, to babysitters.

Unlike the church basements and storefronts typical of early childhood programs, our classroom is large, bright, well-equipped and designed for young children. We're on the ground floor, with a big grassy play yard. Big windows flood our room with light and views of the changing seasons.

One inner wall backs up to a hall with lockers for each child. On the other wall is a long mirror above a low counter extending to a child-sized bathroom. The mirror is actually the one-way glass window of our observation booth often filled with psychology students, teachers, parents, and visitors.

The classroom is lined with open shelves, a changing array of books and games and toys, and the cage of our resident guinea pig, Pepe. Low tables, chairs, and movable display boards help create and change spaces. Clotheslines, suspended from the ceiling, allow temporary hanging of work-in-progress—a crucial accommodation to The Bodyworks! Since a different teacher uses the classroom in the afternoons, much of our paraphernalia must be carted back and forth each day to a small storage room across the hall.

The sixteen four-year-olds who spend their mornings in this room come from families in the broad mainstream of American life. They live in a handful of quiet New England towns near our campus. Their mothers and fathers work as truckdrivers and nurses, receptionists and sales representatives, caseworkers and counselors, clerks and small business people. These little ones, scrubbed, and shining and blessed, appear to be the heirs of the American dream. Yet they are filled with questions, anxieties, and fears. If Gorse children have so many concerns about their own physical and emotional vulnerability, how much more so the children in less fortunate settings!

The Bodyworks, developed in a lab school, has all the marks of that context. A rotating student staff teaches and learns alongside the children. As head teacher, I'm the one consistent daily presence. College students, who spend two mornings a week as my assistants, contribute excitement, energy, varied backgrounds, and fresh perspectives to the children's experience. However, much time and attention goes into updating, supervising, and choreographing their work with the four-year-olds. The Bodyworks could be taught as well or better by a team of two consistent adults. Fewer hands would mean a longer running time, but it would also mean more maturity, more sensitivity, more continuity from day to day.

As you begin reading, you may find the swarm of children as confusing as a Russian novel, a complex "plot" with many subplots. You may leaf through The Bodyworks (Part IV) for a clearer sense of the model, but the children's questions and concerns pop up without respect for my construction schedule. Relax as you read. The story's not neat or linear, but you'll get the gist. It's not necessary to keep everyone straight!

As the pages go by, individuals emerge. There are eight girls: Ani, Shirelle, Cara, Daisy, Maggie, Missy, Rosa, and Tanya; and eight boys: Bo, Clint, Zack, Jogger, Kahlil, Paul, Pip, and Shane. Who stands out for you? Who gets lost in the shuffle? Most of the children are four years old, a few already five. The student assistants are Nita, an old hand, and Terry, who is new. The children call me by my nickname, Sandy. We have been together for seven months when The Bodyworks begins, long enough to know each other well and to have created a learning community that is a safe haven as well as a real-life adventure.

Our school lacks a vigorous diversity. In this way we are sadly typical of many middle-American settings. Our compensation is the wonderful variety of backgrounds provided by the student body and faculty of the college. We try to enrich our blend with children who have special needs. Even in a classroom of "normal" children, one child or several are apt to "stick out"—to themselves, their peers, their teachers. We struggle to balance each child's needs with others'. This is an issue in all our teaching, regardless of the "curriculum" we have chosen. In many ways, individual children become the curriculum for themselves, for their classmates. We can fight that phenomenon or we can weave and dance with it.

The Bodyworks provides an unusual opportunity to dance with differences often experienced as problematical. We can learn from these "problems," grow with them, if we examine our assumptions, if we appreciate the individual whorls within the stream.

The journal may leave the impression that my classroom is a placid pool, where the resident bullfrog sounds off in the silence. Nothing could be further from the truth. My classroom is a creek, full of flowing, spraying, colliding waves, rocks, reeds, and rainbow trout. The Bodyworks curriculum is not a dock jutting out over the water, offering the teacher dry feet and a good view; it's more like a lifejacket: you don't drown but you definitely get wet.

Much of the time you improvise—from a strong center of sensitivity, self-knowledge, and information. As Bess-Gene Holt put it, "It is the early childhood teacher's challenge to fit the truth of the world into the child's system of knowing it."[2] Information is the least urgent; it can be located later. "Research" can be more empowering for children than any amount of precooked fact. ("Don't feed me. Teach me how to fish!")

However, The Bodyworks demands a certain level of maturity in the teacher. It's challenging to handle so many live wires at once. And to have all your own buttons pressed! You may want to arrange ahead for therapeutic back-up, perhaps when there is an identified victim of abuse. More likely, you'll innocently open a can of worms or bump heads with insurmountable difference, and grow from it!

The Bodyworks also asks the teacher to reawaken within herself a sense of wonder. An infant is mesmerized by her own wiggling fingers, enchanted by her own bubbling and babbling. A young child spends long moments poking his tongue into remote pockets of his mouth, prodding and pinching, scratching and stretching, humming, hissing, and growling. Most adults have forgotten these playful journeys. It's up to us to find our own new ways back into the wonder of our physical beings.

Play—exploration rather than competition—leads to new awareness, to expansive curiosity. Play enables us to listen deeply, to hear the whispered wisdom of the body whirring night and day below consciousness, beyond control. This deep listening prepares us to "teach" The Bodyworks. Our deep listening invites children to bring us discoveries and fears, enables them to trust us with questions, helps them grow their own answers.

Have you ever watched a flock of wild geese move through the air? The lead goose opens a channel which eases the flight of those who follow. The teacher is the lead learner in The Bodyworks. Your curiosity and enthusiasm create an energy stream which attracts the children like a magnet. If you're like me, there's a lot about the body you take for granted, or have forgotten, or never knew. I took my questions to the children's section of a good public library. Scanning the picture books and browsing the books written for older children, I got hooked. Absorbing a critical mass of information, I became more and more alert to the complex workings of my own body. This aliveness is where The Bodyworks begins, joining the teacher to the children's vitality. An engaged teacher is like a primed pump, brimming with insights, metaphors, and improvisations at the teachable moment.

What touches children deeply is the teacher's attitude of openness and respect for all life, including the cycles of decay and death. Many adults and children have been taught, explicitly or implicitly, that our bodies are "dirty." We've sanitized and deodorized and compartmentalized essential realities. It's no surprise we've grown up feeling split from our very selves, as well as from the earth and from the web of life which binds all species together. Your confidence—that everyone, everything belongs—will help children develop healthy attitudes toward blood and mucus, farts and feces. "Dirt" is simply matter out of place! In the wisdom of the body, we come home to the wisdom of the planet.

Most children will pick up a number of concepts and facts, but in The Bodyworks the growth that counts is rarely quantifiable. For all my charts and portfolios, I've been guided best by those moments when "the whole child" (that hidden creature we rarely glimpse) suddenly arcs out of the water. Then I've seen the child as a dolphin leaping, a whale sounding. I've brimmed with praising too deep and swift for words. The Bodyworks bursts me out of my narrow enabling role, dunks me into the sea of life. There I find myself buoyant in the current, swimming beside the luminous child.

Please use my journal to imagine yourself swimming with us, diving into The Bodyworks with your children. Sometimes the water's cold and murky, but there's no place I'd rather be. After the Journal, we'll consider what The Bodyworks can tell us about learning and teaching in "The Growing Edge."

II. Journal

WEEKS ONE AND TWO

Warming Up, Outsides

Wading in

It's time for The Bodyworks. Every year I'm ambivalent. It takes so much energy and time and space. Is it really worth it? Is it timely for these children? for me?

Are Paul and Missy ready for this? Cognitively, yes; emotionally and socially, maybe no. Rosa and Jogger need it desperately. Can I address their needs without losing sight of every one else's? What about Clint? Tanya? Shane? There are so many underlying issues in their families right now. I have to remind myself The Bodyworks has built-in safeguards, and so do children. If we pay close attention, we can meet each child at her growing edge. The children's needs poke through every activity. At the least, The Bodyworks helps me address many of them right out front.

Is it parents that I'm anxious about? They're always so supportive, once we get started, but some of them are so needy too. This project puts me out on a limb. There's apt to be so much response from the children, the college students, and the parents–high expectations I can't possibly realize. I'm feeling too lazy to gather and prepare all the materials, deal with all the mess, move things back and forth, make the tough trade-offs, accommodate the absences, address the different learning styles, mesh all the uneven stages of interest and motivation and development so we all keep moving more or less in step. I don't want to have to spark and sustain such a complex curriculum.

At this point in the year I'm tempted to give the children their heads. So much is happening that I don't want to interrupt. I want to observe for a while—to learn from the children, to celebrate with them. It's almost spring, at last. We deserve to relax a little after a long hard-working winter.

I've talked it over with Nita—how wonderful to have her back for another year. She gave me a pep talk, reminding me how deeply the children need The Bodyworks, how ready they are for it. Despite her own senior-year overload, she's keen, committed.

I'll wade in tentatively, give myself some time to get fully behind The

Bodyworks this year. I'm probably just tired, but I don't feel ready to dive in. I'll begin Outsides as an independent project, testing the children and myself. That will simplify my task at first. If it's going well, I'll send the parent letter home and put out the body books.

There's no guarantee any curriculum is "right" or timely. The best I can do is assess my resources and my limits at this point in this year, then take a leap of faith, put on the brakes, or make a detour (or all of those, in any sequence). I can't look over my own shoulder every minute, only reflect and evaluate as we go. At this point in my career, I can trust myself to work through whatever comes up.

Tomorrow I'll emphasize the "science" aspects of the Outsides, hoping we can sidestep some of the issues that come up when the children see the Outsides as art.

Mishaps, worries, fears

Bo's back after flu: "I threw up LOTS!"

A big block falls accidentally on Rosa's toe. She's glad to get a big hug.

Daisy points to her temple, "Sandy, my daddy has a cut right here! Shaped like a 4! A branch got him."

Maggie's older sister appears in the doorway, a plush bunny tucked in her parka, "Logo is sick in the hospital. She's dehydrated. She's 13. That's 91 people years."

Cara drags in, pale and heavy-eyed. "I not sleep. I think about Mommy."

Shane: "I know a guy what wanted to start a volcano and he had matches. He was old enough. He lit the matches and got some oil and put it in the fire and he just got lighted up, his clothes. My mother and my big sister were scared. On '911'."

Someone broke into Kahlil's house. His mother hates the idea of an intruder in her home. Her older boys seem more intrigued by the detective than worried about robbers. Kahlil is not himself today.

Conscious and subconscious fears rise like unpredictable tides in individual four-year-olds and in the group. They're vulnerable and they know it. They worry about accidents and illnesses—"Why can't grownups make me well?" "If something terrible happened to my parents, what would happen to me?"—Disaster holds a lurid fascination for them. We get health bulletins on pets, neighbors, grandparents, TV characters. A contagious rash of "the worries" in the classroom today has been aggravated by the usual physical mishaps.

Circle in a storm

At circle, taking a cue from the weather, I'm reading *Storm!* The children start in on cats and dogs who have died. I have a hunch there's more going on under this surge. We've discussed death many times in the circle. They know I'm open to this. I decide to risk putting off pet-death and see what surfaces next. I can probably retrieve the subject later if I've blown it. I suggest, "Lots of you have important things to say. Let's finish the book and then do some more talking at snack." They listen to the end.

Kahlil: "That's scary!"

Rosa: "It's not scary! It wasn't very loud."

Shane: "Lightning could hit a tree and put it on fire."

Zack: "Or make the tree fall."

Shane: "And if it's near a waterfall and it falls down to the water and the water puts it out. . . . Only one thing can put out water and that's gasoline and that makes more fire . . . I think so."

Pip: "Once my neighbors had a fire and gas was on the tree and the water couldn't put it out."

Ani: "I know a family what had a fire. A big truck was in their yard and the man made a mistake and there was a explosion. They didn't die. But their bird did die. . . . Sometimes basketballs are on fire and they break in half."

Sandy: "I haven't seen that."

Ani: "I DID! Once we went to a fire engine place and I got to ride in the fire truck and push some buttons."

Kahlil: "Sometimes storms have a lot of crashes. With CARS. Because they don't have their wipers on."

Pip: "One of the mother hamsters bit the babies' head offs. And my mom said no more it was too gross but they were my sister's."

Bo: "Some hamsters get dead by lightning."

These comments are flung thick and fast, overlapping, into the circle. No way I can follow up on each child's concern at this point, only offer space to be heard. Later I can check out some stories and respond with sympathy, time for fuller telling, facts. What I can offer now is The Secret Place.

The Secret Place

Since September, we've been taking a few minutes a day to "lie down and put your hand on your tummy. Feel your breath go in and out. Your breath can help you go to the secret place deep inside you where it's always safe and comfortable, no matter how scary or sad, or mixed-up it is all around you." The children settle down right away today. I sing them my words to a melody adapted from the Pachelbel Canon:

The Secret Place

In, out, quiet, slow
To the Secret Place I go.
Deep, still, safe, strong,
Sing the shining inside song.

© Helen H. Johnson

Some of the children sing with me. We all lie there for two or three minutes, then I invite them to "come back into this room when you are ready," and we all go over to snack.

Parents report that some children use this practice at home too. It's perhaps the most valuable tool I can offer in a culture where old values are disappearing, and many kinds of violence are the norm.

This is a confusing, turbulent, and frightening time for adults, battered by rapid cultural change, trying to steer a course between extremes. It's all the more bewildering for young children, who depend on us and may feel our human vulnerability acutely. Our sense of the Secret Place is the context for The Bodyworks.

I'd planned to use circle time to preview the self-portraits. So much surfaced earlier in the day that circle took a different twist—typical! On the other hand, it pointed up the need for The Bodyworks. My ambivalence is dissipating.

"Art" and "Science"

Given the limits of time and attention, I told the circle only that tomorrow we'll start tracing each child's body, the first step in making life-size pictures. I mentioned this will be a chance for the children to work like scientists, looking carefully in the mirror, trying to paint exactly what they see.

This year we've made some distinctions between "science" and "art," which may help the children move toward realism in their self-portraits. To these children, art means free expression. When we approach self-portraits as "art," we end up with a lot of painting-as-process and many unrecognizable products.

In fact, The Bodyworks is science and art and everything else the children bring to it. The model is just the tip of the meta-curriculum that develops around it. For The Bodyworks, the children need to create personal Outsides they can identify with, feel proud of, live with for days and weeks. These self-portraits are going to be hanging in the classroom and later at home, exposing the children to others' reactions. Parents can be quite unaware of the impact of their comments. We need to do what we can to help the children earn self-respect and the respect of others for the "me" in the mirror, the self that I and others see. Another year I could contrast painters' portraits with photographs and scientific drawings. It would be fun to launch another way of "knowing yourself." For now, I've got my hands full and I've drawn the line. I don't want to give the children double messages about "creativity," but I have good reason to aim these self-portraits toward "science" rather than art. I can foresee and sidestep difficulties, but I have no illusions that the path will be clear. We'll muddle through, as always.

Missy's self-image

Missy stops off at the full-length mirror on her frequent trips to the water fountain and bathroom. Today she puts her face close, eyes wide open so white shows around the iris. She rolls her eyes in circles, then arches and collapses her eyebrows over and over. Otherwise her face is expressionless. Before leaving the mirror, she gives herself a warm smile.

What a contrast between Missy's mirror self and Missy's general demeanor. In class she tends to be subdued.

She returns to the easel, overlapping circles in primary colors until they produce a uniform brown, commenting to Terry, "That's me, looking up at the tree. . . . I'm painting the inside of me. . . . I'm painting the inside of my brother now. He's two years old and he cries a lot and he cries real loud."

Her conceptual intentions are complex, far outstripping her representational skills.

She pauses and smiles up at Terry. Terry remarks on her pretty eyes. Missy looks down a little: "My Daddy has blue eyes like you, but my mother has brown eyes like me."

Terry says,"My mother has brown eyes just like you!"

Missy laughs quietly, wrinkling her nose, then grins.

Later she seeks out Terry at the playdough table. "Can you make a big ball? I make better little balls cuz of my hands are little." Terry helps her combine her perfect little balls with toothpicks to make a Bucky Fuller dome.

She's so self-aware, introducing the adult-child contrast when her hand size is an advantage.

At the mirror with Terry, Missy settles in to paint her outline, concentrating on representation. She makes vivid blue eyes, despite her own recent comments that her eyes are brown and her brother's are blue. For the time being, we let this go. She uses the tip of the brush to make a very small mouth, then adds huge oval ears on each side of her head: "My mouth is little because I don't talk to kids much, but I listen a *lot*." (Yes indeedy!)

We can sometimes glimpse a child being aware of her own thinking, communicating her awareness, leaping into symbol. Over days (or minutes!) the same child oscillates, unself-consciously between concrete, abstract, and "wishful" thinking.

Clint: artist and he-man

Clint counts the stripes on his shirt and transfers them to his outline. He adds his G.I. Joe slippers, in camouflage, identifying four black spots as the action figures on his slippers. "I kinda like doing this. It's a lotta fun painting myself. It's kinda neat!" He adds spurs and spikes, "to get up trees better."

At the last minute, he dabs eyebrows, which start to drip as we hang the portrait. He says he wants pupils in his eyes. I suggest he add those tomorrow, when the rest is dry. "Clint, it looks to me like you're interested in lots of things—being strong like G.I. Joe and the men who climb telephone poles AND noticing things carefully and painting what you see."

Clint chimes right in, "Yep, that's me! BOTH of those!"

When a child articulates something he has discovered about himself, we have an opportunity to affirm and reflect that back to him. I juxtapose the "macho" activities Clint shares with his older brothers, and the "artistic" aptitude that sets him apart. He needs early support to sustain his perception of himself as both/and in a culture which may pressure him to choose either/or.

Shane's Vulnerability

For weeks Shane's drawings have troubled me. His pictures show a stick figure with all the right parts, all in proportion, not connected to each other or to the small circle in the "torso" position. He dictates stories involving major calamities, a helpless child, and a missing father.

Shane begins painting next to Shirelle, who's using orange. He reaches for her brush, makes an orange circle, adds yellow and red swirls in it, and extends it until it covers most of the bottom half of his face. With the same technique he covers hair previously painted yellow. As he works, he talks about the fire at his grandparents' house as if it happened yesterday, not a year ago.

Later I speak through a rabbit puppet: "Shane, I'm scared . . . there's a fire in the woods." Shane reaches for his favorite puppet, Fierce Cat. "What's the matter, little rabbit? Are you scared?" In a five-minute improv, Shane at first protects then abandons the rabbit.

In The Bodyworks, the unconscious comes up—fears, perceptions, and messages. In the company of a loving adult, children may work on what comes up.

Daisy

Daisy, our queen bee, usually wears ruffly dresses to school. Today she's wearing pants. She looks long and hard at her outline, then makes tiny controlled strokes to emphasize her puffed sleeves and lacy collar. She tilts her head and surveys the effect, smiles and claps her hands, "Ooh, I *love* puffy sleeves!" and that is that.

Mi Cuerpo

Today in circle we begin learning Sarah Pirtle's song, *Mi Cuerpo,* with simple motions I add to make its bright rhythms dance. Songs get into the blood, carry messages more effectively than speech. In singing *Mi Cuerpo,* the children experience "there's music inside me." Long after, the feeling remains: I like myself, inside and out.

Mi Cuerpo

Mi cuerpo, mi cuerpo hace musica.
Mi cuerpo, mi cuerpo hace musica.
Mis manos hacen pom, pom, pom!
Mis pies hacen bom, bom, bom!
Mi boca hace la, la, la!
Mi cintura hace cha, cha, cha! cha, cha, cha!

There's music, there's music, there's music inside me.
There's music, there's music there's music inside me.
My hands they go clap, clap, clap!
My feet they go tap, tap, tap!
My mouth it goes la, la, la
My middle it goes cha, cha, cha! cha, cha, cha!

Traditional: Mexico[3]

Missy's eyes, Missy's mom

The current crop of "Outsides" hang on the line. Missy bounces in with her mother, who asks "What's up there?" Missy grins, "KIDS!" Mom inspects the row, turns to Missy: "You wanted your eyes to be blue like Daddy's instead of brown like mine." Missy's face closes; her body tightens; she says nothing. Mom walks her to the block corner, kneeling down to say goodbye, but Missy is wooden and doesn't respond.

Parents get so involved with their children's choices. It's hard to help them see how powerful their messages are.

Later Terry says the green shirt Missy painted the day before reminds her of St. Patrick's Day. Missy chirps up, "My daddy takes me to the parade. He really does! Just me and my daddy went." Terry tells her it's time to paint her eyes brown. Missy seems relaxed and enthusiastic as they look in the mirror together, joking about where eyes fit on the face. She paints a very large left eye, a right eye half its size, dramatic eyebrows and thick curling eyelashes.

Much on Missy's mind these days: her pleasure in being with Daddy, her rivalry with her little brother, her desire for blue eyes, her risk of her mother's disapproval. Do her eyes make a symbolic statement within our "science" constraints?

Tanya, Shirelle, Pip

Tanya begins: green eyes, white face, white hair, red shoes and blue pants—in control, if not exactly true to life. Then she goes wildly at her shirt, with so much mixing and experimenting she loses the facial features. Enough for today. She's had a wonderful time!

Shirelle paints her eyes green "to pretend." Blue mouth with orange lipstick, pink nose (giggles), orange pony tail ("just pretend"), sunglasses, dots to indicate knees and nipples, a white-painted face. She invents a scarf around her shoulders.

Her twelve-year-old sister is interested in fashion. This is the first time we've seen Shirelle persevere in painting of any kind.

Pip stares at his eyes in the mirror, pulling down the skin under his eyes. He plans to paint his shirt and pants in camouflage. As time wears on, he strays farther outside the lines. He doesn't want to take a break, though he's clearly tired, slopping the green paint onto his outlined hands. He looks dismayed, then reassures himself by telling Terry, "Soldiers have green hands. Some do. It's camouflage. My dad told me." That points him to the skin on his face, but he agrees to wait until the other paint is dry. He dimples at Terry. "I think you should have to paint yourself!"

The classroom's humming like a top. I'm committed! I'll hand out my letter to parents tomorrow morning. Then I can introduce the Insides at circle on Monday, with the models and books.

Cara's coping skills

Cara's playing among the bright silk squares and even allows Tanya to clothespin a lustrous pink cloth around her. Cara smooths her hair back daintily, pouts her lips, and bats her eyelashes while she places one hand on her cocked hip.

At six months, Cara Sopat came from Cambodia to join eager adoptive parents. She had a very hard time adjusting and cried almost continuously until her first birthday. The pediatrician suspected emotional rather than physical issues. Her parents noted that at age one she discriminated between Asian and non-Asian faces on the television screen, following the Asian faces intently.

Cara insists on wearing pink dresses, preferably emblazoned with Disney heroines like Little Mermaid, Belle, and Cinderella. Her mother has given up trying to get Cara to wear pants for any reason, even snowpants.

In the classroom, Cara's intelligence shows in art and craft, patterning, memory for details. Her language is sparse, with minimal structure. ("Me go bathroom," "Rufus woof Daddy.") At daycare and at school, she tags behind four boys, who tolerate but don't include her.Despite her delay in expressive language, she quietly sways and sings all the words to songs in circle. Her family has provided picture books and toys related to her Cambodian heritage, and she has learned a number of words in Khmer, but she refuses to use these even among Khmer-speaking family friends.

It strikes me that Cara's coping strategies reveal physical thinking: the awareness that she looks "different," the observation that media stars and "pretty little girls in pink dresses" get rewarded, the inference that "proximity" to popular peers may pass as "friendship" and is surely preferable to isolation. For months we've tried to enhance the language skills which will give Cara more strength, more self-esteem, more options, but we fear a backfire if we push.

I watch with concern as Nita invites her to come over for body-tracing, possibly a high-risk activity for Cara. I've asked Nita to work with Cara.

Nita's warmth and charismatic energy illuminate her attractive Hispanic features and she casually introduces Spanish vocabulary into the classroom. All the children love Nita.

Cara lies down easily, saying not a word, but offering small smiles as Nita moves around her. When she stands to look at her outline, she grins delightedly. Nita crouches to look in the mirror with Cara and asks, "What color is your hair?"

Cara touches her own hair, turning to look at Nita. "Black, like you."

Nita meets her eyes. "Right, we both have black hair. What about your eyes?"

Cara moves closer, looks first at Nita's eyes then at her own. "Black."

Nita smiles, "That's right. I have black eyes too." Cara looks in the mirror at her own face, then at Nita's. "What color are your lips, Cara?"

Cara smiles, turning to Nita with a finger to her lips, "Pink."

Nita concludes, "Come on! Let's go paint you now!"

Cara runs ahead, sits and waits, looking back and forth from Nita to the tracing. "What color for your hair, Cara?" "Black." Down to the dress. "Pink." (Of course!) Nita elects to ask Cara what color she wants for her hands. "Brown, like you." Cara chooses two different colors for her shoes, explaining, "Rufus chew slipper! New doggie. Old doggie dead."

She paints without looking up, talks without change in expression. She takes special care to make her eyes big and round, one much larger than the other.

Is this coincidence or did she watch Missy paint? She and Missy have been showing signs of mutual interest.

Zack's wristwatch

Zack has no interest in looking in the mirror. At each stage he asks, "Now are we done?" Terry asks him how long his sleeves are. He points to his wrist, "But I roll mine up so I'm gonna keep 'em that way." He paints an elbow line, to show himself where to stop. He examines wide and narrow stripes in five colors, copies his shirt. Soberly painting his white sneakers, he notices, "My shoes have blue on 'em too," and adds a blue heel.

Zack springs to life, "WAIT! I forgot to paint my watch!" He scrutinizes it. "It has blue, red, a little white, some yellow, and black." He hums, working deliberately, and he likes the results, though to the casual eye the "watch" is a blur of random colors.

Once the circle discussed how to show friends you like them. Other children suggested: send them a letter, kiss them, wink at them. Zack's idea: "Buy them a TV." He has his own TV in his room. His family values extras.

Kahlil's specificity

Kahlil takes his time at the mirror. He fetches a magnifying glass, pronouncing his eyes have a little blue and a little brown, black in the middle and white all around. He paints a blotch of each color. He labels his skin "peach. It's like orange, so you use yellow and red. But that's too dark so you have to mix some white." Smiling at himself and sticking his tongue out at his reflection, he checks his mouth. "Pink—so you mix red and white."

Kahlil paints his hair, eyes, nose, and mouth, and is about to leave when Terry asks him about his clothes. Kahlil has no interest in his clothes, but works meticulously to complete the portrait. After painting black shoes, he realizes he's wearing blue but decides that's OK. He decides not to paint his skin "because it would cover my eyes and nose."

For Zack, the watch was everything. In Kahlil's family, hand-me-downs are the rule, little value attached to clothes as long as they are clean and neat, but much attention is paid to the individual children's talents and needs.

What's on the outside is important to children. Not everything is of equal importance to each child. The child's focal point tells us about his present view of himself and his world. It may indicate directions for our work with him.

Maggie emerging

Maggie carefully paints her pixie bangs. She fills in the pink tights and T-shirt she tie-dyed with her mother, adding a little purple for effect. Her smile shows she's as proud of the painting as of the tye-dyeing, though—being Maggie—she says little. When she cuts, she's sure and steady, so happily absorbed she doesn't notice that cleanup is starting.

Maggie has speech therapy three times a week. She began the year with her head hanging, finger in her mouth, clinging to her mother's hand. All fall, she and I sat down daily to "write a story." For many weeks, Maggie repeated my cues, building sentences about her activities at school. Then she began to offer words of her own. We added other children to the round-robin story.

Maggie's morning warm-up time decreased. Her speech is clearer and more fluent, especially with friends. She still has a hard time retrieving words, but she's now a vivacious participant in circle. In art and crafts she has leaped ahead. It'll be fun to see how she responds to The Bodyworks.

Paul surprising us

Paul wants to paint leaning down from his slouch, but we insist he sit to start. He looks dreamy as usual as he hears the rap about painting from the top down, and starts with his new shoes, which are like Zack's. He paints them to match Zack's. To our surprise, he asks for a lighter blue, so his blue shirt can look different from his blue pants. He stays poised to the end.

Throughout the painting, Paul amazes us with his focus and care, his firm and effective grip. Usually he lets brushes and other tools dangle, with no effort at control.

He helps hang up the wet portrait, commenting: "He looks just like children. Happy mouth and sad eyes."

Until today, I've never seen Paul give himself fully to any project nor make a reflective statement. He uses the third person in his stunning observation about himself.

Letter to Parents

I've used The Bodyworks with about one hundred children and their parents. Despite the parents' range of "progressive" and "conservative" approaches to child-rearing, there has been overwhelming praise for the curriculum.

The single exception came from a couple who had been uncomfortable all year with our school's open unisex children's bathrooms. They wanted to keep their Linda unaware of sex differences to protect her from teenage pregnancy. They forbade her to use the toilet at school.

I explained our strong feeling that four year olds are best served by a family bathroom approach. Even "modest" children soon get used to our open door. Questions come up naturally and supervision is easy.

I said I couldn't in good conscience enforce the parents' ban of our school bathroom, feeling their policy was not in Linda's physical or emotional best interests. I recommended education in the context of the family's love and values as the best insurance against early pregnancy, and mentioned we would do a whole-body curriculum in the spring.

Linda's parents acknowledged my disagreement and released me from any responsibility for carrying out their ban. They said their child would obey them even if they were not present. I don't know if they questioned Linda about her bathroom habits at school. In fact, she spent plenty of time watching at the bathroom door. Uneasy with the adult decision to agree to disagree, I consoled myself with the prodigious growth occurring in all areas of this little girl's development.

Then it came time for The Bodyworks. I arranged a conference to show Linda's parents the books we'd be using. They'd been so supportive and positive about Linda's school experience. I hoped they'd trust me enough to risk The Bodyworks, but they abruptly withdrew her from school. I'm still sad about that. However, it doesn't mar The Bodyworks' approval rating among families who have actually tried it.

Dear Parents:

It must be spring—the birds are singing; the flowers are blooming; the college students are in love; the 4-to-5 year olds are snickering and whispering about "butts," "wieners," "boobies," and "poops." It happens every year.

Shall I ignore them? scold them? distract them—Good luck!—? interpret their behavior as a signal? I conclude that the children are curious about their bodies. It's a teachable moment. Developmentally, they are ready for some new knowledge. My job is to create an environment in which they can raise questions, express concerns, explore feelings. How can this be done in a way that respects their individual needs and differences?

We know that despite their sophisticated use of language children of this age are "physical thinkers." They learn best by doing, by "constructing" their own knowledge. They're working hard to develop a sense of self, and this proceeds from the outside in—from body image, activities, possessions. They're intensely interested in their relative personal power—their self-control and their influence over others. The human body, with its powerful transformations of energy and matter, is a superb subject for these budding scientists to explore . . . especially in spring, when motivation surges like sap and there is a well-established community of trust and cooperation.

Mulling all this over a few years ago, I conceived of The Bodyworks. After cutting out and painting a lifesize self-portrait (the Outsides), each child builds a working model of the Insides.

Day by day, we attach strings, balloons, pipecleaners and more to a cutaway brown paper bag torso, until we have the essential elements: brain, spinal cord, nerves; lungs; heart, arteries and veins; esophagus, stomach, intestine, rectum; bones, muscles, joints; bladder, urethra. Appropriately, in this larger context, we place the penis or uterus-with-vagina.

For obvious reasons, the three hot topics—digestive, urinary, and reproductive systems—overlap and bring gender issues to the surface. We try to walk the fine line between giving children the information they are asking for and referring to parents the questions we feel you would prefer to answer yourselves. It is clear that, if children are to esteem themselves, respect and care for their own bodies—and extend that respect to those of a different gender—they need to come to terms with anatomical differences. Fred Rogers's wonderful song, "Everybody's Fancy," offers the unifying insight. While little boys may still feel left out of the miracle of growing a baby inside themselves and nursing with breast milk, and little girls may still feel deprived of the squirtgun potential of the penis, all children rest easier in the knowledge that "Boys are fancy on the outside, Girls are fancy on the inside, Everybody's fancy, Everybody's fine, Your body's fancy and so is mine."

Most children today are familiar with pregnant and nursing mothers. Fewer are aware of the father's role in procreation. Many parents feel that early education about conception should take place within the family, where it can be linked to the family's love and values, timed and phrased to meet each child's development in a unique way. Most parents appreciate the way we place sexuality in the context of the child's whole body and address our program to children's spoken and unspoken concerns about the "goodness" of their external and internal physical selves.

You can anticipate that direct or indirect questions about sexuality may emerge during this curriculum. You may want to take a look at the good books on our parent library shelves, in preparation for the day when I greet you at the gate with "Maxine asked me today how the baby gets into the mother's stomach, and I told her I thought that was a question you'd like to answer, didn't I, Maxie?"

In fact, this question rarely comes up at school. More commonly, parents report that children announce with satisfaction what they have learned or test their grasp of concepts. Often this curriculum helps parents feel more comfortable dealing with issues that may have been taboo in their own growing-up years, and supports them in offering simple and direct answers as a base for an ongoing and trustful relationship with their children. The Bodyworks also enhances parents' work on nutrition, health, and safety issues.

Along with the models, we will be using books, puzzles, props (bones, X-rays, skeleton, etc.), songs, and lots of conversation in the process of discovering what's inside. I predict that most children will be excited and sometimes impatient during this long and complex project. There's every reason to hope that, at the end, each child will have deepened her sense of the wonder and goodness of her own being and glimpsed the common humanity beneath surface differences in size, gender, ability, color, or culture.

I'm interested in hearing about your and your children's responses to the body project, or anything else. Art, blocks, dramatic play, table games, work with small manipulatives, outdoor activities, investigations of worms and seeds, as usual, will continue. Please do keep in touch.

Warmly,
Sandy Johnson

Ani solves problems

Ani paints her blouse white, wondering aloud about painting white hands—they would blend with the blouse. She uses orange and approaches the fingers carefully, leaving room for nails. She puts pupils in her eyes. Doing her hair, she spatters brown and decides to make freckles, eyelashes, and eyebrows. She stops to look around the room several times but doesn't want to take a break.

Working on the model the children frame and share concerns. They perceive or invent problems and try solutions. Ani's self-esteem allows her to find a creative response to her paint-spattering "mistake." Another child might have crumpled, and we'd have taken that as a moment for learning about frustration, fear of failure, and creative improvisation.

Jogger's dual inheritance

Jogger (Juan) paints his hair dark brown, taking pains with the spikes he specified should "show." He sits on his heels, looking at his work, then dips his brush and boldly extends the arc of dramatic spikes. He paints his mouth a grim straight line, blood red, and he notes with satisfaction, "Karate! I'm small, but I'm sneaky!"

He's chosen brown for his hair. When children discuss hair color, Jogger refuses to be included among "people who have black hair." He asserts that his hair is mixed black and brown because it comes both from his mother (of Polish descent, with wavy light-brown hair) and his father (born in Mexico, with the classical features of his mountain village—high cheekbones, copper skin, and straight black hair).

Jogger's parents say hair color comes up often at the family dinner table. Although Jogger and his three older sisters seem to have inherited their father's hair, the parents want them to identify with both ethnic groups, and "black and brown mixed hair" is a symbolic statement.

I note the "both/and" approach seems focused on hair; culturally the family shows a marked disinterest in Spanish language, cuisine, and customs. Jogger avoids working with Nita when she is here, and scowls when she calls him Juan, his given name. Jogger's mother says of her third-generation Polish family, "We really don't know much about the old country. I'd say we're pretty much plain American on my side."

I decide not to mention Jogger made his hair brown rather than mixed. Was his color choice deliberate or unconscious? He may have intended to "mix" it. Was color sidetracked in his strong statement of form and scale? In any event, Jogger's working out his personal and his cultural identity—perhaps amid some family ambivalence.

I can give him space to do that and can affirm through our multicultural approach, most effectively through the person of Nita, the goodness of all *his potential. I can't push him into identifying with what he may see as a minority group. Jogger has indicated in many ways that he wants to be on top. This is a problematical issue for him since he is the baby of the family, smallest though oldest boy in the class, the mascot of all the neighborhood "big guys." My hunch is that he's launched on a long struggle, which we will not see resolved this year. The best we can do is to plant some seeds.*

Tanya's sadness

I talk with Tanya about making the self-portrait look "real," and she seems relaxed as she repaints her features. This time she makes her mouth "big because I'm sad."

This could be sadness from having to redo the painting, but I think not. Recently Tanya's seemed frazzled. She's talked about feeling sad. I know her family's struggling with expenses, her mother's working overtime, and the children's routines have been disrupted.

I ask, "Anything special making you sad, Tanya?"

"No, just sad."

We leave it at that. She has let me in as far as she wants today, confirming my perceptions. It's important that she used her self-portrait to tell me there's something wrong. I let her know I heard her, I'm available, and I respect her limits.

Bo: "NO PINK!"

Bo (Bowie) bursts out crying when I tell him it's time to repaint his face. He painted "no face" featureless bright blue.

"This project will work better if your Outsides look more like what you see in the mirror. It's different from most of the painting we do. Some children worry that they can't paint themselves. We'll work together. I think you're going to like it when you're finished."

Bo's not buying this. "NO PINK ANYWHERE. JUST BLUE!"

Terry helps him cover the blue with a coat of light tan, as he talks about hating to paint and not wanting to get any paint on his clothes. He dabs some on her. She laughs a little. He does it again.

"That was funny the first time, but not any more. Please stop. Now, what color for your hair?"

He wants "Green! Like The Joker!" but accepts brown with streaks of yellow. Terry asks him whether he wants a pink or a red mouth.

"NO PINK! NEVER PINK!" A bit of paint lands on his nose. Terry laughs gently and makes it OK, then helps him wipe it off when they're finished. He thanks her with a smile. They hug.

"Good painting! You stayed in the lines. That's really hard."

Bo jerks back, "I'm NOT a good painter. Painting is for GIRLS. My little sister paints. Yuck," and then pauses a moment before asking shyly: "Did you tell all the kids that, about being a good painter?"

Jogger "stuffs butt"

Jogger's bragging to Zack that he's faster. "I stuff your butt."

I comment that he talks a lot about butts and ask if he has questions about butts.

"NO."

I follow up, "Most words are OK to use when you're asking questions or explaining things, but the same words are not OK when you use them to hurt people's feelings, to tease them, scare them, or shock them. What's your butt for, Jogger?"

After a pause, Jogger comes up with an answer: ". . . . sitting."

I pursue this: "What about the hole in your butt?"

Jogger takes it further: "And the LINE."

Here's the moment. "Yes, what about the line? The line is where your body starts to make legs, where the part of you that is all one piece divides into two pieces, so you can run and walk and stretch and balance better. What do you think the hole's for?"

Jogger: "Poops."

I ask him,"Why does your body make poops?"

Jogger: "I don't know."

"To throw away garbage. Poops is the garbage that's left over from food, after your body uses what you need. . . . Please don't say 'butt' so much, unless you're using that word to tell us about your body or to ask questions."

Circle: introducing the models

At circle I introduce body models, with a quick overview of systems, explaining the models are like dolls—not like living people. "Just like children play with dolls and trucks and learn about babies and machines by playing, scientists use models to learn about things. Models can help us learn and remember how our bodies work inside.

"Our bodies don't really have baggies and straws inside them. But they do have parts—like the stomach—which hold things, and hollow tubes—like the windpipe—that air and water and blood pass through.

"Most bodies have all the same parts, like hearts and stomachs and brains, but boys and girls each have some parts that are different from each other. On the outside, boys have a penis, so the model of the boy's body has a balloon penis. On the inside, girls have a uterus, where a baby can grow if the girl decides to be a mother when she grows up, so the model of the girl's body has a balloon uterus.

"We have books that can show and tell you lots about bodies." I hold up several. "Each child will be making a model body. This project will take lots of days to finish. We'll do a little bit at a time."

Excited talk rustles the circle.

Bo: "Can you read us that book right now?"

Jogger: "Girls have a line and a bump on the outside too. AND a part on the inside."

As usual, Jogger assumes he's being shortchanged and confronts me. His psychological issue isn't going to be resolved, even if he learns of the male role in procreation, and the group as a whole won't be served by a complex accounting. Besides, in the eyes of these physical thinkers, the line-with-a-bump doesn't hold a candle to the "wiener," not even in Jogger's own eyes. So I elect not to pick up Jogger's challenge this time.

Bo: "Girls have a penis and pee inside their body."

Sandy: "No, boys and girls and babies and grownups all pee outside their body through a little hole called a urethra, and the pee goes into a diaper or into the toilet. On boys, the little hole is at the end of the penis, so you can see it. On girls, the little hole is between their legs, where it's harder to see."

I make minimal responses, moving this introduction along. I don't want to overload the first day, nor let the children's interest in taboos skew the project toward sexuality.

"There are many interesting parts of bodies, and mostly people's bodies have all the same parts whether they're old or young, fat or skinny, dark-skinned or light-skinned, boys or girls. We will learn about *lots* of interesting parts that are the same, like the heart, besides the parts that are different in boys and girls."

Models in the doorway

The body models are hanging in our doorway, spreading excitement to parents as well as children. I stay as free as possible to help everyone explore the models and relate three dimensions to the drawings, diagrams, and photographs in the body books.

From now on, we'll set up a table for body books and puzzles near The Bodyworks project area. An adult will stay near to attract children's interest, follow up questions and comments, and supervise their use of Outside-In. *The flap gimmick initially lures them, but the content is what holds them for extended periods of time.*

Taking turns helps each child's interest develop along individual lines and minimize wear-and-tear on the book. Most children take ten or fifteen minutes each, while classmates hang over their shoulders, kibitzing. Some children linger after their turns, fascinated enough to go through the book a fourth or fifth time. Other books attract attention, but none seems to match the developmental appeal of Outside-In

The children are hooked. They're invested in their self-portraits, intrigued by the mysterious and invisible Insides, eager to own a replica

of the fascinating model. Now they understand why their Outsides must remain at school for "a long time," and they want to share the process as well as the product with their families.

Jogger's mom and the "Happy Face"

Jogger's mother has not stopped in for quite a while. Jogger pulls her over to his Outside. She looks at the fierce painted face of her son, murmuring, "Is that a Happy Face?"

Jogger picks up his cue. "Yep. I'm not smiling cuz I got chapped lips."

Mom underscores. "No wonder my Happy Boy looked so mad!"

Ani remembers it all

Shirelle goes up to Ani at the model, "Look at the boy's penis!"

Ani responds, "Yeah, but LOOK: the girl has a VAGINA!"

Passing them, I add, "And inside is the stretchy place where a baby can grow if the girl decides to be a mother when she grows up."

Ani sticks out her stomach playfully, "I got a baby!"

Yesterday Ani reported to her mother that every child will do a body—boys and girls a little different—and she used technical names: spinal column, bladder. Today she leads her mother to the model and reviews each organ system. She appears to have remembered everything from circle, and she smiles happily, "This project is going to take a very long time."

Shirelle flirts, Clint shows his mom

Shirelle pirouettes up to Clint as he arrives, batting her eyes at close range, and asks, "Do I look beautiful today?"

Clint backs into his mother, who says, "That's a pretty dress, Shirelle."

Clint marches his mother to the model, pumping the heart with a big grin. After he heads for the block corner, his mother stops to say she's read the letter and is excited about the project. "I can't believe all he's learning! Such difficult subjects. I really admire the way you wade in. I didn't know it could be done with kids so young."

Paul: skeletons and people

Paul muses at the model, "If a skeleton had no arms, then people would have no arms."

Paul's working out the direction of causality. He's grasped a relationship between underlying supporting structure and what's visible in a living person. Is he doing "voodoo" thinking, imagining people's arms would drop off if you removed the arms from skeletons, or is he simply limited by four-year-old syntax?

Daisy's enthusiasm, her mom's concern

Daisy's mother stops me in the hall to tell me Daisy came home bursting with information for her family: "The brain tells you it's hot, like when Auntie touched the barbecue. The body has like balloons inside, but they don't go PFFFF all over the room when the air goes out of them. It's not all red and yucky inside—it's pink and nice. Some of your blood gets blue. The boy has a blue wiener."

Her mother's thrilled. "I love these hands-on projects. I'm taking Daisy to the library to follow up on all this. Ages ago her father told her there's a 'bad guy' and a 'good guy' inside her who make her 'do things.' I've been trying to erase the concept ever since."

"Yes, children latch onto an easy out of accountability. Something like that is bound to come up during The Bodyworks. I'll try to help Daisy move toward a sense of free will and responsibility."

Daisy, Kahlil and Pip: puppets explore the models

Daisy, Kahlil, and Pip take animal puppets over to the body books and models, making silly noises while the puppets peek through holes, acting out the children's mixed feelings about taboos being removed. Daisy repeatedly touches the model, especially the penis.

Later Daisy returns, craning her neck to see all parts. I offer to hang the model lower, to make it easier to see. Daisy says, "YES! I'm gonna sit down to enjoy it!" She points to the vertebrae macaroni: "These things are hard on me. I can't break it," and talks about joints and the rib cage. She absorbed yesterday's circle!

Many of the children can be seen and heard "thinking physically." In manipulating and constructing the model, they are posing questions, checking their perceptions, and modifying their own behavior.

Rosa's rainbow dress

Rosa's wearing a blue dress with tiny rainbows and hearts printed all over it, rainbow buttons down the front, and a large hairbow to match.

For three days she's watched other children work, looking hard at the Outsides on the clothesline, lingering over Maggie's and Ani's. She's the last to paint. Does she worry she can't measure up to the most skilled children's work? She's run through her repertoire of avoiding and delaying tactics, and is now kneeling on the floor to paint.

Rosa's mouth is grim as she attacks the outlined shoes, her paintbrush dripping with brown. Nita reminds her she picked brown for her hair, that starting at the top makes the job easier. Rosa mutters, begins the hair, and stops in midstroke. "I wanna do my bow first. It's the top. You shoulda made me do the bow first. Now it'll be bad and it's your fault." Nita agrees pleasantly that the bow is an excellent starting place and asks Rosa what colors she will need. "Well, look, stupid, all of them. It's a rainbow." She paints very carefully, very slowly.

When Rosa gets to the hair, Nita suggests she leave a space around the bow to fill in when the other paint is dry. Rosa starts to challenge Nita's suggestion, but looks at the beautiful bow and visibly decides to risk success, sighing she'll wait. As she paints her dress, Rosa announces she will put in all the little rainbows over the blue.

Nita is torn. We see three options: (1) allow Rosa to attempt the rainbows independently, probably to fail in a big and public way; (2) have Nita commit most of her time (and a large amount of floor space) to Rosa for the next two activity periods so she can succeed; or, (3) urge Rosa to do one big rainbow on her dress, or smaller ones just on the front buttons, a suggestion certain to infuriate her. Even the last option is highly labor-intensive for adult and child, with no guarantee of success.

There's no good way out of this. Rosa so rarely opens herself to a project. Despite her initial attempts at sabotage, we've gotten her this far. Now what Rosa wants can't be had without skewing the whole project—we just can't give her quite that much adult attention. It's sickening not to be able to support Rosa, but she always gets far more than her share of classroom energy. This go-round we have to draw the line, even though we see how deeply she identifies with her rainbow dress (an issue for people far beyond the physical thinking stage).

Nita explains all the little rainbows would take too much time, offers the idea about the buttons, and suggests Rosa could finish the rainbows at home, at the end.

"I GOTTA do the rainbows. You GOTTA let me! Or I'm not doing any more of this stupid stuff. I hate this stuff."

Ultimately Rosa paints rainbow buttons, griping the whole time.

We remind ourselves that part of our task is to help children accommodate to real life—including the limits of teacher and pupil one-to-one time—and we can't take Rosa's anger personally. Less rationally, we know each little skirmish in Rosa's war with the world is a test, and we prefer to help her polish her sense of self-esteem rather than weigh her needs against the group's. We're aware of the irony that with some children we've insisted on realism, while here we've abandoned realism for expedience. The color of a child's eyes may strike an adult as more significant than that of her dress, but Rosa's fierce attachment reminds us that to the physical thinker the dress may be all-important.

Another caveat about Rosa: Our concern for her and our frustration that we can't meet all her needs may appear to her as our irritability, whittling away at her self-esteem. Children need to know adults do disapprove of their behavior at times, but they're quick to interpret disapproval as a rejection of themselves. It's all-important that I do my best and then let go. Otherwise, my attachment to teacher success will confuse and dismay the children in my care.

When Rosa finishes painting, I set her to washing brushes, which she loves to do. I remind her to push the brushes against the sink to see if the water runs clear. She's in control of something important and pleasurable besides. In the sensual flow of the water her whole body loosens. She's half smiling as activity period ends.

Terry cues, Pip plays, a strategy develops

As Pip cuts, Terry shows him how to clear away the excess paper for more control around the fingers. He holds a strip of paper under his nose and calls it his moustache. After his sparkly and playful interlude he returns to the task. Realizing he has to shift his whole body to another angle, he approaches from the other side, using one hand to support the paper while the other hand works the scissors.

Our basic approach is trial and error, with a teacher cuing the child, helping him articulate what he's learning. In this way, the child begins to plan and analyze tasks as he goes and becomes more conscious of the use of tools and the efficient placement of his body. The Bodyworks provides a perfect context for developing awareness of one's learning style and creating strategies for making work easier.

Bo's mother really sees

Bo's mother comes to see Bo's self-portrait and enjoys looking through them all. "It's incredible how each one captures the child. Personalities really shine through!"

Missy's mom tries hard

Missy pulls her mother to The Bodyworks table and sits down to work on the four-layer body puzzle. Mom asks where each piece should go, quickly answering her own questions. Missy wilts, then brightens as she shows Mom a diagram of the digestive tract. Mom stuffs information. "Here's how your body gets nutrients, vitamins and minerals when you digest your food."

Silently I sigh. Missy's mom tries so hard, making time to spend a few minutes with Missy at school before rushing off to work, but the quality time almost inevitably backfires. Mom can't express interest without grabbing the ball. She pushes so hard to make each moment count. It's especially complicated because she and Missy seem, temperamentally, to be so different.

I've made tactful suggestions. At school Missy can follow her own nose, discover her own approach to people and materials. Observers worry because she's usually on the edge, quiet as a bright-eyed mouse. This is Missy's first group experience. She's clearly taking her time, learning the ropes by watching before she jumps in. We've made sure all her skills are in place, set up duos and small groups to make entry easier, whetted other children's interest. Her parents wish she would make friends. I assure them she will, in her own time. We're not neglecting her; we're giving her space to feel her own appetite and follow it. Missy's the one to decide she's ready for friends. Will The Bodyworks play a role?

Cara perseveres

Cara runs to the project area without being called and struggles with lefty scissors. Despite all the right motions, the blades are not cutting through. Finally she sighs, "Wrong scissors. Other one?" Nita checks, "Yes, those are sticky. See if these are better." Success! Cara kneels with her face to the paper, eyebrows together, lips pursed. Periodically she gets up, sighs, and pushes her hair off her face.

Tanya in a hurry

Tanya slashes with her scissors, muttering, "I can't cut too good. FAST, I gotta do things FAST."

Tanya's the middle child. Even before the recent upheaval at home, she had learned to exasperate her parents by being pokey. They recognize the root of her behavior and try to give her more attention, but they're also campaigning to speed up her home chores. Meanwhile, she's transferred the "hurry up" message to school, adding to her long-standing concerns about "success."

I tell Tanya, "It's great to be able to do some things fast, like pick up your toys at home. But some things just need more time, and if we rush them we make lots of mistakes. Writing and cutting are things we just work away at, not dawdling but not rushing either." I say this, but I know my little message won't be the end of it.

We pay close attention to the child's responses, meshing the project with her development. She reveals her "appetite," her growing edges, her blocks, her learning style, and her temperament. We try to reflect her to herself, making our perceptions available for her to explore and test.

Children jump in

Ani's acting bored, lurching and sliding on large paper scraps. Other children ask WHY they have to cut the WHOLE THING.

Terry points to the models. "Each child is going to make one like that. Girls will make one with girl parts and boys will make one with boy parts." Ani swivels around, alert, "What parts?" Terry goes on, "Girls will have a uterus, where the baby can grow inside if . . ." Ani interrupts, "AND A CORD!"

The children cut with renewed interest. Tanya's racing to beat Ani, who seems not to notice.

Ani wonders aloud, "What if your skull broke?"

In a slow exaggerated motion, Bo opens his jaw, "What happens when you yawn?"

Ani announces to Pip, who's hanging around, "If you fall, your skull gets bumped!"

Maggie, passing by, grabs a body book and waves it in Terry's face, "The SKULL, the SKELETON!"

Immediately Tanya's on her feet, "I want to do it now! I want the book before Ani gets it!"

The Bodyworks at work: In the flurry of cutting-out and passing-by, in context or out of it, questions and insights begin to emerge. An invitation has been issued, permission has been given: to share wonders and puzzlements and fears; to seek confirmation; to examine taboos; to dig out under-articulated perceptions, no holds barred. It doesn't take the children long to recognize this rare opportunity and jump in with both feet.

Navigating gender roles

Zack and Kahlil are playing with the small dollhouses.

Kahlil: "Help me! Help me! Help me!"

Zack: "Oh, Mommy's coming. I mean . . . DADDY'S coming!"

In dress-ups Daisy and Shirelle are telling everyone whom to marry. Pip gets independent: "I will marry Santa Claus . . . or the Easter Bunny."

Shirelle, full of scorn: "Santa Claus is a BOY!"

Pip, not to be squashed: "Then I will marry MRS. Santa Claus."

At circle we play "Great Big Tiger" in two lines, alternating the roles of preying-tiger and parent-protecting-baby. Shirelle stomps off: "I am NOT a tiger. I am a Ballerina Mother! I am ALWAYS a Ballerina *Mother!"*

They're learning to navigate complex gender roles and relationships. I'm continuously surprised by disparities in their functioning. At one moment, a child is a master of sophisticated lingo and moves. A heartbeat later she's an innocent.

Missy and Clint share *Outside-In*

Missy told her mother Clint's a nice boy and she might invite him to play. Clint reported to his mother that he likes Missy, too. Missy and Clint haven't figured out how to signal this to each other, or else they aren't ready to. They're a good pair for the body books, but I want to oversee them. Missy backs off fast from social engineering.

The two children take turns with the flaps of *Outside-In,* enjoying themselves and each other. It goes wonderfully well until they hit the soft drawing of a girl and boy about six years old, facing forward, completely nude. There's a little pause, no flap to lift. Then Missy comments: "The girl's turning her head to look at the boy, but the boy's not looking at her."

Time for a quick decision. Is Missy saying that boys are less interested in girls than girls are in boys? that in fact she's noticed Clint doesn't pay much attention to girls? that although she may not act like it she's quite interested in boys, especially Clint? Is she deflecting the conversation away from nudity? In her four-year-old way, is she intuiting that female development moves toward "relationship," male development toward "autonomy"? Or is she alluding to her relationship with her little brother?

Knowing Missy, I suspect any and all of these possibilities are relevant, though largely unconscious. Knowing Clint, I guess the nudity issue is salient. Ready or not, here we are at the taboo.

I jump in, "That's right. And this picture shows the parts of their bodies that are different from each other. What do you call that part of the boy's body?" They squirm and look away. "It's not a word we usually talk about, but it's an important word to be able to use, and both of you know it. What do we call this?" Both, softly: "Penis." "How about this part of the girl's body? What's the name for that?"

This time Clint's less squirmy, and he speaks clearly after a slight hesitation, "It's her vagina."

While not technically correct, "vagina" is the name used for the vulva by most of our school's families.

"Yep," I say, and the children happily continue paging through the book.

Maggie's eagerness

Maggie's eyes are shining, as she pulls her babysitter to her self-portrait, then points to the model, grinning, "I gonna make one."

Sibling illness

Tanya heads straight for the models, as her mother stops to say, "Thanks so much for doing this project. Remember two years ago, when Renee was born and Michelle was in your class? I was so worried about the intestinal blockage in the baby. Michelle didn't understand why we had to take Renee back to the hospital, and then I remembered the 'body' and we took it down together and talked about the doctor opening up the tube and stitching it back, and Michelle relaxed because it made perfect sense. Michelle still has her 'body' hanging on her door. Tanya started talking about hers last night, and Michelle jumped right in. I don't think she's forgotten any of it."

When a sibling is ill or injured, the situation may be emotionally complex for the healthy child. Concern often mixes with relief: "It isn't me," ambivalence toward the patient, and resentment that the other child is getting so much attention. In the midst of the crisis it may be impossible to sort out and release these feelings. It can be helpful to offer the healthy child a cognitive focus. It's a relief to concentrate on the body's self-healing properties. Children are delighted to learn how white blood cells "defend," why blood clots and scabs.

Toilets and research

While Zack looks at *Look Inside Your Body*, Shane peers over his shoulder. I ask, "What do you notice that's interesting?"

Zack points to the bare bodies and the toilet.

Shane huffs loudly, "That's disgusting! You should talk to him!"

"I'm glad you're interested in your bodies, Shane and Zack! When you understand more, they probably won't seem disgusting. You can figure out a lot, like scientists do, by noticing things carefully. You can ask questions. You can look things up in books, too. 'Research' is what we call it when we're trying to find out answers."

In this context children have a powerful, pleasurable introduction to the use of reference books. The subject matter is at hand (literally) and there's a strong drive to know more about it. Sensation, perception, and concept formation—linked by the curriculum—expand within the individual child. The group's energy boosts discoveries and enthusiasms, creating special bonds between children and their favorite books.

In effect, the children are developing a varied repertoire of research skills in the most natural way. These academic skills include: scanning, recognizing, and following up cues, cross-referencing, reviewing, and interpreting pictures and charts and diagrams. The children are also learning that there are books available on complex subjects (including taboos)—sources of information for independent "readers." Above all, they're learning curiosity is legitimate.

At first the curiosity may seem prurient, but attention gets hooked to other topics. (We adults know how one dictionary or encyclopedia entry can launch a many-branched exploration.) Children refine muscle skills that enable them to use books effectively: manipulating pages and placing and retrieving bookmarks.

Shane: "disgusting"

Kahlil and Maggie whisper and giggle at the playdough table. Shane complains, "I hate telling secrets in front of friends and disgusting words." Kahlil and Maggie: "It's private." Shane continues, "Is it nice private or disgusting private? Telling poopee is disgusting private and being alone is nice private." Kahlil and Maggie giggle, "Sorry." Shane scolds them, "Say it not silly. Be serious."

In this unprecedented social situation Shane's clearly disoriented. The old rules don't apply. He's able here to define his limits and to insist his feelings be respected. I'll watch carefully to see if he needs support.

It's crucial to provide sensory and gross motor outlets to release, express, and refuel energy The Bodyworks stirs up. Fingerpaint, clay, wrestling, and puppets may require extra supervision. Water, sand, and playdough beckon.

Obviously not everything can be available every day. The children can learn from being included in these decisions. What do they need? Something to push, pound? Why are they wanting to do this kind of thing right now? Where could it happen in the busy classroom? Who will be in charge of it?

Escape valves for Cara, Missy, Clint, Pip, Paul and Bo

There's general delight in fingerpaint right now, especially since we've put together a double-table for four fingerpainters. "Fecal smearing" is too easy an answer, but no doubt these overtones are present! The children experiment and play, slapping at each other's strokes, laughing delightedly. When they bog down, we suggest variations: fingertips, thumbprints, fingernails, fronts and backs of palms, whole hands. Finally the happy foursome sloshes clean in the bathroom.

Hands clean, Cara and Missy head for the wrestling mat, with Clint and Pip following. The girls lean and rock together, while the boys push and butt each other yet manage to confine their activity to one end of the mat. Paul and Bo approach, growling and waving blue monster-hands, on their way to wash up. All four children on the mat collapse and huddle in thrilled mock-fear, then crawl-chase each other around the mat.

Wrestling provides escape valves for built-up energy. Here even Missy has let go, with Cara as a playful partner to wrestle with the boys!

The Bodyworks shows us the child and provides a context in which to address her issues. It also reveals the child to herself and to her peers. With greater awareness of her body, she develops greater awareness of her "self," and expands her conscious field for playing, experimenting, risking, and adapting. Already Cara and Missy are making leaps.

Rosa cuts and recovers

Rosa doesn't volunteer to cut out her Outside but doesn't object when Terry calls her over. She works intently, tight and twisted even when Terry shows her how to adjust her position. As Terry turns to answer someone else's question, Rosa's scissors continue along to the head, straying onto the hairline instead of the outer edge of hair. Rosa doesn't notice what she's done until the hair slips to the floor like a wig.

Rosa and Terry see the damage at precisely the same moment, and Terry scoops up the fat roll of tape we keep nearby for just such mishaps. Terry mends the back side while Rosa shifts from near tears into anger: "You made me slip. That tape's never gonna work. It's gonna be terrible cuz you didn't tell me to cut the other way." Terry reminds her of all the slashes and tears on other children's work, offering the skillful mending job as a small consolation.

Nearby, Pippin is struggling with the Humpty Dumpty puzzle. I suggest, "Pip, why don't you ask Rosa to help you? She's really good with puzzles." Rosa's almost too far gone to be drawn in, but she drags herself over and soon glows with competence and helpfulness.

Decapitations and amputations in the cutting process may be serious business for some children. On one level they know "I" am not my bodyworks, but there may be a strong identification.

A day off

Time for "a day off," with no work we have to complete. Time for me just to be with the children as they go about their work with blocks, puzzles, sand, fingerpaint, dress-ups, dinosaurs, and all the rest. I want some time with Maggie today, also Pip, Ani, Shirelle, and Kahlil. They're likelier than many to "fall through the cracks" of teacher attention. Even though they don't particularly "need" me right now, they deserve to know they're important, cherished.

I don't even put the body books out—just leave the day open so we can chew our cuds and let the digestive juices work. We've been so busy!

Time to think about our experience so far. I see again how powerfully children identify with their life-size paint-and-paper representations. Some take pains to detail a single feature. Some decide to paint themselves unrealistically. Knowing she cannot represent herself to her own satisfaction, a child may create outrageous distortions which cannot be mistaken for herself, as Bo did. Or she may try to acquire some wished-for power by representing it, like Missy and the blue eyes.

Like Rosa, some children may avoid the self-portrait or deliberately sabotage it, so they won't feel inadequate when wielding a paintbrush. Others may feel real anxiety about the self being represented. In contrast, the confident child takes the opportunity to differentiate and appreciate the symbolic self.

Of course children may be tired or preoccupied or simply have their own agenda. Then motivation tends to surface soon, so magnetic is the invitation to paint a life-sized self-portrait.

In any event, here are precious opportunities for diagnosing problems and offering resources to resolve them. The alert teacher may discover seeds or full-blown bias among the children. Racism, classism, sexism, able-ism, and size-ism rear their heads in children's views of themselves and each other. The "physical thinking" of children wedded to the "image thinking" prevalent in our media culture threatens self-esteem, especially in the child whose physical appearance doesn't conform to the image.

The Bodyworks was created and tested among children predominantly white and middle-class, well-nourished, styled like the power structure. Throughout the year I deal with race, class, gender, nutrition, and personal safety in individuals and in the whole group. Any one of these issues could become a major focus within The Bodyworks, but it's necessary to choose, not to overwhelm children or teachers. The design of the curriculum invites this kind of tailoring to fit each group.

An example: These children have already spent a good bit of time thinking and talking about race, sharing activities designed to heighten awareness and appreciation of differences. The Bodyworks is a natural context for mixing paint colors to match skin tones. This valuable process happens to be time-consuming and teacher-intensive, adding at least one drying day to each self-portrait before features and clothes can be added. I decided this year to introduce tan butcher paper for the self-portraits, providing a more or less "neutral" background. The children were free to paint skin or not, depending upon its salience for them.

As with every trade-off, this one had pluses and minuses. Cara chose to paint her hands brown "like Nita's," to make a proud public statement about her skin—risking some sense of separateness from her adoptive parents. Jogger chose not to address the issue at all. Was this a minus? Perhaps the open-ended structure allowed him time he needed to stay "underground."

Who am I to set a timetable for Jogger? He doesn't seem ready to wrestle with what it means to be biracial in this society. Perhaps he's not comfortable enough to do so in this setting. Perhaps his family is not ready for him to do so. Perhaps race is truly not even an issue for him, though it's likely to be later.

Once again, I've hit the wall of my own limits as a white teacher to understand from inside the challenges faced by children of color. Although I've spent a lifetime trying to recognize and to root out racism in myself and in our society, I can't assume my intuition and my compas-

sion can make the leap to Jogger—I haven't been there in my own skin. All I can do is stay open, keep trying, continue learning to be an ally, keep turning to people of color to teach me how to accompany their children.

My sadness, my frustration, is not limited to race. It comes up most dramatically in relationship to the large issues that divide us: race, class, gender, ableness. However, it's there in many small and subtle moments of my teaching day. There's an essential aloneness in each child, which I can't reach, can't teach. I can only respect and trust this in the child, as in myself, and balance it with its complement, the equally true experience that at some level we are all one. The Bodyworks throws me against that paradox and helps me live with it into deeper understanding.

WEEK THREE

The Brain

Introducing the Method

Ideally, we'd start Insides with something easy to understand and simple to construct, so each child could get hands on fast. However, we must begin with the brain, if the children are to grasp much that follows. I invite a boy and a girl to examine the model, encouraging them to speculate: where brains are, what brains do, how brains work, why brains extend through spinal cords into nerves.

Typically, this leads to talking, moving around, gesturing, demonstrating, referring to books and other resources. In the process I introduce concepts that build on the children's experience of their own bodies. Despite developmental and temperamental differences, the children's questions and responses overlap, amplifying and extending their range. I improvise, shifting emphasis to follow interest.

When the children have some grasp of key concepts (from looking, talking, manipulating the model, moving and observing their own and each other's bodies), I give each child a coathanger with an oaktag head and a paper bag body stapled in place. Most of the front panel of the bag has been cut away, leaving an open torso: the base for the model.

From a basket of supplies and tools, the children select what they need to construct a brain and spinal column. With my help, they plan the work and begin. Conversation and exploration continue. By the end of this first stage of bodyworking, each child has begun to form new concepts, the seeds of a dramatic new sense of self and other.

Ani and Zack begin the Insides, guided by Sandy

Zack remarks, "I'm going to do a boy because I'm a boy, and Ani's going to do a girl because she's a girl." I note to myself that sex differences keep coming up for Zack, saying only: "Yes, when the whole project is finished, in some ways your models will be different, because in some ways boys' and girls' bodies are different. But mostly boys' and girls' bodies are the same. Everybody's brain looks alike, so today your models will look just like each other."

Sandy: "Today we're going to make the brain! Do you know what your brain does?"

Ani: "Your brain is when you're smart."

Zack: "You think. Your brain."

Sandy: "Yes, your brain gets messages and sends messages."

Ani: "Like the phone. You leave a message."

Sandy: "Lots of little pathways called nerves go from your brain to the rest of your body. Pretend you put your finger on the stove. The nerves in your finger would send a message to your brain: 'Hot, Hot, Hot!' Then your brain would send a message back to your finger: 'Move FAST! get off the stove!'"

Zack: "One time my mother spilled hot water on Brownie. Just a little bit. It was a mistake."

Sandy: "What did Brownie do?"

Zack: "He barked and ran out of the kitchen."

Sandy: "Dogs have brains too. Where do you think your brain is?"

Ani taps her head: "Up here."

Sandy: "Exactly. Look on the model. Do you see something that could be a brain?"

Ani: "Why is that string all tangled up?"

Sandy: "That's to show that the brain is full of pathways for messages that are coming and going all the time. See where the string goes."

Ani follows the string with her finger to a hole punched at the base of the skull.

Sandy: "Nice going, Ani, you followed the brain stem down. Can you guess where it goes now?" No answers. I turn the model over to the back. "The string goes down the back. The part of the brain that goes down your back is called the spinal cord."

Ani: "Why does it have macaroni?"

Sandy: "Your real brain doesn't have macaroni. On the model we use macaroni to look like a lot of little bones in a row. Your spinal cord goes through all the little bones on your back. They protect it. Those little bones are called vertebrae. Can you say that word? Ver-ta-bray."

Ani and Zack: "Ver-ta-bray."

Sandy: "We all have vertebrae up and down our back, all bumpy like this macaroni on the model. Feel the middle of my back."

Ani, touching Sandy's back: "You can see little bumps sticking out."

Sandy: Yes. Try reaching around to your own backs. Can you feel your own vertebrae?"

Zack: "Why are there lots? Why not just one big one?"

Sandy: "What an interesting question, Zack! I bet you two can figure out some of the answer. First, let's bend over and touch the floor. . . . Lean way back. . . . Move your head and shoulders in a big circle while you bend over. . . . Your back can move in lots of different directions, can't it?" I touch each child's shinbone. "Now, try moving this part of your leg around like that."

Ani bends her knee and swings her leg: "I go to dancing lessons."

Sandy: "Yes. When you're dancing, you can bend your knee and your ankle, but not the middle, the shin bone. Feel your shin bone."

Zack: "No bumps."

Sandy: "That's right. It's smooth, and it can't bend. It's all one piece. Our backs have lots of small pieces, lots of vertebrae, so we can move in lots of different directions. Look at the model again. There's the head bone—sometimes we call it 'the skull.' Inside is the brain, like a tangle of string, and it goes down the back to make the spinal cord, with the vertebrae to protect it. Where else does the string go?"

Zack points to pieces of string attached to the spinal cord and extending to shoulders and thighs: "Here. And here."

Sandy: "Yes, those are the nerves. The model only shows nerves to your arms and legs, but nerves go to all the parts of your body. The nerves are pathways to take messages back and forth to the brain."

Ani: "So if you put your finger on the stove, it says 'Hot!'"

Sandy: "Or if you put your toe in the ocean, it might say 'Cold!'"

Ani: "One time I went swimming and it was too cold, so I made a castle."

Sandy: "Do you see there's a different kind of macaroni at the end of the backbone? Some people call that the tailbone."

Zack: "People don't have a tail. Only dogs and cats."

Sandy: "You're right, Zack. We don't. But if we were animals, that's where our tail would grow. Can you feel your tailbone, where your back ends?"

Ani: "One time I was sitting on a pillow, and my cousin pulled it out and I fell on my tailbone and I cried. It wasn't funny. He said it was a joke."

Sandy: "It hurts when a bone gets a hard bump! In a minute you'll start making a brain and spinal cord and vertebrae and nerves for your bodyworks. Look in the basket. What do you need?"

Zack: "Macaroni. And string."

Sandy: "Yes. How are you going to get them to stay on?"

Ani: "This one has tape on it."

Sandy: "Right, so get some tape out. Look at the brain. No tape. What do you think is holding the string like that?" No answer. "Look in the basket and find something else that holds things together."

Zack: "Glue!"

Sandy: "One more thing you're going to need. You won't use this whole ball of string, so we'll have to cut it."

Ani: "Scissors!"

Sandy: "Yes, now we're all set. Where should we start?"

Ani (threading a piece of macaroni on string): "I'm gonna to make the macaroni, the . . . ver-ta . . ."

Sandy: "You could do that first, but it will help you remember how the brain works if you start with the brain at the top, then go down the back."

Zack: "That's what I'm gonna do. . . . I can't cut this, it's too hard."

Sandy: "Let's try together. If Ani stretches the string, it'll be easier to cut. Then you can switch, and Ani can cut."

Ani (stringing macaroni): "Remember that picture?"

Sandy: "Which picture, Ani?"

Ani: "In the book. The ballerina picture."

Sandy: "Yes, I know just which one you're thinking of."

Ani: "Why did she get all folded up?"

Sandy: "Good question, Ani! You get *Outside-In*—-it's right over there—and let's look at the picture again. . . You found the page right away! Here's the first picture, where she's standing up dancing. Do you have any ideas why the other drawing shows her all folded up?"

Zack: "I never saw anybody like that."

Sandy: "I haven't either, Zack. I bet the artist was trying to make us think what it would look like if someone didn't have bones. Bones hold us up. Let's try something. Ani, please hand me a pencil. Zack, would you please get me a tissue from the shelf? . . . OK. Can you make the tissue stand up by itself?. . . Ani, you hold the pencil up, and I'll put the tissue over it."

Ani: "Now it's standing up."

Sandy: "That's what our bones do inside our skin, just like the pencil holds up the tissue. A different day, we can look at some X-ray pictures of bones."

Not all children are as interested, as responsive, as patient as Ani and Zack. Teachers have to accommodate big differences among children, as well as fluctuations in an individual child's attention. The method takes this into account, and makes it easy to extend, compress, and take breaks to create a developmental fit. Fortunately, no other organ system is as complex or time-consuming as the brain.

Shirelle: making a leap

Shirelle's taping her vertebrae, glancing across the table at Clint's work. "HEY, mine is JUST LIKE Clint's!"

Terry affirms and extends, "Yes, your bodies look different on the outside, but inside your spinal cord and nerves look just alike."

Shirelle pauses, looks around the classroom with her mouth open, turning to Terry with wide eyes, "Just like EVERYONE ELSE'S!"

Shirelle has made a quantum leap. We can't assume that her insight is deep or permanent or that it will generalize to other body systems. No matter: in this instant, Shirelle has grasped a mystery. She's filled with wondering awareness. As teachers, we try to create the environment in which insights happen. It's a rare privilege to see the process whole, and to rejoice in the midst of the thousand other things that are happening.

Clint, Paul, Ani, Pip: extending and assimilating

Clint, Paul, and Ani are working on puzzles. Ani stretches her legs, flexes one knee and ankle. Watching her joints work, she comments, "If your knee couldn't bend, you couldn't go upstairs."

Paul adds, "Or downstairs."

Clint, his puzzle completed, announces, "My brain's telling me to get up now," and stands up at the table.

Pip, playing with puppets nearby, crouches on all fours, and waves his bottom from side to side: "I have a tailbone like my kitties. I can wag my tail!"

Of the four children, only Ani and Clint have actually constructed the nervous system so far. Paul and Pip have picked up information informally. Each child's comments indicate (1) enough interest to pursue the topic without a teacher's prompting, (2) personal application of the material, and (3) social support and momentum. Assimilation's underway. I note different learning styles.

Ani flexes her leg again. Is she tying that into her ballet theme? My teaching focus was the brain, but the skeletal system was her entry point. I responded to Ani's interest with a concrete improvisation built out of the teachable moment. Now Ani poses a hypothesis to test her new information. She transfers one familiar context (dance class) to another (going upstairs). Ani often works outward from a strong interest like dancing. It's clear she's learned something about bones; it's not clear whether the ripples of her attention incorporated the brain.

Paul doesn't have close friends in school and often seems passive among his peers. Chirping up and adding to Ani's comment, he hints at new readiness. Has the subject matter lit his fire?

Clint, already self-aware, considers reflection. Typical of his age, he expresses his thinking physically. Where will he go with this? I wish I could ride his train of thought.

Pip, full of whimsy, imagines himself a cat. He places himself at the edge of groups, jumping in with appropriate contributions. Unfortunately, other children seldom linger in his magical world. He rarely sustains his connections. Is it that he can't, or that he chooses not to, preferring the richness of his own imagination to his peers' predictable media scripts?

Kahlil talks to the model

Nita drops Kahlil's model as she hangs it to dry. Kahlil wags his finger, mocking: "The brain told you to cry because you fell down, and go get your mommy. Sometimes it tells you you're bad."

Kahlil's exaggerated voice and gestures tell Nita he wants her to know he understands the nature of a model, and is making a joke out of incongruity. Imagine a paper bag behaving like the living child it represents! At the same time, he may well be identifying with the model, and reminding himself it's not "real." He extends the concept of "messages" to the emotional realm, revealing his familiarity with lapses in self-esteem. It's too much to suggest he links "bad" messages with incompetence or dependency, but it's worth noticing his juxtaposition.

Filling the stomach

The children have been told The Bodyworks will take a long time, but they don't really understand we'll inch along, waiting for each child to finish each system before anyone moves to the next. It's important for everyone to get hands on while the meaning of "a long time" sinks in, so we set up a table for group work. Here children discuss what they ate for dinner the night before, choose construction paper to represent each food, cut the paper up into tiny "bites" to place in a small baggie "stomach." They chat about food, match colors, experiment with shapes and sizes. Periodically, a teacher drops by to write down each child's menu, reminding children to "chew your food well" in order to encourage the sustained eye-hand scissor work.

It's a natural moment for nutrition education, but we bypass this opportunity. We give children the chance to develop a conversation themselves, freeing teachers to oversee other areas.

Bo, Daisy, Maggie, Cara: colors, rules, points, cutting

Bo jokes with Maggie, "I had onions for dessert, onions in ice cream."

"YUCKY!"

Daisy parrots: "Chew everything in small bites so you can digest it and you don't choke."

Bo complains, "There's no color for ham."

Maggie offers him a piece of construction paper, which Bo swats out of the way angrily, "NOT PINK! I DON'T TOUCH PINK!" He shuffles through the stack until he finds red. After cutting red "ham," Bo rummages again. "I had a new kind of juice. Not yellow and not orange. Kind of orange AND yellow."

Maggie risks another suggestion, "Use yellow AND orange. In your stomach I bet it turns like that."

After the first few "bites," Bo continues to cut but avoids putting anything more in his baggie. Terry urges him to fill the baggie with his pile of little scraps, but he refuses. Finally she spreads the baggie wide and holds it up while Bo drops in his scraps, pretending to chew and swallow them first. Terry notices that her fingers are smudged with ink rubbed off from Bo's name written on the baggie in marking pen. He smirks, "That's why I wouldn't touch it."

Daisy works for a long time, using her scissors to round off all the points of her small pieces. "I gotta make sure it isn't sharp, so it won't hurt my stomach."

Others come and go while Cara and Maggie spend almost the whole morning at the table.

Bo uses onions for a good laugh, but he's dead serious about pink, as in his self-portrait. So tight is the cultural association of "pink" and "girl" that Bo won't even touch the color. He's not afraid of being "changed" somehow, is he? Is he too uncertain of his masculine identity to risk a "feminine" color? He seems to be concerned about himself, not rejecting actual females. He's fond of his younger sister and plays happily with both girls and boys, in and out of school. He often avoids getting his hands dirty, due to tactile sensitivity, parental values, or both. In any event, he also enjoys hornswoggling an adult when he can.

Daisy tries to please adults, even absent ones. She works at being a "good girl," parroting rules for "digestion" and "not choking." There's no playfulness in her hard work to round off sharp construction paper—she has fully identified with the model.

Maggie enjoys her competence with colors and scissors. In this secure setting, undeterred by Bo's initial rejection, she transcends the usual limits of her speech to risk offering help a second time. She manages to be helpful, not bossy, which would have alienated Bo immediately.

In contrast to Maggie, Cara struggles with lefty scissors. Yet she stays at the table far longer than she needs to. Is she refining her skill, or taking advantage of the chance for low-risk sociability? Probably both.

Circle: children take a topic and run with it

At circle, Kahlil leans forward waving his hand urgently, blurting: "Why do we need a brain?"

"Good question, Kahlil. What do you think, children?"

Clint: "To talk."

Zack: "So if you touch something hot, your brain can tell you to move your hand."

Ani: "To think."

Shirelle: "To send a message."

Shane: "My cousin went to the park, and he touched the fire thing and he broke his little bone."

Tanya: "One of my friends broke his leg."

Rosa: "I know somebody that went in a ambulance. To the hospital."

Maggie: "My aunt. I have two aunts. And the one that doesn't live next to me one time she. . ."

Daisy: "My friend broke a arm and he got OK and his dog got sicker and sicker and his dog died."

Paul: "If something's real cold, you need some hot water."

Kahlil's question probably comes from considerable depth, judging by his earlier "joke." Clint has connected thinking and talking. Zack remembers the example of the brain's functioning and he phrases this in his own way, using complex syntax. Ani remembers Zack's answer during their paired work. Shirelle recalls key words. Shane's got fire and trauma on his mind again. Tanya tops him. Rosa tops Tanya. Maggie jumps in, though she can't get the whole story out. Daisy juxtaposes events, relating them—causally? Paul offers his general knowledge, showing he's awake and wants to be included. The children who've had a turn to construct the brain address Kahlil's question. The others veer off into first- and second-hand disasters.

When is it a "bad word?

I 've managed to "not hear" taboo words sprouting in the past few days. Before an epidemic hits, it's time to tell the whole group what I told Jogger last week.

"Here's another job for your brain. Your brain can figure out when it's OK to say a word and when it isn't. It depends on HOW you use the word. Suppose you want to ask a question, like 'Why do people have a line down the middle of their butts?' Suppose you want to say you hurt yourself, like 'I fell on the rock and I hurt my butt.' Then 'butt' is an OK word to use. But suppose you're mad at somebody and you want to hurt her feelings, so you call her 'butthead.' Then 'butt' is not a good word, and it's not OK to use it in this class.

"Your brain knows the difference, when it's OK and when it's not OK to use body words. Lots of other words too. Pretend I'm really mad at Terry."

I work my face up into grotesque anger, and push threateningly close to Terry, attack her with my voice: "You're green, Terry. Green, green, GREEN. Yeah, Terry, you're GREEN!" The children roar with laughter, enjoying the joke. They get the point.

"So any word can be OK or not OK. It depends on how you use it. When we're doing The Bodyworks, we use lots of body words. Your brains will tell you when it's OK to say words like 'poops' and when not to. You don't need a rule.You can figure it out yourself."

Differing interest levels: Shane, Maggie, Bo, Daisy, Tanya

Shane and Maggie haven't had much time to warm up for the day. As they sit at The Bodyworks table, they squirm and twist to look around the room. Nita tries to tie in their turning, looking, and talking with the construction of the brain.

Maggie offers one-word prompts to Shane, but he shows no interest. He does fill in the bit about "Hot!" messages. When Nita asks if either knows the word for the "little bumpy backbones," there's a pause. From halfway across the room Bo supplies "vertebrae!"

Later in the day, Paul falls on the porch. Shane tells him, "When you fall down, your brain says 'Ouch! Go tell your Mom to get a Band-aid!'"

Shane and Maggie's low interest is probably related to timing. Both children tend to cruise the room when they arrive: greet friends, scan the activity options. We thought they'd like an early start on bodyworks, so they could stick with other activities later in the morning. Hard to predict how children will react, but worth trying: timing is all-important.

In any event, Maggie has absorbed much of the material, and Shane later makes it plain that he's already extending a concept.

It's definitely not too early for Bo: his antennae are fine-tuned to this aspect of The Bodyworks, though he's usually resistant to structured projects.

Tanya and Daisy are eager to take their turns. Tanya touches the balloon uterus, smiling, "THIS is where the BABY grows!" Tanya and Daisy feed ideas to each other. Daisy ventures, "I think the brain is like mail to different parts of your body. A messenger brain. You get a letter and you send it back." Tanya extends, "It says 'Lift your hand and go put it in cold water.'"

Tanya's strong interest in babies shows up right away. Daisy rarely risks sharing her own thoughts, but here she creates an analogy, based on her familiarity with "messages" in the mail from her grandparents in Florida. Tanya connects the new message concept to her experience with a burn in cold water.

Bodies and marriage: Shirelle, Daisy, Clint, Pip

Shirelle takes Pepe out of the cage, flips her over, pulls Pepe's legs out of the way and roots in her fur: "I'm looking for her boobies."

In the line for the bathroom, Daisy announces: "I will marry Willy."

Shirelle follows, "I'll marry my brother Ryan even if he's still a baby."

Clint furrows his brow, "I HAVE TO get married or I'll get OLD, so I'll marry Daisy."

Daisy's quick with a comeback: "No way, Jose!"

Pip joins in: "Then two boys could marry each other."

Daisy adds, "My two dads are married to each other."

Shirelle's mind is on her big sister's changing body. She hunts for sexual markers in another species.

Daisy, Shirelle, and Pip have talked about marriage before. Daisy initiates. This time she proposes the unknown "Willy" as her spouse. As a physical thinker, Shirelle picks her own brother, since they are already part of the same household. Her brother is still a baby, so she deflects in advance any potential snags. (It's unclear whether she assumes he'll become an appropriate mate in time, or whether she thinks marriage is possible for a baby. Most likely, she just realizes there's something fishy about her plan and doesn't want to have to defend it.)

Clint introduces an entirely new concern, probably the fallout from some well-intentioned teasing by his grandfather. He has inferred: it's good to be young; it's not good to be old—old people get sick and die; marriage somehow keeps you young; you should get married so you won't get old. Daisy's his logical choice for a spouse, since the two children's families are close friends. Clint has a real sense of urgency about settling this, like any physical thinker with such inferences.

Daisy likes to play marriage, but suddenly this game is much too close for comfort. Clint has brought his plan up before, according to her mother. To be a good girl and a good friend, Daisy wants to please Clint, but she can't conceive of leaving her parents and her own home. Clint's bigger and stronger and she's afraid he can force her to do what he wants. Loudly and clearly, Daisy rejects Clint's idea, with the new assertiveness parents and teachers have been cultivating.

Pip opts for same-gender marriage again. This time Shirelle doesn't shoot him down, and Daisy's an unexpected ally. Daisy comes from a very traditional nuclear family. With "my two dads are married to each other," she stops the conversation, closing a topic which has become threatening.

Missy's view of herself and her brother

Missy's drawing with colored chalk, sneaking looks at the work of nearby children. She selects blue chalk and giggles at Terry, "When my brother sees something blue, he says 'that match eye.'"

She declares her freewheeling loops and scribbles are "my brother. I'm putting some red near his nose, because he's always got a booboo." She trumpets, "He picks it."

Missy's pesky little brother, with his blue eyes like Daddy's, looms large. Ambivalence toward him spices many conversations. Missy partly defines herself in relationship to him, with an intensity many children reserve for older siblings. Here she scores his inappropriate behavior, relishing its consequences.

Terry casually asks Missy to draw a picture of herself. Missy responds with alacrity, chalking a large blue head with little bows in the hair. In red, she makes a small circle for one eye and the other twice that size. She proceeds with eyelashes, eyebrows, a large red mouth, and small red nostrils, before picking up the blue chalk for a tiny round torso, stick arms, and legs. She observes matter-of-factly, "I made the body too small and the head too big. I'll do another one for you."

In Missy's play with mirrors and magnifying glasses, does she perceive one eye as bigger? Is she making a symbolic statement? "I keep my eye out." She takes her own watchfulness seriously and suggests it gives her a certain power.

Here she sidesteps the issue of eye color by using red for all the features. Most stunning is her relaxed move from scribbling to deliberate representation. Before The Bodyworks began, she seemed far from representational drawing. She's moved rapidly past "egg" people with features grossly misplaced. Now she's conscious of proportion and confident in her ability to render it.

Missy's voluntarily evaluating and offering to amend her own work. In the past, her mother has often demanded corrections in, say, the color of the grass, while Missy shrank and withdrew, passively resisting. Today she's free to express and modify her own perceptions, to trust and please herself.

Missy asserting and testing

Missy's drawing again. "This is my head and here are my ears, eyes, nose, and mouth." She smiles, "And this is my tummy. Now I'm going to draw a picture of my brother." She looks straight at Terry, "Do you want my brother naked or with real clothes on?"

Terry answers, "Any way you want to make him."

Paul reaches for the red chalk. She grabs his wrist and glares, "I was here first."

Paul pulls away, drops the chalk, but creeps his hand back, teasing "I'm gonna take it."

She swivels, almost shouts in his face, "NO, NO, NO!" Paul retreats. She turns back to draw.

Missy duplicates her self-portrait, but her brother is smaller with larger fingers. This is no accident, as she laughs, "I made his hands big because he's always in my things."

This is the first time Missy has made an issue of nakedness. She's aware of a salient difference between her body and her brother's, a feature which will only show if he's naked. She may also be testing a taboo.

Missy has never expressed herself so forcefully at school. She directs her anger at Paul, who's behaving like her brother. She enlarges the fingers she draws and verbalizes her symbolic intent.

Missy's changing before our eyes these days. She's taking risks socially; she's making strong statements symbolically and verbally; she's examining her relationship to family members. Is The Bodyworks the catalyst for her leaps? Or are we seeing the fruit of our careful nurturing? Perhaps she's hit the edge of a developmental plateau.

One thing seems clear: The Bodyworks invites Missy to affirm herself, provides a context for her to represent and articulate her emerging sense of self. The curriculum can offer Missy a safe space to explore family dynamics.

Later in the day Missy's hands are deep in playdough. She inserts a cooky cutter, "Yucky mushroom." Nita plays along, "What does it taste like?" Missy twinkles, looks Nita straight in the eye, throws her a curve: "POOPS!" Nita's fast, "No thanks. I don't want to try that kind." Missy backs off gracefully, "It's really strawberry."

When the taboos are lifted there's testing. After months of rigid inhibition, Missy gives us a healthy sign of readiness to take risks, the mark of increasing independence from adults and alliance with her peers. It would be a big mistake to overreact, perhaps scaring Missy back into her shell. Nita simply draws the line.

Paul and Clint ask questions about appropriate touch

Missy's not the only one testing. Paul, after his out-of-character grab for the chalk, later reached deliberately across the table to touch Terry's breast. Terry looked straight at him, saying distinctly, "That's a private place." He withdrew, with a small smirk. He knew exactly what he was doing.

I assume Paul's behavior "means" the same thing as Missy's. Because it's physical rather than verbal, it may seem qualitatively different. Paul was late to be weaned. This may be a tactic he uses to get his mother's attention. If so, it's natural he would try it here as he begins to feel his oats. We'll watch carefully in case there's more involved than casual testing. If it happens again, I'll check with his mother. Otherwise, I won't mention it, lest she overreact and Paul close up again.

Clint's testing has a different quality to it. On three recent occasions he has touched Terry's or Nita's breast or buttock. They've pulled away firmly, saying "I don't like that" or "Don't touch me like that." I sensed Clint's behavior didn't stem from exuberance or affection, so I talked to his mother. She asked Clint about it, and he said, "I was experimenting."

"What did you find out?"

"I found out people don't like that."

Clint's mother notes he conducts many "experiments" at home: What happens if you put cookies in the freezer? What happens if you put sand on the heater? Certainly, at school I urge the children to experiment.

Clint's mother and I discuss other motivation for experiments with touch. His family is caring for three foster children who've been abused.

No doubt Clint and his brothers have heard whispers. No amount of straight talk is going to quickly banish the questions and fears ghosting the household. Clint's testing the limits that did not protect the girls. His mother will follow this up with the caseworker.

Many children try similar experiments. Does The Bodyworks bring out testing, acting-out, regression? I suspect that many children transfer unanswered questions and unresolved issues to the teacher, even when they know behavior is socially unacceptable. The Bodyworks allows issues to surface.

Grown-ups expect children to distinguish between kinds of touch: to restrain themselves from touching inappropriately, to defend themselves from someone else's inappropriate touch. However, children are aware that grownups casually touch them—in play, in affection, in restriction, in anger—when they may not wish to be touched. Can it go the other way too? Can a child intrude on an adult's personal physical being? Children need adults to model the firm NO to inappropriate intimate touch. I'll deal with this subject during circle time.

Is The Bodyworks putting dangerous "experiments" in children's heads? Just the opposite. The curriculum gives children permission to deal with deep questions. These surface in the company of trusted adults who have time to listen to behavior and the skill to respond firmly but lovingly, without shaming. The children are also testing whether the lines that parents draw apply to teachers as well.

How clear and conscious Clint is about his "experiment"! We don't give children credit for this much awareness. Not all are so deliberate or so bold, but many have questions that emerge in physical form. These questions are the children's best efforts to find out what they need to know, not defiance of adult authority and cultural mores.

In my experience it's usually boys who ask these questions in this way. Boys once had access to breasts for comfort and suckling, and then they were weaned. At this stage, their separation task is different from girls'. If more preschool teachers were male, would girls touch their penises?

Our model-making is currently focused on the brain, but some children need to anchor other concerns which are not necessarily in sync with my planning book. "Everybody's Fancy" goes straight to the hearts of physical thinkers, reassuring them in their own terms.

Everybody's Fancy

Boys are fancy on the outside,
Girls are fancy on the inside.

CHORUS
Everybody's fancy, everybody's fine.
Your body's fancy, and so is mine.

Girls are girls from the beginning.
Boys are boys right from the start. . . .
Only girls can be the mommies.
Only boys can be the daddies. . . .
I know you're a special person,
And I like your ins and outsides. . . .
© Fred Rogers[4]

Jogger wide awake, Paul fumbling

Jogger rushes to The Bodyworks, touches the model girl, and scowls: "Girls have an extra hole AND a bump with a line." Paul slogs his way to the table and slumps on a chair.

Jogger grasps the information right away and hurries to get to work. Terry helps Paul locate a picture of the brain in a book. He recognizes the formal relationship between the picture and the model and, true to his developmental stage, comments, "Noodles!" He doesn't seem to take in what the brain does or how it works, though he relates the message "roads" to the string running through the macaroni: "Car tunnel!"

Paul slumps back, flopping his head and arms onto the table, knocking things to the floor. Facing his own empty model, he drops his eyes, muttering, "I can't do that." Terry says she'll help and lays out the materials, explaining the first step, while he droops over the back of his chair.

Terry turns away to refill the tape dispenser, as Jogger bounces on the balls of his feet: "At home, my brain makes me be wild and think of wild stuff. Not at school, because the things I have to do. At home I never close my eyes. I can't."

"You mean when you're awake. You close your eyes to sleep."

"No, I don't. I never sleep. I stay awake all the time. I can never close my eyes."

"Why can't you close your eyes, Jogger?"

"Because so much going on at my house. I gotta go to bed before Maria and Cristina and Teresa. It's not fair. So I can't close my eyes. I get up first, before anybody else, before even my mom and my dad. Because I never close my eyes!"

Terry finds Paul sitting up straight, proceeding independently with the string and glue.

Paul has amazed us with his alert energetic behavior lately. What accounts for today's slump? Does he feel overwhelmed by the concepts or the company or both? With "Noodles!" he seems to be planted firmly on physical ground, but his "car tunnel" connects to the "message roads." On a single day a child may operate at different levels or stages.

Mastery often comes in flickers and glimmers, rarely in whole leaps without inconsistencies and regressions. It's important for the teacher to be comfortable with this nonlinear process, and to communicate her comfort to the child, who may be confused and anxious along the way. Parents need reassurance too. They're often troubled when a child who can write his own name suddenly begins reversing letters.

Paul's helplessness disappears while Terry's preoccupied with Jogger. Many children need time and space to find their own way. In effect, Terry's body served as a kind of screen for Paul to make his first fumbles out of view.

Sad to say, many four-year-olds are anxious about measuring up, driven by desire for the teacher's approval. With the benefits of pairs or small groups come potential drawbacks. It's important to track the dynamics between children, to offset some of the subtle but significant fallout from our competitive culture. Early school experiences have a huge impact on a child's self-esteem and attitude toward academic work.

Jogger's very first comment tells us he's still not buying gender equality, and he's not pleased: he wants us to know that. Then he reveals his own brain as boss and watchdog. Jogger recognizes the agenda at school and day care is geared to preschoolers. At home the tempo is set by older siblings and their neighborhood friends. Jogger often complains school is "boring." Here he gives us a glimpse of his challenges as the youngest in the family swirl, his sense of the inequities, his fear of missing out on "so much going on." He recognizes the situation is overstimulating, and knows he seeks an outlet in "wild stuff."

His parents feel they're doing their best to juggle different needs and refuse to discuss it. As Jogger's teachers we try to help him straddle his three worlds. Transitions are hard even for adults, and particularly so for a child like Jogger, who is perceptive, analytical, and curious. It takes a great deal of energy for him to accommodate to so many people and such different priorities. The effort makes him restless, irritable, often abrasive. He has claimed early morning for himself. It's probably the one time in the day he can enjoy the sense of being centered, free to rest in his own company.

Bo wants to try

Each morning Bo heads straight for the block corner. It's a challenge to get him engaged in a project, virtually impossible until all the parents have left and other children have settled. Today, he pulls out a chair at The Bodyworks, asking, "Why I'm always last?"

"Usually when we invite you over, Bo, you say you don't like to do projects, so we try to give you time to get ready."

"But I LIKE to work on the BRAIN! I know what the brain tells: 'Hot! Hot!'"

Bo's mother reported he ran a play-by-play during a "sword fight" with his sister, "Oh, no! You got my spinal cord. . . . Your brain is a straw brain."

Nita explains that two children have just begun, telling Bo she'll call him over when it's his turn. He says he'll wait at the table, and he does. Motivation's still high a half hour later, when Bo begins the brain. He's taken in a lot through observing other children and is soon ready to move into the construction phase.

Focused small motor work is always hard for Bo. Nita organizes things so that she can direct most of her attention to him. Despite fatigue and frustration, despite distractions, Bo plugs along. Very near the end, he reaches for small blocks from a nearby table and throws them over his shoulder. When Nita gently corrects him, he repeats the maneuver. Nita shifts into our problem-solving format: "Bo, we need to talk." Bo twists into a mask of silliness, signaling he's unable or unwilling to take responsibility at this point.

Nita leaves the table, telling him, "I'll wait until you're ready to talk." A few minutes later she's back: "I feel upset and nervous when you throw blocks. Do you know why?"

Bo's ready to participate, "Someone could get hurt."

Nita adds, "Right. So tell me, please, that you're not going to do it again."

Bo: "I won't."

The work goes quickly. After admiring it, I take Bo aside. "Some important things happened today, Bo. You decided you really wanted to work on the brain, even before we called you over. It's exciting to see you so interested. You chose to wait at the table, and you were very patient. But by the time it was your turn, you had already been sitting still a long time. Maybe that made it extra hard to do the work at the end. Do you think so?"

"Yeah."

"Now it looks to me like you really need to move around, to climb and jump. But clean up has started and there's no time for you to have your turn playing on the porch. What should we do next time?"

"Give me my turn first!"

"Right! And if you have to wait, then what?"

"Go play and you call me."

"Sounds good to me. Let's just go out in the hall and jump up and down a few times together. That'll let some energy out. . . . What do you think now? Can you handle circle today, or are you just feeling too jumpy?"

"I can. I want to go to circle."

"Good. We'll try it. You can use Secret Place time to relax. If it's too hard to let go, tell me and we'll find another place in the room for you to be. Sometimes it's hard to sit in circle close to other people when your body needs to run and jump. You sure did a lot of good work today."

"I know. I did the whole thing. The brain. I'm gonna show my mom."

It's often a descending spiral for Bo. The less competent he feels, the more he avoids fine motor activity, so the gap between his skills and his peers' grows wider and wider. Today his interest in the brain motivates him to seek a situation that he'd normally avoid and to tolerate frustration. But he needs lots of support to integrate cognitive and small-muscle development.

Ideally, we would respond immediately to Bo's initiative, break his work with stretches and play, to tailor a perfect fit between his ability and the project's demands. We did the best we could. At the end I took extra pains to make sure his acting-out didn't blight Bo's success. I milked the experience with him: What can we learn for next time? Can we anticipate and deflect immediate fallout? I know he feels he chose to do a tough job and did it well. I think he tasted the sweetness of conscious learning, despite the obstacles. I hope he remembers.

Kahlil's own analogy

Kahlil comments to Terry, "My brain's not soft. It's very hard. It helps us think. It's a control tower. It sends a message to your finger when you touch something hot. Because my finger doesn't have a brain. I got nerves to take the message. And vertebrae are the bumps on your back."

Kahlil has invented an analogy all his own, building on his recent visit to the airport, and he reels off what he has heard at school, enjoying his mastery, wanting his teacher to know how much he knows.

Two sides of Daisy

Daisy and Zack are back at books. Daisy flips to lisping-toddler mode, "Daythee doethn't wike bwood."

I stop by, "Daisy, do you know what the blood's job is?" Daisy explains in her normal speaking voice.

"You know lots about the blood, Daisy!"

I walk on, as Daisy turns to a drawing of a naked boy and girl, giggling, "I'm gonna pull Mister's dinky."

Daisy has thoughts and questions that keep pulling her back to the model and the books. Her thinking doesn't fit her ruffly, helpless, good-girl persona. She camouflages herself in toddler talk, but my direct question breaks the spell.

When Daisy turns back to the book, she owns her interest. In time we trust the prurient overtones will fall away, leaving her curious, self-accepting, and assertive. After The Bodyworks, she's less likely to be a victim or a martyr in relationships, trapped in learned helplessness.

Tanya's dream

Daisy and Zack join Tanya and Shane on the porch. Tanya's annoyed when the other children won't follow her orders. In the shuffle of big blocks and ladders, Shane gets hit and demands, "We need to talk."

Daisy and Zack immediately say they're sorry. Tanya refuses to take responsibility, offer sympathy, or talk it over.

Nita joins the children, "What's going on?"

Shane: "Tanya hit me."

Tanya: "No, I didn't. Anyway, I HAVE to hit Shane!"

Nita: "Nobody has to hit anybody."

Tanya: "I HAVE to hit Shane! Because I had a dream."

Nita: "You don't have to hit. Tell Shane you won't hit him again."

Tanya: "I WON'T tell him."

Nita: "If you feel like you want to hit Shane, go tell a teacher."

I enter: "What's up, Tanya?"

Tanya: "I had to hit him. I had a bad dream last night about hitting Shane."

Sandy: "But it's not OK to hit people. You don't have to do what your dreams tell you."

Tanya: "I can't throw my dream away. It keeps hanging onto me."

Sandy: "Sometimes dreams do stay in your mind when you wake up. Maybe you could write a story about how that feels."

Tanya: "I DON'T WANT to write a story."

Sandy: "That's fine. You don't have to write a story. But you do have to be in charge of you. Your dreams are not the boss. You are the boss of what you do, and you must not let yourself hit Shane."

It's impossible to unravel this one. Who hit whom, and why? It's more than possible that Tanya—resenting Daisy's entry onto the porch—took it out on Shane, since Daisy is the queen bee. Daisy and Zack admit they might have bumped Shane, apologize and get on with it. Tanya denies then implies she did bump Shane but is not responsible because her dream told her to. Did she really have a dream, or is it an invention to get herself off the hook?

In any event, this is not the moment to chat with the children about the conscious and the unconscious! The point is that we must control our behavior, override ill-willed dreams and impulses. I hope Daisy was listening, phasing out "the good guy and the bad guy inside."

Missy's reaching out

Missy pulls her mother over to the body puzzle again, peeling layers off until she hits the skeleton. She hits her own leg on purpose. "See Mom, when I hit my leg it didn't hurt." Mom leaves quickly. Missy responds animatedly to Cara's invitation to look at body books.

What does Missy want her mother to say or do? It's unclear. She probably just wants her to play along. Today Mom doesn't try to change Missy's direction, and Missy isn't crushed or disappointed by her mother's response. In fact, Missy moves on with a peer, pursuing The Bodyworks with someone who shares her interest.

Later Missy works with Clint on the brain. When Clint squeezes the heart balloon, she smiles and follows. When he comments, "I'm taking swimming lessons and my heart beats faster when I kick my legs," Missy picks it up, "I'm taking swimming too. We hold our hands on the sides and kick. I wear my Dalmatians bikini and it has spots all over it."

Paired work, swimming lessons, and the shared memory of kicking deepen their bond. There may be a physical sense of proximity and pleasant recall: "Hey, we know how THAT feels!"

Ani, Jogger, and Zack work with new information

Ani's mother reports Ani taught her little sister all about the brain. I thank Ani's mom for sending us the "Body" volume of the children's encyclopedia she's buying at the supermarket, and mention that Ani announced to no one in particular, "The brain is VERY fun and interesting."

Ani cuts up paper food to put in her baggie stomach. I want the children to have more scissors practice. I also want to address the role of chewing in digestion and the problem of choking. "Tomorrow, please cut them a little smaller. That would give you a stomach ache."

Ani looks straight at me. "No it won't. Because that's not real food. It's just paper." She adds, "In the stomach, food turns to lava."

It's great that Ani takes her enthusiasm home. I swallow my opinion of the supermarket enrichment gimmick. The encyclopedia illustrations mix cartoons and large-eyed children with tiny bodies. Color, pattern, and irrelevant decoration cram the pages, making it hard to pursue fact. Perhaps that's the point: In The Body, *nothing below the waist is pictured or mentioned in the text. What message do children get about reference books and science?*

I'd rather take children to the public library, for fun and looking things up. If money can be spared, it's wonderful to follow a child's personal interests with a few good books for her own shelf. Many books and "educational toys" are designed with corporate profits in mind, aimed at parents and grandparents who want to assure academic success.

But let's face it: I'm a professional teacher with a trained eye and my own taste. Unless parents ask my advice, I keep my taste to myself and focus on their loving intent. There's plenty of room at school to offer the children books more to my liking. What's important is that Ani's curious and excited about the brain, and her mother's supporting Ani's interest!

Ani's dry response to my comment about paper food tells me that (1) she's past the stage of simple identification with her model, and (2) she probably suspects my ulterior motive. Her reference to "lava" gives me pause until I realize it's a physical/formal comparison between stomach and volcano and a sound-sense extrapolation from "saliva" in the mouth to "lava" in the stomach! Why not?

Jogger digs into the body books, locating several pictures of brains: "This is a BIG one. How big is my brain? Bigger than this. I got a really big brain. Bigger than Maria, Cristina, and Teresa. Bigger than anybody in this room! Because I'm the smartest!"

Jogger, trying to level his sisters' apparent advantages, has seized upon the brain, which can also offset his small stature among his peers. Perhaps his thinking goes like this: 'Bigger is better. I'm small and young, but everybody says I'm smart. If I'm smart, I have a bigger brain. No one can see it, so no one can say I'm wrong.' Abstract "intelligence" has been rather cold comfort for Jogger. He exults in his potential for dominance-by-brain-size. Despite his sophistication, he's still compelled by physical thinking.

Sitting with Nita at the book table, Zack keeps pointing at the drawing of a naked boy and girl, "I'M this one and YOU'RE that one."

"No," says Nita, "I'm a girl, and girls don't have a penis."

Zack snaps back, "Bad word, go to the bathroom. And you can't use your finger like this." He holds up his middle finger. "It's bad. It means shut up. Who ever had the brains to make THAT up?"

Is Zack checking his assumption that Nita has a naked body under her clothes, an adult female naked body? He slyly makes a statement he expects her to correct. She stops there, without correcting his statement about his own body or alluding to the differences between naked adults and naked children. Zack "catches" Nita violating a taboo, and may relieve his own anxiety with his mock scolding. Then he introduces another taboo, which he probably suspects means more than "shut up." He concludes that people invent symbolic language and credits the brain.

Rosa's awareness of "race"

Rosa heads straight for Nita, eyes shining. Nita's wearing a pink scoopneck shirt instead of her usual black turtleneck. Rosa beams up at her, "You were more brown the last time. Maybe we didn't have so much lights on."

Apparently Nita's skin color is salient for Rosa. Rosa suggests that perceptions change with circumstances. Is she coming from her own experience, or conversations with adults? Is she also hypothesizing that skin color/race is relative? So often in young children, "to like" is "to be alike" in physical terms. Is Rosa trying to diminish the differentness she perceives in Nita, because she likes Nita so much?

Rosa picks several small fights with Cara. Finally I take Rosa aside:

"Lately you seem to be trying to keep Cara away. Do you think that's been happening?"

Rosa scowls. "Cuz I don't know how she got here, from different worlds."

"Cara was born a long way away in a country called Cambodia. Her mom loved her a lot, but she couldn't take good care of her, so she tried to find a family that could. Cara's mom and dad in South Hadley were looking for a baby who needed a home. They heard about Cara when she was a tiny baby, and a friend brought her all the way here on a plane to be John and Jill Worth's little girl.

"Cara didn't grow in Jill Worth's body, so she looks different from John and Jill. She looks like the woman in Cambodia whose body she grew in until she was born. But even though Cara looks different, she's just like you and her mom and dad on the inside. The differences on the outside aren't important."

Rosa interrupts, "That's NOT THE SAME. BODY BONES is not the same as WORLDS."

I try to get through. "I like lots of kinds of eyes—round brown eyes like yours and oval black eyes like Cara's and round blue eyes like mine. The important thing is that we all have eyes—in the important ways we're all alike. Do you understand now why Cara looks different from her parents?"

Rosa snuggles up, "Ummhmm."

"When people don't understand things, sometimes they get worried and hurt other people's feelings. Be sure to ask a grownup if something is bothering you."

"Ummhmm! I will!"

At the gate, I manage to talk for a moment to Rosa's mother. Rosa's parents' close friends are Chinese, and Rosa often plays with their children.

Why is she so threatened by Cara? Probably Rosa is struck by the difference between Cara's looks and her adoptive parents' looks. Lacking precedent or explanation, Rosa infers that Cara is an "alien" intruder, unlike the Chinese children who "naturally" resemble their parents according to the conventions of Rosa's experience.

"Race" is definitely on Rosa's mind, as her earlier remark to Nita indicates, but we oversimplify if we call her behavior toward Cara "racist." By helping Rosa solve the cognitive puzzle of Cara's family relationship, I hope we've eased the discomfort that can sow the seeds of racism.

Tanya puts Cara down, Cara defends herself

Proudly Cara reports now she's keeping tissues by her bed to wipe her nose and is taking her medicine on time.

Cara's seated at the snack table when Tanya pronounces, "You can't sit there." Cara looks up, "I got to. I picked this chair." Tanya sticks it to her, "But I don't want you." Simply, Cara ends it for the moment, "This where me sitting."

Cara, Tanya, Clint, and Shane are playing with blocks. Cara's nose is running again, thick green gobs swinging as she bends. Tanya bristles, "Blow your nose!" Cara's assertive tone is new, "You don't tell me!" Clint defends his loyal sidekick, "That's the teacher's job."

The two boys soon leave, and I sit on the floor with the girls, "It's a good idea to tell a friend when something bothers you, but it's important to speak kindly so you won't hurt feelings. Tanya, how could you tell Cara about her nose in a friendly way, not bossing or hurting her feelings?"

Tanya looks at the floor. "I can't say it. I don't want you to hear."

I continue, "That's a good point, Tanya. We try to say things like that quietly so other people won't notice. This one's different. I'm the teacher and I already know. Cara, how could Tanya tell you so you would feel good about it?"

Cara looks straight at Tanya, speaking in a sweet and unaffected voice, "You say, 'Cara, please blow your nose.'"

There's a lot of history here. Every preschool teacher spends a fair amount of time wiping noses, tying shoes, tracking zippers, while teaching children to do these things themselves. Nose-blowing is a health issue as well as a self-help issue. By midwinter, most of these four-year-olds kept their own noses clean. Chronic infections held Cara back. Her nose was becoming a social issue: "big kids" don't have snotty noses. She was already at a disadvantage due to her language development. It was time for Cara to keep her nose clean. I asked her parents and day-care providers to make sure she completed her courses of medication, and to send her to the mirror with a tissue—hoping visual feedback would help. She was learning quickly, proud of her new skill.

Tanya's harsh comment made me flinch. Was this the consequence of our efforts to teach Cara? Or was Tanya echoing a tone she had heard directed at herself? If I had intervened immediately, that would have ended the mixed-gender play in blocks, a rare experience for all four children. I kept a close eye on the play, which ended when the boys left.

Meanwhile, Clint's intervention had affirmed Cara, boosting her status more than anything I could have done.

When I raised the issue with the girls, Tanya tried to slip away under the cover of tactfulness—a good strategy, belied by her obvious resentment. Cara's poise and confidence brought this incident to a close, as at the snack table. Significantly, her language proved equal to the task.

Is "racism" a factor in Tanya's treatment of Cara? There are other explanations for Cara's relatively low status in the classroom: her language lag, her habit of parallel play near the boys, her lack of connection to the girls, her minimal affect, her runny nose. The runny nose alone would affect the standing of any child in this group.

Children's awareness of differences in skin color, facial features, hair texture varies with their experience. It's likely that some children may associate Cara's low status with her "racial differences." In Tanya's case, we've seen no evidence of such a link; there's every sign she's simply pecking a weaker chick. Cara's growing self-esteem is helping to put Tanya in her place.

We address racism as such when we find it, but among these children it's more likely to be incipient than full-blown. Our most effective preventive measure is the empowerment of all the children and the development of sensitivity and compassion among them.

Circle: tracing a bite

At circle I introduce the digestive tract. I try to set the tone for a straightforward discussion of a loaded subject. "What happens to a bite of food when you put it in your mouth?" Incorporating the children's suggestions, I trace a bite of hamburger from the table to the toilet.

I summarize: "Our teeth chew food up into little pieces so we won't choke. Our spit—saliva—makes it juicy and soupy so we can swallow easily, and it starts changing the food into energy. Food goes down a tube like a pipe, called the esophagus, into our stomachs. Stomachs are like washing machines or blenders that churn the food around and break it up into tiny bits that travel in our blood to all the other parts of our bodies.

"Our bodies can't use everything in the food. Some is garbage we squeeze into a long tube called the intestine. It's very long—as long as this room—all curled up in the middle of our bodies. At the end of the tube there's an opening to the outside. That opening is the rectum. We can feel when our bodies are ready to throw the garbage away, so we go sit on the toilet. We have lots of different names for this garbage we flush down the toilet: bowel movement, poops, stool, poopoo, kaka."

Children giggle, squirm uncomfortably, look away. Nobody is ready to pursue this topic today.

Many children are incredulous that their teacher is inviting them to discuss a taboo subject. If a daring child risks a real question, the discussion can move to sources of real anxiety in young children: "accidents," cleanliness, sex differences. Many four-year-olds are only too aware of the thin line of control that separates them from babies in diapers. Some remember toilet training in the recent past; many can't yet stay dry through the night.

Missy makes her point playfully

Missy sets a hook for her mother's attention, "Mom, I want to show you something." This time her mother follows Missy, who holds a magnifying glass to her own eye and backs up laughing. Her mom gently takes the glass and imitates Missy. Missy takes the magnifier back and presses it against her own eye, looming over her mother, who has crouched down. Missy sparkles and giggles. When her mother turns to go, Missy leads her to the door, still giggling and "spying" through the glass.

In the past, we've guided Missy in explorations with the magnifying glass and the mirror. She's enjoyed the incongruity: her view of herself with one big eye, her huge teacher. Is she simply sharing her fun with her mother, or is she also making a symbolic statement? She seems to be saying: "I'm really looking at me, seeing me as I am, as ME not you" and also "I'M not an object for your observation and correction. I'M one who SEES and I SEE YOU!"

The playful statement may be unconscious, but Missy's body drawings, words, and choices have been telling us she now SEES herself and her family. Her seeing has empowered her. She's embracing her life, leaping beyond the solo self-making in the mirror.

She's determined that her mother recognize this independent person she's becoming. Missy's mother has hoped for this blooming but has tried to control it. Whatever her ambivalence, today Missy's mom yields and follows gracefully, and Missy is giddy with delight.

Families follow up

At the dinner table, Clint mentioned "my beautiful stomach," and his older brothers howled their derision, setting up a family conversation about appreciating the body.

Maggie lost her first tooth and asked about the blood. At school she shows me the empty socket and proudly states, "The heart sends blood all around the body."

Bo and Shane share what's on their minds

Shane missed two days of school, so Terry takes him out in the hall to catch up. Bo asks, "Do you have your Turtles T-shirt on?"

"No, I'm wearing Batman." Shane pulls up his sweatshirt to show the logo.

Bo smiles with satisfaction, "I got my Turtles."

Shane shrugs, "At least I'm wearing Batman."

At the window, Bo looks out at new green shoots where we buried a squirrel and planted bulbs in the fall. "Sandy, the squirrel's gonna make some flowers. When animals go to earth, they make flowers."

Shane's face is blank as Terry traces the bite of hamburger, but lights up when she asks him about his dinner. "YUM! Roast beef, cheetos, bread with mayonnaise, and KoolAid!" He chooses colors to match his menu, warming, then looks shyly at Terry. "Do you know where I live? If you know where my house is, you could visit me. Well, if you go down this street and turn . . ." He's explaining it with his hands when I walk by. He clams up, mumbling, "Am I done yet?"

Bo and Shane touch base after Shane's absence. They share the glory and power of their superheroes, agreeing on the relative status of their emblems.

Bo glimpses the garden. In September and October, he was obsessed with the death of his grandmother. Apparently our work with "the great circle of living and dying" has stayed with him. In The Bodyworks context he expresses new comfort with physical processes.

Shane's disinterest in digestion (or discomfort with the topic) disappears when he can specify his menu and express it in concrete terms. He relaxes into time with Terry, and in the construction process he expands. He breaches his own shyness to invite Terry to visit, removing the physical obstacle by explaining how she can reach his home. My entry shatters the intimacy, and all he wants to do is flee.

Other kinds of bodies

Pip wants me to touch his ribs, "See if you can feel under: my Chinese food I ate last night." After poring over the pictures in *Spiders*, he goes up the climber, extends bent arms and legs, jumps and scrambles along the floor. "See I'm a spider dropping down. See I made my drag line."

Rosa brings her book about beavers from home. She shares it with Shane, then pulls out puppets. This time, she chooses Fierce Cat, and Shane eggs her on. "You can fly . . . in this basket . . . fly faster . . . now I'll get gas . . . but you're running out of gas so you're too slow. . . ."

In a series of crises and resolutions, Rosa's racing around the room acting out Shane's directions. I intervene. "Cat is out of control. What can you do to keep Cat in control, but still have fun?" We generate ideas. They elect to move the puppets to the dress-up area, where limited space and numbers will contain the excitement.

Later Rosa invents a move she calls "the trap jump" on the minitrampoline. Soon other children copy her. When the game moves on, Rosa drags herself, griping, to The Bodyworks table and glowers at me, "You watch out or I'll toast you."

As children investigate their own bodies, we see waves of curiosity about other creatures. The Bodyworks books motivate looking up other topics as well. Pip assimilates his "research" by acting out spiderness. Rosa's play with Shane is less about "cats" than about transcending physical (and interpersonal?) limits, a sense of aliveness which later inspires an acrobatic maneuver. Her pleasure and vitality attract children who often keep their distance from Rosa's intensity.

Is Rosa anxious about meeting her own high standards in constructing the brain? Once again she manages to be last. When she's finally lassoed, she spits out a scenario of physical revenge.

A lovesong to the brain

Every day this week Kahlil has talked about the brain. Today he calls me over. "Did you hear that, Sandy? . . . You DIDN'T? It was about our brain. We made a song. Shane said he couldn't build his truck again. It broke. So Clint and me sang a song." (His clear boy soprano slips into soft rock.) "'My brain, my head, I know . . .' and we ended with 'YEAH!'"

Sandy: "Sounds great! Would you do the whole song for me?"

Kahlil: "We can't. We can't remember the whole thing."

Clint: "It's too hard."

Sandy: "Well, you could try. Like the Lego™ truck, like you told Shane. It might not be exactly the same, but your good brains can do something wonderful again."

Kahlil: "Yeah! Maybe we'll be famous. When we grow up. AND when we're kids, like Nintendo Guidebook."

Clint: "A 1, a 2, a 1, 2, 3."

Kahlil: "NO! NOT THAT!" (He shifts to soft rock.) "Why didn't you know that you LEARN in your head?"

Clint: "It's nice when you have a dream in your head. It isn't hard to do"

Shane: "And it's all in your brain, and you can see it in your brain."

Kahlil: "How would you know? Nobody would know when you're even imagining."

Clint: "Now this song is really good if you're just learning, when you have something with Legos™ and you just can't do it again."

Shane: "And it's all in your mind. If you play with Legos™, you can watch TV at home, you can see it too. It's all in your brain, with your eyebrows!"

Kahlil (bringing it to crescendo and close): "IN YOUR HEAD . . ."

Sandy: "That was wonderful. Thanks so much for singing it for me."

Kahlil: "You wrote it down in your notebook, so now you can sing it to us!"

Sandy: "I wrote the words, but I didn't write the tune. I'm not sure I can do it."

Kahlil: "Try! Try!"

Clint and Shane: "Try, we want to hear it!" I improvise a tune in the same mood and tempo, using words from rough notes. The trio links arms.

Kahlil sighs, "Yeah. It's a really good song. We wrote it."

What a leap to see! All the more significant for the boys because they shared it. Kahlil daydreams of their role models. Collective improvisation is rare and intoxicating. These three boys have a new relationship with the brain, with themselves and each other.

Urgent concerns voiced at circle

Yesterday no one pursued the digestive tract. Today I ask in a general way, "Any questions about bodies?"

Bo: "Sometimes you could have loosey-goosies."

Zack: "Sometimes you could get loosey-goosies in your pants. Sometime you could get loosey-goosies on your floor."

Sandy: "Yes, that can happen to anybody, children and grownups. Diarrhea happens if you're sick. You eat too much of some kinds of food or you eat food that's spoiled. You can't help it if you have diarrhea. People understand if you have an accident."

Ani: "Sometimes it's not comfortable to get it out."

Pip: "Sometimes when I sit on the toilet I can feel it pushing."

Zack: "Sometimes you pee and poo at the same time."

Bo: "Girls don't pee. They don't have a penis."

Sandy: "Girls do pee. Girls and boys pee through a small hole called a urethra. In boys the urethra is at the end of the penis. In girls, the urethra is between their legs."

Paul: "Girls have a baby in their belly."

"When they grow up, some girls decide to have babies. The baby grows in a special place inside the woman's body called the uterus. Girls' bodies are fancy on the inside, just like boys' bodies are fancy on the outside."

So rare for Paul to say anything at circle. Is he asking for a review? Again I say lightly that some women choose not to become mothers.

Jogger adds a note, "Boys have boy bodies. Boys can have a gun and big bullets!"

Jogger jockeys for position, linking male sexuality and weapons. Can I let this one go in front of the whole circle? No. *Ironically, I have to assert the sexes have equal rights to blow heads off.*

"I don't like anybody to have guns, but girls can have guns too, if they want to."

Shane jumps in, "Boys can have bigger bullets! Boys can save girls."

Shane, so full of fears and without a father, needs male heroes. I'll ignore the sizes of bullets.

"And girls can save boys, too."

Tanya sits up straighter. "I saved my sister when she fell off the porch."

I smile at her, then at Clint. "And Clint saved his brother from swallowing a penny. Boys can save boys. Girls can save girls. They can save each other. It depends on who needs saving and who's near to help."

Shane proposes, "Sometimes the mother has to go to a meeting and the dad could take care of it."

Shane's pulling together all his inferences about two-parent families. Perhaps he's even projecting himself into the future.

"Yes, Shane, after the baby is born, if mothers and dads live in the same house, they can both take care of it. Dads and moms are both very important."

Suppose I can't control my bowels? What if I have diarrhea or constipation? Is it OK to urinate and defecate at the same time? How do girls pee? What compensates for the lack of a penis? How can boys compensate for not being able grow babies in their stomachs? Is there a hierarchy of gender?

The children risk raising their urgent questions. I'm uneasy answering. It feels unfair not to tell the boys they too have a procreative role, but temporary oversimplification best serves the group. With children this young, the next step needs to be taken individually, in the context of family expectations and values. It's clear to me that this is the parents' role.

There's something to be gained from the interim emphasis on the female role in procreation. Children see pregnant bellies and nursing breasts. It's important to affirm the female body's powerful potential without implying it's necessary or sufficient for a girl to choose motherhood. We may help offset the deficiency some girls feel in themselves—and some boys feel in girls—due to the absence of a salient organ like the penis.

It's easy to see how a sense of deficiency may arise in little girls in our culture, especially in the stage of "physical thinking." An early sense of lack may be deepened and complicated by many experiences with dominant men and boys. It's also easy to see how the presence of a salient organ may contribute to a sense of innate superiority in small boys.

Low self-esteem and high self-esteem tend to perpetuate themselves. An early imbalance based on gender differences impairs both boys and girls before they recognize the full range of human potential in themselves and each other. An early focus on the female role in procreation may help to preserve the balance nature intended. For our own health and our planet's, we all desperately need to learn to balance the power to generate and nurture life with the power to control and direct strength.

WEEK FOUR

The Digestive Tract, The Lungs

Planning the week ahead

From the mysterious, hard-to-construct brain, we move on to the digestive tract—familiar, accessible, and loaded. It comes next on the construction schedule because the design of the model requires us to place the "food tube" in the torso first. Since we've already filled the stomachs, the installation won't take long. Then we'll go on to the lungs.

Why the lungs next, when many children are probably thinking about the urinary and reproductive systems? Children do pursue hot topics on their own individual timetables, but it's time to cool the group focus.

There's a deeper reason to juxtapose the digestive tract and the lungs. Here we can bridge from the individual human body to the vast all-encompassing body of Earth. Earthworms and seeds will help the children glimpse the web of life.

Most children view excretion with contempt and disgust, often with anxiety. "Waste" is a topic our culture avoids. Worms are the lowliest of the low, linked to death and decay. I'll try a different spin. We'll dig for worms, examine worms, appreciate worms as Mother Earth's digestive tract. We'll see how worms also work as lungs, making the earth loose so air can circulate and seedlings can sprout.

I won't call the worms "Transformers," though: Mattel Corporation owns that word, as far as children are concerned. Worms are exciting in their own right, as long as I don't frame them as "Transformers."

We'll also examine, sprout, and uproot seeds. The seeds will introduce the carbon-oxygen cycle linking plant life and animal life, and they'll demonstrate the magical and mysterious "growpower" of all living things.

This is the point in The Bodyworks I hunger for and also fear. I get wound up because I have a big agenda.

I want to help the children glimpse the great circle of food and breath, the mystery and marvel of it. Even a brief experience of that radiance will sustain them for years to come, giving them a conscious and subconscious sense of homecoming, of oneness with the earth and all life-forms.

Why try to link their aliveness to the life of the planet? Isn't it enough to help them come home to their own bodies, to each other?

No. That link is the very essence of reality.

But it's a reality so complex that very few adults even try to grasp it.

Exactly! Because they didn't begin when they were children.

Can The Bodyworks help children grasp the connectedness?

Yes. Children know it's the heart of the matter—they are born mystics. The Bodyworks can give them a little "science" to corroborate their deepest inner longing and belief. We're all one, inseparable from the universe that to adults seems a thing apart. That's a piece of the solid truth that can shift our collision course.

So this is my agenda. It's a concept that won't ring true unless it emerges from the children's experience. I have to create an environment in which this is likely to happen.

All I can really offer is provocative juxtapositions in every sensory mode: sounds, images, smells, tastes, and textures. Then the children's neurons may create synapses—the living stuff of germinating concepts. I cannot transmit truth. I can shape only the conditions for it to sprout.

I needed this journaling today: to clarify my own intention, to stoke the fires of my own curiosity, and to open me to the teachable moments. An old song reminds me: "Keep your eyes on the prize. Hold on." What shall I hold onto this week? My hope, my intent:

I intend to help protect (or restore) in each child the sense of the goodness and integrity of the body. This should be a birthright, the experience of the body as wondrous, sacred. Not so in our culture, where bodies become objects on the market.

I intend to nurture the sense of wonder, not to teach facts. Especially now, as these children learn to harness their bodies to work at what they choose (write their names, throw and catch, ride a bike), it's crucial that they get in touch with what's occurring outside consciousness and control, as real and free as a horse, a butterfly, a thunderstorm, a river, a tall maple running with sap. We too are temples of mysterious intelligence and energy.

I intend to awaken curiosity and courage, the freedom to discover one's own questions and to ask them.

I intend to honor the shared humanity beneath surface differences.

I intend to reveal and celebrate the web of life. Geologists describe "forces that build up" and "forces that break down" the body of the planet. So too among plants and animals, and within the individual child. There's a constant cycling between life and death, between eating and being eaten. I hope to cultivate reverence for all of it.

I intend to affirm power.[5] *Most four-year-olds are passionate crea-*

tures, enthralled by power. Our culture tends to recognize it in only one form: dominance, power-over. This power is a dead end for us interpersonally, internationally, ecologically. As a teacher, my dearest hope is to help children experience power as cooperation, power-with. And, beyond that, to celebrate with them the root power: power-within. We don't understand it, can't control it, but we do participate in it with every breath: "Growpower."

I intend to offer a few "facts" that may stick. At best these will stimulate awareness, motivate exploration, anchor new experience and information, and facilitate communication with peers and adults.

No wonder I'm wound up. Strange how it relaxes me to face my agenda again, admit to myself that this is what I'm trying to do. I feel energy and trust bubbling up.

It took me years to name "growpower." No one can explain what scientists call "Life" and believers call "God." Children today urgently need a concept free of reductionist rationality and sectarian overtones. "Growpower" embraces the sense of wonder at the root of the will to live, the grace to love.

I'm excited because I've seen it happen over and over: children turn toward this concept like sunflowers following the light. I know this concept is simple and elegant enough to carry in their minds and hearts for a long time. They don't outgrow it, they grow into it and it grows with them.

I'm scared because there's nothing simple or linear about "growpower" or the taboos it touches: God, sex, and death. All I can do is throw open doors and windows at once, let the concept loose—knowing it will stir challenges I can't fully meet.

I also feel peaceful, because no one has all the answers. Children need most to know the search is life-giving and joyful and can be shared. The nightmare that haunts most of us from early years is that we are alone, stuck in our ignorance, cut off from the mystery of life and from each other. Somehow, when we name "growpower," we can celebrate the particles of our understanding and the enormities of space around them. We become both believers and scientist-explorers voyaging on the vast sea of experience.

Yes. Now I'm ready for tomorrow. It's against all the rules, but I'll have to start with a lecture. I'll take it as far as they can stand it, and work the rest in as the week allows.

Sandy's lecture (with fiddlers): Growpower 101

At circle time we pass around a stack of small cups.

"I'm going to give you one of the most powerful things in the whole world to hold in your hand, and then put in your cup." Solemnly I place two or three tiny alfalfa seeds on each child's open palm.

"It's a seed. It has GROWPOWER. Growpower is what knows how to live and grow and change and turn something into itself. Like you. Before you started to grow in your mother's body, you were even tinier than this seed! When it was time for you to start to grow, the growpower in you knew how to grow into you. And it still does.

"You're still growing and changing all the time, getting bigger and stronger, learning new things, because you have growpower. Your growpower knows how to use food and air and sun and water to keep growing hair and fingernails and teeth and all the other parts of you.

"The seed in your hand knows how to grow into alfalfa, the clover cows love to eat. The seed's growpower knows how to use water and sun and air and soil to make roots and leaves and flowers. Nobody has to teach it how. The most amazing part is how all the different kinds of growpower fit together on Earth. Each plant, each animal, each person, is part of Earth's growpower."

A few children call out. "Even dogs?" "Even bears?" "Even sharkses?"

"Yes, EVERYTHING that was ever alive is part of the growpower. Even dinosaurs!"

The magic word. They all look up, alert.

"Even DINOSAURS?!"

"When dinosaurs were alive, they had growpower too."

"Just like the seeds?"

"Just like me? I got some too?"

I push on. "Everybody stand up and look out the window! Growpower's been working over in the corner of the yard where we buried the squirrel. Remember when we talked about the big circle?"

They nudge and jostle until everyone has a chance to see.

I review the fall curriculum: "The oak tree makes lots of acorns. A few of the acorns start growing into new oak trees, but lots of extra acorns feed the baby squirrels in the oak tree. The baby squirrels eat the acorns, they grow into big squirrels and have their own babies, and after a long while, it's time for them to die. When the squirrels die, the little earth creatures, the worms and grubs and beetles and bacteria, know it's time for them to do their job. They start chewing up the squirrels' bodies. They turn the squirrels into food for the earth. The oak trees suck all that up into their roots and that gives the oak trees energy to make acorns for the new baby squirrels.

"It's like a circle that keeps going around and around. The earth feeds the tree and the tree feeds the squirrel and the squirrel feeds the earth and the earth feeds the tree and the tree makes new acorns for the new squirrels and over and over."

"OK, let's go sit back down in the circle."

I could stop here, but I haven't gotten to the worms yet. I've got to introduce the worms before we head down to the digging pit! I hope they can hold on a few more minutes.

"So when we're learning how our own bodies work, we're also learning about how we fit into Earth's growpower with other animals and plants. The worms are really important. You eat food to give your body energy, but your body can't use all of it. So your body makes the leftovers into poops and squeezes it out to make room for new food. The worms' job is to take all the leftover garbage—like banana peels and chicken bones and poops—and swallow it and change it into food for the earth.

"Each of us has one big food tube to do all the work for our own body, starting with chewing and ending with pushing out the poops. Mother Earth doesn't have one giant food tube. The earth has lots and lots of small food tubes that all work together. That's what a worm is, one of the earth's little food tubes. The worm feeds the earth, the earth feeds the plants, the plants feed us, and when we die we feed the worms, and it keeps going around. Another big circle of growpower."

"You've been doing a lot of listening. Let's stop and do some Swing-Swing-Stretch and Loud Noises! Before that, put your seeds in your cups, and move your cups out of the way!"

I pull out the tambourine and we go to it.

"Here's a new song. At the end of each line I sing, you call out loud, 'GROWPOWER!' "

Growpower

I once was a tiny seed (GROWPOWER)
So very small indeed (GROWPOWER)
Didn't become a tree (GROWPOWER)
I grew right into me (GROWPOWER)

Can't tell you how I know (GROWPOWER)
But I know how to grow (GROWPOWER)
There's a super plan (GROWPOWER)
In sky and sea and land (GROWPOWER)

Seed by seed, bit by bit (GROWPOWER)
One puzzle we all fit (GROWPOWER)
We're in the mystery (GROWPOWER)
Know how to grow and be (GROWPOWER)
Part of Mother Earth (GROWPOWER)
Even before our birth (GROWPOWER)

"The next one's a song AND a dance. First I'll teach you the song."

The Great Circle

From plants I receive.
To earthworms I give.
Earthworms give to plants.
In circling we live.

"Now we'll dance it."

We pair the children up and arrange the pairs in a double circle, one partner facing in, one partner facing out.

"When we sing the first line, about receiving gifts from the plants, stretch up high and spread your arms over your head like the branches of an apple tree, then take a bite of apple. When we sing the second line, about giving to the earthworms, squat down and creep your fingers on the ground. When we sing about the worms helping the plants grow, reach out and hold your partner's hands and slowly stand up together. When we sing about all living in the circle, keep holding hands and make a little circle with your partner. Then let your partner's hands go so the outside circle can slide to the left, and everybody meets a new partner."

Most of these four- and five-year-olds don't know left from right, but they feel which way our dancing circle always turns. It takes a few dry runs for them to get the idea of switching partners. We hang in there, dancing deeper into the concept of biodiversity through motion and words appropriate to young children: "In circling we live."

After our break, they look relaxed. I'll try to squeeze in the rest. They retrieve their cups, and fiddle with the tiny alfalfa seeds. I've assured them that if a seed gets lost, we'll all help find it later, or I'll replace it. Maybe no one's listening, but remarkably the circle is quiet, absorbed in the magical smallness of the alfalfa seeds. I'll take my chances with the remnants of their attention, if any. I've been sowing concepts by the handfuls. Who knows which will sprout in these young minds?

"There's another growpower circle in the air. When we breathe air in, we use some parts of it, and we breathe the rest out again. The air we breathe out isn't good for people and other animals anymore, but it's just right for trees and bushes and grass, all the green creatures. So the trees breathe in the air people and animals can't use. They use that air and change it and send it back out again. Then it's perfect for people and animals to breathe all over again.

"Back and forth, around and around. Growpower and cooperation. That's how it all works. You and I and that oak tree are part of Mother Earth's lungs!"

"Thanks for doing so much good listening. I'm just about finished talking! Everybody, take in a big breath. Now, BLOW! Blow out—you're sending air to the trees. Now breathe in—they're sending fresh air to you. In and out, back and forth, around and around. You can feel it! We're all part of the growpower circle!

"I'll sing you a chant, an old tune from the Native American people, with some words I wrote. If you catch on right away, just sing it with me. Stand up and we can move it while I sing it. Start the rhythm with your knees pumping up and down, 1, 2, 3, 4. Tip your head down and make big circles with your arms going frontwards like this, when I sing 'breathe out.' When I sing 'breathe in,' tip your head back and make your big arm circles go backwards. Keep the rhythm going with your knees, just like your lungs keep the rhythm of your breath."

Breathing Circle

The trees breathe out, breathe out, breathe out
What we breathe in, breathe in, breathe in.
Then we breathe out, breathe out, breathe out
What trees breathe in, breathe in , breathe in.
The trees breathe out, breathe out, breathe out
What we breathe in [two quick inhales]
Then we breathe out [two quick exhales]

What trees breathe in [two quick inhales]
Then trees breathe out [two quick exhales] . . .

© by Helen H. Johnson

"The mystery is nobody has to learn how. The growpower in the earth and the trees and the worms and you and me knows how to keep the circle going. It's fun to think about it, to say thanks to the earth, and to be careful and kind to the earth and all our growpower partners. So this week, while you're building food tubes and lungs for your bodyworks, we'll be watching worms and seeds do their jobs in the earthworks. NOW: We'll go down to the digging pit and get some soil to make a garden. We need plenty of worms to go in it."

This is way too much teacher talk, but I can't find a way around it, and I get away with it, more or less, every year! We'll keep coming back to the concepts, but there needs to be an overview at the beginning. Amazingly, even the most restless children absorb a lot of it. They sit more or less still, fingering the seeds and cups, dreamy or fidgety—but deeply engaged by the whole concept of growpower.

Shane's afraid of worms; Paul helps

Down at the digging pit we have four child-sized shovels, four garden trowels, and the clear plastic water table. There's much activity, much excitement. Some children run off after a few spadesfull, others settle. We find not only dirt and worms, but also grubs, stones, spiders, roots, sticks, grass, and insects I can't classify or identify. Shane stands on the periphery, his face and body full of ambivalence. I offer him a shovel.

"No thanks," he says.

"We'll wash our hands later, and most of this dirt will brush off our clothes." I suspect this is not his issue.

"I don't care about getting dirty," he frowns. I'm surprised he volunteers his real concern. "I don't like worms."

"Lots of people don't like worms, usually because they don't know them. All the children in this class will learn to hold worms and feel ok, even if worms aren't their favorite."

"Not me," says Shane. "I won't ever touch 'em."

"Maybe not today, but someday soon. I'll make it easy for you. It's my job to help you try new things."

"I don't want to try. I don't want you to help me. I'm afraid of them."

"Lots of people are afraid at first. Children and grown-ups. Nita told me she was afraid before, too. But I showed her how to touch them and now she's not afraid anymore."

"Nita was afraid?"

"That's what she said. I bet it'll only take you three days to learn not to be afraid. We can start you today or wait til tomorrow. Which do you pick?"

Shane turns around with his head down, turns back and whispers, "I don't want to." His lip is trembling.

"It'll be easier if you start today. Let me show you what we'll do. Paul, please bring me a worm." I mound dirt in my palm, putting the worm on top. I ask Paul to let me hold his finger for a minute, and I quickly touch it to the worm on top of the dirt in my palm. "How did it feel, Paul?"

"It went too fast. I couldn't even feel it."

I reach my hand out to Shane. "It'll be quick, and it'll be over. It doesn't hurt and it doesn't feel slimy. Come on and try." Shane holds back, but he's ready for this step and we both know it. "You can close your eyes if you want." I take his reluctant finger and touch it rapidly to the worm.

"That's all?" He's incredulous. "I did it?"

Paul contributes, "Good for you, Shane. You touched a worm."

"Tomorrow we'll do the next part," I say. "It's gonna be easy, Shane."

"I touched a worm," Shane says wonderingly.

It was fairly easy with Shane. He was ambivalent, not all negative. Paul was handy—Paul, who is far less confident and competent than Shane in most areas, as Shane is well aware. And Paul had the good grace to cheer Shane on. If Shane had been more reluctant, if Paul had been less kind, I would still have proceeded, for several teacherly reasons. Four-year-olds have lots of fears. Many are huge, vague, intractable—like nightmares. It's important for them to know they can take little steps to whittle their fears into manageable size. It's often easier to do this at school than home, in daylight, in the company of peers, guided by a relatively detached teacher.

Worm phobia, however incidental it may seem in our modern lives, is symptomatic of all the aversion to dirt, decay, creepiness, and death that separates us from the earth and each other. It's not too much to say that helping children learn to handle worms is one step in helping them learn to handle the darkness inextricably wound into the human condition.

The next two stages of the cure should be relatively painless, now that Shane's launched. Tomorrow I'll put the mound of dirt on HIS hand, place a worm on top, and remove the worm before he can feel it wiggle. Finally I'll hold his hand on mine and put a worm right on his palm.

Rosa on my mind

Rosa's on my mind. She gnaws at my attention like a dog on a soup bone, steadily working her way to the marrow. It's been one thing after another.

We walk over to the greenhouse, each child holding a knot on the ropes we use for field trips; I emphasize traffic safety as we cross each street. At the greenhouse there's a can of herbicide on a low counter. I point out the skull and crossbones as the sign for poison: Don't swallow! Don't even touch!

On the way back to school, we stop to run in the field. Rosa stands still, looking up at clouds in a gray sky.

Sandy: "Anything special on your mind, Rosa?"

Rosa: "I'm just thinking about a little boy who didn't get to grow up. His mama didn't take good care of him. She put poison ivy in his juice."

Sandy: "That's a scary idea, Rosa. Sometimes mothers make mistakes, but usually they take good care of their children. Poison ivy can make you very itchy and uncomfortable, but it won't kill you." *Her mother's a nurse. Does Rosa know about anaphylactic shock?* "If someone's very allergic to something, like a bee sting, his throat might swell up and he might not be able to breathe, but I've never heard of that with poison ivy."

Rosa: "It's TRUE. The little boy DIED!"

Sandy: "I can see poison ivy is really on your mind, Rosa. Would it help to run around with Pip and some other friends?"

Rosa: "No, I just want to think about the little boy. It's TRUE."

Sandy: "That's up to you, Rosa. Let me know if you're feeling stuck and you want some help."

I suspect there's a kernel of truth and the rest of it is spin-off from Rosa's potent imagination. She seems dominated by fear. Her father's young brother was killed in an automobile accident when he was nine. Although this happened before Rosa was born, for her it's living history. The subject comes up in the extended family: the worst could and did happen. No mother or father could prevent it. In Rosa's mind, this may mean any possible threat is probable and needs to be guarded against.

She spends her energy controlling what's near, and despairing of controlling what's far away. The world is full of scary possibilities even adults can't control. I try not to scoff at her fears, but to help her see that the probabilities are slim, that she can learn to live without being obsessed by those probabilities. I encourage her not to suppress her fears but to balance them with interests and delights. We work at this to-

gether. She knows I respect her choice to stay stuck when she chooses, or when she's so flooded she has no choice at a given moment.

So I hug Rosa, leaving her to wander in the corners of her complex mind.

Soon we're all back on the knotted ropes, headed back to school.

Pip: "Why is Rosa so mad?"

Sandy: "You'll have to ask Rosa, Pip."

Rosa scowls at her friend and his gentle question, and then relents. "I'm NOT mad. I'm sad." She doesn't say why.

I lead a small-group chat about the confusing look of sad-mad, how we can often read in a face that something's wrong, but we can't always tell what the person's inside feelings are.

Back at school we have a picnic snack. Rosa's still quiet, self-absorbed. She's in so deep that she can't yet run it off. She resists when I draw her over to a bench, then she launches the conversation: "You don't believe me, Sandy. But you're WRONG. You wait and see. IT'S TRUE. The little boy really did die because his mama put poison ivy."

Truth is a major issue between Rosa and adults. Her parents tell her "Lying is bad," and she wants to please them, but she wants also to honor her own truth, to retain her self-respect. Our impasse has the elements of a power struggle, but at some other level it seems to be Rosa's struggle for integrity.

How do I know what is and isn't true in Rosa's story? What I do know is that Rosa at such times is trapped, reactive, unable to participate in school life. In the midst of it she projects her mad-sad on the people around her, raising a cloud of smoke and dust that follows her. Increasingly, the cloud will define her.

I try again to help her straddle her worlds. "Rosa, which kind of 'true' is it? Is it the kind of true that other people can see and touch, like this bench we're sitting on? Or is the kind of true that's inside your mind, so other people can't see it and touch it?"

Rosa sits there, arms crossed, chin tucked, eyebrows tight together, head turned, fuming and refusing to talk.

Sandy: "I know: Let's ask your mother about it when she comes."

Suddenly Rosa's face shifts and she's more than ready to talk, trying to pull me off the scent. "NO. We won't talk to my mother. It's true, but SHE doesn't know him."

Sandy:"That's unusual. Mostly mothers know their children's friends. I'm sure if a little boy died, your mother would know about it."

Rosa: "Well, she doesn't. Because . . . I only met him at the playground and I played with him, and she was watching my little brother and she didn't even see the little boy."

I feel as wily and intrusive as a prosecuting attorney on TV.

Sandy: "Then how do you know he died?

"Because he told me. He knew it was going to happen, and he told me before it happened. And it did, and he died."

I'm uncomfortable with this. I don't like to probe. I don't want to force a child who's not developmentally ready to distinguish magical from rational thinking. I don't want to expose Rosa in a "lie." For all I know, this child is a psychic and there is a plane of reality for her which is unavailable to me. All I can do is muddle through, trying to balance myself, hoping to help her bridge her worlds.

"You know, Rosa, there are different kinds of true. There's a true that lives inside our feelings, where storytellers and songsingers and poetrymakers go. The kind of true they tell is VERY VERY important, as important as the other kind of true. It's just different. You're a wonderful storyteller and songmaker. Maybe when you're a grown-up that can be your job. While you're a child, you can keep looking for the inside kind of true. I'll help you write down your stories so you can share them. Feelings-truth is very important, Rosa, but it's different from eye- and finger-truth like the bench. Part of my job is to be sure you know which is which."

She doesn't say anything, but I think it sinks in. Her face eases a little. Inside my own head, I keep hearing the refrain of a song: "You can't kill the spirit. It is like a mountain. Old and strong, it lives on and on and on."[6]

At pick-up time I include Rosa in my conversation with her mother. I say Rosa's been thinking a lot about poison and children and mothers, and we've been talking about different kinds of true. I hope Rosa will feel her grown-ups are allied in her behalf. Privately I tell her mother more about the day.

Rosa's daffodil

We're using garden catalogues to find pictures of the flowers we saw at the greenhouse, and mixing colors to match. Rosa wants blue for the leaves of her daffodil. I explain today the job is matching, and after she finishes it she can paint flowers and leaves any color. She says she'll use red and yellow for leaves. I explain growing plants need green in their leaves because the green comes from chloroplasts that use the sun to help make food for the plant. In the fall the leaves change to red and yellow and brown because the chloroplasts die and then the leaves fall off. I send her out into the yard to check on the dead leaves: What color are they? What color are the leaves attached to the daffodils blooming next to our classroom?

Rosa comes in beaming, "The dead leaves on the ground are brown and yellow, and the leaves with the flower are green, so I'M going to paint MINE some green and some brown and some yellow."

Perfect. Why do I do this to myself? Most children seem to be comfortable with my science-through-art projects. In October they paint brown trees for our leaf-collection mural, and then create blue trees and purple grass to their hearts' content when they're on their own. Not Rosa. Rosa knows she can drive me to the brink wondering if I'm warping her with double messages about artistic freedom and scientific objectivity. Why don't I settle for something lower risk, like cutting-and-pasting catalog pictures? So what if cutting and pasting gets boring, and the children don't learn much about flowers? They don't have to learn about everything, from me, this year! She's pushed that button too: What these kids need is lots of play. But most of their school day is self-directed play. And the thing is that everybody else enjoyed the project from start to finish. Rosa just gets me going on myself. I'd better watch it, or soon she'll be running the classroom.

After Rosa serenely completes her giant daffodil with its red and yellow AND green leaves, she joyfully calls me over: "See it?! I DID it! Mine looks just like 'em!" She's radiant, smooth and graceful, her voice lilting.

I share her pleasure: "Just like 'em!"

Some of her resistance may have been due to anxiety that she wouldn't be able to meet her own standards of realism. Or mine. I wasn't even thinking of that. Oh well, we got her over the hump this time anyway.

Rosa heads into the bathroom to wash up, pausing to scowl in the mirror. She mutters to her reflection, "That's the LAST time I'll EVER do THAT." She turns, sees me watching her, and quickly pastes her smile on.

I can let this one go . . . but I can't: she knows I know, and if I pretend otherwise, she'll have to test with renewed vehemence. I check my heart. While I'm not innocent of the desire to pounce, I'm not feeling like a cat with a mouse at this moment, so I can proceed. I make sure my voice is gentle, matter-of-fact, not blaming.

Sandy: "What did you say, Rosa?"

Rosa: "I SAID I liked it."

Sandy: "It didn't sound like that to me. And it looked like you changed your face when you saw me. That makes me wonder what's going on."

Rosa looks chagrined, but not ashamed, "Yep."

I go on: "It's really OK with me if you don't like projects. But my job is to make sure you try out a lot of different things, so you'll know how to do them if you need or want to. Anyway, I thought your face looked happy while you were actually painting and after you finished. Maybe you liked the painting part; you just didn't like me telling you that you had to paint."

Rosa: "YEP. You got it."

Sandy: "That's OK. I understand that. Lots of times I don't like it when people tell me to do things. But sometimes, when I let it go, I really have fun anyhow."

Rosa shoots me a small grin: "Yep. Me too."

Sandy: "I know, we're a lot alike! I love you lots, Rosa. Could I give you a hug?"

Rosa throws her arms wide and looks deep into my eyes, a broad grin on her face. "SURE!" Our hug is big, long, close, and genuine.

We know our respective roles in the dance and we play these out, but beneath there is an ocean of love and we both know it.

Hypothesis about Rosa

With Rosa I need to be very clear, very sure of my own center. I will never really know the truth of her, the reasons for her behavior, but I do need to decide how I can best serve her as a teacher, given who she is, given who I am at this time and place where our paths intersect. To some degree, I must simply proceed by the seat of my pants, improvising as I go—but there's a risk that Rosa will push my buttons and my response will be reactive and less than she deserves.

I need to find a North Star to orient me in those moments when we are smack in the middle of everything and Rosa fires a salvo at someone or everyone or me in particular, or she mutters (with eyes blazing) words to the effect that the emperor has no clothes. I already have a hypothesis about Rosa—that's what's gotten me most of the way through the year—but she's challenging my equilibrium again. I have to own my guiding hypothesis, check it, modify it, and dump it if need be.

How can I "explain" Rosa's behavior?

I could say, "Hey, there's no problem!" She's big for her age, loud, energetic, forceful, physical. She's deeply interested in good guys, bad guys, guns and knives and poison—themes which, in our culture, hold little boys in thrall. If she *were* a boy, maybe she wouldn't stand out in such high relief? Not true. I've taught boys with Rosa's intensity, her instinct for the jugular, her obsession with danger—and the boys haunted me too.

I could say, "She's got an overactive imagination. Lighten up, Sandy, she's just yanking your chain!" I could ignore her. No, I couldn't. I could *pretend* to ignore her? Hah! Rosa would not be fooled. And what would be the message to her and to the other children if I ignored her? "Rosa, your behavior is normal; it doesn't call for a response." Or: "I don't know what to do with you, so I'll let you rot alone." Or: "You've got a problem, kid, but it's not *my* problem."

I could say, "This child just needs to know who's boss." I could shut her up, sit on her. Shove her rough edges into the nice round hole I've made for her.

I could go the other way and say: "There's something deeply wrong with Rosa. It's probably her family." Maybe it's unresolved grief—the death of her young uncle—passed on to Rosa. Maybe she's being abused and she's crying out for help.

I could ask myself why I have such a strong reaction to this child. It's almost a chemical thing. I was a child like Rosa on the inside, but I held it in, turned it on myself. It took me years to unravel that. Does that make me more, or less, qualified to respond appropriately to this child? Probably both.

Each of these hypotheses has appeal, and they all let me off the hook. Any one of them makes solid common sense and yields a course of action I can explain and defend, if necessary.

But there's another hypothesis—much murkier, much harder to support, and much more compelling—that hooks me firmly to wrestling with Rosa.

What if Rosa's issue is not a problem? It's a gift. Or, as is usually the case, a double-edged sword. Rosa is extraordinarily sensitive to the essential energy of a situation, a person, an image. She functions like a kind of psychic sponge, absorbing "the vibes." If there's anything under the surface which is false, threatening, or simply ambiguous and unsettled, Rosa knows it immediately. Like the canaries sent down a century ago into mineshafts to detect poisonous gas, Rosa sends early-warning signals that danger's lurking.

Why is she pulled by negative energy, when so much positive energy surrounds her? Because negative energy means threat, and Rosa's deepest instinct is for survival. Part of her gift is the sense of the wholeness of the bodymind, where physical and emotional survival are one and the same.

Once she picks up the scent of danger, she's stuck with it—*in* it—until she can release her anxiety through mental manipulations or physical/emotional discharge. Meanwhile the perturbing stimulus becomes a magnet, clumping together other free-floating anxieties. Rosa's like a snowball rolling down a mountain.Once the process is underway, it's very difficult to uncover and release the original nucleus of her concern—whatever bit of grit got inside the very permeable membrane of Rosa's psychic skin. Meanwhile the ball keeps rolling, gathering enough mass and speed to trigger an avalanche. It becomes almost impossible for Rosa—or the adults who love her—to put on the brakes.

Rosa is a very powerful receptor. Most of us function well with two or three local channels, pulling in the information near us. A few of us have cables which give much broader scope. Rosa's like a huge radar disk, sucking in a complex array of signals from a vast magnetic field. A child with this kind of super-sensitivity is continuously bombarded, her circuits overloaded—yet she's too young to have mastered the controls. She's constantly spinning, scanning, trying to discern the truth.

If we lived in another time, another place, we'd recognize Rosa's gifts. We'd apprentice her to the tribe's shaman and train her for a lifetime of community service in the healing arts: bringing outer and inner worlds together. She'd be taught to read the clouds, the flights of birds, the subtleties of breath and pulse. She'd grasp the meaning of dreams, pattern her understanding into songs, stories, dances for the tribe. She'd learn to ground herself, to open and close at will the doors to that dimension between life and death where matter and energy interpenetrate and transform.

But Rosa lives in the United States of America, in 1994, and she's only four-and-a-half years old. What can I do to help her keep her gift intact, to help her grow one year older and stronger and more at home with herself?

We don't even have a name for her gift!

So I'll begin by naming it. Rosa, I call you "the inner ear." You're a sensitive membrane that vibrates in response to invisible waves. You're the delicate cilia that move the fluid, signaling us to adjust our positions, to realign.

Now, Rosa, what can I do for you? I can continue to offer you (and the other children) experiences, concepts, and tools to deepen your faith in a coherent universe: the awareness of breath in The Secret Place connecting you to other life cycles; the wheel of the water turning through skies and oceans; the wheel of the seasons and the food chain binding us to animals, plants, and soil; the pulse of rhythm and melody; the sense of belonging in circle dances and creative movement with peers; processes for resolving conflicts; practice at observation, listening, speaking. These are the ancient things you and all the children hunger for, the immersion in the elemental ongoing mystery of life and death, before and beyond the gyrations of contemporary "civilization."

I can help you learn to manage transitions, when you're especially vulnerable. It's then that you need grounding: soothing water play, stroking Pepe's warm fur, sweeping up sand, a hug or a kiss.

I can keep watching you like a hawk. I can try to keep my own eyes clear in the heat of each moment, and I can turn to the long cool view of my colleagues. All together, we've been watching you for almost two years. We've seen you grow steadily more relaxed, more communicative, less impulsive, more aware of yourself and others. We've seen you make and keep friends, explore new activities, and begin to take risks on projects. We've seen you playing, bubbly with delight. We've seen you willing to compromise and make amends.

I keep in close touch with your parents. Your parents and teachers hold you in a net of love and concern, protecting you from gross errors in judgment, helping us focus on the trajectory of your growth over time.

Even so, you challenge us all to the roots of our collective wisdom. I've recommended therapy for many other children. Why not now, for you?

To begin, there are few good children's therapists in our area. The best have long waiting lists, and give priority to children with severe problems. When teachers suggest therapy, this often stirs defensiveness in parents. The child suffers not only from that but also from tension in the air between the parents and teacher. It may be years before cumulative feedback from caring teachers can guide parents to the help a family needs—for usually it is a family, not just a child, in trouble. Knowing this, I err more often by suggesting therapy than by burying my head in the sand.

Why am I so reluctant to suggest therapy for you, Rosa? Therapy is usually seen as a fix for what's broken. You're often angry, always intense, but you're not "broken," Rosa. The potential for damage to your view of yourself—and your family's attitude toward you—is very great. You're four. Most four-year-olds are gripped by issues of passion and power. This developmental tide will probably ebb a bit when you're five, shifting you toward cognitive and motor tasks, helping you balance. Your peer group will become more predictable, less volatile—and your little brother will probably challenge you less next year, when he's three.

There's this too: Most therapy takes place in a sealed compartment of safe time and space. What I wish for you is a wise companion in the classroom, at your side in the midst of the fray. Someone who helps you learn from your choices, using them to develop self-awareness, self-acceptance, and a balanced view of your immediate environment. Someone who modifies the classroom to make it work for you. Someone who mirrors you as you move, without judging. Someone who holds the thread as you grope through the labyrinth.

If I could wave a wand, Rosa, I'd produce a teacher-therapist for you. In our culture, maybe that's a contradiction in terms; there's no such breed of cat. This year, in this classroom, I'm all you've got. I'm no therapist and this is not a controlled environment.

Oh, there's the rub. Classrooms could be powerful therapeutic environments. Appetites are visible. Vulnerabilities are visible. So are the attractions of the community of peers. We've learned the wisdom of mainstreaming children with special needs, supporting them with advocates and resource rooms. When will we learn that *all* children have special needs? They all need advocates. Our culture doesn't take time to listen, to hear, to know each child, to wrestle with each child for the realization of her fullest potential, to love each child. Parents can't do this job alone. The African proverb puts it forcefully: "It takes a whole village to raise a child."

I mourn for you, Rosa, and for myself. We all need the village, children and parents and teachers too. We each yearn for accompaniment—someone to face with us the struggle of what it is to be fully ourselves. We shouldn't be facing the mystery alone, trying to unravel the riddle alone. We need each other's eyes to see through the mirror, as the barrier dissolves between the knower and the known.

So I will be here for you, Rosa, inadequate as I am. That much, at least, is clear to me: I'm called to you, by you, in a special way. Each time this happens, I'm awed but less afraid. The essential act of authentic teaching is presence: showing up, being there. Accompaniment is the next step. So much depends on timing. I can't create the moment when readiness and resources meet, but I can recognize it and respond as fully as I am able.

With some children, no matter how I pretzel myself into position, the big moments don't seem to come. The children aren't ready, or I'm not. Our wave lengths don't match. The best I can do for them is to lay low, keep my eyes open and my ego out of it. At the very least, I can give them clear space, not abrasion or resentment. Beyond that, I have to trust that another teacher, a coach, a scout leader, or a neighbor will be there when the time is ripe.

Daisy helps Paul; Ani remembers Oz

Paul and Daisy are discussing the placement of the food tube. Paul sticks one end of the black plastic strip onto the middle of the head of his bodyworks.

Daisy corrects him: "No, it can't go there! That's where the NOSE is."

Paul shifts it over to the side.

Daisy's still not satisfied. "That's too close to your ears. The food tube goes down where your MOUTH!"

Paul looks at her, confused, and Daisy holds the model up in front of her. Suddenly Paul breaks into a big grin. "Right here!" he says, putting the strip in place.

"Right!" says Daisy. "I knew you'd get it!"

On the floor next to them Ani's been looking at a book. She puts it on the table where they're working, pointing to a diagram of the brain. She starts to flop around, hitting her own head with her hand: "I'm the scarecrow in the Wizard of Oz. He couldn't walk good. When he got a brain, he could." She shows them the nerves and blood vessels in the picture. "My brain goes to my NOSE! It looks like nose monsters!"

Daisy has fully grasped the correspondence of model and body. She can abstract and transfer her understanding. Paul hasn't yet made that leap. He has to be led through each step, gently, glimmers of insight fading in and out. Daisy's interest carries him along, and she deepens her mastery as she "teaches" her classmate. This is a new role for Daisy, who's the baby at home. Paul's flash thrills them both.

Ani independently follows up her curiosity about the brain, aroused last week. She remembers the Wizard of Oz, miming her new appreciation of the Scarecrow's behavior. It hits her that the brain is related to the workings of her nose, but she isn't ready to pursue that yet. Another child might have gone directly to "boogers," but the edge of Ani's insight turns abruptly into an association with the fantastic shapes of the diagram.

Difference in heights: Ani and Bo

Dressed in assorted finery, Ani and Bo look in the mirror. Ani hugs Bo, towering over him. "I'm taller. My whole head. You're only to my chin."

Bo says nothing, but his eyes drop. The two children shift back into dramatic play as I hustle to say, "You know what, Ani? I think you're the perfect size and shape for you, and Bo's the perfect size and shape for him. And I'm the perfect size and shape for me. There are wonderful things about being taller and wonderful things about being shorter. You know what's crazy? Sometimes kids, and grown-ups too, tease each other for being a different size. Later on somebody might tease you for being tall like the people in your family, Ani. Bo, you might get teased for being short like your mom. Just remember you're just right for you."

Ani whirls on me, eyes flashing, "I will NEVER be teased. NO ONE will tease ME. I will tell my mom!"

Bo says nothing but thanks me with huge brown eyes.

For physical thinkers, bigger is more—extra status for this confident girl, shrinking self-esteem for this vulnerable boy. Ani meant no harm. She's protective of her good friend Bo, but Bo's already painfully aware he's shorter than his own younger sister. It's likely Ani and Bo will remain at opposite edges of their peer group in terms of size, and both may suffer, especially in adolescence.

I can't change any of this, but I can prepare them to think in different terms. My intervention felt heavy-handed. In circle we could make a list of things tall people do easily, things short people do easily, things where height doesn't matter. A list might help all the children deepen respect for themselves and their peers, and take the edge off their smallness relative to adults.

Experiments with Pepe: Missy, Tanya, Shirelle

Missy, Tanya, and Shirelle wander away from playing doctor to sprawl on the floor in a clump by the bookshelves. Shirelle turns to Tanya. "You're always bossing me. My sister bosses me."

Tanya justifies. "But there's only one doctor and one nurse for each doctor."

Missy initiates, "Let's go get Pepe out."

Shirelle rummages through the books, extricating the one about guinea pigs. "I'm gonna look for the twin of Pepe."

Missy scooches over to Pepe's cage and pokes at his rear, changing her plan. "I don't want to pick him up. His bum's too fat, THAT bum."

Tanya picks up Pepe and flips him over: "I'm gonna find Pepe's boobies."

Missy tactfully instructs her. "Yeah. Boys have boobies, but they can't. Babies can't drink milk from 'em."

There is much that tempts me to intervene, but this time I don't. Missy's loose and easy with two peers. Nothing like this happened before The Bodyworks, though now it's almost commonplace. Shirelle directs some resentment of her powerful big sister at Tanya, who needs her friends to size her down a bit. And Shirelle, who showed no interest in books before The Bodyworks, is doing some "research." Missy's working through some taboo about "bums," and she and Tanya are both curious about nipples.

Adults rarely hear such classic child talk. The Bodyworks invites these concerns into the shared space, removing some of the shame and guilt associated with curiosity about the body. Rather than informing or moralizing at every turn, teachers can notice interests and misapprehensions and provide guidance. Had Tanya handled Pepe roughly in her nipple hunt, I would have stepped in. I will watch carefully, however, to be sure that our respect for Pepe—and other creatures, wild or tame—holds up under the onslaught of curiosity.

Maggie and growpower

Children wander over to the worm and sprout farm, peering through magnifying glasses, holding up rulers. If one child is willing to supervise the worms, we put a few on a tray to observe and handle.

Whole curricula have been developed around seeds and earthworms. I could be helping the children measure and graph sprout growth. We could be setting up experiments with too much and too little sun, too much and too little water. We could test the worms' dietary preferences with different kinds of table scraps, and track worms as they explore: sand, gravel, water, mud.

Not this year. I'm missing a lot of teachable moments, but I'm relaxed. It's a good trade-off. When I'm frantic and exhausted, fatigue becomes the curriculum. I've learned this more than once. I hope not to have to learn it again. In our stress-filled culture, children need the classroom to be peaceful, centered. I need to have energy free to respond to all the unexpected challenges in the children's lives and my own. This is no excuse to get lazy. It just means I have to order my priorities very carefully. Each year I think we'll do earthworms and sprouts before The Bodyworks begins, and something else squeezes out the time.

Meanwhile the children get a lot out of mucking around, with minimal supervision of the worms and sprouts. Each day some child may uproot one seed to examine closely and leave on a tray for others to look at. This is a cherished privilege—children are rarely allowed to "pick." Mostly, they act with self-restraint, under peer pressure. At least once a day, some child comes to me oohing and aahing over the way a seed has split or the first visible tip of green. Such is the marvel of unfolding.

Today Maggie has been sitting at the clay table, where she can see and hear the action at sprouts-and-worms. She's been poking and prodding at the clay, rolling little bits, not producing anything—unusual for Maggie, who likes to create little figures. I sit down next to her and take some clay in my hand. She looks up. "Clay has no growpower," says Maggie.

I remembered in time just to listen. There was no problem! Out of Maggie's full sensory engagement with the clay—her dreamy, receptive solitude—came insight important enough for language. Another small miracle. Later I'll invite Maggie to be in the news at circle. She's ready for a spotlight and the whole group will enjoy starting a list: What has grow power and what doesn't?

Clay seems to be particularly conducive to fruitful reverie. Is this because clay is real earth, with its own deep evolutionary history? We often use playdough instead of clay, since it has many similar tactile qualities and is so much easier to clean up. Here's one more reminder that "alike" is not "the same." Although our playdough is homemade, natural materials have different effects than their synthetic counterparts. We'll keep using playdough, but we'll open up the clay more often. It's more than worth the trouble.

"Over the Mountain": Tanya, Zack, and Jogger

Tanya, Zack, and Jogger are in line to "go over the mountain" of the big arcade climber.

We restrict young children to the lower bars of the big climber. Many children move like mountain goats and can easily handle this challenge. But in a group setting even the ablest child can become distracted and careless. Usually by spring I feel the four-year-olds are ready to scale the heights, and it becomes a rite of passage to "go over the mountain," with a teacher to spot and coach.

Tanya goes over awkwardly, but she makes it on her own, and I'm waiting to hug her, singing "Tanya went over the mountain." Zack starts, hesitates, backs down before I can help him. It's the third day he's tried.

"I'm here to help, Zack. I think you're ready."

Zack looks down at the ground, backing away. "Uh-uh."

"Maybe later today, or another day. Just let me know."

Jogger starts strong, but at the top he panics. He looks around wildly, unwilling to ask for help.

"Here I am, Jogger, right under you. I'm here to catch you, but you're not going to fall. Just stop for a minute and make a plan."

Jogger scowls at me, gripping tightly, then negotiates the turn and heads down, dropping with a flair. "It was a cinch," he calls out. He joins in singing the song, but avoids a hug by spinning past me and back into line to do it again. Zack has been watching the whole thing.

"Zack, did you see how Jogger stopped and made a plan, and then it got easier for him? I'll help you whenever you're ready."

Zack blanches. He joins the end of the line again.

"Zack, you can go to the front of the line. The people who've already gone over the mountain always give the next turn to someone who's still trying," I intervene.

Zack starts, clutches the climber at the third step, hangs on.

"Good going, Zack. You're still on. Take your time. You know you can do the first four steps. You've done them lots."

He lifts one foot to the fourth step, his hands trembling.

"Zack, you're shaking. That makes it dangerous. Put your foot down for a minute, and stand there till you feel steady."

He steadies.

"Now, use your breath, like when you go to the secret place. Just feel your breath go in and out, feel how safe it is. When you feel safe, try that next step again." He climbs slowly but confidently to the next step, hanging on tight. Then he takes another step and starts to wobble.

"Wait. Use your breath."

One more step and he's at the top, looking down. His face changes. "I can't turn around. I gotta come down."

"You can if you want to, but if you want to try going over, I'll tell you what to do. First, just lean on the bars. Feel your whole body, how the climber holds you up."

Little by little, coached at each move, Zack begins to trust the process and trust his body. There's one moment of panic as he turns to go down.

"Stop, Zack. Lie flat on the bars and breathe till you're steady."

As Zack starts down, his face flushed with excitement. "Sing it! Sing 'Zack went over the mountain!'" He lands on two feet, wild with pride. "I did it! I did it! I'm gonna do it again!" The next time there's hardly a hitch, and he himself pauses and breathes without coaching. "My mother's not going to believe it!" he shouts. "I went over the mountain!"

Zack's strong mind has generated disaster scenarios that inhibit him. His personal supply of violent videos doesn't help. This is a big day, a big beginning! I just hope his mother, who worries a lot, can celebrate his triumph.

Zack's experiment with worms

Jogger, Tanya, and Zack have migrated to the digging pit. I sense an energy shift among the children and turn away from supervising the slide to see Zack positioning his shovel to bring it down hard. "I'll cut him! I'll cut him! DIE, worm!"

"Stop, Zack!" I yell. "Don't kill that worm!"

He pauses long enough for me to reach him and gives me a disgusted look. "It's just a WORM! There are millions of worms! They don't really die. They make two worms if you cut 'em. I hate it when you won't let us do the fun stuff!"

Tanya and Jogger watch and other children gather. I speak to them all. "*Sometimes* both pieces of a cut worm live, but sometimes only one lives or they both die. It's OK to kill to eat. But it's never OK to kill for fun or just to see what happens."

"Scientists do stuff to see what happens." *Zack's father's a scientist.*

"They do, but first they have to plan so they don't hurt anything when they do experiments. Sometimes creatures get hurt anyway, but that's very different from killing for fun, or just to see. We'll talk in circle about this. Only five more minutes to play outside!"

Always a sticky wicket, loaded with double messages. I encourage children to try things, to "see what happens," but I don't condone killing, "even" worms. Many children have heard about "regeneration," the perfect umbrella for curiosity plus sadism and the relentless righteousness that goes with ridding the world of creepy-crawlies. Since Zack shows a fair amount of blood lust anyway, it's tempting to swoop down and throw a little guilt his way. After his experience on the climber, he might have mercy on the vulnerable, but children and adults often backlash after a close encounter with their own vulnerability. Instead of feeling compassion, they relish the turn of the tables. Zack probably picked up some of my bad vibes, even if I didn't lecture him. That was one reason to postpone further discussion, to depersonalize the incident. If it hadn't been Zack, it would have been someone else—inevitably. I needed time to collect myself before bringing this complex subject to the whole group.

Shane and Shirelle at worms

Shane has gotten over his worm phobia. He and Shirelle are at the worm walk. It's a sheet of clear rigid plastic balanced across two chairs so the children can observe the worms from above and below, with magnifying glasses to make it even more interesting. I put a pile of dirt at one end, a pile of sand at the other, and a puddle of water in the middle. Now the water, sand, and dirt are all mixed up. Some worms are taking their chances and freefalling off the edge. Others are stretched out, thin and passive.

These worms have given their best for interspecies communication and they deserve some R and R.

"Time for these worms to get a break."

Shane groans, "But we just got here."

"Well, dig out a couple of fresh ones if you want. A lot of children have been touching these worms, and they don't look very comfortable to me. Please take them down to their home in the digging pit."

All year the children have heard me talk about our responsibility for taking care of the creatures we bring in. I've told them about the time I didn't take good care of some worms and they all died. I don't have to say more.

When Shane and Shirelle come back, I ask them what they noticed about the worms.

Shirelle says, "They don't have eyes."

Shane asks, "Can they hear me talking?"

"Good question. I'll tell you what I know and you can help me explain it later, at circle. Worms don't have eyes or ears or noses, but they have special skin. They can't hear the way we hear, but they can feel the vibrations that sounds make. Do you want to know about vibrations?"

Shirelle gets out while the getting is good. "I'm going to dress-ups."

Shane proves his loyalty. "I'm going where Shirelle goes."

It's always a challenge to match the depth of the answer to the depth of the question. Shane's relationship to Shirelle is more important than almost anything in his life right now and he follows her around like a puppy. I finally figured out how to explain vibrations to children, and it's hard to muzzle myself but best to wait until there's real interest.

Voices on Tape

All during the year we add to the tape of classroom songs. At the year's end I give a copy to each child. "Please remember not to clap. The clapping's so loud it makes it hard for the tape to catch your voices."

"The tape CATCHES OUR VOICES?!" Ani marvels.

Uh-oh. I'm in over my head on this one—one of those things I say without thinking. Finally a child hunts me down.

"The tape doesn't really catch your voices; it just records the sounds you make."

I don't want to get into it, but my explanation's no explanation and Ani won't let me get away with it.

"How can we talk?" she asks.

"That's a good question. The Bodyworks doesn't show how we talk. What happens is that air goes into a voice box in our throats, called the larynx. Put your finger on your neck, on the bump. We call it the Adam's apple."

We all feel the bump. Children turn to each other, comparing bumps. "Your vocal cords are in there, and the air moves them, like my fingers move my guitar strings. They make sound waves." *This is more than enough for everyone.*

Not Ani. She pursues."There's no water."

"Right. The waves go through the air. We can't see them, but they're like waves in the water."

"Then the tape catches the waves."

"Something like that. I don't really understand how it works, but I can try to imagine it with my mind. Let me think for a minute. . . . Imagine a sound wave leaves a print on the air. Then imagine a tape machine makes an invisible picture of the wave print, and turns it back into sound when we play the tape."

"I'm bored of this," Shirelle contributes.

"It's a lot to think about. Ani could look up some more in her encyclopedia. Let's tape our songs now."

Oh, brother! My world—just like the children's—is filled with little black boxes I take for granted but don't understand. Maybe now I'll push myself to learn more about sound and electricity, subjects that scare and swamp me. I don't want to squash curiosity to hide my own ignorance. As I stretch toward the children, my own fears get worn away. I think I'm out of the woods for the moment.

Shane pipes up. "You said worms hear but they don't have ears. How can they?"

Here we go again. I was ready for this earlier, but he wasn't. He just filed it away for a more convenient time. Now I have to give it a stab with the whole circle.

"I'll try to explain it: Worms hear by vibrations. That means they can't hear the sound, but they can feel the sound waves in their bodies. We can feel sound too, a little. Try humming and putting your fingers on your Adam's apple. . . . Did you feel your vocal cords vibrating? I'll come around with my guitar, so you can feel the wood vibrating when I play the strings. . . . Let's experiment. Let's see if we can *feel* the sound when we can't *hear* it. Nita, please close your eyes. Terry, please put your hands over Nita's ears so she can't hear. Put Nita's fingers on my voice box and see if she can feel anything when I hum."

A broad grin breaks over Nita's face. "I felt it!"

"I want to do it! I want to do it!" Everyone wants to do the experiment. We repeat it around the circle.

"Now we know worms can hear by feeling the the sound waves. Maybe that's how they know when a robin is walking on the grass trying to find them!"

I got to try my explanation after all. One child's question-in-depth was the lasso that ultimately caught even the children who were "bored of this." I missed my chance to mention how deaf people enjoy and develop special sensitivity to sound vibrations.

"It's the perfect time to tape 'Dig, Dig.'"

And it is. The children sing their hearts out, full of new respect for what's unseen.

Dig, Dig

Dig, dig, under the ground,
Below the growing green.
Far down under the ground,
Where sun is never seen.
Thirsty roots and seeds asleep,
Crawling worms and things that creep.
Down, down ever so deep,
The world of underground.

by George Garlid, Lynn Olson[7]

It's going so well that we tape another one, moving with it to release some of the built-up energy.

My Roots Go Down

CHORUS
My roots go down, down to the earth.
My roots go down, down to the earth.
My roots go down, down to the earth.
My roots go down.

I am a pine tree on a mountainside.
I am a pine tree on a mountainside.
I am a pine tree on a mountainside.
My roots go down.

I am a wildflower reaching for the sun. . . .

© Sarah Pirtle[8]

Taking care of worms

I turn off the tape recorder. That's it for circle time today. I'll respond briefly to the worm-cutting experiment and bring it all to a close.

"I was going to talk to everyone about taking care of worms and leaves and grass and spiders, and all the other creatures we share the earth with. We all belong here. We all have a place. We don't always understand how something fits, but we know that it does fit. We might feel big and strong, but we can't kill what's little and weak. Not for fun, not for experiments. We have to think hard how the Great Circle works. We can remind each other if someone forgets.

"Time for your secret place. Lie down, feel your breath go in and out. The trees and grass, all the green creatures, have sent you fresh air. Now you send back to them. Down there under our school, under the ground, our little sisters and brothers the worms are helping the earth breathe, so the roots can go deep, so the fruit and vegetables can grow, so we'll have plenty to eat. Lie there for a minute. Feel the Great Circle move through you as you breathe in and out.

"Now, open your eyes and stretch and sit up. . . . One last song for the tape."

This one's a favorite, bluesy with simple syncopation. It shifts the mood, gathers the energy and grounds it.

Lots of Worms

Well, there are lots of worms way under the ground,
Lots of worms that I've never found.
I'll bet they're way down there, a digging' around
'Way under the ground.
[REPEAT VERSE 1 AS A CHORUS AFTER VERSES 3, 4 & 5]

I dug the biggest hole I ever did dig,
The biggest hole. It sure was big!
And when I got to the bottom, you know what I found
'Way under the ground?

I found a worm to go on a fishing pole
Down in the bottom of that deep, dark hole.
But I left him alone 'cause he liked his home
'Way under the ground.
[REPEAT CHORUS]

I found a bumpety bug with big black dots,
Thirty-three legs and twenty-two spots.
But I left him alone 'cause he liked his home
'Way under the ground.
[REPEAT CHORUS]

I found an old sow bug curled up like a ball.
He didn't move from there at all.
So I left him alone 'cause he liked his home
Way under the ground.
[REPEAT CHORUS]

It's hard to balance needs. To prepare this generation for survival we have to articulate a new ethic of interdependence and respect. Where do we draw the lines? These children will have to deal, individually and collectively, with complex moral issues. It's urgent that we help them get ready, not oversimplifying with gooey sentimentality but developing in them the expectation of mutual responsibility. Music takes us to the joyful heart of the matter!

Paul scribbles

Paul's scribbling on pieces of paper, cutting them up.

I marvel at the progress he's made since his self-portrait. He used to drift through the day; now he commits to activities. He's a long way from mastery of pencils, crayons, paintbrushes, and scissors, but at least he's handling them with more and more satisfaction.

"Happy Birthday" from Clint and Paul

Clint and Paul giggle over a baby doll spread out on the "kitchen" table. After singing "Happy Birthday" they shove a bite of pretend birthday cake into the doll's mouth. "Chew it up, Baby!" orders Clint.

"He can't. No teeth!" crows Paul, "Just spit!"

"Swallow your cake, spitty baby," Clint proceeds. "Swallow it down your tube to your belly."

"Gooshy, gooshy, juicy, juicy in your tummy," Paul pumps the doll's middle. They trace the birthday cake all the way from fork to toilet—diaper, in this case—with great hilarity.

I didn't know Paul had it in him to sustain any focused play with Clint, much less to contribute appropriately with so much gusto. Paul often seems to be out of it. Here's proof he's taking in plenty.

Paul knows he's growing

On the playground Paul comes over. "I growed a lot."

"Yes, Paul, you certainly are growing a lot."

"We went to our friends and last time I swinged in their baby swing and now I'm too big. In Connecticut."

"You're growing in so many ways, Paul. Too big for a baby swing, but just right to be making friends with other boys who are four."

He runs off, smiling

Bo and the worms' work

Bo's looking out the window again. "Hey! Flowers! Where we buried the squirrel one time."

Other children come over to see. Do I use this moment to review concepts? I hold my fire. They are smiling, happy. Most turn quickly back to other activities; a couple remain, pensive. Bo speaks up. "They shouldn't use coffins. Coffins make it hard for the worms to do their work."

I stand there with him for a while. Nobody's saying anything. Another minute goes by. Bo says, "I remember the name. I'm glad we put the yellow . . . daffodils. The baby squirrels eat the nuts. Acorns."

Bo's grandmother died in the summer after a long illness. All fall he was ambivalent—wanting to talk about death, wanting to shut out his thoughts. The day we buried the squirrel was a very emotional day for him. Months have passed. While the worms have been working to assimilate the squirrel's body, Bo's mind—conscious and unconscious—has been chewing on his experience, making use of our concept of the Great Circle of life and death. He doesn't mention his grandmother, and I don't either. I don't speculate why we use coffins, or tell him about cremation and other cultures' ways of handling dead bodies. Instead, I take a quiet breath, celebrating the peace that shines from this child in this moment, feeling blessed to stand beside him.

Jogger and the daffodils

Jogger asks if he can pick a daffodil for his mother.

"Thanks for asking first, Jogger. I wish I could let you, but I can't. The flowers are for us all to enjoy at school. You're a great painter. How about a picture of a flower for your mom?"

"Then if I take it home and put it on her wall by her bed, she's gonna take it down. I hate this crappy day."

"I'm sorry it's a hard day for you. Want a hug?"

"No." Jogger moves away.

Later Terry puts a hand on his shoulder, gently restraining him as he nudges and pushes in the line for the slide. Jogger turns and bites her, and she erupts, "NO!"

I arrive, calling, "What's up?"

Silence for a minute, then Terry states, "Jogger bit me."

"I did NOT!"

Terry goes over the whole story. Jogger keeps his face tight, turned away, and repeats his denial. I ask if it bothered him when Terry put her hand on his shoulder.

"She pushed me."

Terry offers, "I'm sorry if it felt like a push, Jogger. I was trying to remind you to be careful. Next time I'll use words instead."

He says nothing. I come back to the biting. "I want to believe you, Jogger, but sometimes you tell me what you wish had happened, not what really did happen. Want to get all this over with now?"

He keeps his head turned, blinking back tears, but grunts assent.

"Tell Terry you won't bite her again. Tell her you'll stay in control."

He does, and spontaneously gives me a big hug.

Many children bite as toddlers but quickly learn to curb this impulse. Occasionally biting persists into the preschool years. It seems to me that children who continue to bite tend to be small, highly verbal, and intensely frustrated by their lack of control, especially in significant relationships. Jogger's bite dismays me, but it doesn't shock me. Poor little guy. So much for him to manage. It's amazing he doesn't snap more often. I'm glad he could offer a hug, and I'll watch to see if this is a prelude to an opening. I wish we were in closer touch with his parents, but they keep communication perfunctory. I'll keep reaching out.

Zack's mom wants advice

Yesterday Zack flew to the gate to meet his mother and dragged her to the climber to show off his achievement. She protested, "But Zack, you're *afraid of heights!*" He proceeded smoothly over the mountain as she blanched.

"See, Mom? I *can do it!*"

She looked doubtful, but hugged him when he hugged her.

Today, she took me aside. "I've been thinking about Zack's fear of heights. He's afraid to ride his two-wheel too, but he's probably ready. He wanted us to take the training wheels off and we did, but he fell and now he's scared again. His father wants to put the training wheels back on. What do you think?"

"Well, I haven't seen him with a two-wheel. I don't know if he's ready or not. Lots of five-year-olds aren't. What does Zack think?"

"He thought he was. His friend across the street doesn't have training wheels. But Zack took a couple of spills and now it's a big deal. When he tries to ride scared, he falls. If we put the wheels back on, won't he feel like he's a failure?"

"Zack wants very much to succeed. Here we're working to help him feel more comfortable taking risks, giving himself time to 'practice.'"

"I know. It seems to be working. At school. What are we doing wrong at home?"

"Maybe nothing. Teachers have a cleaner slate to work with. It was much harder for me to wait with my own two at home. The peer group is powerful motivation. Zack expects everything to come as easily to him as letters and numbers do, and he clutches when that doesn't happen. There was no magic formula yesterday—just being there for him, trusting him, a little coaching at key points. Reminding him to use his "secret place" breathing. Helping him stay in his body having the experience instead of flipping out to the expectations and fears in his head."

"He's told me about the secret place. Do you think we should try it with the bike."

"It's up to you and Zack."

"I think it's worth a try. How do I do it?"

"Would you like me to talk to you and Zack about it together?"

"Would you? I'd really appreciate that!"

I called Zack out to the hall.

"Zack, your mom and I have been talking. She's so happy that you went over the mountain, and she was thinking maybe that could help you with your two-wheel. Do you want some ideas from me?"

Zack looked from my face to his mother's. "Maybe. Maybe tomorrow," he said. "Can I go back to blocks?"

"Sure, Zack. Let us know if you want some ideas about your bike."

"Bye, Mom," he called over his shoulder.

There's a lot going on in Zack, between Zack and his mother, between Zack and his father, probably between Zack's mother and Zack's father. Zack's mother senses some of this is at the root of Zack's fear of his two-wheel. I'm reluctant to give advice, especially about a situation I haven't observed firsthand. It's not so simple just to plug a "solution" into a new context. I want to encourage Zack's mother to observe him, learn from him, but I don't want to jeopardize what's working for Zack at school. I try to walk a fine line, leaving the control in Zack's hands. His response makes it clear he needs that control. It's better to acknowledge this than try to manipulate him, setting us all up for some passive-aggressive games.

His mother needs control too. Thank heavens I didn't use her question as a jumping-off place for my own larger questions about Zack's emotional development! One small step at a time. I wonder if Zack will bring the subject of his bike up again.

Jogger farts, Sandy belches

As we settle into circle time, Jogger farts loudly and begins to laugh. After a split second, several other children laugh too, and others follow—some forcing it. Pulling a trick out of my own childhood, I belch loudly and deliberately, then seize the shocked silence. "Does anybody know the names of those noises we just made?"

In the titters around the room, Pip giggles, "You burped!"

"That's right, Pip, I did. Does anybody know why people burp? I was doing it on purpose, but mostly we burp because we have to."

"When you drink soda," Shirelle laughs.

"Sometimes. Those bubbles go down in our stomachs. We burp to get them out. Sometimes when we eat fast or talk while we're eating, we swallow air down our food tube and that makes bubbles we burp out. Sometimes our stomachs have to work hard, if we don't chew our food enough, or if it's very rich or spicy or full of chemicals like junk food. Then acid in our stomach makes bubbles we burp up. What about the other noise you heard?"

Another titter. This time it's Paul who calls out, "Gas."

"That's it, Paul. Some people call it a fart."

The children smile and squirm, some starting to mimic the noise. "Now you know what makes a burp. What makes a fart?"

No takers. Finally Cara puts her hand up. "Not nice."

"You're right, Cara. Most people think it's rude to burp or fart. A fart's like a burp, but the air comes out the other end of the food tube, out of the rectum. The food has already been in the body a while, and it's turning into garbage. You know what we call body garbage: poops or stool or bowel movement. Some air bubbles from the rectum smell like poops. Gas means your body had to work hard."

Several children comment: "Yucky . . . gross."

Daisy blushes. "But if you can't help it."

"Sometimes you can hold farts in, but when you can't, sometimes you get embarrassed. Especially if people laugh."

"I like it when they laugh," chortles Jogger.

"Sometimes people do it on purpose to get laughs. Lots of people laugh when something happens they're not expecting. It depends on what you're used to. In some parts of the world, it's very polite to burp when you're finished eating—it's like saying "Thank you, that was delicious!" to the cook. Sometimes in a family, people let their burps and farts come out, and they laugh when that happens at home, but not at school or a restaurant. We need to know what's polite and comfortable for the people we're with. Today I burped on purpose in circle so we could talk about it, but usually I don't. When I say 1-2-3, everybody can make noises like burps and farts. Then I'll put my hands up for STOP, and after that we'll try not to make those noises anymore at school."

Burps and farts are dear to many children's hearts—amusing and confusing. Children love knowing why these taboo noises happen. I would have raised the issue, if Jogger hadn't set it up for me. My theater trick shifted the focus to a slightly less taboo topic, making a curriculum point memorable. Some years, with some classes, I wouldn't risk this introduction.

Kahlil and the rib cage

Kahlil and Zack stand side by side, each blowing on a set of model lungs. Kahlil touches a pipecleaner rib, "These things are just like the bars on Pepe's cage."

I stop to chat. "You're right, Kahlil! The rib cage is what protects the lungs and the heart. And guess what? It's curvy! The ribs can move to make room for a deep breath!" I place their hands so they can feel their chests expand, and leave them excitedly trying it on each other.

"Here," they say. "Want to feel mine?"

The boys were playing with the model as with any toy, but it stimulated some analogic thinking. I risked an extension. This time it worked out just the way I hoped.

The limits of the model: Rosa and Clint

At the table Rosa and Clint discuss whether the two straws are supposed to be nostrils or nose and mouth. Terry refers the question to me.

"What a great question! You're really using your brains. You know you can breathe through your nose *and* your mouth, so your air tube must go to both your nose and mouth. You're absolutely right! The nose is the main way we breathe, and the mouth is the main way we eat, so I made the model with straws for the nostrils, but our bodies are much more interesting and complicated than the model. It's great you figured that out! We leave some things out of models to make them easier to build and understand."

I didn't offer to add a third straw for the mouth, and they didn't ask. I breathed a secret sigh of relief—easier not to create a modification or explain why not. Meanwhile, important points were made: the children's own experience is a prime and trustworthy source of information; a model is oversimplified. If time allows, I'll invite Rosa and Clint to share their discovery with the circle.

Fences and ribcages: Zack and Daisy

Zack solemnly brings me a broken piece of fence from the block corner. "I don't know how it got broken," he says.

Daisy looks up from playdough. She squeezes her ribs, thoughtfully examines her knuckles, slides the fingers of her left hand through the thumb and pointer of her right. "These things are hard on me. I can't break it," she muses aloud.

During The Bodyworks we notice a widespread interest in fences and enclosures at block play, whether or not the children articulate their awareness of the protective function of the skull, the rib cage, the vertebrae.

Clint sees the breath

Clint's blowing into the "lungs" again.

"You look like you're having fun," I comment, letting him know he's important to me and I'm glad school is fun for him. He makes it a dialogue. "I can't see my breath. But in the winter I can."

"I bet you can see it today, too. Come look." I breathe on the mirror and the vapor clouds my reflection.

"That's neat!" He stays at the mirror a while, breathing on it, writing on the misted surface, blowing again.

There's a lot we've stopped seeing. The Bodyworks points children's attention to phenomena they've noticed, framing their experience. We don't have to stuff them with concepts and facts. We can notice and affirm the children's own exploratory process, perhaps extend it a bit, not rush to turn searchlights on the magic. It's hard to know when to intervene, how, with what. I think this time I hit it about right, sharing Clint's pleasure briefly, trusting him to follow the thread in his own time. I'm glad I stopped, glad he took the opportunity to tell me what was on his mind. I'd never have guessed.

Goblins and Growpower

At circle Tanya requests "The Goblin Song."

"It's been a while since we've talked about goblins. Does anybody remember what I told you about goblins?"

Ani: "They're not real. They're in your mind."

Sandy: "Sometimes everybody has mean feelings, scary feelings. Those feelings are hard to understand, so we make up a picture in our minds about the feelings, and what we imagine is what people call "a goblin."

Rosa: "But a LONG time ago maybe there really WERE such a thing as goblins."

Sandy: "People THOUGHT so, but they were just imagining. If people didn't understand something real, like if an earthquake happened, they imagined goblins did it. Then scientists began to figure out what was actually happening."

Rosa: "NO. It wasn't goblins that made a earthquake. It's because the earth changes."

Sandy: "Right."

Rosa: "The dinosaurs went away because it got too cold."

Tanya: "They fell on the ground and cracked it."

Sandy: "That's an interesting idea."

Rosa: "I get goblin feelings like I don't HAVE to do what people teach me. I can figure it out myself."

Despite her resistance, Rosa's learning how she ticks. Her sharing may help other children connect with their own feelings, far more effectively than anything I can say. I wish Jogger were ready, but he won't let anybody in (not me, anyway). Sometime soon I need to review the crucial difference between feelings and action, but this is the moment for some moralistic spin-off for Rosa's sake. Maybe timely for other children too?

Sandy: "Yes, you can figure out a lot. But it wastes a lot of time if you try to figure *everything* out. Like if you tried to figure out how to drive a car, you might have a wreck. You can learn by figuring things out *and* by learning from other people. Both ways are good. What song do we always sing right after the goblin song?"

All: "This Little Light of Mine!"

Sandy: "Right! Because I don't want us to let the goblin feelings get too big. I want us to feel the love and the light inside too. Singing helps us feel like little candles glowing inside, full of love and not scared."

After we sing, I lead a movement-and-imagination exercise, then pull out Eric Carle's *The Tiny Seed.* "This book is all about 'Growpower.' It's something else we can't see, but we know it's real from what it does. We can't see the wind, but we can see it blow the leaves, and we can feel it in our hair."

Aaargh! "Growpower" is invisible and internal, but it acts upon and has an impact on the real world. How is this different from goblins? I can't resolve this for the children. It's a matter of belief, partial knowledge, like contemporary science, continuously revealing to us how much there is that we don't know. I try to give the children some tools to help them balance their "imaginary" fears. Yet it would be irresponsible to deny all credibility to the invisible energetic dimension. Modern science teeters on the same borderline. I share what we "know" and leave room for what we don't.

I've explained earthquakes to the children in terms of plate tectonics, but that's just a hypothesis some scientists dispute. It doesn't "explain" why the earth's core is full of molten elements. Who knows why? It just is. We can chart a sunflower's development from a seed, but we can't analyze or replicate "growpower," the life force so real and essential to the sunflower. It's so "messy" among four-year-olds, so paradoxical. I could sit on them ("No more 'Goblin Song'. It's time to sing about spring flowers.") but that wouldn't help these children with their gargantuan human task. At least I can give them room to speak what's on their minds. So here I am, telling them there's no such thing as goblins, except in the mind, but growpower is real.

Rosa and the seesaw

Rosa nuzzles up to me. "I get a lotta goblin feelings when I watch 'Land Before Time.' "

"Can you tell me some more?"

"Littlefoot's mother dies cuz Sharptooth bites her on the back."

"That sounds sad. What happens to Littlefoot?"

"His grandma and grandpa didn't die."

"So he goes to live with them?"

"Uh-huh. His mother never comes back. Not even one time."

"Usually mothers don't die when their children are little, but if they do, other people in the family take care of the children."

"I know."

"But it's still sad to think about it."

"It's not the same as his mother. The grandparents isn't the same."

"If that video gives you goblin feelings, probably it's better not to watch it very much."

"But it's my favorite."

"Well, goblin feelings are OK unless they get too strong, and it's hard to think about anything else. Like a seesaw. It's fun to go up and down, but it's not fun if one child gets stuck in the air, and the other child gets stuck on the ground. It sounds like sometimes your mind is like a stuck seesaw. I know that feeling too. Let's get some blocks, and I'll show you what I mean."

I build a little seesaw and we move some fat pegs around on it. Very crude—it keeps falling down. "I can't get the blocks to work today, but do you get the idea? Our minds are like seesaws that can get stuck on sad things and scary things, so we have to give ourselves other things to think about and to do. That's our job. We're in charge of the seesaw. Suppose we think about the hard stuff all the time? We miss all the fun things."

"But everybody has to die. Even if they get old then they have to."

"Yes. We all have to die when it's time. But we have to live while it's time to live. Then when it's time to die, we'll be ready. Wouldn't it be sad if somebody just thought about dying and never had any fun?"

"Because if I get to be a old lady and I always thought about the bad stuff, it would be sad. I wouldn't do any good stuff."

"Right! That's why you're learning to balance the seesaw. So you can live a lot. Then when dying time comes, it'll be OK. How about a hug? You give great hugs!"

Rosa's mother likes the seesaw idea. She adds: "I keep telling her not to have all those bad thoughts. I tell her to have good thoughts. It's driving her crazy. It's driving *me* crazy. I know you said it's normal for kids this age to be interested in death, but you know Rosa—she's just hammering away at it."

"I know. It's easier for me, because I'm just her teacher. She goes home to you at the end of the morning! One other thing—some children are extra susceptible to TV and I think Rosa's one of them."

"We don't let her watch anything but Sesame Street and Misterogers and the Disney channel and Nickelodeon. Animal shows sometimes. No cartoons. Some videos."

"Good for you—it's hard to hold the line on cartoons. But even Disney shows and 'family entertainment' can be too much for a child like Rosa. Those images get into her mind and she can't get them out. Like 'Land Before Time.' "

"She watches it whenever I let her. She never gets tired of it."

"That's what she said. I told her maybe she needs a rest from all those scary feelings."

"I tell her it's bad to watch it over and over, but I've got enough battles with her. I just give in."

"I sympathize! Keep trying. Meanwhile we can help Rosa name thoughts and feelings clearly: 'scary,' 'sad,' 'all about dead stuff,' 'happy,' 'easy,' 'peaceful,' 'smooth.' It's tempting to label everything 'bad' or 'good,' but I bet that gets her deeper in the hole."

"Then she thinks she's a bad person."

"Yes, it feels contrived. But let's help her make distinctions without using 'bad' and 'good.' We can say, 'Even when you do the wrong thing, I know you're a good person.' It's subtle, but it adds up in Rosa's mind. This may sound ridiculous, but it feels to me like she's waging her own war with light and darkness, at age four."

"Four going on forty! That's how I've been feeling, but I couldn't put words on it. My sisters tell me to lighten up—kids outgrow this. My husband thinks I'm overreacting. Rosa doesn't get to him the way she gets to me. Thanks!"

Cara runs fast

Cara's breathing hard, her eyes sparkling after a chase game with Clint. She takes my hand. "Clint chase me, not catch! I run fast! Tummy go up me running fast!"

"I saw you—you really did run fast! When we work and play hard, our lungs and hearts work extra hard to give us energy. Sometimes we feel a little uncomfortable if our bodies need to slow down or stop. Was your tummy telling you to stop?"

"My's tummy up here! Not hurt me. Running!"

"Just excited and full of energy! I'm glad you noticed that, Cara, and told me about it."

She gives me a happy smile and squeezes my hand.

I was sure Cara was simply sharing something of mutual interest—not a worry, but an observation. Still, I had to check it out. Cara's using words to volunteer personal experience!

Cara makes lungs

Cara runs in. "Lungs!" she calls.

Her mother's grinning. "She made them herself! She hunted up baggies, straws, and tape, but we had no nylon net lying around the house. That's what the scraps of paper doily are all about. She said they're 'pockets for air.' " Cara's mother is beaming. "I'm going straight over to the Odyssey to buy *Outside-In*. She can't stop talking about that book."

Momentum's building. Did it begin with Cara's self-portrait, when Nita was so warm and confident about her own dark skin, straight black hair, black eyes? We've seen Cara keep her nose clean, assert herself to Tanya. make a bridge to Maggie, reach out to Bo, carry her excitement about the lungs home and back to school again.

On the playground she still follows Clint around like a puppy. That role works for her, even though the adults hope she'll outgrow it. At least Cara's taking new risks with other children. She got Pip to chase her and later beat Shirelle to the swings.

Most significant, Cara's face has opened up. She smiles more, makes eye contact. Her speech is limited, but now it's illuminated by expression and gesture. Other children respond differently to this new animated Cara. Hard to believe she's the same child. No doubt these changes have been ripening all year, but The Bodyworks has given her a boost—holding Nita's bright mirror up to "racial" differences, addressing classmates' concerns, opening a new channel for her intellectual curiosity, inspiring her with delight in her own inner workings. It's a thrill to watch her emerge.

Kahlil makes lungs too

Kahlil also runs into the room with "lungs" he's crafted at home. He asked his mother for "something with a lot of little holes in it to catch the air when I breathe in my lungs," and they hit upon cheesecloth. His mother whispers, "Please tell him the rib cage goes around the back too. He said it couldn't, because you didn't say so. Around our house you are the ultimate authority!" She twinkles, while I groan. "In fact, you're a local hero, since Gabe read your letter to the parents and saw 'wiener' in print. Kahlil can't do much with the spelling software, but he's now mastered 'Go poops' on the computer. The Bodyworks motivates him in unexpected ways! By the way, Gabe says he got ripped off because he didn't get to build his body. I know you've got your hands full, but is there any chance he could visit during vacation?"

"I'd love to have Gabe visit. Let's see where we are next week."

Kahlil, like Cara, shows the crucial relationship of concept and material in the experience of a physical thinker. The concept of homology helped guide the design of The Bodyworks. Biologists describe the human arm, the bird's wing, the horse's foreleg as roughly homologous in origin, though differently adapted. I chose familiar materials with properties that would express function in the Bodyworks model. Although nylon net did not meet my criterion of availability, I included it because, to physical thinkers, the medium is the message. Kahlil and Cara each grasped the significance of the nylon net and improvised an appropriate alternative. I couldn't have devised a better test for mastery of a concept.

Kahlil's claim that his mother must be wrong about the rib cage will be familiar to many parents of young children, whose teachers are their idols. It's inevitable that The Bodyworks, like any curriculum, may leave gaps and distortions in information, or honest differences in interpretation and opinion. Close communication between home and school can help to bring these to light, gently leading children to dig deep for their own truths.

And, while some may not welcome "Go poops" on the computer, there's no denying that The Bodyworks perfectly matches the whole language approach, and engages the whole family.

Cara offers help

Bo is blowing into the straws to inflate the lungs. He steps back and runs his finger down the model's esophagus to the stomach, along the intestine to the anus. "The bag has a hole in it," he comments to himself.

It's probably the right moment for me to check out his understanding of the digestive tract. Before I can engage him, Cara brings over a book open to the respiratory system. "Lungs," she tells him, "breathing!" He looks at her, at the diagram, at the model. "Yep," he says.

I use my moment simply to affirm Cara's initiative. "Thanks for bringing the book over, Cara. You noticed Bo was interested in the lungs."

She smiles, eyes shining. Bo wanders away.

There will be other moments to follow up on Bo. It's important to make space for Cara's initiative, not crowd it with my own agenda. It would have been nice if Bo had thanked her, but prompting him would probably have backfired this time. She seemed more than happy with the limited outcome.

Bo is up to it

Doing the lungs will challenge Bo. He's interested—in fact, eager—but placing and punching the holes and twisting the pipe cleaners into position may be too much for him. I arrange for him to work with Nita, without a peer partner, and I talk to him about the task ahead.

"The rib cage is tricky, Bo. Lots of stuff to put together in a small space. Nita's ready to help you if you need it. Remember how you've learned to work: Use your mind to be in charge of your hands. Keep your eyes on your hands. Go slow and take breaks. Stop to see what you've done and plan what's next."

"OK," Bo grins. "I didn't get tired waiting this day. I played till Nita called me."

"That's another thing you remembered from doing the brain! Great!" I watch from a distance. *His effort is visible in overflow behavior: tongue between his teeth, squirming in the chair.*

Nita urges a break halfway through. Bo's reluctant to stop, but agrees to jump up and down a couple of times with her, and takes a sip from the water fountain. He completes the rib cage and calls me over, beaming.

I don't want to set Bo up for failure by making much of the difficulties inherent in the task; on the other hand, he has a long string of frustrations behind him. It's tempting for an adult to do the fine-motor work for him, assuring short-run success, but Bo would know exactly how much success was his own. What he needs—and now seems ready for—is learning how to learn. We can support him best by offering strategies to reduce distractibility and impulsivity, improve his eye-hand coordination, and build self-esteem based on positive experience.

Ani invents a sphincter

Ani's at The Bodyworks table watching other children work, idly twisting a pipe cleaner from the basket of "ribs." She glances down at her hands, bends the pipe cleaner into a circle and wraps the ends together to close it. Twisting the circle in half, she produces a figure eight and bends that over; now she has a double circle. She squeezes it together, stretches it out again, repeating these last two steps several times. A lightbulb goes on. "Look! Hey, look! I made the muscle you go poops."

I confirm. "You sure did, Ani. Great! That's just what happens. The sphincter muscle opens and closes the anus to squeeze the poops into the toilet." The children at the table look at Ani's invention. "Neat!" No one seems embarrassed.

Later in the morning Ani comes over to tell me what else she has been doing. "I watched the worms on the tray," she says. "Two times they fell off. I caught 'em."

"Thanks, Ani. Those worms can move pretty fast. I'm glad you rescued them. Sometimes the person in charge forgets to watch carefully."

"You said to see where the wormses head is, head are. I know which end. The head is the movest end. I made you a picture," Ani says, holding it out to me. She has worked very carefully with watercolors and a fine brush, producing a giant red spider with eight black legs bent in half.

"You and I really like spiders, don't we, Ani?" I smile and hug her. "This picture's a real treasure. It shows how much you know about spiders! It reminds me a lot of a daddy longlegs I saw out on the porch this morning."

"That was it," says Ani.

I could have done a little rap contrasting human, worm, and spider anatomy—somebody told me a daddy longlegs isn't really a spider anyway—but that would have been overkill. Ani didn't need me to teach her anything at that moment, just to celebrate a rich morning of self-directed learning.

Teacher play

Being around Ani and other creative children gets my juices running. Sometimes I want to strip off my teacherly apron and play, explore, experiment—with no responsibility for anyone else. I'm playful with the children at school, but I can't be a child among them. I make plenty of time for that at home.

Some of that play leads to new things for the classroom. Next week I'll try out two of my latest brainstorms. I dragged out an old kneesock and cut a small hole in the toe. When I inserted a tennis ball at the cuff and squeezed from the top of the sock, the tennis ball moved slowly through the hole in the toe. Voilà! The perfect demonstration of worms and human "food tubes."

After I introduce the ball-in-a-sock, I'll ask the children to imagine they're fish, with water always pressing on their bodies. The children know how good it feels to swim—it's easy for them to identify with fish. They'll be able to guess what's pressing on people's bodies all the time: air. From that point, I can suggest that for a worm it's natural to be surrounded by soil. Maybe to a worm it feels as good to tunnel through the earth as a backrub feels to us.

Then we'll play "worm tunnel," with two lines of children on their hands and knees, facing each other. I'll be the worm inching along on my belly, while the children are the little clods of soil rubbing my back. They'll love it, and so will I, and by the time we've all had a turn to be the worm, I hope we'll feel more connected to our little partners.

The worm tunnel will be a big hit—it's just like my old car-wash standby. I'll still have to be teacher-in-charge, but it'll feel like play.

Kahlil chooses his time

Kahlil's middle brother, Ari, was building a bodyworks when Kahlil was born with an intestinal blockage requiring immediate surgery. Today his father reminds me how he used the bodyworks to explain to Ari why newborn Kahlil had to stay in the hospital for a few days. Ari grasped the baby's problem and the surgical solution and relaxed. Four years later Ari still keeps his bodyworks hanging on the back of his closet door. Now Kahlil's father confides that his wife has been hospitalized for exploratory kidney surgery. Although the bodyworks doesn't include the kidneys, he suggests we might add kidneys for Kahlil. I tell him it does sound like a good idea, but I'll need cues from Kahlil.

Kahlil's working alone at a puzzle when I sit down with him. "I'm sorry your mom had to go to the hospital."

"My dad's gonna stay home from work to take care of us. Maybe he can take us to visit her after two days."

"I hope he can. I bet she misses you and you miss her."

"Yeah."

"Your dad said he talked to you about the problem with your mom's kidneys. He thought you might want kidneys on your bodyworks. I'd be glad to help you."

"I don't want to."

"If you change your mind, you can let me know."

"OK."

"Maybe later you could make a picture for your mom."

Kahlil looks up from his puzzle with a slow smile spreading. "Right now," he said. "I'm gonna make her a picture of a flower. She likes flowers."

Kahlil's older brother was reassured when his dad used the bodyworks to explain his infant brother's medical problem. The timing was perfect. Kahlil's response is totally different.

To begin with, the patient is his mother, not a newborn brother he's never met. The intellectual explanation about kidneys may have helped him manage some of his anxiety, but the real issue for Kahlil is emotional. He misses his mother; he's worried about her. There's not even a clear diagnosis and treatment plan. Later Kahlil may be interested in constructing kidneys for his bodyworks. Right now he just wants his mother. The next best thing to seeing her is to express his love and longing—making a card will comfort him. He will feel he's helping her, too.

His dad and I will keep in touch. It's important not to overload Kahlil cognitively or emotionally. For now, he may need school to be the safe space where he can afford to forget home troubles. Kahlil may hold himself together until the crisis has passed, not because he's in denial, but because this is how he copes best. After the initial stage of the crisis, we may see some acting out. Until then, we can err as much by being intrusive as by ignoring the problem.

Had Kahlil responded positively to the invitation to construct kidneys, I might have had all the children add kidneys to their models. The priority was to address Kahlil's needs as quickly and personally as possible, to let him lead in defining the immediate problem and evolving a solution.

Nostrils, dragons, bracelets, cages: Clint, Shirelle, Pip

Clint and Shirelle are constructing lungs. Pip's hanging around nearby. Shirelle comments: "I have nostrils. Spotty has nostrils. So does Calico!"

Clint adds: "Not only persons and dogs and cats. Horses have nostrils too. I've seen 'em. They have two. Nostrils. All the time animals have two, and persons. Not only one nostril."

Pip has his own angle. "What if a dragon? What if fire's coming out his nostrils, then he breathes air at the same time?"

An unanswerable question. There's a short pause. Shirelle, fiddling with the pipecleaners in the basket, offers, "You could make bracelets out of this!"

Clint holds a baggie lung in place while Nita tapes it around the straw. He looks at the book open on the table. His eyes go back and forth from the diagram of lungs to the model hanging from the doorway to what he is holding. "The breathing tube is one in the middle, together, then it turns into two because one for each side."

The lowest common denominator here is "nostrils." Each child has relevant experience and interest, and makes the generalization to other species. Otherwise, the children are pursuing their idiosyncratic paths: Shirelle's interested in adornment, Pip in personal fantasy, Clint in function and structure. Wisely, Nita doesn't teach any content. Each child engages the subject in an individual way, the group sharing interests within the framework of general information about breathing—the developmental process at work.

Shirelle's ready to put her lungs into her model: "I'm putting my lungs over my tummy, cuz I like 'em here."

At this point, Nita begins to "teach," and Shane chimes in: "You can't put 'em there, Shirelle! They gotta have the 'tector. The cage."

Four-year-olds have learned that things and people can be manipulated. It's important to give them room to explore their power, without encouraging delusions or allowing bullying. Shirelle needs to learn the elements of her body are more than internal jewelry to relocate at will. Discussing the function and location of the lungs is a small step in deepening her self-esteem.

Tanya counts out

Several children are arguing about who will play with which puppet. Tanya keeps assigning roles with a counting-out rhyme learned from her older sister, and always manages to make it come out the way she wants. I step in: "What's happening?"

"Tanya always does it, and it always lands on me," Missy says. Others agree.

"Here's another way to work it out," I offer. "Let's count how many people are playing." I fetch paper and number strips from 1 to 5. Each child traces or copies a number I've written. "Hand your paper to Tanya and she'll hold the numbers where you can't see them. Then you each pick, and the person who gets Number One chooses her puppet first. You keep going until all the numbers are used up."

Tanya scowls. "What about me?"

"You get a number also, and you choose when it's your number's turn."

She looks at me witheringly but makes much of collecting and holding the numbered strips and chooses the Butterfly puppet. When Missy tries out the powerful Pink Cat for the first time, attempting to "save" Tanya from the alligator. Tanya shrieks, "DON'T save me! The butterfly can save her own self!"

Tanya's peers have begun to resent her machinations and soon will exclude her unless adults step in. Family disruptions leave her vulnerable right now. Otherwise, I might have let her learn by experience the limits of bossiness or taken her aside for a quiet talk. I could've demonstrated to all how the counter-out can stretch or shrink a rhyme to suit herself; instead, I gave Tanya's friends a new and empowering tool but left her in a key position.

While Bodyworks expands self-concepts in one corner of the classroom, in another corner children are constructing themselves in quite a different way. The approaches reinforce each other. We may as teachers divide development into different domains, but children are all one piece, with many ways to nourish themselves. Before her Bodyworks experience Missy played it safe at school. Her emerging sense of self allows her to take new risks in imaginative play with her peers. In the world of puppets, a clever cat may outwit an alligator and a fragile butterfly may escape on wings alone.

Sand in Shane's eyes

Paul's vigorously excavating a hole in the sandbox. Shane scoots behind to retrieve a dump truck, screams and rubs his eyes. Paul looks around, alarmed but unaware he's caused the problem. I lead Shane inside, inviting Paul to help. "Shane, it'll be OK," I say reassuringly. "Don't rub your eyes. That'll make it worse. I'll hold your hands for you." Shane continues to scream.

"Your body knows how to clear out the sand. That's your tears' job—washing out the sand. Sit on my lap and let your tears work. You can help by blowing your breath out like this—whoooooo. A nice long soft blow. Make a little sound like the ocean to help you relax while your tears do their job. If you relax, the sand won't bother you as much. Paul and I will breathe with you." After a few minutes his eyes are mostly clear. Paul wipes Shane's cheeks with a tissue. "Now, it's almost finished. Your body knew just what to do."

Shane leans against me. "There's still some. A little bit."

"I'll wash my hands and lift your eyelid to help." He reaches to rub his eye, and I gently cover his hand. "That'll rub the sand in deeper." I wash a measuring cup and tilt Shane's head over the sink, explaining the water will wash the grit out but it might hurt a little. I keep the rhythmic breathing going with him. He winces but doesn't scream as I pour. Paul hovers, looking anxious. "Paul, please get Shane a tissue. . . . You dry off his wet face for him."

Paul's delighted to help. He knows somehow he's involved, even if he doesn't understand what happened. "I'm sorry you got sand in your eye," he says.

"But my eyes fixed me!" says Shane. "They know how."

"And you helped: you kept your hands away, and used your ocean breathing to relax," I add. I escort both boys back to the sandbox, reminding them to pay attention to what everybody else is doing nearby.

Until now Shane has overreacted to the least jostle; he was almost hysterical the day he fell and cut his knee. Before today, he didn't take much comfort from "ocean breathing" or my steady reassurance. Did his new awareness of the body help him calm down and trust the clearing process? Paul was shaken by the accident and would have been even more so, had he felt responsible. Letting him watch and help led both boys to a satisfactory closure.

Walter Cannon, M.D., wrote his classic Wisdom of the Body *about the body's capacity to regulate itself and restore equilibrium. Cannon's wonderful title returns to me when I try to guide children through the small and large pains of early childhood. We can often support them by engaging the quieting breath and helping them observe the body's wisdom in action, especially if they know "the body works."*

Tanya's babies have to breathe

Throughout the year children take turns at "The World," a shallow tray of sand on top of rolling shelves filled with boxes of small accessories: animals, people, shells, stones, sticks, feathers, miniature tools, oddments of all sorts. Each child has a whole activity period to work alone, creating "a happy world, a scary world, a mixed-up world, any kind of world you want to make today." I affirm the creative process by watching and listening, reminding other children they're welcome to watch but not to touch or make comments. I write down the World-maker's "story of the World" as she describes what she's built. In the bustle of the busy classroom, children go deep into their Worlds, treasuring the opportunity to play out what's on their minds.

Tanya always gets the babies out first, all four of them. Her mother reports that she has real rapport and concern for her infant sister, young cousins, neighbors, the babies she befriends in the supermarket. Today she groups the babies closely together in the sand, enclosing them in a clear dome she's made by upending a round glass goblet. Tanya tells me that she's keeping the babies safe. At the end of the hour, she props a little stone under the goblet. "I gotta give the babies some air. For their lungs. They gotta breathe," she observes.

Yesterday in dress-ups Tanya was acting the part of the frenzied mother at supper time. I asked her if the daddy would be home to help soon. "No, he got poisoned by broccoli," she told me. She went on, "I know where it goes when you eat stuff. Afterwards it goes to your poops. I know it myself. My mommy didn't tell me." She goes on. "My daddy drinks too many beers. Mommy tore up her wedding picture cuz she was mad at him."

No wonder Tanya's frantic. She's using The Bodyworks in at least two ways. She feels empowered by her new information, especially since her mother's too overwhelmed to provide the informal teaching that underlies routines in a stable household. In addition, Tanya uses The Bodyworks on the symbolic level, working through her sense of vulnerability by assuring her babies "can breathe." I hope The Bodyworks will give Tanya some fresh air in the suffocating atmosphere of her home in this time of stress.

Rosa and the little head with the blood

Rosa's a whirling dervish today, stirring up everyone in her path. Terry sits her down to do the intestinal tract. Rosa shoots her a withering look, and a loud comment to match: "I KNOW THAT! I know things YOU don't even know. Like how we got here. My mother didn't even know, but I DO! By Mother Nature and the Weather! Besides I can't do my food tube because I don't have enough green beans I ate for dinner in my stomach. So I'm gonna cut some more. Get me some green paper and some scissors."

Rosa feels she should know everything and she hates to be told anything. She often puts up a big smokescreen to hide what she doesn't know. Here she may also be dodging failure. All the other children have used adult help to install the "food tube." That doesn't get Rosa off her own hook—she wants to do it solo or not at all. So she's trying to control us by distracting us with a demand for green paper. She's also letting us know she's been thinking about The Bodyworks. I'm dying to hear her hypothesis about Mother Nature and the Weather, but first we have to calm her down and help her face the task at hand. Time to give poor Terry a break.

Rosa has turned her chair around backwards and is in snapping turtle mode: arms tightly crossed across her chest, shoulders hunched high and rigid, neck sticking out. She whirls to confront me, catching sight of her Insides at the same time. A small smile escapes her. "Lookit my brain I did. It's great. I like my brain I did!"

"You really did do a terrific job." After we admire it for a few seconds, I shift. "You said you didn't want to make a brain, but after you did it you were really happy. Like the daffodil."

Rosa's smile fades. She smells the bait. "Yep."

"Are you ready to try the food tube? Terry will help you—it's long and tangly."

"I GUESS so. I hate it when she helps me."

"Please give it a try. Remember the brain. You needed help, but it was worth it. Terry, Rosa's going to try."

Poor Terry's probably not up to this, but I need to check on the worms and it's important that Rosa not monopolize my attention. She's so stirred up today, I'm tempted to postpone the whole thing, but that happens too often. We've got to help her learn to function within the parameters.

From worms and sprouts, I can see things going downhill fast. Rosa will recognize my brisk authoritative manner even if she doesn't salute it. "Excuse me for interrupting you, Terry. Rosa and I need to talk. Please work with another child for now."

I lead Rosa over to a quiet corner and sit down on the floor with her. "Enough, Rosa. You're using all your energy one way. What would you call it?"

"Fussy."

"Time to tip the seesaw. Terry can't teach you if all your energy and hers are being used for fussing. Take a break. You need to be by yourself a while. Call me when you feel ready for something besides fussing. The way you're acting makes me think maybe you have something on your mind."

"I been thinking about stuff. That's why. Know what I saw? A VIDEO! I didn't see the tape, but I saw the BOX at the video store. With like a little head with some orange hair sticking up, and blood coming from here." She points to the corner of her mouth. "It think it's called Bloofairy. I think there's another scary feeling about a girl that's holding a gun in her hand. On the box. I thought: my seesaw is stuck on the yuckies."

This is the cultural context of The Bodyworks. Before Rosa can give herself to The Bodyworks, she has to shake off the goblins that haunt her. This child and her classmates live in the imaginary terrain we've projected—where the body is victim ("the little head with the blood"), the body is aggressor (Power Rangers), the body is object (Barbie). What happens to children who can't be at home in their own minds?

What about the children caught in the cross fire in housing projects, the children sleeping in bathtubs to dodge stray bullets? What about the middle schoolers my daughter teaches in rural Georgia? Young dealers who bring their beepers to school, the boy shot dead for "sassing" his cousin, the eleven-year-old impregnated by her best friend's father? What happens to children who can't be at home in their own bodies?

"That really does sound like a scary picture to think about. What are you going to do about your seesaw?"

"I COULD think about GOOD things. About Care Bears™. Care Bears™

are real nice for other people. They like it when you think about nice feelings. I could think about . . ." She runs out of gas.

"Is it hard because the scary pictures are very strong and you don't have such strong pictures of happy stuff?"

"About the little guy, he had a knife in his hand too. The gun wasn't so dangerous. You can go to the hospital and get fixed. But knifes is even dangerouser, because you can't get it fixed. AND. He had a gun. Too. I'm thinking about a boy when he growed up he got something what some other guys stole but then he was captured and he got away. That's the best part. I got it. Maybe I could say, 'I love people,' and that would make the seesaw go THAT way."

"Good idea. It might help, but just saying 'Love' isn't as strong as some of those scary pictures in your mind. You need to make a picture of what love and happy look like. Can you think of a time that's really happy? What's in the picture? Is there a story that goes with it?"

"All of it's colored rainbows up in the sky with pink in it. And the sun is shining bright and he decided he was gonna take a walk. He met a couple of friends, and they play, and after a while it's time to leave. 'Goodbye! See you next time!' And he was really happy. He really loved someone and he saved their life. That made the seesaw go the other way . . . BUT—when I'm working, it goes back."

"OK. Let's try to make one strong picture you can use when you're working, when your mind seesaws to the yuckies. We can take turns trying out some pictures that make us feel good inside."

"How bout a HEART? It's pink, and EVERY single day even when it dies it sprays its perfume on."

"Great idea to put the smell in. That helps it be more real. How does it feel to touch it?"

"It feels squeaky and slobby, cuz those are mostly how hearts. And every time somebody picks it up, it falls all over their hands and makes their hands slobby and if they don't get it over soon it's gonna stay on them forever."

"Does it make any sounds?"

"It goes deedle, deedle, all kinds of sounds."

"How big is it?"

"As big as the whole world! But when it was a baby it was so small, then next springtime it spreaded. It even opened its home."

"Does the heart have a taste?"

"Like sugar, so yummy."

"My turn. My favorite picture for real is the one of Mother Earth over there. I'll try to make up a picture in my head too. I'm imagining a creature that's spinning lots of silver threads. All the threads together make a shining web that's invisible, but it connects everything in the whole world. So you and I are connected, even when we're not in the same room."

"I never thought you'd be connected! But sometimes Babyhugs and Babytears pull hard. . . . OK! It worked." She leans over to give me a big hug, her body loose, her face radiant. It's all out of her for now.

Who knows what helped her the most—the verbal release or the body contact? She sat in my lap, leaning against me while we talked. I kept my breathing deep and steady. She's as porous as a sponge—almost as if she has no skin.

The horrors—manufactured images and real-life—are affecting us all, but most of us stuff them into the subconscious; Rosa can't. Even one glimpse sets her off. Her loss of control in the face of a violent image is linked to her sense of being vulnerable when she has to cope with a new task. These feelings amplify each other, becoming one and the same.

I want to rant and rave at the corporations ripping off our children's minds and our own for the sake of big bucks. Nothing signifies love and hope as powerfully as the commercial images express violence and terror. Children's most fundamental emotions are hooked, bought, and sold. There are always a few sappy rainbows, unicorns, and pastel teddybears (usually pitched at girls), but the love-and-joy dreck doesn't have a prayer against death rays and rampages and specific unspeakable interpersonal crimes, with pictures in full view at the video store, the supermarket, the TV news, previews. We can't keep Rosa away from those images unless we lock her up. All we can do is help her build some psychological dikes to hold back this bloody ocean.

I tell Rosa's mother about the residue of graphic violence from her stroll through the video store and suggest we help her strengthen her positive images. Her mother nods, "I didn't know what it was, but she told me first thing this morning she had to talk to you about something. That must have been it. Who would have guessed?"

"I know. She was whirling, but it didn't come out for a couple of hours. It must have been eating at her since last night. Anytime she mentions she wants to tell me about something, maybe you could remind her when you drop her off—and let me know too."

There must be some way we can help offset the violent media. The images are scarring Rosa and the other children. What about the children who have to run the gauntlet of real guns and drugs?

After work I sit in the kitchen with my colleagues, and they help me generate a list of beautiful and complex images to add to my favorite, the view of Earth as seen by the Apollo astronauts. Not much, but a start: snow crystals, seashells—especially the spiral of the chambered nautilus, the head of a sunflower, dandelions gone to seed, milkweed seeds packed into their cradling pod, growth rings of trees, bare branches against the sky, water-drops strung like beads along railings and roofs, rocks in pools, feathers, constellations, galaxies, the spiral of water swirling down a drain, honeycomb, sunlight dappling water, shadows on snow, wave prints on sand.

Perhaps these images will never have for Rosa's generation the power they have for us. Perhaps these children will always see the world through a film of plastic, by the flickering light of a video screen. Perhaps this list is just for teachers, to console us while our blue-green planet spins toward doom. I recognize this is a possibility, but I won't let my seesaw get stuck there. I don't have the answers, but I'll keep groping along, and I will hold before me the radiance of Rosa's face like a small flame in the darkness. I believe in growpower.

Rosa and The Bodyworks

What, if anything, does this have to do with The Bodyworks? Rosa's issues have been here from the first day; she isn't any more reactive than usual. Perhaps The Bodyworks helps me see how she voices the concerns of all the children: the integrity of the body, the oneness of body-mind, the thin line between "fantasy" and "reality." I'm angry with our culture, which scares children for profit, attaching to products their capacity for love and dreams and honor.

The Bodyworks opens things up. Am I playing with fire? I'm focusing on Rosa, but I'm really asking myself again if The Bodyworks belongs in the preschool classroom.

Yes. I *am* playing with fire. We always are—we who call ourselves "teachers" or "parents," as if we had the wisdom, the discipline, to be models for anyone else. We grown-ups don't know what we're talking about, really. For most of history the threats to people came from beasts, weather, disease, famine, marauders. In our time, much of what threatens us has sprung from our own hands. Radiation, toxins, the proliferation of deadly weapons, the degradation of the environment: the list is endless.

Yes, Rosa, it's a terrifying time to be alive. We've forgotten how to live and die in harmony with nature, and we don't know how to put the genie back in the bottle. I invite you and your classmates to ask real questions about the realest thing you know—living in a body / mind—while revealing that I have few answers. I urge you to observe, to wonder, to apprentice yourself to a mystery.

You're so young! Yet already you're enthralled by what passes for power in our culture, the kind of power which will betray you. Intuitively, Rosa, *you* already know that your vulnerability as a child, as a female, is only one aspect of "safety." The safety of your spirit is deeply at issue. We're fighting an undeclared war for the survival of the spirit in a civilization given over to power games.

Maybe it's always been so: the lords at war for the bodies, minds, souls of the people. But in earlier times and places, the people were deeply aware of their fundamental kinship with the four elements, the Earth and all her animals, plants, minerals. Alienated as we are, our bodies can still bring us home to the truth of interdependence.

The more aware you are of your own true being, the microcosm of a mystery you apprehend but can never control—the more powerful you'll become: a true partner in the dance of life on this planet, not easily fooled by naked emperors.

So it's no wonder, Rosa, that you keep coming up for me as we invent The Bodyworks. Ultimately this curriculum is all about the roots of wisdom and true power: energy, awareness, insight, and experiential knowledge. It's about relationship: the muscle and the bone, the finger and the hand, the nerve and the brain, the person and the planet. It's about the integrity of the whole—the thin permeable membrane of skin between us and the larger life in which we live and move and have our being.

Oh Rosa, I can't stop to remember all this in the midst of the classroom when you balk and spin and threaten rebellion. I must focus on the other benefits Bodyworks brings—the construction of concepts, community-building, the small leaps of understanding—but deep down I know it's the sense of wonder that keeps me going.

Every day I stand here pointing to the open gates. Don't trust my knowledge or the false gods. Trust only the light which comes to you in the Secret Place of your own being, the breath moderated by trees, the heat moderated by worms, the great circle in which we dwell together before and after videos and politicians. I'm a servant of that circle, neither model nor magician. Nothing but a struggling grown-up who stops sometimes to remember where I came from, where I'm going, why I'm here—and to accompany you, as far as I can.

I've answered my question. You keep coming up for me because you need The Bodyworks to affirm your intimate experience of being alive. The Bodyworks recognizes your whole self as a source of vitality, information, understanding, connectedness, adventure, expansion, power within. It's hard for you to believe the "inner ear" is a gift, cherished by our tribe. That's why I'm called to keep doing The Bodyworks, wrestling with you, Rosa, and all the children seeking their true names. Empowered from within, linked to others, you will not be cogs and consumers, but co-creators.

WEEK FIVE

Bladder, Urethra, Penis, Vagina Bones, Muscles, Joints

Circling the Urinary Tract

At circle we're discussing the urinary tract. Actually, I'm performing a dramatic monologue.

"When your body has used up all the vitamins and minerals in the milk and water and juice, you need to throw away what's left over. So it all drips down into a little bag called the bladder. When the bladder's almost full, your nerves send a message to your brain: 'Better empty your bladder.' And your brain sends a message to your bladder: 'OK, hang on for a minute. We're not ready yet.'

"Then your brain tells your legs, 'Hey, legs! Walk to the bathroom. OK, arms! Pull down those pants. OK, urethra muscles! Loosen up and open that hole. Now, bladder: get ready, get set, and GO FOR IT! Send that pee right into the toilet!'

"After a little while, your bladder sends a new message back to your brain: 'I'm all empty again, feeling good, ready to hold some more pee.' And then the brain says, 'Great job, bladder. Now you arms and legs, pull up the pants. Eyes, you check to see if any drips got on the toilet. Hands, you wipe up and flush and then wash yourselves with soap and water. Terrific teamwork, everybody! Let's go back to play.'"

"Isn't it amazing that you can do all that? When you were a baby, you couldn't. You had to wear a diaper until you learned to do all those things. And sometimes, when you're sleepy or sick or busy, you forget what you've learned and maybe have an accident. Everybody, even grown-ups, sometimes has a little accident. But then you can just clean up and dry off. No big deal."

The children are leaning forward, eyes wide, mouths gaping, hanging on every word. The dramatic tension has built to its peak. It's a high point of my career on the teaching stage. Time to break the spell and ease the audience into an interchange.

"Different families use different words for urine. Lots of people call it pee. What do you call it?"

Zack opens. "I forgot."

Cara volunteers, "Tinkle."

Daisy gets silly, "TWINKLE!"

Cara changes her tune to echo Daisy, who's generally right, "Twinkle!"

Paul chimes in, "Police? Cherry tree?" *(Maybe "police" comes from his unconscious. This discussion breaks the rules.)*

Zack veers back. "I remembered the brain because my brain told me to." *The brain is relevant but safe!*

Given the group's visible anxiety, I'm about to release energy with a movement activity when the discussion takes an abrupt turn.

It's Pip. "We thought we were going to have twin babies. But they *didn't grow right.*"

I follow up, for the sake of the others: "So they didn't get born. They stopped growing inside your mother's body."

Daisy tosses in, "My aunty had a baby."

I ask matter-of-factly, "Where did it grow?"

Daisy, "In her tummy."

Now I can follow up. "We call that special place the uterus. And you grew inside YOUR mother's uterus."

Jogger scowls, "Girls go pee in their butts."

"No," I say gently, "Your penis is in front. That's where your urethra opens out of your bladder. A girl's urethra is in the front of her body too. And she has an extra opening in the middle of her body for the baby to be born, if she ever has a baby. Boys and girls both have a rectum in the back, where their bowel movements, poo, comes out."

Two months ago Pip's family was in turmoil. His parents carefully explained his mother's miscarriage of twins. At school Pip seemed deep in fantasy play, without chatting about home. He kept his family's loss hidden. It was too hot to handle. Now it's pushing out into the light. Pip, who rarely speaks up at circle, goes only so far today. He says nothing about his feelings, and I don't ask. This is his tentative beginning.

Daisy recalls her aunt's experience, perhaps smoothing over the jagged truth Pip has introduced.

Jogger, with three big sisters, knows exactly how and where girls pee. Perhaps he's trying to reduce the double fanciness.

Terminology

Every year I raise the terminology question for myself. "Penis" and "vagina" are not analogous structures. "Vagina" is not the correct term for the external female genitals, only for the hidden opening. However, it's the word most families at our school use for this area of female anatomy. Similarly, the word "penis" doesn't include scrotum and testicles, but commonly refers to the male anatomy. Should The Bodyworks at school lead the way toward more accurate terminology at home, differentiating vulva, labia, vagina, uterus, penis, foreskin, scrotum, testicles?

I want (1) to encourage children to express their own concerns and to ask questions about the human body; (2) to give them a vocabulary which is generally understood; (3) to help children grow comfortable using this vocabulary so they can keep clean and healthy, defend themselves, ask for help, satisfy curiosity, make informed decisions, etc. I don't want to confuse children with too many names and technicalities. "Penis" and "vagina" seem to hit the middle ground, with "pelvis" as a comprehensive term for the whole "private" region of the body.

Pip and Daisy, pursuing the subject

For the urinary tract, I pair Pip and Daisy. As the two compare the girl model and boy model, Pip states the obvious, "Boys have a penis. Girls don't."

Daisy pouts, "But I want a penis."

Pip comforts. "But girls have something on the inside where babies grow. We were gonna have two babies. But we lost 'em, both of 'em. One was growing smaller than the other and we lost it. Then we lost the other one. We were going to have babies and that's," he points to the uterus on the girl model, "where they grow. I want a green balloon for my penis. My penis isn't green, but that's my favorite color." He steers toward urination: "So the bladder gets full."

Terry quizzes, "Where does the liquid go when the bladder's full?"

Pip knows. "It goes out of the bladder thing and down the tube and out my penis. Then I go pee."

Daisy pursues her topic, "Why don't I have a penis?"

Pip returns to his teaching and comforting role. "Because you got a opening between your legs. You're fancy on the inside, cuz you can have babies, but I'm not. But I'm fancy on the outside, cuz I got a penis."

As they work, Daisy keeps asking her question and Pip patiently answers each time, finally elaborating. "Girls are fancy on the inside. It starts like a tiny little egg and ours went into two. But it's a tiny tiny egg and it grows into a little baby."

When Pip leaves the table, Daisy tries Terry, "Why can't I have a penis?"

Terry turns the question back. "What do you think?"

Daisy sighs, "Because girls have a place where babies can grow, but boys don't. They can't be mommies. But they have a penis." She sits there for a long time, fingering the balloon uterus, gazing off into space. Finally she pushes her chair back from the table. "Boys have a penis. Girls have dresses."

It must be a relief to Pip to release his knowledge in conversation. It's comforting to be the comforter. He puts his knowledge of female anatomy, learned in a time of grief, to good use on Daisy's behalf. For these few moments, Pip seems older than four—no trace of the whimsical little boy who so often plays around the edges. The whole experience seems rich and reassuring to him.

Daisy, on the other hand, is only beginning to come to terms with male "fanciness." She's been fascinated with the penis on the model and in the books. The internal invisible uterus, with its potential for childbearing, is far less attractive to this four-year-old girl than the handy decorative equipment of her powerful older brother. Finally she tries to console herself with her fancy female wardrobe. For now it's the best she can do, but it doesn't satisfy.

Daisy and Pip: What does a penis feel like?

Ani and Kahlil are working on the urinary and reproductive systems with me. Daisy circles back, commenting, "I know what it feels like to have a penis."

I gently correct her. "You and I and Ani are girls, so we can *imagine* in our brains what it feels like to have a penis, but we don't really KNOW."

Daisy scowls, insists, "I KNOW what a penis feels like. I have a brother and I change his diapers." Daisy turns on her heel, heading for dress-ups.

There's no baby at Daisy's house. Frustrated by her lack of a penis, she's making a proprietary claim nonetheless. Has she helped with—or watched—a diaper change? Her big brother is four years older. Has she touched his penis? First she asserts that she knows what it feels like to have a penis. Then she insists she knows how a penis feels to the touch. Is this immature syntax or a significant shift in meaning? My antennae go up. In all likelihood Daisy's just trying to work out a more satisfactory relationship to her "missing" piece. Maybe I should have left her some space rather than rubbing her nose in reality again. In any event, my gut sense is that Daisy's curiosity and desire to possess a penis are normal for her temperament and development, not indicative of abuse. I'll keep a special eye on her anyway. Daisy usually gets what she wants.

This may be her first reckoning with an arbitrary and absolute obstacle to "having it all." She wisely heads for dress-ups, where she can create and control her own fantasy universe.

Pip's on the floor, stringing beads. "MY penis feels like seaweed and lobsters. Soft AND hard. Sometimes it's soft like seaweed. It's hard when I go round and round with it." Nobody says anything. After a pause he continues. "What if girls had a penis?"

I have an answer to this one. "Then they wouldn't be girls, they'd be boys."

Pip checks to see if it works in both directions. "What if boys had a uterus?"

"Then they wouldn't be boys. If they had a uterus, they'd be girls."

"But what if they DID?"

"Then they'd be a boy-girl, but there isn't any such thing. We can't be both."

Pip sighs, "There are only TWO openings."

I confirm, "Yes, on you, because you're a boy. On Ani's model, right here, there are three, because she's a girl."

Pip, so authoritative and mature moments ago, is back to onlooking. In his whimsical style he shares perceptions about his penis. Does he have questions about different states and sensations? His equilibrium was short-lived. Like Daisy, he's now puzzling over his own "missing pieces." It's no coincidence that Pip is hanging around the table. He has a lot on his mind.

Bo's cat, Shirelle knows, Zack relaxes

Bo's cat had kittens. Bo's mother brings them to school for a visit. "The Bodyworks couldn't have come at a better time for us! You should have heard Bo explaining to Lucy how the kittens could squeeze out. Young as Lucy is, her artwork's already more sophisticated than Bo's. Yesterday she drew a picture of me with 'that little hole.' My mother thinks it's too early for all this, but I disagree. When everyone lived on farms, children grew up seeing birth as a natural thing. The Bodyworks helps fill in the gaps."

Many parents report that Bodyworks spreads through the whole family.

Shirelle's eager to begin. "This is the womb and this is the crotch, with THREE holes. Some stuff I talked with my mom and some stuff I already knew, like food and poos."

Pip looks up from the kittens. "That one has a yellow spot because it's young. It'll have black spots when it's old."

In Pip's family, blonde babies grow into brunette adults. Pip's own hair has streaks of dark brown. Has he inferred the same thing happens among cats?

Zack, sitting next to Shirelle, is quite straightforward about the bladder. Shirelle looks away, refuses to say any key words. When Zack names the uterus, Shirelle says "Blah, blah, blah" and won't even point to it on the model.

Zack suggests he blow up his balloon penis. "Just a little."

"We're going to leave the penis balloon like that. For the heart, we'll use strong red balloons and we'll blow those up."

Most boys, most years, ask to blow up the penis balloon. I've decided it's simpler not to. This is my boundary line for realism. If I can avoid it, I don't want to deal with the differences between flaccid and erect penises, much less the potential "popped" penis balloons. So far I haven't had to. The boys, while disappointed, let the issue go.

To my surprise no child has ever mentioned differences related to circumcision or size. If circumcision comes up, I'll explain it's important to keep the penis clean. Some families ask their doctors to cut the skin and fold it back to stay, but others choose to fold it back during bathtime. If size comes up, I'll say it isn't important—like arms and legs, penises come in different sizes, but they all do the same job.

His work done, Zack heads off, grinning."My brain's telling my bladder to go to the bathroom. See ya later!"

Shirelle, who spends a lot of time with Shane and Clint, froze up when Zack came to the table. I'm dismayed, since she began with such enthusiasm. I wonder if she feels inadequate around Zack, who often jumps ahead verbally and acts impatient with children who take it slow. Ironically, Zack seemed more comfortable with Shirelle in this context than I would have expected, maybe because Shirelle is "no threat" intellectually. Ah well—win some, lose some.

Soldiers

Kahlil, Shane, and Jogger are marching around the classroom with instruments. It's an impromptu parade, respectful enough of other activity that I don't have to intervene.

Kahlil sings out once, "We're wiener soldiers!" Out of the corner of his eye, he catches my look. Quick substitution. "We're SUPER soldiers!" The other two pick up his refrain.

The fences may be down, but there are limits and Kahlil knows it. He couldn't resist a tiny test, however.

Boys often allude to the phallic properties of weapons. During the Gulf War and for months afterward, the association of sexuality and violence was particularly disturbing. Four boys played out in the block corner their impressions of war as presented on television. Together, they dictated many stories to me that semester.

A few excerpts illustrate themes that lie just under the surface in more peaceful times. "Everybody in the whole universe stupid their butts off . . . [The soldiers] stepped in dog poop. And then they weren't looking where they were going. They bumped into a truck full of water. They stepped in dog pee . . . They had a peace world . . . Happy eyes . . . happy hugs . . . happy noses . . . happy snot . . . happy blood. The whole universe happy story . . . And then when they got there in another room there was a rainbow and they blowed it down and the whole earth burned its body apart. . . . 'Aiee ya yiee!' This guy in 'The Gods Must Be Crazy' says 'Aiee ya yiee!' . . . I busted your face off and your eyeballs. Ah, shot their butts off. Majorly buttkicking is back in town! . . . Monster Iraq! Rackety, rackety, rack! . . . The whole universe of girls are fighting. They excited their butts and wieners off. . . . Want to know what the world's, the whole place is gonna look like when the war's ended? It's really gonna be messy!"

I hope The Bodyworks helps to exorcise and release some of the effects of media exposure.

Kahlil and birth order, Tanya and sibling rivalry

Tanya's looking at illustrations of babies in the womb. "How big is this baby in the tummy? Who felt it? *I* felt it when Michelle was in." *Michelle is her younger sister.*

Kahlil asserts, "*I* felt it when Ari was in MY mommy's tummy. *His brothers, Gabe and Ari, are both older.* "Lump bump, lump bump, lump bump."

Tanya asks, "Who felt it when YOU were in?"

Kahlil pauses, then reluctantly admits, "Maybe . . . Gabe."

It's hard for younger children to admit their older siblings have a history that precedes them. Kahlil's home is filled with pictures of the family without him. He tries to imagine he was there before his middle brother arrived on the scene but has to concede his oldest brother must have been around, cozily bent over his mother's stomach before Kahlil himself was even born.

Tanya has climbed into my lap. She fast-forwards pages. "I want to look at the pictures of the tiny babies in their mother before they get born. They are THIS TINY! But my baby is this big now, and I am the BIG SISTER! The milk and juice and water make the pee. And the yuckies make the poo."

"What you eat makes your poo. Hamburger, bread."

Tanya flicks the model's penis. "It's dancing wiggly!"

"Yes. Now we have to help everybody else clean up."

"NO. I'm NOT cleaning up."

My sympathy's ready. "Some days it's hard. It's hard for big sisters when babies are sick."

That's the opening Tanya needs. "And my big sister got a Barbie house AND a Ken for her birthday. It's NOT FAIR!"

Clean-up is ending, children are gathering at the circle, and Tanya's still on my lap, curled up like an infant.

She needs this time. It's so hard in her family, with flu on top of everything else. Added to her interest in babies today is the poignancy of her position as middle child: her hazy memory of simpler times, when she was still the baby; the painful jealousy of her older sister (not only forever oldest, but a recent birthday girl besides). The other children don't complain about Tanya dodging cleanup. They know they get laps when they need them.

"Everybody needs a lap sometimes," I remind the circle. "Be sure to let me know when YOU need a lap."

Rosa offers, "Or you can play by yourself."

Shane puts in, "Last year Rosa needed it. Every day! She doesn't need it so much this year." *Children are acute observers of each other.*

Daisy has her say. "At home, my big brother didn't want me to play. So I had privacy upstairs by myself."

"Yes," I comment, "that's another good thing. You can give yourself some special time when you need it."

Daisy continues, "You can play by yourself. Or if a friend comes you can tell them." *It's hard to be rejected by your big brother. You have to develop a repertoire of responses.*

Missy observes, "At my home I can play with myself or you can tell someone if you look around in the rooms and find them." *Missy lives in a big house. Her parents are often busy.*

Pip brings us back to Bodyworks. "Sometimes boys can go pee sitting on the toilet." *Is Pip noting a way in which boys and girls are similar, or becoming self-conscious? He's the only boy other than Paul who usually still sits to urinate. I'll try to hit a reassuring tone, in any case.*

"Yes, Pip. Big boys and daddies too, especially if they need to go poo too."

Ani observes, "Sometimes you poo but no pee."

Clint volunteers, "SOMETIMES people have to pee a LITTLE." There's a pause. He adds, with his head down, "When you're not on the toilet."

We've discussed this. "Even grown-ups, sometimes."

We're leaving circle. Pip mumbles, "And there's fish inside my penis and DUCKS!"

Is Pip back into whimsical mode or is he looking for metaphors? One thing for sure—he's asking himself a lot of questions about sexuality. His parents will have to decide how far they want to take it this time.

Jogger alone

When the circle talks about nursing babies, Jogger shouts out, "That's GROSS!"

After circle, he careens from activity to activity, very unlike himself. Intermittently he pauses, subdued. He seems to be seeking contact, pulling, lurching, grabbing, and moving on.

I take him aside, sit him on my lap and ask a few leading questions. His eyes are opaque, his body stiff. Soon he gets down, refusing a hug. He's not going to let me in today.

Not letting me in is Jogger's habitual stance. It often feels personal, but I doubt that it is. I don't think Jogger lets anyone in. Am I imagining since we started The Bodyworks he seems more vulnerable beneath his swagger and pounce? Some of what's going on for Jogger is definitely a sense that in the baby department, female bodies have a competitive edge. In every arena, Jogger strives to be Number One. All year long, his appetite for dominance has made him restless. He chafes against our cooperative norm. Like Daisy and Pip, he may be facing the longterm limits of personal power: the arbitrariness of gender.

I can't read his mind. That may be a good thing. On the other hand, I have to try to imagine what it's like for him, being Jogger, being the baby brother of three sisters in a busy family, being biracial, being small for his age, being shuffled from caregiver to caregiver.

It's no surprise Jogger seems to feel he's different, unique. I suspect his big brain is busy wondering about the invisible insides, which account for yawns and heartbeats and babies and also for plans and problem-solving, wishes and dreams, moods and behaviors, relationships.

If so, this is an enormous undertaking. Jogger's not ready to communicate, but I'm guessing the scent of self-knowledge is strong in his nostrils and he's hunting it down like a bloodhound. He's precocious, alone, probably lonely in this process—which is essentially solitary no matter when it's launched.

Jogger knows I'm here for him, but I'm not the person he wants. Who does he want? If I could figure that out, maybe I could get some support for him. He's brilliant, and struggling, but I can't get a handle on specific issues. I have to admit I feel this child is somehow neglected—not physically, but psychologically. He dictates stories full of adults who act like buffoons—they step in dog poop and knock each other senseless, they fall into deep puddles of pee and drown. Is this cartoon version of life all Jogger has to sustain him? I have no sense of ill will being directed at him, just a feeling his emotional needs aren't being met.

In my father-in-law's family small children were left unsupervised for most of the day, building the independence so highly respected among Norwegian immigrants. Maybe Jogger's family's choices are aimed at the development of qualities they value. Maybe I'm temperamentally and culturally biased. Maybe Jogger's parents are coping with private problems, and keeping busy is the best they can do. These hypotheses don't ease my heart. My colleagues agree Jogger's not a happy child. His parents don't want to discuss it. What can I do?

At the very least, I can refrain from forcing my unwanted companionship on Jogger. I must keep close watch but stand aside for now. He's only four, but I see him as a tiny warrior, launched on a lonely existential quest, a small silhouette against a huge sun. I didn't devise this challenge for him. Much as I'd like to, I can't get him off the hook.

So much for my romantic notion of every child's right to a happy childhood. So much for my romantic notion of my role as a teacher, making my class safe and fun for every child. It's not much fun for Jogger, here or anywhere, and there's apparently nothing I can do about it except watch for more objective signs of trouble. No fair!

Rosa's radar

Rosa has been wound up the past few days. We manage to resolve each incident, but five minutes later there's something else. Finally I ask her mother if anything's up at home. She tells me Rosa's grandfather's been in the hospital for four days, but her parents haven't told Rosa.

"This is going to sound funny, but I'm relieved to know there's a 'reason' Rosa's been acting up all week. I bet she knows there's something wrong, even if she doesn't know the specifics. It's under the surface, but it's coming through her pores and driving her wild. I understand why you don't want to worry her, but I bet it will be easier if you tell her something rather than nothing. Hasn't she had questions?"

"Yes! We haven't lied, we just haven't told her the truth. I take turns with my sister, sitting up at the hospital, so either her children are with me or mine are with her. When Rosa asks why her cousins are spending the night again, I just tell her Auntie Jeannie has to go somewhere. But it's been hell. My dad's hemorrhaging from the stomach and the doctors can't figure out why. He's in intensive care, going downhill."

"What a hard time! Well, it might be easier for you as well as Rosa if you tell her something that will explain all the changes in routine and the feelings she's picking up. Something like, 'Grandpa's sick. The doctors aren't sure what the problem is, so he's in the hospital and Auntie Jeannie and I take turns keeping him company. Why don't you make a picture for him?'"

"I could tell her his stomach is bleeding."

"Probably just as well not to get into the specifics at this point. I bet what's really bothering her is the fact there's a secret and she smells a rat."

Ani experiments, Maggie shares, Pip pursues

Ani comes to school with a plastic bowl full of water, smashed berries, grass clippings, mud, and twigs. "Look what I made. A experiment."

"Terrific. Let's put it on the playdough table, so other children can see it. I'd like to hear more about it."

"It's a collision." Ani sits down, and looks around the room. Finally Daisy comes over.

"What did you make?"

"Soup," Ani answers.

"Oh," Daisy responds politely. "It's good soup."

Ani probably did make a model of a "collision," using what was at hand to imagine the parts of a human body crushed in a car. When Daisy came, Ani changed her tune to "soup." Did Ani lose interest? Or did she realize she was in too deep? Was she simply following her own metaphor through to its natural conclusion? Or did she anticipate that Daisy would be disgusted? Who knows? The only sure thing is that Ani is increasingly interested in observing, experimenting, recording, and reporting.

Ani and Daisy sit at playdough, scanning for signs of action elsewhere. Maggie and her mother walk in, beaming at me. Maggie sticks out a Polaroid photo. "When I was born."

Her mother prods, "Show Sandy the other one, too."

Maggie sticks out another photo. "It stayed. A long time."

"Maggie, I'm so glad you brought the pictures for me to see. This must be the one of you right after you were born. What a wonderful picture. Your mom and dad look so happy to be holding you!"

"We were!" her mother affirms. "Tell her about your bruise, Maggie."

Maggie has clearly heard the story many times, and she's rehearsed it for me. "The doctor pulled me out. My face got a bruise. A long time it showed. Not now."

Her mother supplements. "It was a forceps delivery. All Maggie's baby pictures show a big purple and pink blotch on her face. It didn't completely fade until she was two. She used to ask about it when she looked at the pictures, but she never understood until she did her Bodyworks vagina yesterday. She came home asking to see her baby book."

Maggie's still beaming.

"That's a really interesting story, Maggie. I can see the bruise in both of these pictures, but it's all gone now, so I never would've known. Thanks for telling me about when you were a baby."

This is a big subject, momentous enough to move Maggie to speak. Most children and adults are deeply fascinated with their own lives as stories, the mystery of continuity in a growing and changing self. The Bodyworks has helped Maggie understand a haunting image from her own story, and to embrace it.

Pip intercepts me. "My penis is like seaweed."

"Your penis is like seaweed?'

"NO. I was just telling a story. It's really like fish."

Pip's parents report he keeps a running inventory of his observations of their bodies. "Daddy has fur," he announced to his mother after "the boys" showered together. His parents have been offering him all the information he seems to want. He clearly wants to communicate with me. No other children seem to be listening. I take a stab at his meaning.

"You mean the sperm?"

"No."

Maybe so, maybe not. In any event, it's not the direction he wants to go. I try to speak to the concern which may lie under many of his recent comments.

"Sometimes people are really interested in parts of bodies. Sometimes people wish they could have ALL the fancy parts."

This one hits the target.

"YES!" says Pip, sighing heavily.

The Skelly Game and Personal Safety

At circle, I reach behind me for "Skelly," a plastic model of a human skeleton about the height of a toddler.

There are oohs and ahs, comments too thick and fast for response. I let it roll for a second.

"What's THAT?"

"That's a skeleton!"

"I'm SCARED of skeletons."

"I LOVE skeletons."

"Skeletons can eat your blood."

"I saw one at Halloween."

"Is it a real one or pretend?"

"Children, this is Skelly. Skelly is a model made out of plastic. Skelly's like a doll—that's why I named it Skelly. Skelly never was alive. We use Skelly to learn what our bones look like under our skin."

"How did he get deaded?" Shirelle asks.

"Skelly didn't die, because Skelly was never alive. At Halloween, some people like to scare each other with toy skeletons, but I don't want to scare you. I think if you understand how your bones work, you probably won't be scared of skeletons."

"Is it a boy or a girl?" Jogger wants to know.

"I'm not sure. Boys' and girls' bones look alike. There are a few little differences, but I can't tell one from the other. Let's play a game with this model. I will touch one of Skelly's bones, and you try to touch the same bone on your own body."

I point to the hand, and all the children immediately point to their own hands. Then the foot, and everyone gets that. Spirits are high, as they call out, "That's my hand!" and "I know! That's the foot bones!" They laugh when they touch their own teeth. Almost everyone recognizes elbows, knees, and shoulders. I try the vertebrae.

"It's on my back!"

"The BUMPS!"

"Like the brain, where the string goes."

"Does anybody remember the name of those little bones?"

Zack, Kahlil and Ani call out, "Vertebrae," with Jogger a beat later, his face scowling, "I knew that."

"You didn't do the cage." It's Shane, ever concerned about protection.

I point to Skelly's ribs. Jogger yells out, "The ribs!"

I keep going with the clavicle, the hips, the jaw . . . coaching and adding little comments "Now, I've got a question." I touch Skelly's thumb. "Is it OK for someone to touch you here?"

The children touch their thumbs. No one says anything. *It's that word 'OK.' That's a red flag. They know that something's coming, but they don't know what.*

Then a child calls out, "It's OK. If they don't hurt me. One time my cousin pushed it way back."

"How about if someone touches you here?" I point to Skelly's skull.

"That's OK!"

"Yeah, you can touch people's heads."

I put my hand on Skelly's pelvis. "What if someone touches you here? Is that OK?"

The children look down at themselves and squirm. Ani speaks up. "That's your privates."

Clint laughs but no one joins. He forces it, long and loud.

Clint's experiments with touch at the beginning of The Bodyworks cued us to his questions about personal safety. The foster children in his home were abused. Many children—and adults—signal distress with inappropriate laughter.

"Ani knows a word for this part of the body. She calls it 'privates.' Does anybody know other words to use?" Silence. A couple of suppressed giggles. "Most grown-ups call this bone the pelvic bone or the pelvis, or sometimes the pubic bone. Try saying, 'the pelvis.'" A few faint mumbles.

"Usually we don't talk about this part of our bodies or touch it in front of each other, but it's an important word for you to know. Everybody say, 'pelvis.'" They do. "Another time, to help you remember: the pelvis." They repeat "pelvis" in fairly normal voices. "Is it OK for people to touch you around your pelvis?"

Heads shake no. Ani calls out again, "Nobody can touch you there. My mom said."

"Right, Ani. Usually no one should touch your pelvis, or your vagina, or your penis, or the other parts of your body that are near there."

Daisy pipes up. "I can't let 'em. My mom said."

"Yes. Your moms and dads have told you these are parts of your body other people shouldn't touch. Sometimes it's OK. Like when your doctor gives you a check-up, or if a grown-up helps you dry off after your bath. But usually it's not OK for people to touch around each other's pelvis. Those parts of your body are private, just for you. You already know that. Other people just shouldn't touch you there—not your sisters or brothers or friends or even grown-ups."

The children are wide-eyed, all ears, and then a surge of what-ifs break the dam. Daisy's first. "What if a grown-up touches your bottom?"

"If your clothes are on and you're around other people, it might be fine. Sometimes grown-ups pat children on the bottom the same way they give you a hug, to show they love you. But if you don't like it, it's not OK for them to touch you that way."

Daisy follows up. "Spose they PINCH you?"

"If they do something you don't like, tell them to stop. If they don't stop, tell another grown-up."

Voices burst out, asking variations of the same question. "What if no one else is home?"

"If no one else is home and the grown-up won't stop, go in a different room or go outside or go to a neighbor's."

They've already thought of this. Several voices push. "What if grown-ups don't listen?"

"Then find another grown-up and keep telling different people until somebody does listen. It's the same thing if a child touches you in a way you don't like, even if it's a big kid, even if it's a babysitter. That's not OK, and you need to get help."

Zack offers, "If no one's home, and you can't get out of the house, you can go to your 'Secret Place.'"

"Yes, it's a good idea to go to your Secret Place whenever there's a problem. But first of all, try to get help. If there's no one to help right away, tell somebody as soon as you can. What if somebody says 'I'll give you candy' or 'I'll give you a present if you let me touch you there'? That's not OK. You say, 'NO.' Everybody practice. Look right at my eyes and say 'NO' in a strong voice."

Their voices ring out. "NO!"

"Try it again."

Louder this time. "NO!"

"Say, 'LEAVE ME ALONE!'"

They're eager to practice this. "LEAVE ME ALONE!" Their faces are shining.

"Suppose the person says, 'It'll be a secret. We won't tell anybody.' You say 'NO.'"

No urging is needed. "NO!"

"Some secrets are good, but secrets about touching are not good. Tell a grown-up if someone wants you to have that kind of secret. Keep telling grown-ups until somebody helps you. Suppose you're playing doctor with a friend, and it doesn't hurt and it feels kind of good. It's still not OK. Change the game. Go where some other people are."

Shirelle volunteers, "Sometimes my cousin teases me and tickles me. He's nine."

"Is he touching your pelvis, or other private parts of your body?"

"No."

"Then it's not quite the same, but if he won't stop teasing, you need to get a grown-up to help. He's older and bigger than you are and it's not OK for big kids to pick on littler kids."

"Then he calls me a baby. And he won't let me play. If I tell."

"That's hard, because it's fun to play with the big kids. But you still need to make him stop if you don't like the way he's touching you. He might call you a baby, but he'll probably leave you alone if you tell him 'NO' in your strong voice and look right at him. Feeling safe is more important than doing what your cousin wants."

I have to wind this up for today.

"All of you know the difference between private touching and other kinds of touching. You just can feel it. You will know if someone ever tries to touch you the wrong way, even if it's somebody you really like. If it's just teasing and tickling but you don't like it then you tell them to stop. Go get help if it doesn't stop. You're in charge of your own body. Don't let people bother you. Not even grown-ups! You know when it's not OK."

I always feel I'm walking a tightrope when I deal with this subject, but the Skelly game seems to be a natural and effective introduction. Apparently, most of the children have had some instruction from their parents. It's still important to bring the issue out into the open, not only for the sake of the children whose parents haven't discussed it, but to strengthen the message and invite further communication. The intensity of the questions, the number of both boys and girls who have clearly thought about their own vulnerability, make me uneasy. In the absence of other indicators, high interest in the topic is not necessarily significant, but it's important to follow up individually with children who seem especially invested in the subject of appropriate touch. At the very least, this is an opportunity to help children learn to be more assertive, a safeguard against many kinds of violence. Tomorrow I'll read the children a book about appropriate touch, and leave it out on the shelf. That will help individual children take the initiative to pursue this difficult topic, and it may give me further feedback about specific concerns.

After the children have left for the day, Nita has tears in her eyes. She pours out her story.

"I WISH I had had something like The Bodyworks! Then maybe my parents would've talked to me. They didn't tell me ANYTHING. We didn't even have a word for anything below the waist. When I was nine, I was riding a bike downhill and I crashed and I really got bruised. That night I saw blood on my underpants and I thought I was bleeding to death! I didn't want my parents to worry so I didn't tell them. I figured they couldn't do anything anyway.

"I kept changing my underpants and hiding the dirty ones in my closet. After a couple of days, I figured it was about time for me to die, so I went out back and dug a grave. Then I filled up my Barbie lunchbox with food, and went to sit in the grave until I died. I didn't know anything about dying—I guess I figured dead people might get hungry.

"My mother found my dirty underpants and called me inside. She said, 'Now you're a woman and you can have babies,' and she gave me some sanitary napkins. I told her I was going to die because I hurt myself on my bike, and she laughed."

"That's all she ever said. My friends told me the rest and I asked my grandmother if it was true and she said yes. My mother never told my little sisters either. I had to tell every single one of them myself. Oh, I WISH somebody had told me! It feels so good to be teaching The Bodyworks. I know this sounds silly, but it feels like I'm getting a second chance."

Nita's pain is not unique. Every year, Bodyworks opens the door for college students to share their memories. Although each story is different, many report the absence of informal conversation between parents and children about body facts, including excretion, sexuality, and death. Often students express concern about the education of younger siblings—and gaps in their own. They make extensive use of the materials in our resource library, including books intended for the very young. It's clear that in the process of true education, distinctions between "adult" and "child," "teacher and student," fall away. Valid curriculum ripples outward, touching people in unpredictable ways, changing lives.

Zack crashes his bike

At the door Zack's mother asks him to tell me the news.

"You tell her. I gotta play," he tosses off as he heads for Kahlil.

She fills me in. Yesterday Zack crashed his two-wheel and was in a lot of pain. He told her it was his pelvic bone, and then admitted it was his testicles that hurt. They followed up with a trip to the doctor, which was reassuring rather than traumatic, because Zack had the language.

Zack's mother continues, "Zack is too shy to talk to anyone else in the family, but he tells me all kinds of things. I LOVE the Bodyworks! The other day, he said 'My food goes down inside my body and out the back! Can you believe that, Mom?'" She chuckles. "There are some concepts he simply can't accept yet, however! He insists that daddies have boy babies and mommies have girl babies." "Do you remember how shocked I was when I enrolled Justine and discovered the open-door unisex bathroom here? I can't believe it's only been six years. I can't thank you enough for educating us as well as our child. It's changed our lives. We still have a long way to go, but look how far we've come!"

It's wonderful to know that Zack is able to use his information in a crunch, despite his strong sense of privacy. At the same time he makes it clear he's not ready for more facts. He has invented his own way to explain and to evenly distribute the mysteries of procreation. However, the topic has been opened up at home, and he can return to his mother for further information when he is ready.

Of course I remember Zack's mother's struggle. It was my struggle too—to respect her perspective, to reexamine my own, to find a bridge between us. She said in her family no one ever talked about sex. She called herself "old-fashioned," but felt this was the price for protecting her daughter. She had taught Justine never to look at herself or touch herself "down there." She was worried that the sight of little boys urinating would make her daughter curious, and lead to teenage sex.

I told her how much I appreciated her directness, that I too had been taught to ignore my body "between your legs." As a mother and teacher I had come to believe it was healthier for young children to learn about bodies—their own and each other's—in as natural a way as possible. They need straightforward names for all the body's parts. If they've seen other children's bodies from the beginning, they're much less likely to be driven by curiosity into "playing doctor" in childhood and are better prepared for puberty. It's hard for a girl of any age to protect herself if she's ignorant about her body or ashamed to talk about it.

All this made sense to Zack's mother, and her trust grew. She began to question many aspects of her own upbringing, to see that the values were solid but the methods had some very negative effects. She realized she wanted her children to speak up more, to take risks, to reach.

The partnership between parents and teachers of young children is tremendously important. When it's working, we all grow. Zack's mother's commitment to her children has opened her life in all kinds of ways. Today she's a strong advocate in the public schools.

Zack's News

I mention to Zack that I'm sorry about his bike crash and glad he's fine. To my surprise, he looks me in the eye and says, "Me too! It really hurt. But the doctor checked me."

I suggest very tentatively, "You know, Zack, a lot of children get hurt on bikes and they're afraid to say anything. You don't have to, but if you could, I wish you'd tell the circle what happened to you."

"Sure," says Zack.

At news time he comes to the front of the circle and tells the group. "I crashed my bike and it really hurt me, and I was scared. So I told my mom it was my pelvic bone and she took me to my doctor and he had to feel all around to make sure I was OK. And I was. But it was good touching even if he touched me there because he's my doctor."

Children ask questions. Zack describes the whole accident in detail. He says it still hurts a little, but the doctor says it will go away pretty soon. Other children are waving their hands in the air. Everybody has a first- or second-hand bike story to tell. At the end I wrap it up, "Thanks a lot, Zack, for telling us about what happened to you. It helps everybody to know that other people have been through it. We don't worry so much when we can talk about things like this."

Zack smiles graciously. "You're welcome," he says.

It seemed a little risky to suggest to Zack that he talk to the group, but I'm confident he could've said no. It's great he felt ready—no amount of talk from me could have made the points so effectively.

Rosa's release

For two days Rosa's been acting like a normal energetic child. I mention it to her mother, who says, "I told her about my dad being in the hospital. She didn't ask a lot of questions, just told me she KNEW something was wrong."

What a relief for Rosa: her intuition is confirmed. The inner and outer realities match. She doesn't have to bear the unknown alone. The lonely dread was worse than the reality—and there was no way to hide that reality from Rosa's radar. Now she can get on with the business of being four years old. Something's wrong, but the grown-ups know about it and are taking care of it. She doesn't even want to know the details at this point.

Pip and the stretch

Pip's looking at the books and the models again. He asks with urgency, "But how can the baby come OUT?" and before I can answer, he grimaces at the balloon vagina, "That's TOO SMALL!"

"When it's time for the baby to be born, the mother's vagina stretches. See how this balloon can stretch to make a big opening at the top. That's what a mother's body can do."

Pip fades off to playdough. There he keeps an ear cocked, twisting and turning, following the conversation at The Bodyworks table. When the word "vagina" comes up, Pip cranes his neck and grabs his crotch at the same time.

Pip's favorite aunt is hugely pregnant. He's worried about her. His family's recent experience with miscarriage has made him extra sensitive to gestation and birth. Many children wonder and worry about the passage of the baby. It's to help alleviate distress like Pip's that we use a balloon to represent the uterus. A stretchy balloon makes the whole process easier to understand and less problematical for all the children. (It also reduces "balloon envy.") Despite the potential for confusion, no child has ever suggested that the girls' balloon is really some sort of interior penis.

Sprout Sandwiches

When we started the worm and sprout farm with many different kinds of beans and seeds sowed at random, we reserved one patch for alfalfa sprouts, with a sign that said "No Picking Yet." Today we've harvested them for snack. The children can eat them as is or make "sprout sandwiches" on saltines.

Daisy's enthusiastic, even before tasting: "Oh goody, I *love* sprouts. I ate 'em at my aunty's house."

Paul follows. "I hate 'em. I had 'em once. Yucky."

I remind the children of our basic classroom approach to food. Everybody tries a bite, however infinitesimal, because "This might be your magic day. People are always changing, especially about food. Lots of times they like something after they try it a few times, but they don't know unless they taste. You might get a surprise."

Somebody usually offers a bit of personal history on the subject, affirming or contradicting. The other rule is that we talk only about food we like. If a child tries a taste and doesn't like it, she doesn't have to finish, just say "No thank you," if more is offered.

In our school many children are picky eaters, quite uninhibited about expressing distaste. Our approach encourages receptivity to new foods and new cultures, sparing the feelings of classmates and parents who have prepared special treats. (Even so, someone always blurts.) Many children love the sprouts. Maybe it's their personal relationship to the growpower involved!

Tanya draws a baby

For months Tanya, hunched over paper and pencil, has been trying to draw babies. Her schema for drawing people, the classic egg-with-limbs, does not match her perception of how babies look. Invariably she crumples her paper, frowning and muttering. She wants no help, no encouragement. She tries to conceal the whole process. It's her private battle, and her self-esteem is much scarred.

Today she drags her feet as she pulls out a chair. Half lying on the table, she rests her head on her left hand as she draws with her right, sighing heavily and pausing often. Suddenly I hear her. "Look! Look! I made a baby! It's me. Crawling. When I was a baby!"

Sure enough! She's figured out how to show a baby crawling—a round head, a horizontal torso with four lines sticking out under it, two near the head and two near the back. To produce this drawing, Tanya had to "invent" the torso. Recently she constructed lungs for her bodyworks, and a few days ago she was quite concerned about fresh air for the babies in her "World." I wish I could've watched her mental processes preparing her for this breakthrough. Probably the torso arose naturally out of the need to house the baby's lungs. In any event, Tanya is ecstatic. No doubt her achievement will boost her self-esteem, fuel more exploration and more discovery. She identifies the crawling baby as "me . . . when I was a baby." Perhaps the whole process has deepened her concept of the continuous, ongoing self. Bravo, Tanya! Once again a child's deep and singular interest—babies, in Tanya's case—has been the leading edge for her growth.

Naked people

Kahlil and Shane are standing near the Bodyworks table, giggling and singing in full voice. "Happy birthday to naked people. Poopy birthday to naked people."

They want to be heard. There's a question they're asking. What is it?

Nita invites them to spell it out. "Want to talk?"

"Yeah," they say in unison.

Kahlil takes the lead. "Like where you go to the bathroom."

Shane chips in, "Poop and pee."

Ani walks over from the drawing table. Nita, Kahlil, Shane, and Ani discuss anatomical differences between boys and girls. Shane asks his big question. "How do dads go to the bathroom?" *Shane doesn't know his father.*

"Dads go to the bathroom just like boys," Nita informs him.

Kahlil adds from personal experience, "They have BIG POOPS."

Shane states, "They have a big penis." *Sounds like a statement, but it's probably a question.*

"Dads are bigger all over than boys. All the parts of boys keep getting bigger—arms and legs and penises and all the rest—until they're grown-up," Nita fills him in.

"BIG penis!" comments Kahlil. There's a lull. Kahlil has another feature on his mind. He touches the model. "They have fur right here."

Nita keeps pace. "Yes, hair that looks like fur. How about moms?"

It's Shane's turn to be the knowledgeable one. "They don't have a penis, but they got fur . . . hair."

Nita answers the unasked, "Grown-ups' bodies are bigger than children's and they have more hair. When you grow up, your bodies will be bigger and you will grow hair too."

The boys smile at her, and drift off to big blocks. Ani goes back to the drawing table.

Ani didn't seem to have any questions of her own, just general interest. She must've felt comfortable joining the boys and her presence didn't inhibit them. Taking this initiative is different from being assigned to paired work or being surrounded by both genders in circle.

Bo's broken leg

Yesterday Bo's mother took me aside to say he'd been up late and wasn't 100% but seemed OK. She urged me to call if he or I needed her to pick him up early. When he's off center, he goes into physical overdrive, careening from one thing to the next. His mom and I agree he must learn how to manage these hyper-cycles in school.

Bo raced into the room. After resisting projects all year, now he hustles to The Bodyworks, saying "I don't want to be last. Not any more." Yesterday he chattered a mile a minute, "Am I doing MUSCLES and JOINTS today? I know what my joints are! Like I'm riding my bike or sitting on my chair and my knees are like this and my hands are like this. That's my joints doing it." All day long he struggled to drag himself from the brink of disaster. Bo and I had a good hug at the gate, celebrating with his mother how much he's learned to stay in control.

His father called at 7:30 this morning to tell me how the day ended. Bo's babysitter was concentrating on Lucy's potty-training, and Bo felt he couldn't wait any longer to use the toilet. Noticing the storm and screen windows out for spring-cleaning, he stood on his window ledge to urinate, lost his balance and fell to the ground. Fortunately, he grabbed a curtain on his way down, so he landed on his leg instead of his neck. The doctor predicts three weeks in traction, three months in a body cast. Bo's father sounded exhausted, but relieved too: "He's Bo. We knew something like this would happen sooner or later. Thank God, it's only a broken leg!"

Bo, immobilized for more than three months. All the children are buzzing, and so are their parents in the hall. Concern is mixed with gratefulness at being spared, and guilt for being glad. At circle I start to discuss Bo's accident, and each child interrupts.

"I had a infected ear, one time."

"I was all clogged up."

"I went to the hospital and they showed me a old cast for a arm."

"One time my sister went to the hospital."

"My dad burned me with a cigarette on my finger a little. It was a accident."

"At Riverside Park. A man in the line. Burned my arm. With a cigarette. He wasn't looking."

"So all of you can imagine how Bo feels. His leg hurts a lot and he has to stay still, and he can't go home for a long time. What can we do to help him?"

"We could send him a toy. Like a staple-paper."

"Only if he could use a toy with his HANDS. Not his leg."

"Good thinking. It would have to be something he can enjoy when he's lying down."

We agree we'll write stories and draw pictures and put them all together in a book for Bo. I end circle without explaining how bones heal. Everyone seems eager to move around on two good legs.

During activity period, I set out a box full of medical paraphernalia from our supply closet: doctor and nurse jackets, johnnies, stethoscopes, casts. There are no takers today. A kind of denial reigns. I suspect everyone at some level fears "contagion."

For now we'll concentrate on helping by making the book for Bo. I can expect to see a determined focus on wellness for a while. Dramatic play may come later. Questions may be long in coming. Assimilation takes its own time and I can't hurry it. On the other hand, here we are in the middle of "doing bones" for The Bodyworks. I can't avoid the subject of Bo's broken leg. I'll have to feel my way into this.

Clint's sculpture

Clint has been alone at playdough for quite a while, totally absorbed. I watch him out of the corner of my eye. When he finally looks up and stretches, I walk by. "You've been working hard, Clint. Do you want to tell me about it?"

"It's a person."

"It sure is. It really looks just like a person. I'd love to hear more it."

"These are the milkies."

"Just like the nipples on your chest. Boys and girls both have nipples."

"And that's the belly button. And the peepee. If it didn't have a brain, it would be dead. If it didn't have bones, it would be SLIME!"

"Thanks a lot for showing me your person, Clint. It's exciting to see how you are using what you know about bodies."

Clint picks up the plastic storage bag and tosses it up. "This looks like a air bag. My lungs fell off. I can't breathe." *He's teasing, and prolonging our one-to-one time.* "Guess what my mom does at work. She's a nurse. And WE are learning about bodies." He pauses, picks it up in a new tone. "I have to be careful not to stop my peepee."

"What would happen?"

"It would die. Then it would have to go to the hospital. Not me. Just my inside. I'd rip my body open. Yeah. I think."

"Your body knows how long to hold your pee and when to go to the bathroom. All the parts of our bodies work together and they work very well. Once in a while if something goes wrong we have to go to the hospital. It would be handy if we could just send one part, but we can't. Our real bodies are not like a playdough sculpture or a model. Our insides all stay together and work together."

Bones, muscles and joints

Several children are attaching rubber-band muscles and brass paper-fastener joints to cardboard arm bones. Missy speculates, "I know why we have arms, so we can reach things and pick things up. What if we didn't have arms?"

Paul asks Terry, "Where are your muscles?"

"Where do YOU think, Paul?"

"Your mouth."

"How do you know?"

"Because you can talk."

Terry exaggerates the movements of her jaw and lips. "Yes, my muscles help my mouth move, so I can talk. Yours do too. We have muscles in the same places."

Paul keeps going. "Your hand's bigger. You have a thumb."

Terry meets him where he is, "Grown-ups and children both have hands with thumbs, but they're different sizes."

Missy picks up where she left off. "If we couldn't bend our fingers, how could we pick things up?" She tries picking things up with stiff fingers. *This is a rhetorical question she's trying to answer herself.* Cara hasn't said a word. Now she's watching her own hand with fascination, as she bends her thumb and index finger to meet in a circle, opening and closing the gap.

Clint turns toward Terry, motioning from his fingertips to his wrist, "Do bones go from here to here?" *He worked with a teacher several days ago to measure his fingers. He knows the answer. He's just checking.*

Terry knows he knows. "What do you think?"

Clint has set her up. "I knew that when I was four years old!" *Way back before his fifth birthday last week.*

Terry tells him what he wants to hear. "You must have been a smart boy!"

"I still am!" Clint launches a methodical investigation, bending his neck, shoulder, elbow, knee, ankle, wrist, fingers. He counts from the wrist up his index finger. "I have four joints on my finger. Knuckles."

The spirit of inquiry is contagious, especially when the laboratory is so personal, so accessible. At least some of this activity probably spun off from the song I taught them yesterday, my adaptation of "Dry Bones." We do it with a rhythmic clap and gestures on the chorus.

These Bones

CHORUS
These bones, these bones have muscles.
These bones, these bones have joints.
My brain tells them to move.
Bones, muscles, and joints.

Chinbone connected to the jawbone,
Jawbone connected to the headbone,
Headbone connected to the neckbone.
Bones, muscles, and joints.
Neck . . . back . . . shoulder . . . collar
(CHORUS)

Collar . . . shoulder . . . arm . . . elbow
Elbow . . . forearm . . . wrist . . . finger
(CHORUS)

Collar . . . chest . . . rib . . . back
Back . . . tail . . . hip . . . pelvic
(CHORUS)

Hip . . . thigh . . . knee . . . shin . . .
Shin . . . ankle . . . toe . . . NO BONE!

(new words © Helen H. Johnson)

Often when I borrow from a traditional source I have to translate, sterilize, secularize, tone it down. That's standard operating practice in the folk tradition. Still, it gives me pause, and sometimes I just can't do it. It wrenches me a little to sing my own new words in place of the old chorus. I console myself that we're prolonging its life since it seems to have died out even as a "camp song." I hope the ancestors approve.

After the children learned "These Bones," we played "People to People," a movement game they loved. I paired up the children, got a rhythm going on the tambourine and called out body parts for them to touch with their partners. "Back to back, back to back," then "Elbow to elbow, elbow to elbow" or "Toe to toe, toe to toe" When they got the hang of it, I made it more complicated: "Elbow to knee, elbow to knee. . . . Nose to shoulder, nose to shoulder." Periodically I tossed in "Partner to partner, partner to partner," and everyone had to switch partners.

Ani's analogy

When the chuckles die down after "The toe bone's connected to NO BONE!" Ani puts up her hand at circle. "If you had no bones, you would melt like ice cream."

She was initially fascinated with the Outside-In *illustration of the hypothetical ballerina folding up for lack of bones. Apparently she's come up with her own way to envision a change in state, perhaps borrowing from her beloved "Wizard of Oz." Her remark tells me Ani's assimilating information.*

Pip's time out

While I'm washing my hands, Pip comes over to the sink. "Sandy, I didn't come out of my mother's stomach. I came out of her MOUTH." He hustles to the snack table without waiting to hear what I might say.

Pip is probably telling me, "I need some time out. I'm worried about my aunt. I think having a baby hurts. What if maybe I hurt my mother by being born? I don't like that thought. I know things can go in and out of my mouth without hurting—and for right now I'm going to pretend to myself that's what happens when babies are born. Please don't tell me any different."

Poor Pip. He's had a lot on his mind—the miscarriage of twins, the near due date. He's been getting new information at home, and probably picking up anxiety from the adults. He's been wrestling to make sense of what's happening in his family and how he's connected to it. He's had enough for now. I won't follow after him trying to help him sort his feelings out, reassuring him. He's drawn a line for himself. I'll respect it.

Mixed feelings about Bo

For two days the box of medical paraphernalia has had no takers. Children and parents still buzz about Bo's accident. Compassion for Bo and his parents seems to be mixed with relief "it's not me," and some sense "he deserved it." I suspect the conflicting emotions make it harder for the children to come to terms with Bo's fall. While it's important that everyone learn from Bo's accident, it's also important not to judge, nor to leave the false impression that accidents only happen to children who act impulsively. At circle I feel like I'm high-diving into a can of worms. "A lot of us have been thinking about Bo and his broken leg. Does anybody have any questions?"

Daisy jumps in. "My mom says Bo's wild. That's why he got hurt."

Jogger grins, "He is. Bo's really crazy."

Tanya intones, "He shouldn't do that."

Ani speaks up, "Bo's not crazy. He's my friend."

Zack's eyes grow big. "I would NEVER do it."

Shane agrees. "Me neither. It's DANGEROUS. It's NOT SAFE." Other children are nodding their heads.

Are they eager to distance themselves from Bo's accident and therefore from Bo? Until the accident Bo was everyone's friend, appreciated for his vitality, warmth, and generosity. Now only Ani expresses her loyalty to him. If I comment on that, I'll add to the problem: guilt and widespread stuffing of feelings, leaving plenty of residue to backfire on Bo.

"It sounds like a lot of people think Bo made a mistake."

Rosa calls out, "He should've waited for his turn."

"I've been thinking," I offer, "about how hard it is when I need to go to the bathroom and somebody else is using the toilet. Sometimes I feel like I might wet my pants, and I really don't want to. I wonder if Bo was feeling like that." No one says anything.

"Bo's babysitter told him to wait until Lucy was finished. What if he couldn't wait anymore? We know the babysitter didn't want Bo to fall and break his leg, but she didn't tell him what else to do if he couldn't wait. Maybe he was worried she'd be mad at him if he wet his pants."

Jogger comes down harshly, "He could've waited longer."

"He could've gone outside," Kahlil offers.

"He could pee in a jar. One time I did." It's Shane.

"It's the babysitter's fault," Zack decides.

"Our job isn't to decide whose fault it is. Maybe Bo and the babysitter were both trying to do their best. Our job is to show Bo how much we love him, even if we think he made a mistake. And it's important to remember not to climb where it's not safe, even if grown-ups fuss, even if you might wet your pants." *The children are taking this in.*

"Bo's mother says he feels really bad he climbed up on his window. He said to tell everybody in this class not to do it. He loves the book we made for him. What else can we do to help him feel better?"

Ani says, "Bo loves the triceratops."

"Ani, you've really been keeping Bo in your heart, haven't you? That's what friends do for each other."

Cara says, "And the tiger. He loves the tiger too."

"Every day he gets 'em first if he comes first," Zack says.

"Good noticing! That's another thing friends do for each other. What if we lend Bo the triceratops and the tiger while he's in the hospital? You would miss having them in blocks, but that would be a special way to let Bo know how much we miss him. I could take them when I go see him."

Jogger dissents, but only a little. "But I like the triceratops too. And I would NEVER get a turn." Everybody else is shaking their heads "yes," with excited smiles. *The sense of community begins to heal.*

"I bet Bo will get surprised!" Daisy anticipates.

"And he'll be HAPPY!" Kahlil says.

The air is clear. Maybe it's time to shift into cognitive gear. "I'm excited about our plan! Now: does anyone have any questions about broken legs?"

"Why do they have a cast?" Ani asks.

I pull two unit blocks off the shelf, and then a double unit. "Let's pretend this long block is a leg that's smooth and solid, all in one piece? It's like the top bone inside your leg, your thigh bone. If it breaks into two pieces, like these two blocks, the doctor fits them back together. If the person tries to walk, the two pieces of the bone wobble and break apart again, like this.

"Suppose we tried to glue these two blocks together. You know they'd keep wobbling if we moved them while the glue was wet. The glue has to set first. It's the same with your body. The bone has to set.

"Bodies don't use glue. We make new bone cells to grow the broken pieces back together. Some of you've seen a soup bone or a steak bone. You can see some reddish-brown stuff inside. That's called the marrow, where the new cells are made inside the bone.

"It takes a long time to grow the pieces of bone back together, and it's too hard to stay still all that time, so the doctor makes a cast to keep the bone from moving. Sometimes if it's a big break, a cast isn't enough, and the doctor uses some wire and pulleys to help you hold still. That's called traction. Bo has a cast and traction."

Ani puts up her hand. "I'm going to see him at the hospital. Me and my mom got him a present."

Jogger adds, "Me too. I want to see his cast and his traction."

"He's going to be real happy he can have the triceratops and the tiger,"

Pip says. "But he has to only play with them in bed."

It's a relief for us all to have faced the conflicting feelings. Now we can support Bo more fully, and move ahead with our learning and doing.

Cara and Maggie puzzle it out

Maggie's working on the four-layer body puzzle. She puts the skeleton on the bottom, adds the organs over it, then muscles/nerves/blood vessels, then skin/clothing. She sits quietly, looking at the finished puzzle. Then she dumps it out and starts over. Cara's watching. This time Maggie puts the nerves on the bottom.

Cara asks, "Why you change it?"

Maggie hypothesizes, "Like ribs. Protect. Skeleton. Protect messages, like bumps in your back."

We ordered the puzzle from a catalog. When it arrived, I was disappointed it wasn't self-correcting. Different systems could be layered in any sequence. Then it struck me: any arrangement is essentially an oversimplification. The puzzle's flexibility invites the children to think about relative positions.

Cara and Maggie are both children whose language is delayed. Here they are using the puzzle to inquire, to express, and to explain complex thinking. Maggie's used her Bodyworks experience with vertebrae and rib cage, to think through the challenge posed by the puzzle. Clearly Cara has done some thinking on her own, is testing it as she observes Maggie. Not only do the two children persist in their own intellectual activity, they recognize each other as peers in the process, bridging silence.

Jogger punches a hole

Jogger orders, "Give me the hole punch."

"We don't have the hole punch on this table today."

"Get it. I need it."

I ignore his tone. "What do you need the hole punch for?"

"Because I gotta have a little hole. At the end of my penis. My . . . urethra. I gotta have a little hole for my urethra."

"Good idea, Jogger! I'm glad you thought of it. It's neat you remembered the word urethra too."

"You should've thought of it."

"Well, I'm glad you did. We need good ideas from everybody."

"Hurry up and get me the hole punch."

"I think it's in the writing caddy, Jogger. You can borrow it if someone's using it."

"It's not fair that girls have the bump AND the line."

"I know fairness is important to you. Fairness doesn't always mean the same number. Some things are just different."

"I still don't think it's fair."

I have a lot of reactions to this exchange with Jogger. He's got some live issues eating at him. I chose to focus on the task, not to comment on his rudeness, but I don't like to be ordered around. I don't like to feel helpless to help this child. He managed to turn my sincere praise into a jab at me. My guess is Jogger's innovation came from his passion for precision and also from his desire to out-fancy the girls. Would it be better for Jogger if he had a male teacher? Probably. I wish there were more men in early childhood classrooms. But I'm not sure resentment of his three big sisters is all that's eating at Jogger.

It's interesting to me how many children remember the word "urethra," even though it's not part of the vocabulary I stress. Maybe it should be. The "urethra" is the part of the urinary tract that boys and girls have in common, a safe place to rest. It's a straightforward functional part too—a hole like other familiar holes: drain holes in sinks, holes in milk jugs where liquid pours out.

The Fancy Parts

Missy and Cara put their hands up at circle. Missy speaks for them both. "We want to sing "Everybody's Fancy."

Everyone joins in with gusto. When the last chorus dies down, several hands wave, requesting a repeat.

Pip suggests, "Somebody could be a boy AND a girl."

Assent ripples around the circle. "SOMEBODY could."

"No," I say, without qualification. "Everyone's either a girl OR a boy. You can't be both."

"But there COULD be," someone says.

I'm not budging. "No. Only pretend. Real people are one or the other. That's just the way it is. A girl is a girl and a boy is a boy. Anyway, people's bodies are a lot alike, and most things you can do whether you're a boy or a girl."

I'm not getting into hermaphrodites, transsexual operations, or cross-dressing if I don't have to. If the children have heard about these phenomena, they'll say so. That's not where the issue is coming from. Some theoreticians suggest penis-envy's built-in, maybe womb-envy too. What I know is these children have heard a fundamental message of contemporary culture: You can "have it all." You should "have it all."

That message works powerfully to affirm individuals, to end pervasive discrimination and inequity. Here I see the downside: beyond frustration, a fundamental sense of inborn inadequacy in both boys and girls. Is this part of the human condition, or primarily a function of culture? In any case it contributes to subtle or full-blown conflict between the sexes. I suspect it's linked to western civilization's addiction to power without limits. Children and adults, we've inherited a false picture of life. It's hard to relinquish the fantasy of omnipotence, but it's time to replace it with the wisdom of balance.

There are murmurs of dissent. Jogger holds out one last hope. "A ALIEN could be a boy and a girl. Both."

How true. Time to shift into the affective realm. Name the yearnings, allow them space, and move on. I am not going to solve the problems of western civilization today. I'm a product of the same culture as the children. And I still wish I had a penis for picnics and camping trips.

I lean forward confidentially. "Sometimes I wish I had ALL the different parts."

A loud wave of "ME TOO" comes from the circle. *The moment is poignant—such a relief for boys and girls to share this feeling with each other, with a trusted adult.*

"I'm glad I'm a girl, but it would be fun to have a penis AND a vagina. But it can't happen. Anyway I'm glad everybody has one of the different parts. And I'm glad we all have the same other parts. I really like bodies!" I pull out my guitar. "Let's sing *Mi Cuerpo* now and dance together!" *We'are all feeling good. We've faced the facts together. The common yearning unites rather than divides us. Now we can celebrate.*

During activity period, Cara and Missy are standing under the bodyworks hanging from the line. Cara looks up and grins at Missy. "There's a 'gina."

Missy spots another one. "I see one too."

They giggle together, walking up and down the line, pointing out each vagina. Daisy, Rosa, and Maggie join them.

None of the other children seems to notice.

I wonder who's in the observation booth. Suppose it's someone who has no clue what this project is all about! Is this getting out of hand? Or is it simply a step toward healthy gender identification? Probably both. More or less the same thing has been going on in boys' locker rooms for years, they tell me. Not in female locker rooms—girls are supposed to be modest, their fanciness hidden. Hopefully this is just the fizz of freedom, and it will run its course in short order. What will I do if it doesn't? Redirecting is a cop-out and will just push it underground. I have to trust the children will respect and probably welcome my old standby: "Enough is enough."

After a few minutes, the novelty wears off, the girls disperse. *Whew!* A half hour goes by, the room humming as usual.

Kahlil and Clint stroll over to the array of bodyworks. Kahlil looks up. "Hey, look at that penis," he says to Clint.

"Yeah," says Clint. "And look at that one."

"Yeah," says Kahlil. "There's another one."

Pip comes over to ask, "What are you doing?"

"Looking at penises," Kahlil tells him. "Want to look with us?" Pip looks up.

"We could count 'em," Clint suggests.

Kahlil shakes his head. "No, let's just look at 'em." The boys walk the line, noting each penis as they pass. They stand around for a few seconds, with their arms around each other's shoulders. Then Kahlil and Clint go back to the big blocks, and Pip moves on to the clay table.

Whew! And I'm exhilarated by this one glimpse of girls feeling good about being girls and boys feeling good about being boys—in full view of each other, without any overtones of superiority or inferiority!

Missy's dad blushes

I mention to Missy's dad that she seems to have lots of curiosity about bodies these days, and may bring questions home. He blushes. "Well, if she makes the mistake of asking me, I'll tell her to ask her mom."

I may be wrong. Missy does have questions, but she may not bring them home. Children often choose to protect their parents. It may serve Missy better not to put her dad or her mother on the spot. It's likely they'll give her books—better than nothing. I catch myself feeling annoyed with Missy's dad, until I remind myself: Probably Missy's parents had no one to truly receive their questions large and small. Child or adult, this is what we yearn for—someone to listen while we struggle to know our own deepest questions. That takes big courage. Answers are easier, in many ways, than daring to ask and to hear the questions.

I yearn for every child to have parents who love her and provide not only food, clothing, shelter, but time and presence, too, openness to the child's unique moment in the world. How hard I tried to do that for my own children, and how often I failed to deliver! Just like my own parents. We each do the best we can, and it's never perfect.

Often the best we can do is to recognize our own limitations and try to get out of the way. It may be very hard for Missy's parents to deal with the direction her growth is taking. They're thrilled with her new social appetite, but probably aghast at some of the curiosity and mischief set free as she emerges. They may feel very ambivalent toward me and The Bodyworks. It's greatly to their credit they're following Missy's lead.

In the end, we're all still children, and our own children are our best teachers, motivating us to grow for their sakes in ways we'd not imagined possible. Time for me to find more compassion and less judgment for Missy's parents. This is an ongoing problem—to see the child, love the child, advocate for the child, and not to blame the parents.

Caroline, the worms, and the cows

Thinking about Missy and her parents, I'm reminded of Caroline. Ten years ago, before The Bodyworks, Caroline showed her mother and me how a child constructs her own meaning and puts on the brakes when she gets ahead of herself.

Caroline was playing with plastic bricks next to two boys who were inventing "worm houses." The boys broke off bits of clay and rolled them into long "worms." They took big hunks of clay and made balls, then pushed their fingers as far as possible into one side of each ball and probed from the other side until they had made several tunnels through the clay. They had a grand time working their worms in and out of these houses.

Caroline watched, fascinated, as play progressed. She gave up her brick project and sat there open-mouthed, focused on the clay worms and houses for the rest of the activity period.

After school Caroline was sitting in the back seat of her mother's car as they passed the pasture on their regular route home. Suddenly she piped up. "Mommy, are there mommy cows and daddy cows?"

"Yes, Caroline."

"Mommy, do the daddy cows have a penis?"

"Yes, Caroline."

Caroline was quiet for a while. Then she jumped a level. "Do the daddy cows put their penis in the mommy cows to make baby cows?"

Caroline's mother felt herself blushing. "What do you think, Caroline?"

"I think so. Do they?"

"Yes, they do."

Silence from the back seat for a long time.

Finally the big question came winging forward. "Did my daddy put his penis in you to make Allie and Pete?"

Her mother was holding her breath. She hadn't anticipated anything like this so soon." What do you think, Caroline?"

"NO WAY! That's GROSS! My daddy would NEVER do that!" Caroline firmly closed the door on a concept she couldn't yet handle.

I'll never know what led Caroline's thinking in that direction, though it seems likely the worm houses played a part. What I do know is that children of this age have big questions, whether or not they ask them out loud. They use all available resources to fashion the best answers they can. The Bodyworks doesn't put these questions in children's heads. It does give them permission to expose some of their questions to the light of day, in a setting with a teacher prepared to respond. Many young children wonder about sex, death, God. My job is to try to respond sensitively, without imposing my values on them. It's hard. It scares me sometimes, knowing how much they trust me, knowing how little I know. I just keep muddling through, and the memory of Caroline reassures me. In many ways, the child's in charge.

Sidewalk superintendent

Our new custodian generally leaves the building before I arrive, but today she waits for me and spends part of her lunch hour telling me how fascinated she is with "these paper bag bodies hanging in your room." She makes a particular point of saying she's glad to see "The boys are boys and the girls are girls," because she believes "They gotta learn it early, or it's too late to do any good."

Tanya and the hippity-hop

Tanya's lying on top of a big hippity-hop ball on the grass. She calls me over. "See, this is my big stomach. When you have a baby inside." She stretches her T-shirt, trying to shove the hippity-hop under it. She points to the rubber loop handle. "And THIS is my neck with a hole in it!"

Tanya's doing more than symbolic play here. She's also demonstrating her capacity to think analogically, even explaining away that anomalous hole. I love to watch children using the classic tools of good early childhood programs—blocks and books, dolls and balls, paints and sand—that allow them to construct, to represent, to invent, to experi-

ment. So many contemporary toys are suited for only one use, intended to create consumer demand for other products. How can children learn to do science if the scripts are all predetermined?

Kahlil gets respect, Daisy gets squelched

Kahlil's father tells me he's holding his big brothers' attention at the dinner table each night with tidbits from The Bodyworks. They were intrigued to hear "Your skeleton sticks out of your skin: your teeth!" When Kahlil described the hair standing up to plug the pores like birds fluff up feathers, they all agreed to check it out the next time they got goosebumps.

Another tribute to the genius of Outside-In, *the direct source of these memorable images. There is nothing like a good book!*

When Daisy tries to capture dinner table attention, her big brother pointedly tells her that his bodyworks is still hanging on his wall AND the heart balloon still pumps. She begins to describe the working of the brain, and he overrides. "I already KNOW that."

Her mother winces when she tells me. "We're going to have to gag him. I didn't realize until now how much curiosity my little girl has."

And it's no accident that Daisy has been consistently fascinated by two parts of the body: the penis on the boys' bodyworks, the brain on her own.

Playing with Skelly

After circle Ani can hardly wait to examine the skeleton more closely. She's especially interested in the spine, ribs, kneecaps, elbows. I pull a package of X-rays from the shelf. She immediately recognizes the spine, the skull, the arm, the hand, the foot, and spends a long time comparing the X-rays to Skelly, touching her own body.

Ani's been doing a great deal of skillful representative drawing. I wonder if she's thinking about her struggle to represent three dimensions in two.

Daisy stands on one foot then the other, sighing dramatically, until Ani finishes with Skelly. When it's her turn, Daisy carefully nods the skull "Yes" and "No" and discovers she can manipulate the jaw, making Skelly "talk" to a gathering audience of children.

Shane gets into the act. "I got double joints. Want to see 'em?" He bends his thumb to his wrist and palm, back and forth.

"Oooh," the crowd says.

Shane prolongs his moment. "My mom's got 'em too. In her shoulders!"

The Skelly game evolves. The child holding Skelly moves a bone and the other children mirror the movement with their own bodies. This game goes on all morning. Long after other children have had their fill, Daisy plays on alone. I ask her, "Why do you think Skelly collapses when you stop holding her up?"

Because it's not alive," Daisy answers immediately.

Exactly. And because it doesn't have muscles."

Daisy's very aware of her effect on others. Her gestures and facial expressions often have a practiced quality. Here she becomes a kind of puppeteer, in the limelight as usual. However, she perseveres long past the social pay off. Daisy's been struggling to resolve the conflict between her desire for autonomy and her desire for approval. Maybe she's playing these issues out with Skelly: What moves me? Who moves me? Who am I beneath my smile and my pretty dresses?

At home Daisy talks about her model. "I have puffy arms because I was wearing my blue blouse. AND: I have a BRAIN!" Daisy comes to me with a book open to the human eye: scientific illustrations show the eyeball inside and out, its muscles, nerves, and blood vessels. "I want to do my eyes on my body," she tells me.

"What a *wonderful* idea, Daisy. I'm so glad you're interested in your eyes. I wish we could add them to your model, but it's nearly the end of the year. We still have to finish everyone's muscles and bones and hearts. Let's talk to your mom and see if your family could help you work on your eyes at home. What could you use to make an eye?"

"A little ball," Daisy says.

Daisy's been chiefly concerned with friends and with all the dramas of friendship. Since The Bodyworks began, her coquettish behavior has decreased markedly. It seems to be dawning on her that she herself is a person of many layers, great complexities. In September Daisy would have been the first to squeal and squirm if anyone had mentioned "eyeballs." Now she's hooked, cognitively as well as socially and emotionally. She wants to go deeper. Whether or not her parents follow through on her "eyeball" project, she's begun to alter her role of "pretty little girl" at home as well as at school.

Committed as I am to emergent learning, I'm so frustrated not to be able to help Daisy. If we started earlier in the year, we could custom-build a bodyworks for every child. But I've never found a group ready for this project before spring—or is it me? I don't feel ready to do The

Bodyworks until we have a deeply-rooted and self-regulating classroom community. Trade-offs, trade-offs. I can't take Daisy much further this year. I have to be content to see her make a big leap, and to imagine her soaring.

Little details

A scattering of comments from around the room:

Zack looks up at his bodyworks on his way to the water fountain. "Hey!" he says, "My hands. My bones are backwards." He's right. Terry helps him switch.

Paul looks over from his work with nuts and bolts. "He put 'em on wrong," he says to himself.

Shirelle and Shane are playing with puppets. Shirelle comments suddenly, "There's blood all over your body, BUT NOT IN MY HAIR!"

Missy hops across the classroom with a big smile. "My bodyworks has only one leg, so I'm gonna have to hop on one leg."

Maggie's at playdough, poking holes with stiff fingers. "If you couldn't bend. Your finger all one piece."

I call the hospital to check on Bo. His father reports Bo was probing his ribs. "I'm trying to feel my lungs."

Jogger's worried about getting his bodyworks home. "What if it doesn't fit in my mom's car?"

I ask, "Do you fit?"

He still seems a little concerned. "I gotta wear my seatbelt. I don't know if I can stand up. Maybe I'm too tall."

"If your bodyworks is too tall, you can make it sit in a seatbelt too."

Cara approaches Ani. "Want to play with me?"

"No thanks. I'm sorry." She takes Cara into her confidence. "I have a infected finger."

Tanya overhears. "My sister almost cut her finger off when she was working with my mom's scissors."

This is all Rosa needs. "My BROTHER got blood because my mother had a sharp fingernail."

Paul scoots over. "One time I scraped my knee and it got blood and we put a bandaid."

Jogger and Zack are dressing up.

Zack wears high-heeled silver evening shoes, carries a silver pocketbook, and drapes a lace shawl across his shoulders. "I'm all metal, so nothing can hurt me."

Grabbing a plastic banana from the fruit bowl, Jogger puts on the big workboots. "I'm all swords sticking out of my body, cuz if I eat guns swords stick up and if I eat 'em twice, guns stick out of the swords. Once I ate banana guns. We can't put any bombs there cuz this wood won't protect them. The wood needs to protect itself and it can't unless the bombs are not there, unless they're on top."

At circle we do several old finger plays, newly fascinating as we observe the workings of our joints. "Lots of creatures have bodies with many of the same parts we have. But different kinds of creatures use those parts in different ways, depending on where they live and what they do to get food and stay safe. Monkeys have tails, so they can live in trees. We don't have tails, but we have a special kind of thumb that we use for many different jobs. Our thumb can bend across from our fingers. Does anybody want to try an experiment? We could use duct tape to keep our thumbs from moving around."

Nobody says anything. I bait the trap. "I'm going to do it. I've done it before and it's really interesting." I hold up the roll of duct tape and Nita tapes my thumb flat.

Ani looks dubious, but she can't resist. "Me too."

After about a half hour, Ani and I agree to take the duct tape off. "I'm glad to have my thumb back," I admit.

"Me too," says the young scientist, "but I'm glad we did the experiment."

Other children come over to watch us bend our thumbs.

Gabe spends the day

It's public school vacation week. Last week Kahlil's big brother Gabe asked if he could come in to make his own bodyworks. He blushed. "I know I'm ten and everything, but you didn't start doing it until after I was in your class. Ari still has his hanging on our closet from two years ago, and I keep looking at it. Now Kahlil's all excited about his, and . . . I feel left out." What teacher could resist?

When Gabe showed up, looking sheepish, his father took me aside. "Gabe's embarrassed to ask you, but he wants to know if his cousin Frank can come too. Frank's thirteen and he's Gabe's hero, but when he called last night to invite Gabe over for the day, Gabe said he couldn't, because he was coming to do his bodyworks. Frank remembered seeing Ari's bodyworks at our house, and he said he'd like to do one too if you'd let him."

"I'd love to let Frank come, but I'm short on clothes hangers. And I really don't have time to work with the big boys, or answer questions at their level."

"We've got the clothes hangers. The questions won't be a problem—I discussed that with them already. I told them I'd try to answer those later, and we can go to the library this afternoon to follow up."

So Gabe and Frank spent the morning with us, working hard to complete their models. The little ones buzzed around the big boys, who graciously commented, "You guys are really lucky. . . . This is the neatest project I've ever seen. . . . You sure are learning a lot. I didn't know half this stuff. . . . You ought to come teach my science class at junior high."

Shane visits Kahlil: the fallout

Two days ago Shane was excited about playing at Kahlil's house after school. Yesterday his mother left a message that Shane wouldn't come to school because he was afraid of Kahlil. Today she brought him clinging and sobbing, and she demanded I protect him from Kahlil. It took a long time to get to the bottom of the story, which involved a toy sword and Shane's memory of an older boy who used to live in Kahlil's neighborhood. Shane was convinced this older boy was "inside" Kahlil and had "commanded" Kahlil to kill Shane with the toy sword.

Kahlil's mother was resting in bed after getting out of the hospital, and Kahlil's father was fixing dinner in the kitchen while the boys played. Shane's mother was furious. She felt the children had been inadequately supervised, resented missing a day of work to deal with Shane's trauma, and was determined not to be late. She said she had told Shane no one could live inside anyone else's body except Jesus, and if he gave himself to Jesus he wouldn't be afraid any more, because Jesus is the answer to all fears. She put Shane in my arms, pried his fingers off her neck, and strode away, saying, "Don't go near that kid, Shane. I mean it. Tonight I'm taking you to prayer meeting and you're gonna get saved if you know what's good for you."

I sat with Shane a long time, holding him close, reminding him we keep it safe and fun for everyone at school, laying the groundwork for the day. "You know, Shane, some days are hard. You had a hard start. On days like today it's good to do something you can count on. What do we have in this room that's really easy for you?"

"Nothing."

"I've seen you do puzzles really easily. Let's go over here and do a couple together."

"I don't want to. I want to go home."

"That's not a choice. Your mom had to go to work. You're going to stay at school. You can do something or you can do nothing. I think you'll have a better day if you try doing something easy for you, like puzzles, but it's up to you. I can sit with you a while longer and then I need to work with other children."

After a while, Shane said, "Pattern blocks. I can do pattern blocks."

"Great idea!"

When I left the table, Shane said, "Don't let Kahlil come over here!"

"I'll talk to Kahlil, Shane. I'll tell him you're not ready to play with him yet. Later today, or tomorrow, we'll all talk and figure out how to make it better. You're already doing a good job, starting to work with pattern blocks. That's a big step."

"I can stay here all day."

"If you want to."

It was a beginning. At least we pinned down the specific fear. But it's a mess involving two families, starting at home. I can help Shane and Kahlil find their way at school, but whatever happened, I won't be able to unravel it. Maybe Kahlil was acting out some of the stress built up over his mother's hospitalization. His parents and I will watch for other fallout. Shane's response troubles me much more, because his anxieties are not new. They're massive, long-term, embedded deep in his family's circumstances. I've tried everything I know how to do at school. His play, his art work, and his peer relationships reflect profound disturbance in his emotional life. I can give him room to express some of that—in sand and water and dramatic play, in clay and paint, in World-building, in puppets, in stories. But he has some enormous questions I can't answer. His mother has been quite firm from the beginning that she cannot or will not deal with the questions Shane's asking in words and behavior. She's told me that Shane doesn't need outside help, that she can't afford therapy and doesn't approve of it. Her church is a real support to her. Perhaps she'll let me write a letter to her pastor, describing some of my concerns about her son's development and suggesting that Shane very much needs a loving adult male presence in the flesh as well as in the spirit.

This is one of those times I feel sad, mad, and helpless. I've done all I can do and it's not enough. I hope The Bodyworks offers Shane some comfort, some trust in the integrity of the body. Could The Bodyworks have triggered Shane's anxieties? I don't think so. His issues have been apparent since the beginning of the year.

It can and does happen, however, that The Bodyworks reveals children's hidden agendas. With The Bodyworks, it becomes harder for parents and teachers not to see, not to hear what's on children's minds and hearts. Bodyworks may rub our noses in the double messages we give children, confront us with paradoxes we prefer to ignore. I find children are relieved and much more trustful when we face paradoxes with them than when we offer simplistic answers. Often the best and only answers we can give are not verbal—a hand to hold, a quiet moment to share, a walk in the park, a sunset, a candle at dinner or bedtime, an evocative photograph or painting or bit of music. Shane's mother is giving him all she has to offer. She can't provide him with a father, but maybe her pastor can find a "Big Brother" to help this little boy.

My model is me: Shane, Shirelle, Tanya, Paul, Zack

Shane, beginning to construct his fingers and toes, insists on doing EVERY joint too. "I need 'em ALL." He also notices the small bones of the wrist in an illustration, and thoughtfully examines his own wrist, but is persuaded to let those go. It takes him a solid hour and a half without a break, working one-to-one with Terry, to finish—to do so, he elects to skip outdoor time.

Doing every bone and every joint is hardly a digression. It's crucial to a physical thinker, especially a child like Shane, who feels so vulnerable in the world. It's important to support him in this symbolic empowerment process.

Many of the children want not only all the fingers and toes but all the muscles too (especially the boys, confirming the persistence of gender stereotypes). To the extent that they really identify with their models, "integrity of function" is at stake. On the other hand, many of them don't have Shane's unique sense of urgency or the staying power that goes with it. I wish we could let them all proceed at their own pace and stop when their energy runs out.

However, I need to bring this project to a close and give us all some time to hang out together, before some children (and all the grown-ups) burn out. My solution is to help each child construct one complete arm/hand and one complete leg/foot (without wrist or ankle bones), sending extra materials home so parents can work with the children who want symmetry. I'll explain to the group we experimented with Shane's model, and it took too long to put in all the details.

All the children take off their shoes happily. They like measuring toes, looking at their feet. *It's a novelty and a good sensation to be barefoot at school.*

Kahlil fidgets, complaining, "I'm bored." Then we attach the foot. He grins from ear to ear, "It's SO NEAT! This is THE BEST THING!" He looks at his model hanging from the line, then bends down to his shoe and feels his toes inside it, one by one. "Yep," he reports brightly, "five." At the gate, he runs to his mother, "Today we did my foot. And we're gonna do HEARTS! NEXT!"

Ani, overhearing, says to me, "I'm gonna be sad when it's over and the blood is gone and there's no more to do."

Shirelle observes, "My toes are little but the bones are SO LONG. Why can't I make some more joints? I got more joints."

Tanya finds a way around the limitation of one-foot-only. While she's waiting for Paul to measure with Terry, she cuts duplicate "toes" to match the ones Terry helped her make and even punches all the necessary holes through the heavy oaktag. All the while she negotiates to be allowed to do all the joints. Finally she leaves the table peeved, "I'll make Aunt Susie help me when I stay over her house. SHE'LL let me do the joints!" *In the end, my hard-nosed tradeoffs may help The Bodyworks brim over into families, amplifying and extending it.*

Paul's mother reports he fell on the driveway and cut his arm. Instead of crying, he said eagerly, "Now I'm gonna see if my blood works, if it makes a plug for the hole. And I gotta change my bodyworks. I gotta put a cut on the arm and a Band-aid."

When we move Zack's model, the bladder falls out. He jokes, "Quick, quick! Stick it back in my bodyworks. Or else my bodyworks won't know when it's time to go to the bathroom!"

The children move back and forth between levels of abstraction. In many ways, the bodyworks becomes a doll, an opportunity for symbolic play. And, like a doll, sometimes it acquires an energy of its own.

Levels of understanding

It's my turn to ask the children a question at circle. "What's 'energy'?

Jogger leads off. "It makes you run fast."

Zack follows with "Food!"

Clint contributes, "It makes you ski down all the hills."

Missy looks at Clint. "When you swim."

Paul goes for it. "A scooter."

Daisy tries, "Like when you're walking and eating."

Pip has other things on his mind. "I got a guitar and a thing to it. See?" From his pocket he pulls a 'guitar pick' made of a folded Band-aid.

All this time Kahlil has been putting his thoughts together. "When you walk to your friend's or somewhere. Energy's from your body, in food, through your heart."

Jogger now shifts his emphasis. "If you eat food if you're going jogging."

Shirelle, who rarely participates in circle discussions, takes a stab at this topic. "It makes you not sneeze."

Pip comes around to the subject in his own good time. "Energy is from your heart."

Ani finally gives back part of my original explanation, "Like gas in your car."

Kahlil completes her analogy. "Like in your body—food and air."

This is a complicated topic. I vaguely remember from some ancient science textbook, "Energy is the capacity to do work." Or was it "the potential to do work"? In any case, "energy" is an elusive concept. Often we use it to describe mood or tone, as well as power and fuel. It pleases me that so many of the children can come up with biologically-based bits of answers, in their own inimitable phrases. I'm confident that a scientific concept has begun to take root. If only I'd done a "pre-test," this might be part of the "post-test."

"Questions" and Putting on the Brakes

I've started a regular Bodyworks question time at circle. I just ask, "Any questions about bodies today?" I'm keeping a list of what the children ask.

The children pay close attention to each other's questions and answers. The depth of their listening moves me. Their faces say: "I'm not going to miss a minute of this. It's all about me, my SELF, in some powerful way, and it's about other people too—my friends and my teachers. About US. There are questions I was afraid to ask, and questions I never knew I had. I'm not alone in my wonderings."

Some questions are brand-new. Others are requests for review, or check-ins to affirm the questioner's own unspoken answer. The children also use the circle to release themselves from the grip of private experience, and to seek reassurance. I note how many of the questions arrive in statement form.

Some samples of recent initiatives

Cara: "Find out about back bones." *Many children are still learning the difference between asking and telling.*

Paul: "What's your tail bone?"

Shane: "Why the food pipe's so long?"

Clint: "What if your rectum closes before you get all the poops out?"

Shirelle: "What if you eat too much candy and the doctor has to open you up?"

Daisy: "Why do we have cheeks?"

Pip: "Sometimes if you lose all your teeth, you get some round thing so you can chew."

Maggie: "If something stuck in your throat?"

Zack: "What makes your voice?"

Jogger: "What if you had no teeth? You could only eat soup. What comes before your windpipe? What does the flap look like?"

Cara: "Why we got foots?"

Paul: "What about the connector? What if the connector's rope breaks?" *It turned out he meant "elevator."*

Rosa: "Can we sing the bone song? What's your pelvic bone? What does your pelvic bone do?"

Sandy: "Your pelvic bone is important. It holds your hips together, so you can walk and move around." *I was pleased with my answer to that one, since I hadn't thought about it until she asked.*

Shane: "You should talk to people. I don't like it when people tell me poopees."

Sandy: "Thanks for reminding everybody. Bathroom words are for the bathroom. Dirt is something in the wrong place. Like hair and butter. Hair in butter is dirty. Butter in hair is also dirty! Your body's not dirty, but poopees and poopee talk belong in the bathroom."

Tanya: "Why do we have a balloon in our body?" *This one led to a review of key concepts.*

Sandy: "We don't really have a balloon inside our real bodies. We just use a balloon to show what a heart is like, to show how it pumps blood all through our bodies. When you make a model of your body, it's like a doll. A doll looks like a person, but the growpower's missing. We can't make growpower and put it in. We can't make something come alive. You know the difference. What can you name that has growpower?"

The whole circle offers answers to my question: "A baby . . . a puppy . . . a dandelion . . . a worm . . . an alligator . . . grown-ups." *They got it.*

Pip: "Where's a bird's belly button?"

Off the top of my head: "There isn't any, because the bird comes from an egg."

Pip reminds me, "*I* came from an egg inside my mother."

"Yes, you did. What a good question. I've never thought of that before. I'm glad you did! The egg inside your mother and the egg outside a chicken are different kinds of eggs, but I don't really know much about them. I'll have to look it up for you. You're helping me learn something new!"

My colleague's sister runs an embryology lab. She says there is indeed a point of attachment of amniotic "capillaries" to the developing bird. Pip was in the ball park. If these children were older, we could go spinning down the corridors of evolution: dinosaurs, birds, mammals, and more. A simplified trip would make sense even to these little ones. But it's the end of the year, and I don't know enough to toss off these concepts without a little preparation. Maybe next year. Another tie-in to the perennial dinosaur craze.

Ani: "Why do we need to drink milk?"

Sandy: "Milk is full of a special mineral called calcium that helps bones grow strong. Calcium is what's in shells and bones and chalk—it's hard and white and strong."

The next day, Ani asks: "Where does the milk go to the bones?"

"First it goes to the stomach. The stomach sends it into the blood and then into the bones."

Two days later, Ani comes back with a follow-up question: "Why does the milk go to your stomach first?"

"There are lots of things in milk like calcium and water and fat. Your stomach's job is to start breaking the milk into parts, so the blood can take the vitamins and minerals where your body needs them. Your brain tells your blood to carry the calcium to the bones, just like a river carries boats full of things to different places." *More or less, I guess. I still don't fully understand metabolism!*

Tanya: "Why do we got shoulders?"

"To connect our arms to our bodies. The shoulder's a special kind of joint so our arms can move all around. Let's try different ways to reach high . . . low . . . way in front . . . way behind . . . all around in a big circle. . . . It's our shoulders that let our arms do that. Suppose we didn't have shoulders. Hold your arms out stiff like they're stuck to your neck. Now try to reach down and pick up a pencil off the floor."

Tanya listens intently. She's been pursuing the whole matter of connection, function, ever since she expanded her representational schema to include crawling babies.

Shane: "What if you had no neck?" He demonstrates.

Clint: "Once in a restaurant at the airport I had to go to the bathroom and my mother went with me, and she scratched me with her fingernails. It was a accident."

Sandy: "Clint, aren't you going to pick your grandmother up at the airport today? Maybe that's why you're remembering what happened. Our brains put things together like that." *Maybe when Clint's grandmother visits, his mother gets nervous. Maybe she was nervous the day she accidentally scratched him in the airport bathroom. His real question might be: Why's my mom so uptight, and when are things going to settle down? But I can't go any farther on the strength of what he offered.*

Missy: "At my babysitter's I got sick and I was gonna throw up and I had to lie in her bed and my daddy was coming and I throwed up and it was all yucky."

I aim at the questions that might be behind her statement. (What's throwing up like for you? Why do we throw up?) "Sometimes it tastes yucky in my mouth after I throw up. Then it feels good to wash my face and rinse out my mouth and brush my teeth. Throwing up is one way your body can clear out food that's not good for you."

Zack: "You got weird toes in your sandals. Your toenails."

Sandy: "My toenails look thick and yellow, don't they? When I was a little girl, my feet looked like other people's, but they started to change. They feel the same and they work the same, but they look different. Like my hair changed from brown to gray. Now my feet look just like my Dad's. I liked them better the other way. People tease me sometimes and tell me to wear socks. It hurts my feelings. I just keep telling myself I'm glad I've got two feet and ten toes and they take me where I want to go. My feet don't have to look like the commercials!"

Maggie raises her hand. "My mom. Got brown teeth. So she didn't smile. When she was little."

"Your mom has a beautiful smile. I'm sorry she used to feel so bad about her teeth. If somebody makes a big deal about of my toenails or my teeth, then that's not a person I'm going to hang around with. Do any of you have parts you don't like so much?"

Daisy: "I bumped my pelvic bone on my bike seat. I got a bruise." *This could be simply a sharing of information. I bet she's also worried about the bruise.*

Sandy: "A bruise is the place where some blood gets stuck. When you get a hard bump, some of the littlest tiniest blood vessels break and a little blood leaks out under your skin. Then your body grows new little blood vessels, and extra blood cells."

Cara: "Smashed your head. If you. On the floor. You see the bones?" *Is she wondering if the eyes can see inside the skull? Has she heard the phrase "crack your head open" and wonders what it looks like inside? Who knows? I won't pursue the gory possibilities unless she does. Meanwhile, I'll aim at reassurance, for her sake and the others'.*

Sandy: "The skull bone is very strong. People fall all the time and hardly ever break their heads open. Sometimes they break the skin on their head, and they go to the hospital and get stitches. Usually when people break bones, we can't see them because they're inside our skin. That's why doctors take X-ray pictures."

Rosa follows up in her own inimitable way. "If someone was really stubborn and did something really bad and chopped a person, a doctor could see the bone. If someone else did something really stubborn, cut something off, the doctor wouldn't know what to do and then the mother and father gonna be very sad if it's their little girl." *Impulse control is an issue for Rosa and so is willfulness. She's heard plenty from her parents about both subjects. She can imagine what might happen if she went too far. Cara and Rosa are not alone. Most children fantasize about mutilation to some degree, especially in these days of emergency rescue dramas on TV. It helps to get the fears out into the light of day.*

Sandy: "Lots of times people feel like hurting someone or doing something dangerous, but they usually stay in control. All the children in this class are getting very good about keeping things in control. If your feelings get strong, ask someone to help keep it safe."

Ani: "I got pus in my infected finger, and my daddy put a needle in it and soaked it in hot water with medicine and if it doesn't get well I have to go to my doctor."

Sandy: "Your dad is letting the pus come out. Pus is all the extra white blood cells that have been fighting the germs to help you get well."

Sandy: "On May Day, we're going to have a special visitor to help you plant marigold seeds. He's my husband, and his name is Mark. He's very very tall, taller than I am."

Shane: "Is he your Daddy?"

Paul: "He's your grandfather!"

Shirelle: "What's a Maybe Day?"

Zack: "That bone on the Bodyworks table. Is it a fossil? Is it from a dinosaur?"

Sandy: "No, it's not a fossil. My husband bought it at the grocery store, to cook in the soup. It's a bone from a cow. Do you know the difference between fossils and bones?"

"Nope." He's twisting around to look at Kahlil.

"You could try to figure it out, or I could tell you, or we could look it up together. Let me know what you decide." *It's taken Zack so long to get out of his head and into playing with other children. He gets pumped full of information at home. I like to give him the luxury of choosing how much he wants to know at any given moment.*

Maggie: "Clay don't got growpower too. But your nose. But not by itself. Your whole body gots growpower."

After circle, Rosa goes to the bathroom. Through the open door I see her get down off the toilet and waddle over to the mirror without pulling up her tights, holding up her dress. She calls out, "Hey, Sandy! My private parts are bigger too!"

Jogger: "When blood goes through your body you can stay alive. If your blood doesn't move too long you die. If your heart stops pumping."

Sandy: "And your brain keeps your heart pumping all the time. You don't even have to think about it. Your brain's always working, even when you're asleep—keeping your heart beating, keeping your lungs breathing in and out, making new cells, sending your food to all the parts that need energy. Your brain knows how to do all those things and lots more, all at the same time."

Jogger doesn't say so, but he loves The Bodyworks. It's giving him plenty to think about, and an introduction to model-building—which may be a perfect channel for his intellectual curiosity and a useful retreat in his busy family. His daycare provider tells me he constructed a spinal column from bits of cardboard and bright neon tape.

Paul: "The white blood cell fights dragons."

Sandy: "Tell me some more about your idea, Paul."

"I saw it in the book."

"Oh! Yes, one of the books has a picture of white blood cells fighting dragons, but that's pretend. The person who drew the picture was trying to help you understand the white blood cells are good guys fighting germs. There's no such thing as a real dragon in your body or anywhere else. The artist is pretending the germs are dragons."

Pip: "Where does the head bone go?" *In the song, we begin with the head bone and end with "The toebone's connected to NO bone." Pip's question is more than whimsy. It's also his aesthetic appreciation for symmetry and his cognitive grasp of equivalences. Why isn't there a parallel statement about the head bone, since the top of the head is as free as the tip of the toe?*

Cara: "I really want a baby, and I'm gonna name it Pepe."

Missy: "My friend Debby touched my private parts and I screamed for my mom. My mom was upstairs and she didn't hear me, but Debby stopped and I put my clothes right back on and I told my mom. Later."

Another day, Missy reports: "I was thinking about a scary thing. My friend got a SLIVER in her private parts and it was bloody and it hurt and it hurt a whole week and she had to have a SHOT!"

Shirelle: "Muscles are bad."

Sandy: "What makes you think muscles are bad, Shirelle?"

"Because some people have big muscles and they're really strong and they can kill people."

"EVERYBODY has muscles. We need muscles to move. Our brains tell our muscles to move our bones. A person could USE a muscle to do a mean thing, but the MUSCLES aren't bad."

"You don't get muscles when you use a Nordic track." *Aha! Shirelle's mom wants to be fit, but still keep the dainty look.*

Kahlil: "One time I saw a baby with no eyes."

Sandy: "You mean a blind baby? Some people's eyes don't work right, so they can't see. Usually, blind people learn to use their ears and nose and fingers extra well. There's a way to write books using little bumps that blind people learn to read with their fingers. Sometimes they have special dogs to help them get around, or long canes to feel what's ahead."

"This baby had NO EYES on his face. I saw him. My mother knows his mother."

"Once in a while, when a baby is growing inside his mother, something goes wrong and the baby is born missing something people usually have."
I checked with Kahlil's mother. Over a year ago he did meet a family friend whose child was born with no eyes. At the time, he said little about it. Here it is, needing to be dealt with at a different developmental stage.

A rash of questions about appropriate touch: "What if the babysitter picked you up and touched you if you didn't come to bed on time?" "What if the babysitter said . . . ?" "What if you were asleep and a grown-up opened your door and touched you?" "Like you said if a grown-up made you touch him, to take your hand away. What if he wouldn't let your hand go away?"

Over and over, I reiterate, "If it's the wrong kind of touching, you'll KNOW it. Then you tell a grown-up and keep telling until somebody believes you and helps you. Even someone who loves you could make a mistake and touch you the wrong way. Then you must tell other grown-ups and keep telling until you get help. There are no secrets about this—secrets are not safe."

It's impossible at circle to know if a child is hypothesizing or calling for help. I try to follow up the group discussion with an aside to each child who asks questions about personal safety: "If there's anything else you want to ask me or tell me about touching, this is a good time." On the other hand, it's important not to make mountains out of molehills.

Often a child is just checking. Bo once said, "My sister had diarrhea and she smelled all yucky and her bottom got all red and my mom and dad had to rub this salve all over it."

"And do you think that was good touch, taking care of her?"

"Yep."

"It sounds like it was to me too."

Other times children are trying to assimilate media experience. Recently Shane told Nita, "Sometimes people peel the skin off a dead person," and went on to describe layers of flesh and blood and bone. I asked his mother about this, but she couldn't imagine where he got it. Weeks later it turned out that he got out of bed and walked quietly into the room where the babysitter was watching a video about dissection for her anatomy class.

Then there are the children who blow a new concept all out of proportion. Rosa's mother ruefully reported she was listening to the car radio when a bulletin came on about a rape. She quickly changed the station, but not before Rosa's radar had picked up the vibes attached to the word. "What's rape?" she demanded. Her mother gave her a simple answer. "It's when a man hurts a woman." Later, Rosa and her two-year-old brother were arguing in the yard and he hit her. She ran inside, screaming, "Make him stop raping me."

Often after troubling questions someone in the circle says, "I'm tired. I want to go to my Secret Place." It's important for the children to recognize when they've had enough, to signal that to the group and to have us respect it.

Zack's mother reports he's brimming with questions at home:

"What is time?"

"Could time ever stop?"

"Does love grow?"

"Does everyone sleep except one Native American?"

"How far does the universe go?"

WEEK SIX

Circulatory System, Review

Heart Math

Shane and Shirelle are drifting today. I delegate to them the organization of the yarn for veins and arteries. They pair each red piece with a blue one, gather nine pairs into a bundle, and hand it to me to knot for temporary storage. Cara offers to do the next knot. Other children arrive to kibitz, help, correct, and they count lengths of yarns, pairs, number of children. I show them how to use the pegboard to track the running total of bundles.

Heart of my heart

Shirelle and Zack are the two lucky ones to begin The Heart, that coveted big red balloon. As they work, other children cluster around.

Shirelle huffs, puffs, stretches the neck of her balloon. Finally she calls, "Look! Look! Everybody look! I blew it up myself, all by myself!" These balloons are tough. Not every child can inflate them. It's a real achievement. I restrain my spontaneous applause since others won't be able to clear this hurdle, but I hug and congratulate her.

Halfway through installing veins and arteries, Zack launches a review. "The blood takes the fresh air from your lungs to your heart, right? Then your heart pumps it all over your body. Then it's blue cuz it needs more fresh air." *Zack likes to get it straight and keep it straight.*

Daisy's hanging around. "What about your eyeballs? Do they have veins and arteries? Do the veins and arteries go BEHIND YOUR EYEBALLS?"

Maggie stands near the hanging prototypes. She squeezes and quickly releases the heart several times in a row. "Like you're scared."

Nita asks her, "What does it do when you're not scared?"

Maggie slows her pumping. "But if you run, like this." She squeezes rapidly over and over.

Paul can't wait. "Can I blow up my balloon now? I'm never gonna get my turn."

Daisy comments, "Zack's is a penis, but not mine. I got a uterus." *Today she's matter-of-fact, seems reconciled.*

Kahlil eases in. "I gotta have veins to my penis. My penis has veins. I've seen 'em. I want one of those big heart balloons for my penis instead of that little one."

Pip follows me. "After I do my heart, can we do Daddy bodies?"

Seeing the blood vessels, hearing the heart, pumping iron

Daisy's at the mirror, pulling down her lower eyelid to see the arteries. Maggie joins her. They stand at the mirror together, gazing into their own eyes, then they look at each other and giggle. They move away, looking at each other's eyes.

Jogger and Ani take turns with the stethoscope. They listen to their own hearts and then to each other's.

Kahlil is at the sink with the "heart pump," a long coil of plastic tubing, a bucket of red-dyed water, and a rubber infant aspirator bulb. He tries to pump the "blood" up, but the bulb won't stay on. He plunges a turkey baster into the bucket. Success! I go over to help him with the long tubing.

"I'm sorry it keeps slipping, Kahlil. I couldn't figure out how to make it stay together. A real heart is all connected. I'll can hold it together to get you started. It's tricky."

"Hey, it's working."

He works for half an hour, learning to control it. I place the bucket on the floor so he can stretch the tube up to his chin.

"That's as long as you, Kahlil!"

"Cool," he says. "I sure am tired. Pumping."

"Now you know why the heart has to be such a strong muscle."

"Yeah! Really strong!"

"Your heart pumps almost a hundred times every minute. All day and all night. Your whole life."

"A HUNDRED TIMES!"

"That's millions and millions of times!"

"MILLIONS? That's more than a hundred!"

I'll stop there. It would be fun to dazzle him with some more statistics but he's dazzled enough. It's a rare four-year-old who can grasp a hundred, much less a million. I can't visualize a million either. The children love the big grown-up sound of the numbers. Me too.

Clint speaks up

When Clint's mother hugs him goodbye at the door, she signals me out to the hall. She looks exhausted, as if she's been up all night. "I've just got to tell you what happened. I still can't believe it. Neither can my husband.

When we finally got the kids to bed, we stayed awake talking for hours. It's The Bodyworks." She stops, seeing my worried face. "I mean, it's incredible! It's wonderful. It's amazing. The whole thing." She grins.

"You know how quiet Clint is? I mean at home. With the two big boys, he never gets a word in edgewise. Well, last night at the dinner table those two got started on this horrendous racist joke, making faces and everything. They heard it on the school bus. My husband shoots me this look, warning me not to go ballistic, they're just kids, you know: make my point, but go easy. I'm taking a deep breath before I jump in, and all of a sudden there's this little voice from the end of the table. It's Clint. Clint looks straight at his big brothers, and he says clear as a bell, 'I don't like it when you talk like that. It's not funny, what people look like.' So there's this stunned silence, and then he keeps going.

"Clint says, 'Some people look different on the outside, but we're all the same on the inside. Everybody's got a food tube and all that stuff. Like when we saw that old guy the other day that only had one arm, and I started to be scared of him, and then I thought he eats food and it goes down and makes poops and pees just like Daddy, just like everybody.'

"So at this point, Clint stops, and we're all looking at him, and my husband and I both have tears in our eyes. My husband tells Clint he's really proud of him, and then he starts a little lecture to the big boys, way over Clint's head. Hah!

"Clint waits til his father's finished spouting off about democracy and prejudice, and then Clint says, 'Besides, suppose somebody captured you and made you a slave just because you had a different color of skin? Like they took the people from Africa and put chains on their legs.' And then he just keeps going, all the way from Africa to slave ships to Harriet Tubman and Rosa Parks and Martin Luther King. I mean he talked for about fifteen minutes straight. All that stuff you did with the puppets and songs in January? I mean, to tell you the truth, Clint didn't say much about it, and I figured he's too young anyway.

"Who would've believed he was storing it all up like that? I mean it was in his own words, he really understood it, and he pulled it out of his hat at the perfect moment, all hooked to The Bodyworks. It really blew my mind. You should've seen his brothers' faces. Their mouths were hanging open. You know they think he's only four and a half, he's still a baby."

"My baby! He sure got us thinking. I mean, there's a lot of stuff I don't know that I should, my husband too. The five of us sat at the dinner table for two hours. Nobody even tried to turn on the TV. We just talked about a lot of important things we usually don't get around to."

"So I just wanted to thank you. Not only for what you've been teaching Clint, but for all of us. 'A little child shall lead them,' like it says." There are tears in her eyes.

There are tears in mine, too. "Thank you for telling me! And thank you for sharing Clint! He's a remarkable little boy. Very few children could put all that together, much less speak up to their big brothers. You and your husband are doing an amazing job with your family—don't give me all the credit! The crucial thing is we're working as a team. I hope each child is getting what he needs from all these seeds we're scattering by the handfuls, but sometimes I wonder. The feedback helps a lot."

Clint's mother gives me a hug. "Well, there's no doubt Clint's getting what he needs from you, and he's bringing it home to us."

Early childhood is a lot more than the Eensy Weensy Spider and crayons and graham crackers. Little kids are taking in huge gulps of contemporary culture, thanks to big brothers and TV and trips to the mall. They are left with deep impressions, ideas, and attitudes that may not surface for years. A whole informal education, usually miseducation! It's a constant challenge to articulate values and concepts the children can use to sort out their experience. I try to offer hands-on projects, as the grounding for social knowledge that's age-appropriate and flexible—empowerment, not a guilt trip. What a treasure Clint's mother has given me—this glimpse of her son holding a sense of history up to his experience of bodies, his education moving him to act from the heart.

As Shirelle sees Bo

Terry's doing a research paper on the dynamics of this group of children. She asks each child to tell her what they especially like about Bo.

Shirelle dictates: "He does wacky things. He does silly things. Right when he comes in the classroom he plays in blocks because he likes me. He has short hair, like me, and he's littler than me. I'm five and he's four. He talks to people when he's not sposed to, and when he's singing. When he dances, he holds the Valentine and does wacky things like the goblin."

She shakes her head and arms, miming Bo dancing like the goblin.

"I love him. He karate-kicked me, you know! He's cute. His whole body. And you know what's very cute? His hair is so long and it's messy. No. It's short and he messes it up. He says he likes it messy. And then he fell right on his face on the floor. Messy hair! Oh, he's so cute! I feel like banging my face on the floor right now."

Tells us plenty about little girls with sisters in junior high, too!

Still sprouting

Every day Rosa checks the remaining sprouts, usually commenting on the growpower. Yesterday Ani was nearby when Rosa crowed, "These beans sure are outgrowing!"

Ani looked up with a grin. "They sure are!" Today Ani arrives with a bag of birdseed for us to plant.

Following-up on Shane and Jogger

Shane's mother says he's not worried anymore that Kahlil is going to kill him, but she's not letting him go over there to visit again any time soon. She's decided to ask her pastor to take a special interest in Shane, and to sign him up for a Big Brother. *Hooray!*

Jogger's working with me. He tells Kahlil and Clint in my hearing how he used a knife without telling his parents, cut himself, and snuck to the bathroom for a Band-aid. He lifts up his T-shirt to show his friends some scratches on his chest.

"Wow!"

"See where my dad put a Zorro mark with the mercurochrome?"

I butt in. "Jogger, those are really deep! What happened?"

"Me and Rod and some guys were in the woods. We got a fort. Rod got the tools to make it. His dad lets him borrow 'em.We don't wear our shirts. I got scratched in a lot of bushes, but it didn't hurt ME." He pulls up his shirt again.

"Who's Rod?"

"One of my friends."

"How old is he?"

"TWELVE! Next year he's gonna be a TEENAGER!"

"How old are the other guys?"

"Twelve like Rod. But Eddy's only ten."

"Do you play with Rod a lot?"

"Every afternoon after daycare. He's my friend. My dad says he's better than a babysitter."

"What does your mom say?"

"She says Rod's kind of rough, but he's a good kid and I don't have any brothers, so."

I'm not overprotective. I know children sometimes use knives in secret. I know Jogger needs some relief from his three sisters, and Rod may be a godsend. But it's unlikely that a five-year-old boy should be tagging along in the woods with a bunch of twelve-year-olds. Maybe in the mountain village where Jogger's dad grew up, but not here. I suspect Jogger knows he's in over his head and he's calling for help. At last, there's something I can do—"facts" I can follow up. I never thought I'd be glad to see a cut and some scratches; maybe now I can get Jogger the help he needs.

Stories from the heart

Missy runs up. "I know all about my body!"

"That's wonderful, Missy. What would you like to tell me about your body?"

Her face falls. She can't remember a thing. "Um," she stammers, "I didn't want to tell you anyway."

At the playdough table I take dictation from children who want to tell about their hearts.

Shane offers, "I was gonna get a drink. I'm thirsty. The heart I know. Pumps blood. The brain. The brain makes you think. And the blood that fights germs. The ribs. Protect your heart. And the place that they hold the air and those straws that you blow in. The blood things—what goes through them and it goes back to the heart to pump new blood."

Kahlil is next. "OK! I know that the 'testines are as long as our class. And the heart beats. And I know, I know, I know . . . that mine pumps. Pumps. Blood. It goes through the veins. I know that the blood that was up if you got hurt—the hole in the blood—your skin—and you put a bandaid on it to help it."

Missy comes back. "I gotta tell you about my heart. I have a heart pumping. Pumping blood. My brain says, 'There's a hole, there's a hole' and you put a Band-aid on and the blood dries up. Your knee is bent, from your bones. Your blood goes down and down to your foot. If you bend your foot, cuz you move your foot. If you want to walk. That's why the blood goes down and down. Because you can move your foot."

New Shoes

Certain people are wearing new spring sneakers and need to be noticed. Others' faces fall. I comment to the circle, "You know I really like new shoes AND old shoes. I like the way new shoes look so clean. No wrinkles. Bright colors. But lots of times new shoes don't feel so good. I love the way old shoes feel all soft and comfortable, fit my feet just right—I can see and feel the places my own toes go.

Shoes are really important to children, almost like extensions of their own body. I felt so sensitive when I came up with my warm inclusive comment—until I remembered later that children's feet are still growing, and some children wear tight outgrown shoes or hand-me-downs until their parents can afford new ones. Pride goeth before a fall.

How will they know it's you?

Nita's research paper relates to self-concept. She interviews children and asksg them to draw self-portraits. She begins, "Suppose I wanted you to meet a friend of mine, and I couldn't come over to introduce you. What could I tell my friend so she would know who you are? What do you look like?"

Missy responds immediately, "ME!"

Nita persists, "I couldn't say the girl with the purple hair and the yellow eyes, could I? Could I say Missy has brown hair, brown eyes, and a pretty smile?"

Missy snorts, "You could say she has pretty teeth! You are so silly!"

Nita asks, "Do you like being silly?"

Missy pulls herself up and poses dramatically with one hip cocked, her chin jutting out. "NO!" She stomps off.

Maybe Missy's not in the mood. Maybe she sees the limits of her reply. Whatever the reason, she draws her line with a joke. And then she makes it clear that although she may choose to joke and be goofy, no one is to trivialize her. She asserts herself easily these days.

Rosa responds to Nita with familiar delaying tactics, finally drawing while she talks. "I have brown hair and brown eyes. . . . I don't like when people will laugh at me." She colors her eyes pink, while she mutters, "Eyes, eyes, eyes, eyes." Then she moves on. "Lookit what a big mouth. Is that what looks good? Here is pink and purple teeth because I want 'em to be that way. I might be playing ring-around-the-rosy." She finishes coloring rosy cheeks. "Now wait. You're gonna have a shock of this. Look!" With a flourish she writes a large R on one of the cheeks. "Now HERE it is, the Rosa you're gonna show the people!"

She despairs of creating a realistic portrait and covers her tracks by flaunting pink eyes and teeth. Perhaps pink triggers an association with her name, Rosa, and ring-around-the-rosy. She's triumphant when inspiration hits. She allies the totemic power of her own name with the power of written language: her initial emblazoned on her portrait face.

Probably it doesn't occur to her that there's no comparable initial on her actual cheek.

Cara laughs at the whole question, dismissing it as absurd. Anyone can recognize her, she tells Nita, "Because I'm your friend!"

"But," says Nita, "there are some other children around who are my friends too. How will the person know which one is you?"

Cara looks at the ceiling then directly at Nita, leaning close to offer her solution. "*I* know! You say one of my friends her name Cara. She have long hair. She have blue shirt and you can see her pink pocketbook. Maybe she see my new shoes!"

It's inconceivable to Cara that her important relationship to Nita is not self-evident. She suggests her name, intrinsic to her self-concept. Finally she chooses clothing as an objective attribute but recognizes that a stranger might not know her shoes are new.

Ani sees Ani seeing Ani

For almost three weeks, Ani's been trying to go "over the mountain." The first few days she gets in line with the other children and starts up confidently. No big deal. Then she freezes on the third or fourth rung, refusing all offers of help. Finally she backs down, head hanging, and stands a few yards away, watching, eventually scuffing off to the swings. She won't talk about it.

I can feel how much she wants to do this and I can feel her fear. She's losing her nerve. Do I let her work this one out or do I intervene? So much comes easily to her. I've never seen her at a loss. Has she ever before faced such a big gap between her expectations and her performance? I'll give her more time to find her way through the labyrinth.

The next couple of days she runs to the play yard, approaches the big climber, and veers off to join friends in a chase game. I watch her laughing and calling to the others. She runs big circles around the climber, her eyes pulling toward it and cutting away.

I'm afraid to intrude, afraid I'll push her further underground, or worse: "rescue" her, deprive her of the chance to learn to rescue herself. Maybe what she needs most is my confidence that she can handle this alone. Hard to tell. It's the end of the year and I'm tired of watching children struggle. I want the good feeling of bailing someone out. I want to be a hero.

But that's not all that's going on. I know Ani. Independence is not her problem. Maybe this time she needs to learn she can accept help. Maybe it's her turn to try the middle ground, neither soaring solo nor bailing out, but leaning a little, trusting, risking.

One morning while we're still indoors, I take her aside. "Ani, I've got the feeling you'd like to go over the mountain. Am I right?"

She's quiet for a moment, then mumbles, "But I can't. I tried and I can't."

"You tried and you couldn't. But someday you'll be able to."

"No I won't. Never . . . Maybe when I'm seven."

"I think you can do it. This year. While you're only five."

"I can't. I CAN'T! I TRIED! I CAN'T DO IT. EVERYBODY ELSE, BUT NOT ME."

"I think it's hard for you. I think you need some help. Will you let me help you?" I can't see her face. "It might take a few days for you to relax, but I'll help you remember to use your breathing."

"But what if I fall? I might fall."

"I don't think you'll fall. All these years I've been helping children go over the mountain, no one has ever fallen. But if you fell, I'd catch you. That's why I'm there."

"I'm scared."

"Yes. Do you want to keep carrying that scared feeling around with you, or do you want to try to get rid of it? I think there's a deep-down part of you that knows how to go over the mountain already. Your arms and legs are strong, and I've seen you jump from high places."

She looks up at me, knowing it's true. "Like the sawhorse," she says.

"Yes. For some reason, the climb's harder for you than some children, but other things are easy for you. Like what?"

"Like writing. And pictures. Making stuff."

"Yes, like cutting. Scissors are easy for you, but some children need help with cutting. They have to practice a lot."

Ani looks around the room. "Like Paul."

"Right. But going over the climber was easy for Paul." She's looking at me now. I put my arm around her. *The shift has happened. We're not out of the woods yet, but her will is engaged and she realizes she trusts me.* "Remember the butterfly. She didn't just change from a caterpillar overnight. She had to eat lots and lots of milkweed."

"I brought her some," Ani said.

"You sure did!" We smile at each other. "Then she had to find a safe place to stay and be very still while the chrysalis formed. Remember how long she stayed in there? Remember how she looked when she finally split it open and crawled out? She couldn't just fly away! She hung there like a lump of wet tissue, waiting for her wings to dry. She was so beautiful when she was dry! But she still wasn't strong enough. She had to open her wings and close them over and over, until she was ready to fly."

"And then we put her on the tree, and then when we went back she was gone. To Mexico," Ani remembers, "because of winter."

"So today you and I will spend a little time helping you practice going over the mountain. We'll just keep doing it every day until you're ready."

Ani goes quiet again. "But I'm still scared."

"That's OK. You might stay scared for a while, but then you'll be ready."

The days grind by. Some mornings she cries with fear, frustration, and rage as she inches up the climber, clings, and finally backs down. The other children watch with distress, fascination, and self-satisfaction visible on their faces and audible in their comments and questions.

Finally I begin taking Ani outside for five minutes in the middle of the morning, so we can work alone together. I coach her, as I coached Zack earlier in the spring. Her mother's amazed she's tried it in the first place because mother and daughter have "always been afraid of heights."

Who knows what fear of heights is? Or fear of snakes, or fear of crowds, or fear of drowning or public-speaking? Some fears seem almost universal. Some show up in individuals in earliest infancy. Maybe Ani picked up her mother's attitude, although her sister shows no sign of it. In any case, who am I to be mucking about in a fear so deeply rooted? If I had not made a thing of going over the mountain, this never would have come up.

That's true. It would never have come up. Here. But it would have come up sooner or later in Ani's life, this fear and perhaps others like it.

There's danger in marking any developmental benchmark, even if it's within the reach of most children. What about the ones who aren't there yet? Someone may be hurt. Yet, whether or not I frame certain achievements, the children take their own notice. They all know who can zip, who can tie shoes, who rides a two-wheel, who has lost a tooth. We can't pretend these markers don't exist or ignore the passage of individual children. What we can do is to ensure that many different kinds of achievement are noted and valued. That children learn to be comfortable with differences in pace, style, gift. That these become the basis for a compassionate community, not a hierarchy.

So what do I do about Ani? Suppose, no matter how hard we both try, she just doesn't make it over the mountain? This is the first time I really may have misjudged a child's readiness to this extent. What kind of damage have I done? What about the other children watching her daily ordeal? I wish I'd never gotten us into this.

And I realize it could happen again. I'm bound to blow it from time to time. Generally I err by helping a child face fears rather than err by ignoring the monster that has come out of the closet. Some of those monsters evaporate in the course of development. But many just go deeper, changing their faces, spreading their toxins. I've seen enough of that in children and adults.

Time to face it. I've done my best to recognize, to evaluate, to intervene appropriately, and this time it isn't good enough. The butterfly's wings aren't dry. Forgive me, Ani. Forgive me. Now what can we salvage?

Today Ani and I are out at the climber. For the second time she's made it to the top and a little beyond, but she can't make herself turn around to go down the other side. She's not crying. She's learned to look down without panic, but she's rigid as a stick, her stiff arms holding her upper body off the bars, her face hard and set. She's stuck.

I can't trust myself to read her body or her thoughts. I'm not afraid of heights. But I have my own fears, and former fears. My gut tells me most of Ani's fear has worn away, leaving a very strong habit. I sense she can get out of that rut now, if I break my own rule never to physically boost or push a child who's stuck. This is the moment for a strong and risky intervention. Even if it backfires, I don't think it will be much worse for Ani.

"Ani, look how far you've come. You've done the hardest part. Rest your arms on the bars for a minute and feel how solid you are. It's time to try something new to get you going. I'm going to move your arms and legs a little to help you start the turn." As I talk, I firmly shift one of her legs, following up quickly with an arm, then the other leg and arm—rotating her body a quarter turn before she quite knows what's happening.

I place my hand on her back as she starts to wail, soothing her with my voice. "Use your breathing, Ani. Feel your body in the new place. You can do the rest yourself." She stops crying, shoots me a furious look, risks looking down, and starts to revert to her old position.

"Feel how your body knows how to go back to where you were? You can move the other way just as easily, and then you'll be on your way down the mountain."

"You turn me around," she says, glaring at me.

"Not this time. You can do the rest yourself. You know you can. Feel it. Up to you which way you want to go down. Back the way you came or the rest of the way over the mountain?"

She hesitates, shifting first one way and then the other. Tentatively, she edges into the new territory, and then she moves decisively. She's around and starting down. She looks below in disbelief, and then up at me as I sing the first notes of "Ani went over the mountain." She swings through the bottom bars and lands feet first on solid ground. I scoop her up.

Abruptly she pulls back from my hug. "I didn't really do it. You helped me. I didn't go over the mountain all by myself." *She's right. Ani will never take the easy out. I probably would have rerun it anyway.*

"That time I gave you a little push, but you did all the hard parts. *Now* you're going to do it again, all by yourself, so you'll know for sure you can. And to help wipe out the old scared feeling."

"Not right now."

"Yes, now. So you'll really believe it. It'll be easier if you do it again right away." She looks at me, reluctant but wanting to believe, needing to know. *Cross my fingers. OK, Ani girl, you can do it!*

She climbs up slowly, pauses at the top, wobbles, steadies herself, soberly makes the turn. She's halfway down when she lets herself believe it. "I DID IT! I REALLY DID IT! I WENT OVER THE MOUNTAIN MYSELF!" She flies into my waiting arms for a long warm hug, and then she speaks urgently. "I gotta go inside and write a story. Right now."

Ani beams as her classmates cluster around her with congratulations, but she calls out, "Nita, I gotta write the story of I went over the mountain."

As Nita takes dictation, Ani draws: the arch of the climber, the rungs, herself coming down, me waiting for her. The sky is blue.The yellow sun shines. At the bottom of her picture, flowers grow from vivid green grass. Ani leans back in her chair, radiant, looking at her picture while she listens to Nita read back her story out loud.

"Today I went over the climber by myself. And Sandy and the teachers were proud of me. And I always practiced on it but now I have it. And I wasn't even scared on the top when I turned around. And we went in, then I wrote a story about it and Nita was writing about the story and I drew the pictures and I like drawing pictures and Nita did it good. When it was clean-up I cleaned up very good. When it was time to go home and I told my mom about it. When my Daddy comes to see me at swimming and my sister too I told them about it and they saw the story and that really is going to happen. And then they hardly couldn't believe me and my dad made a joke that 'you couldn't do that,' and he was joking and I told my friend Stephanie. THE END."

In her story, Ani reports, reflects, and anticipates. She projects herself into the rest of the school day, predicts her family's reactions, savors in advance their amazement. "And that really is going to happen!" I'm ready to burst with delight (and relief). This child has triumphed over her fear. She's recognized her own need to capture the moment in some tangible way, and to produce a "proof" of her achievement. What a day!

But Ani's not finished. After Nita hugs her and moves off across the room, Ani pulls out another piece of paper. She's intent as she draws herself sitting at a table. Then she draws "a piece of paper" on the table. Purposefully, she reaches for her first picture and pulls it close to the work-in-progress. Looking back and forth, she fills the "piece of paper" in the second composition with a miniature copy of the original picture: Ani has drawn herself drawing herself going over the mountain.

I'm dazzled. Dazzled! Close on the heels of Ani's physical breakthrough comes this dramatic perceptual shift. Does the second drawing record her discovery, or is the drawing a revelation in process? Perhaps a little of both. There's no way to know. In any case, I've witnessed one stage of the essential unfolding of human consciousness. Ani, newly manifest. Behold, speaks her picture, I am Ani, many and various and yet one and the same. It is I who climb—I aware of myself climbing, I remembering the climbing, I making the story, I keeping the story alive in a picture, I who will hand it on. I am the one who does and the one who knows my doing. I am I, aware of myself being aware. I am the story alive, telling myself.

Ani would have come to this dawning sooner or later. Did The Bodyworks help it happen sooner? Did it nudge her to notice, represent, retain, and share her insight? I think so.

Tanya and Zack: different priorities

I'm impressed watching Nita work with Tanya. She holds her interest with a series of questions, skillfully making the point that the blood is a transport system. As they attach blood vessels to each organ, Nita concludes, "These arteries and veins deliver the food and take away the trash."

Tanya looks doubtfully at the partially inflated heart balloon. "But why's my heart so small? Everybody else got a big one." *Tanya's rivalry with her sisters makes her especially conscious of differences in status. To a physical thinker, size equals status.*

"Your balloon's not small. It's just not all blown up, because it needs to work like a pump. If it's too full of air you won't be able to squeeze it, and it might pop. Everybody got the same size balloons. Maybe some people blew theirs up a little bigger. We can blow yours up bigger if you want."

After they hang up the bodyworks, Tanya says to herself, "My backbone's tired, cuz I'm not using it." *Nita is talking to Zack at that point and doesn't respond to Tanya. I'm tied up with someone else. Bound to miss a few—I wonder what Tanya is thinking.*

Zack is tremendously excited over the X-rays. "Where's the broken one? I never broke anything. HEY! That's a 'KULL!" He jabs his finger at the eye sockets, calling Tanya to come back to see what she's missed. "A PIRATE has a 'kull and crossbones." He forms a pirate insignia with his own body, arms crossed over his chest, hands clasping his shoulders. He squeezes his eyes tight and opens his mouth to complete the picture. *Lots of complex cognition going on here. Zack is "reading" the abstract X-ray, recalling a symbol, making the association, and breathing the life of his own body into the symbol.*

Gambits, plans, and parent participation

A number of parents report their children eagerly share their new knowledge with anyone who will listen. Paul, who is normally shy with strangers, met a visitor from Canada at a christening party. He told her all about his brain, heart, lungs, and digestive tract. She listened, spellbound, and made a point of telling his mother he was a stunning tribute to his school.

Tongue-tied Maggie grabbed the phone to give her grandmother all the details of her bodyworks.

At the dinner table Zack thanked his mother for serving milk, "Because we need calcium for our bones." He went on, "It would be too hard to eat if we didn't have shoulders," and demonstrated with his arms held rigid. For his finale he tossed off, "Platelets clog your blood."

Zack, Clint, Kahlil, Shane, and Shirelle have been planning where they'll put their bodyworks on the great day they can take them home:

"I'm gonna keep mine downstairs. Not in my room."

"Mine's going in my room."

"Mine's gonna be in Mommy's room so she can look at it."

"We're gonna put mine in the dining room."

"I want mine in my room where I sleep."

Shirelle's mother brought in some old X-rays to add to our collection, saying it's the first time Shirelle's ever been excited about "school things."

Daisy's grandmother offered to lend her X-rays.

Zack's father dropped in for the first time. He looked with a scientist's interest at our assorted X-rays, and puzzled over one for a long time. Finally he concluded, "*Now* I see! This is obviously a badly broken adult femur, but the diameter's no bigger than a child's. It must be a spontaneous fracture from advanced osteoporosis."

Pip's grandfather asked if he could borrow Pip's bodyworks to show to his pinochle buddies.

Bo comes back

Bo has stunned the doctors with his quick recovery. He's out of the hospital in his half-body cast, and he wants very much to come to school. His mother doesn't feel he's ready to return full-time, but he wants me to visit him at home.

She tells me several classmates went to the hospital, were stunned almost to silence at the sight of their friend in traction, and left quickly after awkward moments. The exception was Jogger, who watched with clinical detachment when the nurses shifted Bo's position and changed bandages. He was full of questions about the procedures, despite Bo's groans of pain.

Jogger's intellectual curiosity outstripped anxiety and compassion. Perhaps this was his defense.

When I arrive, Bo's still in bed after a nap. He's been sad and lethargic, in stomach pain due to severe constipation. At first he won't look at me or say anything. His mother has told me privately that he's humiliated by the diaper under the big shorts pulled over his cast. He's afraid people will notice.

"Could I sit on your bed and hold your toes a minute?"

He nods OK. His mother bustles around, easing the awkwardness. She persuades Bo to show me his belly-board scooter. Finally the old Bo emerges, glowing as he demonstrates "belly-scooter bowling" on the living room floor. We agree he'll visit school as soon as he's feeling up to it, which turns out to be one day later.

The children are excited when they hear him in the hall. "Wait, everybody! Remember our plan. We have to give Bo time to get loaded up on his belly scooter and feeling ready to come in."

There's a long pause, then Bo's mother pokes her head in the door and draws me aside. "He wants to come in, but all of a sudden he's afraid."

Bo's pale face looks up at me from the floor. I plop down on my belly beside him and we inch toward the door. As we enter the room, the children shriek and swarm toward Bo, whose face tightens. On our bellies, the two of us are surrounded by jumping feet. I grab a rubber dinosaur and take on a deep dinosaur voice. "Hey, I've had adventures! I've got lots of things to tell people, but I don't want to start yet. It feels kind of funny to be coming back on my stomach. Why don't you kids go back to what you were doing and I'll come over to where you are."

Bo looks at me gratefully, but the children are slow to disperse. I direct them. "Shane and Shirelle, please go back to dress-ups. Cara and Missy, weren't you doing a puzzle? Kahlil, I think you were in big blocks. . . ." They reluctantly return to their activities.

As the room settles down, Bo heads for the book shelf, where Ani greets him. Little by little he begins to connect with other children. Suddenly Jogger appears and pulls up Bo's shirt. Bo lies on his stomach, defenseless, looking like he is on the verge of tears. *And probably fearing his diaper will show.* "Did you like that, Bo?" I ask him, using our standard classroom formula.

"NO!"

"Then tell Jogger, 'Get out of my shirt. Beat it, Buddy.'"

"Jogger, you lie down on your stomach in front of Bo, so he can look you in the eye and tell you how he's feeling." The room is dead silent.

Bo tells him.

Jogger has a quick comeback. "But I just wanted to see your cast."

I intervene again. "It's OK to be curious, Jogger, but you can't mess around with other people's bodies. You can *ask* if you want to see something, and maybe they'll let you and maybe they won't."

There's a pause, and then the hum of activity begins again, subdued at first. Bo resumes his circuit of the room. At circle time his mother says Bo wants to tell everybody something. Bo speaks for himself. "Just be careful. Don't try dangerous stuff." *He's back, even if it's only a visit. We're all together again.*

Ani's bladder

Ani's mother reports Ani drank a big bedtime glass of water with a satisfied smile, "That'll fill my bladder up fast and go out my urethra." *A sophisticated new version of the old bedtime stall?*

Ani asked about "baby eggs." After being told about the sperm meeting the egg, she went further: "How does it fertilize the egg?" She stopped short of asking about intercourse, though that may be in her mind.

Last week at school we suspected Ani had wet her pants, but she said nothing and we ignored it. Her mother confirmed that there had been a small "accident," but Ani was quite relaxed and straightforward about it.

Our tall young scientist is still a five-year-old. It's good to know she can allow herself a "mistake" now and then.

Taboos returning

Clint, waiting in the bathroom line, turns his head as Rosa settles on one of the two toilets in our open bathroom. "I can't look at Rosa's private parts."

Zack avoids using the toilet, saying "I don't need to pee. I tried."

Fine. The novelty has worn off. They're ready to return to taboos prevailing in the world outside the classroom. However, they return protected by experience, concepts, and language for dealing with sexuality.

Paul breaks through

Paul's awake at last. He's alert at circle, can follow directions for bodyworks, and enjoys fiddling around with many kinds of materials. He's even holding up in some high-powered play with peers. But he's often at a loss when there's a problem to solve. More messing around is the answer, but I want to see if I can jump-start him. He's lost so much time in his prolonged "infancy."

I swallow my aversion to the Ninja Turtle book he's brought to school. Might as well begin where he is.

"Hey, Paul, let's see if we can build a Turtle."

"OK, if you want to. I got my Turtles book."

"I know. That's what gave me the idea."

I put the bin of notched disks on a table and pull out chairs for us. He sits, hands in lap. I pick up a big disk. "Maybe we could use this for the shell. What could we use for the head?" He fumbles around in the box and comes up with another large disk. He can't align the slots to attach the two big disk. He goes limp, slumps further into his chair.

Paul's a bright four-year-old. Is there some perceptual motor problem? Is there learned helplessness? Maybe I have to begin at the beginning, not with problem-solving but with modeling. I narrate my process as I select a triangle for the head and slot it on, then add four small circles for the feet. "Should we put a tail?"

He nods. "They gotta have a tail."

I stick a small triangle in place. "There's my turtle. Your turn. Which turtle will you make?"

"I'm gonna do Donatello. He's my best one." Paul is animated now, trying to copy mine. He picks up an additional triangle "for the neck," but he can't insert it. He stabs at each notch on the body disc. Finally he dumps it and fumbles with the small circles. Many minutes later he has his Donatello.

He seems to have more trouble orienting up and down than left and right. Yesterday he was making a birthday card for his mother. I got out the rubber letters for him to copy MOM. He wrote WOW, then inverted the model letters to match his work. He saw the mismatch. Maybe he thought orientation was irrelevant as long as everything matched. Maybe he just didn't want to go to the effort of rewriting.

If Paul were another child, I would assume this is some form of "mirroring" and will correct itself with maturation. But with Paul, I'm not so sure. He can answer questions about where his neck is, my neck is, turtle's neck is, but in construction he seems confused. For most children the more concrete operation is the easier one. Not for Paul. Like his former daycare teacher, I have questions about this child. His perception seems on target, but he can't act on what he seems to see.

Three days later I try again to figure out what's going on with Paul. I put a big rubber giraffe on the table in front of us. "I've never tried to draw a giraffe before. Where do you think I should start?"

"Giraffes have long necks," he says.

"They sure do. If I start with the neck, I've got to remember to put it in the middle of my paper, so I'll have room to put a head on top and legs on the bottom."

Before beginning to draw, I get up from the table to deal with a paint spill. When I get back, Paul pushes the paper at me. "Look!" he says. "I made a giraffe!"

And there it is, the long neck, a small oval head, and a lumpy rectangle with four leg lines in perfect proportion. "Wow, Paul! That's terrific! I didn't know you could draw giraffes."

"It's my first one."

I mentally muzzle myself, resisting the temptation to "teach Paul something" by articulating the process that led to his breakthrough. How do I know for sure, anyway? Maybe it was just the miracle of readiness. I won't stop watching for perceptual motor difficulties, but I'm much less concerned. He's on his way now. I'm sure of it. It's likely The Bodyworks has helped him wake up to his own body, which opens him to turtle bodies, giraffe bodies, the whole universe of structures:

parts in relation to wholes. He was for so long at the threshold. Now he's walked through the door.

Cara's stomach ache

Under the big climber Cara and Missy are playing with Clint. Missy announces proudly, "I can SWIM. I did it at my lesson."

Clint looks at her approvingly. "Neat!" His face falls a little. "I can put my head under water." *They've hit the swimming connection before. Missy has definitely made some points.*

Cara sparkles. "Pretend we're in JAIL!" *She has a brilliant idea and she puts it right out.*

Clint picks it up immediately, directing the girls: "Let's climb through the bars and escape." He goes through.

Cara calls after him, "You get us out. Right?" *For all her changes, Cara is still Clint's sidekick.* Missy starts to follow him.

"Not yet, Missy. You have to wait till I come get you!" He turns to Cara. "Cara, you have to call my name, OK?"

Cara begs in a small, pathetic treble, "Clint, save us!"

When it comes to role-play with each other, Cara and Clint are stuck in the ruts of their long-standing relationship: the helpless lady and her knight. Elsewhere they've outgrown those roles. Missy's potentially a catalyst for change. She and Cara have become good friends, and their play is often loud and vigorous. Missy and Clint have connected indoors over bodyworks, books, and puzzles, but they have no fixed script. Clint may be ready to try something new.

At snack time Clint invites Missy to sit next to him, but Cara won't move over to make room even when he asks her. Cara's face is heavy with grief as she tells Nita, "I want Clint to sit next to ME!"

Outdoors Missy and Clint are playing Dalmatians with a batch of other children. Cara trudges over to me, dragging her feet. "Me tummy ache."

"I'm sorry you don't feel good, Cara. Here, climb in my lap.You know sometimes when our feelings hurt, we feel hurt in our bodies too, but it's not the same kind of tummy ache as when we're sick. I've been noticing Clint and Missy getting to be friends, and when they're playing together sometimes you get tummy aches. I bet it was hard for you at snack today. When our feelings are hurt, we don't need medicine. We need love. I'm glad you came over to get some. It might take a while to feel better. Maybe it would help if you think about the new friends you'll have next year in your new school."

Cara has just visited kindergarten. She brightens. "New school have THREE chairs in dress-up!"

After a while, I go on. "Lots of times you and Clint and Missy have fun all together. You could play Dalmatians with them right now."

"No," says Cara. "Stay here."

"You can sit in my lap as long as you want."

After a few minutes she runs off to swing.

Until the day she worked on her self-portrait with Nita, Cara's face rarely gave cues to her feelings or thoughts. Even under the cloak of Clint's protection she seemed blank and unresponsive. Children rely on many nonverbal cues in their play with each other. Cara provided too few, and they avoided her. Her sparse language exacerbated her difficulties.

As The Bodyworks moved forward, Cara seemed to trust increasingly that, whatever her "differences," she was deeply "the same" as others. She belonged. She took the risk of letting her feelings show. We watched her begin to glow and sparkle, and the other children caught her fire. With the joy of her new capacity for relationship comes the inevitability of pain. The eternal triangle hurts, at four or fifty.

The Spirit of Inquiry

The children and I are learning a lot about the spirit of inquiry. It takes constant vigilance to protect the circle in which real questioning and answering can flourish.

Before I introduced the concept of growpower a couple of weeks ago, I asked, "What's the most powerful thing in the world?" Hands flew up and answers fountained forth, without interruptions. We were on our way. Shane was last to speak. He took me by surprise with "Stones." I asked him why stones were so powerful. Shane knew exactly. "Because nobody can break 'em, not even with a saw or a sword."

Clint raised his hand to offer firsthand experience to the contrary. "At Grandma's. She has a pile of rocks. And I banged one rock on this other rock, and I busted it open."

Jogger broke in. "They can with a jackhammer."

Other children were waving their hands. Shane was looking at his lap. For Shane's sake, I wanted to stave off further challenges. "Tanya, why do you think butterflies are so powerful?"

"Cuz they have long tongues and they're beautiful and if you touch their wings something might happen."

Zack burst out, "If you touch butterflies' wings, they can't fly. The dust comes off. The . . . scales."

Tanya immediately swiveled to peck on a weaker chick. "Maggie said trees. Trees aren't powerful cuz a saw can break 'em."

The tone of discourse was definitely deteriorating. We had begun innocently enough, with me exploring Shane's thought and Clint contributing relevant data, but we were descending fast into the vortex of competition. The downward spiral had to be checked.

"Stop for a minute and notice what's happening to our circle. We don't push on each other's bodies, but we're starting to push on each other's ideas. That's not OK. We have to be careful with people's feelings even if we don't agree with their ideas. If we put down each other's answers, we won't feel safe sharing our thoughts. We have to make it safe and fun for everyone to offer ideas. Our job right now is to really listen to all the ideas. We can let our brains work quietly for a while, growing some ideas bigger and stronger, dropping what we can't use. If everybody gives ideas and everybody listens, we'll all have much more to work with."

These children are four and five years old. I didn't want to leave the impression that all ideas, opinions, feelings, and facts should be dumped into one big slush pile. There is a time for sorting and weighing, finding solid ground to stand on. But when it comes to these earliest experiences in the community of discourse, my priority is safety, power-with. I want each child to speak and to question without fear, to listen creatively, to respect and trust the collective evolutionary process that enriches the community.

Apparently the children took it all in. A true spirit of inquiry is building. A process has evolved. When I ask the circle, "Does anyone have a question about bodies?" many hands go up. I gather all the questions first, writing each one down as it comes.

This approach allows each child to be heard quickly, before time and distractions chase away the original intent. It gives each child the dignity of a pause, an entry into my little yellow notebook. It gives children time to think while the questions settle. It provides feedback for me on many individual children, and it allows me to frame the ensuing discussion, focusing on the likely high spots before attention wanes. The children accept the fact that we can't answer every question every day. Our process makes questions important in and of themselves.

Many questions strike me as shallow, bids for a moment in the sun. Many questions are repeats, although some may represent a new grow-

ing edge for the child who's asking. I'm wary of my own appetite for novelty and the cultural norm of competition—Who can ask the newest, most interesting question?—so I take care to allot time for reruns as well as "new" questions. Increasingly I refer the children's questions about their bodies back to the circle of peers, guiding the discourse, offering less and less input of my own.

Here are some recent questions and answers from the circle of children.

Why do you got a tongue?

So we can talk. / While you're talking, if you didn't have a tongue then you can't. / Or we can't lick ice cream. / Or we can't taste things.

Why do we have eyes?

Like you couldn't go across bridges with no railing.

Why do we have fingernails?

If you didn't have any fingernails, you won't be able to scrub 'em. / It protects your skin. It's not a good place for poison ivy. / Keeps blood from falling out. / Then you couldn't put fingernail polish. / It gets dirty with fingernails and you have to clean up. / Fingernails are like a shell.

Why do you have fingers?

You don't pick anything up. / You can't dig. / You can't use a shovel. / You can't do this if you're working at the Chinese restaurant *[pantomime of waiter balancing a heavy tray on fingertips]*. / You can't eat something.

Why do we have toes?

You couldn't walk without toes. You might slip and fall. / You won't be able to tiptoe. / Then if you were going roller skating, you couldn't put your toe to stop.

Why do you have hair?

Because then you can move your hair, that if it's in your eyes. / To keep your head warm. / To keep your skin from getting dirty on your head. / For people to pull his hair. / Then if you had a long hair that your pony grows down to your face and then if you didn't have hair you can't make it out your face with a barrette. / So if you're going down a waterfall, people could just reach down and get it.

Why do you have energy in your body?

Because then you can run and hop. / So you can jump real high. / Or then you could jump rope.

Why do you have a brain?

To think. / Your brain helps your body work. / Your brain tells all the other parts of your body what to do. / To listen. / Talk to people.

Why do we have eyebrows?
Your eyebrows can move, that you can see. / If you're mad, you can just make a mad face *[knits brows into a scowl]*.

Why do we have a face?
To see. / Or we won't be able to talk / You can smile *[grinning broadly]*. / To eat.

Why do you go tippy toes?
So you can walk on 'em because if your feet get cold. / So you can lean.

Why do you have breath?
You wouldn't be able to breathe. If you have old air, you wouldn't be able to get new air.

I love to see how the questions and answers evolve. Periodically I call the children's attention to the way they build on each other's contributions. I can't resist interpolating a few questions and answers of my own, but very few. At this point the children's process is much more important than any concepts or facts I could offer.

A Rosa is a Rosa is a Rosa

Bodyworks has generated a great deal of physical awareness and energy, helped to affirm and expand self-concepts. As it happens, the current media craze amplifies these effects. Disney must have just released "A Hundred and One Dalmatians" on video—and, of course, a lot of merchandise to go with it. Everywhere I turn I see spots. Most of the children are "playing Dalmatians" on the playground, in the block corner, everywhere.

"Dalmatians" contrast dramatically with autobots, transformers, dinosaurs. The players act more like the young animals they are imitating: more expressive, more joyous, more spontaneous. The resulting drama is less predictable, more chaotic. There's another major difference: two strong female characters. Stereotypes, to be sure, but a change of pace from the simpering damsel in distress.

Rosa alternates between the roles of Perdie, the quintessential good doggie-mother, and Cruella de Ville, the evil dognapper. In the role of Perdie, she crawls around yipping and nipping her mischievous puppies into submission. "I used to have a hundred puppies and they kept coming and coming and now I have bazillions. See, I'm really good and I win everything. Sometimes I don't want to do it even, but they make me because I'm so good at it."

In the role of Cruella, Rosa takes a long feather duster and inserts it into a cardboard tube, pointing it at a puppy and viciously spitting out stock phrases, "Say your prayers, sister!" She seizes a long string of beads from the dress-up jewelry to use as a whip but, after a reminder from me, her gestures are controlled, symbolic. *Whips and leashes are never allowed.*

Deep into the Cruella persona, Rosa gathers scarves and ties and begins binding children's hands and feet to chairs and to each other. I ask Shane, Pip, Missy, and Cara: "Is it OK with you when Rosa ties you up like that?"

They wag and bark at me, "Woof, woof! We like it. It's a fun game!"

"Well, it doesn't feel safe to me. If we had an emergency, like a fire, you couldn't get out right away. I'll show you the way to make it LOOK real, but keep it easy for you to get out quickly if you need to or want to."

As the days go by, I keep close watch over the Dalmatians. It's good to see that, for all her intensity, Rosa respects the limits and occasionally takes a turn as a puppy. Other children try other roles too, all but Paul, who's stretching just to keep up with the action. Missy surprises me with her vehemence as Cruella.

Rosa's giving Terry a hard time. I walk briskly over to investigate, but before I can say a word, Rosa beats me to the punch. "Take your shirt off, Sandy!" *No doubt some adult has responded to her agitation with "Keep your shirt on, Rosa!"*

At circle I tell the children that everything keeps changing, going around and around. "Just imagine! Right now I'm breathing in a little crumb of air—scientists call it a molecule of oxygen—that's been going around for hundreds, thousands, millions of years. At the very beginning, that little molecule was in space, then in the water, then plants started to grow and breathed it in and out. Dinosaurs breathed it too. The little molecule of oxygen kept going around. Maybe a cave man breathed it in and out, then more trees and people until . . . Suppose it went in and out of Harriet Tubman? And then more trees and people, maybe even Martin Luther King? There's no telling how many people and plants sent it around and around, until finally I just breathed it in. My lungs are sending it into my blood to travel all through my body."

Harriet Tubman and Martin Luther King are our heroes. Rosa's eyes are shining. She voices the wonder. "It all just goes around and around, like a circle." Then she starts the downward slide. "How did all those people die?"

The children have heard my answer many times. "Mostly they died because it was time. Their hearts stopped beating, their breath stopped coming and going."

Rosa comes back to her concern. "And maybe there was HARM."

"To some of them, yes. But usually they died just because it was time."

Ani shifts the topic. "The dinosaurs died because it was COLD."

In thumbprints, Rosa is smearing paint around the paper. I give her a little demonstration of how to make letters and patterns. Rosa leans back in her chair while I wind it up, then she looks me in the eye. "You're going too far, Sandy. I don't care and I don't care. That's the rule of me."

You can't fool me, Rosa. You do care and you do care, and you get overloaded. You need to do some messing around. I get it. I note she didn't fume and fret over this one. She'll have to modify her "attitude," but for now it's enough that she recognizes her need and keeps her cool. She's come a very long way.

It's been one incident after another with Rosa today. The latest is a solo variation on the Dalmatians, in which she's overturning chairs, jostling tables. "Daisy's dog is lost. I gotta hunt him."

By this time in the year, most children can effectively apply the brakes for each other, complaining that someone's too loud, and so forth. Today there's a lot of intensity and energy in the air. Rosa could magnetize the group. We could end up with a massive out-of-control dog hunt. Time for a little preventive maintenance. "Well, you have to hunt him more slowly and quietly."

"Well, I can't. I gotta find him in a hurry, or he'll escape forever."

"Rosa, do you think Daisy's dog is really in this classroom?"

She makes a face. "Nope."

"Then the hunt is a good game, a pretend, and you can keep it in control. If you don't keep it in control, I'll do it for you."

She sputters and spins her body away from me, outraged. Moments later she's back at it, ramming chairs against tables, calling out at the top of her voice.

"It's too much, Rosa. Everyone's getting upset, and sooner or later, someone is going to get hurt. I'm making a safe space for you to take some time by yourself." At the edge of the room I create a nest with pillows and books and puzzles. "Would you like to talk about it?"

Her face is tight. "No, cuz you'll say Daisy's dog isn't really lost."

"It's up to you. When you feel like you're in control, let me know."

Rosa curls up in the pillows, turning her face away. A couple minutes later I check. She's still curled up. I keep checking every five minutes or so. She's relaxed, doing puzzles, looking at books, not ready to emerge. Finally she calls out to me, "I have a loose thread." *This is her way to reconnect without risk or capitulation—and it is a rich metaphor too.*

I snip the loose thread off her buttonhole and sit down among the pillows. She climbs into my lap, snuggly and relaxed. Finally I dare say, "I've been noticing a lot of days you get very mad when I say something about you pretending or playing a game. Does it feel like I'm telling you that what you're doing is silly or not important—is that what makes you mad?"

"No."

"You know that I love make-believe. I think pretending's important for children, grown-ups too. But we have to remember it's a game. We have to keep it in control. Do you know why? Because it's important for you not to scare yourself too much, *and* because when you scare yourself too much, you can hurt other people. My job is to help you see what's happening, so you can control yourself."

Rosa puts her arms around my neck and gives me a big kiss. "I know. I really love you, Sandy. You're my best teacher I ever had. I'm gonna miss you when school's over." *Oh, and I am going to miss you, Rosa. That's part of what's going on in all of us right now. Around the edges there's lots of talk about the end of the year. We're not ready to let go, none of us, and the grief's building up.*

Shane and Zack have agreed to disagree in blocks. Zack stalks off. Rosa sees Shane's eyes filling with tears and she goes over and pats him on the back. "I know it's really tough to be sad, but sometimes you just gotta let it go and think of the good things of life." *It'll probably be years before she can fully walk that talk, but she's on her way. Bravo!*

Bodyworks rampant!

The wrap-up of bodyworks construction's moving along smoothly, almost anticlimactically. I don't have to keep such close track of it. I can stop now and then to take a long look around the room. The real action is everywhere else. The curriculum seems to have taken root in every cranny of consciousness and unconsciousness. Over several days, I note the sproutings of The Bodyworks in the children's free play.

Tanya's talking to Terry: "I have kids at home. Pretend. But I pretend it's real. Their names are Clint, Zack, Shane, and Bo. My husband died. His name was Kahlil. He ate bad broccoli." *Another one of Tanya's husbands falls victim to bad broccoli.*

This time Tanya's in dress-up. "A baby popped out," she tells Daisy. "A flower. A head."

It's the glory days of warm spring, not only for children but also for bees, ants, and spiders. Everyone's full of questions about bugs. Zack brings in a book with a diagram of a honeybee's body and a tulip from his mother's garden so we can see the pollen. At circle I have a wonderful time playing the role of a zealous bee happily gathering nectar until a scared child swats me and I sting. Back in teacher persona, I copy the diagram from the book onto the easel "because trying to draw it helps me really see and remember all the parts." I deliver a running monologue of my thought process as I sort out and combine geometric forms to produce a clumsy facsimile of the original. The children offer suggestions, encouragement, and corrections. *They identify with my struggles with representational drawing.*

Maggie and Ani are a rare pair in dress-up. Ani wears the white coat with the stethoscope, looking very much the doctor, while Maggie lies "in bed" on the table, her shirt pulled up. Ani applies "a turneykit" to Maggie's wrist. Then she reaches for the plastic drill from the toy tool box and holds it to Maggie's stomach. Maggie says, "Just a checkup." Ani tells her imaginary assistant, "Cut her head off."

Kahlil loads his thumb with black tempera from the saturated printing sponge. His print is very wet. He places a clean piece of newsprint over the first one, then peels it off to see the second edition. He settles in for a long session of thumbprints, testing to see how many generations he can get from a single fat blob.

Every year, eternally hopeful, I set up thumbprints during The Bodyworks. It's always a flop: the different patterns of whorls are far too subtle to capture the children's attention, even with a chart, a magnifying glass, and a teacher to help. I juice up the possibilities by adding Ed Emberly's drawings of whimsical thumbprint creatures, but most children give these only a perfunctory try. They're far more interested in experimental smearing than designing, and fingerpaints are more satisfying for this purpose. Occasionally somebody really flies with thumbprints. Kahlil's not exactly flying, but he's extending and discovering. And thumbprints are a low-energy activity for the teacher, something I especially appreciate during The Bodyworks.

Pip has dead-and-alive on his mind. In dramatic play, he explores cannibalism. With the dinosaur puzzles he focuses on the lower layer, where the bones are printed. "This is when he's dead." He works long and deliberately, cutting out large pieces of construction paper. Finally he tapes it all together and holds it up, beaming. "It's a Easter bunny," almost as big as its creator, with separate segments for "his body, his head, his ears, his arms, and his legs."

Missy, Cara, and Tanya rush in early each morning to claim the big blocks, once a territory dominated by boys. Instead of towers and runways, they concentrate on fences and other protective enclosures. *The signs of empowerment are clear in what they do, where they do it, and how they hold their ground.*

Missy goes out on the porch with Paul, Zack, and Maggie. She runs over to the pyramid ladder, climbs to the top and smiles down at Paul and Zack. Zack shouts to Paul, "Let's chase the girls."

Missy leaps from the ladder and huddles with Maggie in the corner, her eyes crinkling with laughter. Zack calls over, "Don't touch the tire. We're making a trap."

Missy grins, hops onto a sawhorse, extends her arms, and proceeds across with the easy grace of a tightrope walker. At the end she turns to look straight at the boys, her eyes flashing and her smile triumphant, daring them without a word. Zack and Paul look at her soberly. "I'm not afraid to jump," says Zack slowly, and carefully climbs up onto the sawhorse, hesitating long and hard before his leap.

Missy hasn't developed these skills overnight, but it's only since The Bodyworks began that she's exhibited them at school. The timid observer has disappeared. In her place we see this energetic child, whose playfulness makes her popular with boys and girls. Zack himself has come a long way from his trembling efforts to go "over the mountain."

Shane and Kahlil hide behind the playhouse. When I approach, they poke their heads over the roof. "We have no bodies!" *They can take my perspective enough to understand that, from my vantage point, their bodies are hidden from the neck down. A classic demonstration of a classic developmental shift.*

Shane, Paul, and Jogger collide while they're running down the hill, and fall laughing in a heap. They begin to unscramble themselves. "Hey! Don't hit me on my pelvic bone."

Daisy, overhearing Terry talking about an interview with the Human Services Department in "the state of Virginia," pipes up "*I* know about the state of vagina."

The whole room's humming with energy. Crawling and chasing games abound. The children make themselves into deer, mice, rabbits, dogs—fluid and quick—in contrast to the slow-grinding transformers and robots. There's a lot of body contact and high-energy physical play involving both boys and girls. *Is it the weather, the increased awareness of bodies, the removal of taboos, the widespread emergence of strong new personalities? Probably all of the above!*

The deep roots are sending up new sprouts too. Right before "Secret Place," we do a little yoga to smooth out the energy. These days many children are coming up with their own new stretches. Shane contributes My Kitty, lying down in a crescent, which he contrasts to the classical yoga Cat pose. Maggie shares A Table, face up, back rigid between supporting legs and arms. Ani displays The Cecropia in honor of the moth we were privileged to observe just after it emerged from the cocoon. Shirelle shows us sit-ups—she's thinking about what to name them. Even Paul's practicing The Tree, and I can hardly believe his poise when I look around the circle of balanced bodies. *He was so floppy and droppy before Bodyworks began.*

Cara giggles as she walks under the bodyworks hanging from the line. She calls me over. "Look. It's fun! They tickle."

"Are you in a leg forest?"

Cara loves the whole experience, and repeats it each day for several days. "Look, I'm in the leg forest!" *It's often terrifying for small children to be in crowds of adults. Here she can enjoy a pleasant sensation and play with a humorous concept.*

In dress-ups, Clint playfully pinches Missy on the bottom. Neither child sees me see it. She grins to herself and says nothing to him. I elect not to put a wedge between these two in the bloom of their new friendship. Later I ask Missy, "Do you like to have your bottom pinched?"

"NO."

"Then tell your friends not to do it. Sometimes we're afraid to tell friends we don't like something, in case they won't want to play with us. But that doesn't work. It makes things uncomfortable. We need to tell friends how we really feel, especially if they touch us in a way we don't like." *I suspect Missy* did *like it some, felt it as playful and affectionate. There's no need for her to lose innocence over this, but it's important to affirm her ability to draw lines for friends.*

Shirelle's in the book corner with Shane. She stretches out on her side on the floor, throwing one shoulder back, cocking her hip, tossing her long hair, and batting her eyelashes at him, saying nothing: the classic Hollywood vamp. *I can't put the blame for this on The Bodyworks! Shirelle's been doing this all year. I'd like to strangle the adults who think it's cute to ask little girls, "Who's your boyfriend?"*

Jed, an eight-year-old Bodyworks alumnus, spends a morning as a classroom helper. When Terry calls Tanya over to work on a project, Tanya heaves a heavy sigh, sets her shoulders, and scuffs over to the table. Then she catches sight of Jed. She sits down next to him, head bent. She tilts her chin, rolls her eyes up, and shifts into a husky "shy" voice when she's introduced. Jed asks if she's ready to start. Tanya produces a dazzling smile, tosses her hair, lifts one shoulder, and offers breathlessly, "I guess so."

It's not just Shirelle. The stereotypes are everywhere, and they are powerful.

Rosa brings in a huge nightcrawler for everyone to examine. She tells us "There's fifteen screaming babies inside it." *If a hundred and one Dalmatians, why not fifteen nightcrawlers?*

Maggie and Ani are at the writing cart again. Maggie draws and cuts out a cat and a frog. Ani spends a very long time on her bird: beak, tail, wings. *Comparative anatomy again.*

In dress-ups, Pip and Paul are stuffing their shirts with plastic fruit.

I ask, "Are you playing pregnant ladies?"

Paul answers, "We got big breasties."

Pip confides, "We really are pretending to have babies." Some things have changed for the better. *When I was growing up in the forties and fifties, lots of girls went through a cowboy phase, but boys never tried out "pregnant." I'm glad they can now. Pretending lets out a lot of the steam.*

Zack's own myth

It's Zack's turn to make a World today. He chooses a very small plastic figure wearing a red cape, and builds an elaborate set. Zack calls it "a mixed-up World," in which "a little red superhero with a blue horse" contends with a dinosaur, a witch, a vampire, skeletons, an octopus, and more. The little red superhero enlists the aid of other creatures. Finally he triumphs. "First he was just a toy. They found something wrong with him and they threw him away. But Mother Nature gave him Super Powers."

I dare to say, "Did the little red superhero practice going to his Secret Place? Is that how he got in touch with his Super Powers?" *Ugh. That popped out of my teacher mouth. I shouldn't have said it. Zack's World is no place for me to intrude my agenda.*

Zack nods excitedly. "But FIRST, he was a KID!" He meets my hug more than halfway. *Thank heavens I shut up in time. Wow! This little old man is growing down at last.*

"That's a very interesting story, Zack. I'm excited about your World. I think you know a lot about being a strong person in a mixed-up world. That's really important to me." He dashes off to invite friends to see his World and hear the story.

Later I explain to the circle that snack's late, ". . . because there were so many interesting things going on today . . ."

Zack interrupts, "Like my story. It was interesting AND important."

"Yes, Zack, it was a very interesting story."

He persists, "And IMPORTANT. You said it was IMPORTANT TO YOU!"

Tears of joy spring to my eyes and my biggest grin spreads from ear to ear, "Yes, Zack. It WAS important!" *Zack never mentioned growpower or worms in his World, much less the food chain or interspecies cooperation. He's done something far more significant than return to me the concepts Bodyworks offered him. He has made them his own: Super Powers.*

"Assessment Time?"

I don't need to prove to myself or anyone else what these children have learned. There isn't a way to test this kind of learning anyway. It's already deep in the children's pores, their bones, their hearts, the very way they see themselves and move through the world.

Yet I'm interested in knowing what sticks out for each one right at this point, or at least what they can articulate in the midst of everything else that's calling for their attention. Some years I do this "assessment" in a vacuum, with no props to tickle the memory. Some years I send all the bodyworks home and ask the children days later what they remember. This year I take each child aside with her bodyworks and ask her to tell me what she remembers about it. I write everything down verbatim.

Shirelle: "Well, I know her's me. Well, my body. I decided I was gonna make my body. Then I made these . . . some are called . . . well, the veins carry blood to your heart to get more air. Your stomach is when some food is left it slips down into this thing. Then you have to go to the bathroom every time when I go home. That air—out of your mouth. The black stuff I forgot. The spinal cord so your brain can come down your back. Your brain tells you when it's hot or cold."

Pip: "Once there's this little boy named Pip and then he was walking along. THEN he went to a friend's house and his mom let him. And then he was playing with the friend and then the friend went to his house. And the friend was Kahlil! And then the body was walking along. And then his bones is moving, like a jungle. And then his feet is like a jungle. Stop like a jungle. And then his heart was being faster. And then his brain was thinking and his heart was stopped beating faster. And then he has muscles. They moved. They moved like this: like 'HI' and 'BYE.' And then he's getting fresh air, a lot of fresh air. From outside he's getting a lot of energy. Then the food." Pip giggles. "He doesn't have much food, because he has a little bit. It's like getting crunched up. And then he chews it all up. And he gets sick." He gives me a broad grin. "I think that's the end."

Tanya: "She has lungs. They blow air in and out. She has a heart that pumps. And she has a mouth to talk. And she has eyes to see. And she has a nose to smell. And she has ribs, rib cages to protect the lungs. She has hands. They can move their muscles. And she has legs—to move her muscles. And she has toes to walk. And she has a tummy. Tummy's job is to get all the food. It goes down your throat into your tummy. And she has. Food goes into your tummy and it gets all scrambled up. And when it's not food for your body, it comes out your bunnies. The brain. It sends messages. And it sends when something's hot, it sends messages. 'Hot, hot' and then you move it. If you have a baby . . . here. Pee."

Zack: "Once upon a time, I don't know about Zack. I don't know about that body. The heart and the veins and I remember everything . . . I remember the lungs and the heart and the veins, and the stomach, and the rib cage, and the veins and the heart and the intestines, and the esophagus, and the arm bones, and the fingerbones, and the other arm bones, and the feet bones, and the leg bones. That's what I remember. And the bladder and the penis and the bottom. The lungs breathe in and out. Like this. You're breathing. Heart's a little out of air. The stomach has the food in it. Your body grinds it up. Through there and out there. Are you made of all this stuff, Sandy? Do you really have paper? NO!"

Daisy: "A heart. It pumps your blood around your body. Oxygen. Blood cells carry the blood. Lungs. They hold your air. Ribs. They protect your lungs. Bones. They make your body so it doesn't go flat. Food goes in your stomach. It goes all around to your body. Go bathroom. Milk goes to your bladder. Toilet. Your womb. Your vagina. Food goes down in your stomach and goes to your body, and then goes here to the opening the junk comes out. My feet. My legs."

Paul: "The heart. It pumps. Goes like this. Those blow up. What is the blue? Food. It's grinding up." He points to the bladder. "Penis. Down to his foot. Spine. The brain tells you to move. He's touching your pencil with his foot." He stretches the muscles, moves the foot over. "How old is he? Four. If you're four, that makes him four."

Cara: "Sandy, I got different color shoes. I DON'T got 'em. Me put my new shoe and my old shoe. They're different! A heart. Pump bump pump bump. Making the blood! Bones! Move! Lungs. Air. Get a new air. Food. In the tummy. Going in the bathroom. Orange juice. For a baby come out. Know what I call my baby when I done? When I grow and have a baby? Bone!" She laughs out loud, and flashes me a huge smile. "Nothing else!"

Clint: "I worked a really lot of time to do it. I have blood. It pumps air in and it does lots of things to help you. Well, some people don't know about it, but some people do, and some people know about it when they're one years old. A bodies do lots of things that help us so we can walk. We got muscles so we can do lots of things. You got arms and you got legs. But mostly we are doing stuff for our bodies. Inside we do lots of things. Like your brain tells you move and the bathroom, to go to the bathroom. Your blood goes all over you when you drink stuff, even when you're playing. Your old blood it stays in your body and then it has to go out for lots of years—when you're a grandma. And then it gets more so you can live more, if you're a grandma or a puppa."

Maggie: "I don't know! The heart. Pumps. Air. Air! Food. You poop."

Jogger: "I have a heart. The heart pumps blood. What you call the thing that goes thick, thick, thick? The platelets! My brain. It tells me what to do. The brain's the boss. I need clean air. I don't need bad air. I don't need dirty air. The lungs. I have bones. The bones keep you up. If you didn't have bones, you just fall down. A nose. I have a penis. I got joints. You can bend. I got muscles. They keep you strong. And what helps your muscles and becomes your insides—milk! Food goes through your pipe all through your body and then things they make energy. Squeeze, squeeze, squeeze. Poopoo!"

Shane: "It has blood cells. They deadly germs. And you have blood to get all the food down. Into your blood. And the nerves come up to your spinal cord. And then to your brain. And you have nerves. But sometimes butter gets stuck, when you're old. And THEN you have parts, that used-up blood. Blue parts. And the bony places. And the bones are like jails, and like bars. And your brain thinks, to everything. And if you eat food, healthy food like milk, it goes down to your body and what's your bony place in your mouth and you stick in it? And you have a Adam's apple. And your Adam's apple sticks up. And you clean your body real clean. And you should brush your teeth and drink milk. Cuz it's healthy. Food gets all crunch-ded up, like in pieces, and then your brain tells you to go to the bathroom. The End."

Rosa: "She's a little pain in the neck. Me. Cuz I needed to put some hearts on the blue. That's the same way the dress looked-ed. Heart. It pumps and brings blood AND your lungs. They breathe in and out. And your tummy. It chews up all the things and then it goes through the bloodstream. It gets a little tired and it goes into your rec . . . plod. After it's been plod a little bit, your brain tells it to go down and it goes down. It goes into the toilet when you go. The heart really pumps the blood. But the lungs breathe in and out to give this ockagen to the heart. It's to keep this birdcage from things that are not good for it. The platter. After it's in the platter, it goes into the toilet." She reaches over for the magnifying glass on the table. "Pee goes out from, that's where your vagina. That's where your baby grows. Your belly needs to be strepped open to get the baby. But how DOES it? . . . Anyway two legs. I don't want to talk about that. The bones hold your thumb. If you didn't have a thumb you could only pick up like that." (She demonstrates with four fingers.)

Kahlil: "I like heart. Pumps the blood. White blood cells. They fight the germs. Blue veins make the blood thick, thick, thick. I like my body! I like my feet. I also like my brain. The brain tells you to go poops. The stomach. It crunches the food. Lungs. They get the fresh air. I got it what's inside the blood—the blood carries new fresh air. The SHIN. Your anklebone's connected to it. My foot bone's connected to it. My elbow's connected to this arm."

Ani: "I know about the bones. The muscles. The joints. In your fingers. I know that . . . I forget. Leg bones. We have special kind of bones, the thighbones. I don't know what else. The arm bone. The skin bone. The blue things if you get a cut, like a car driving through your body, it'll come to your cut and block it up. My mom messed up on the skin when she was reading that book I brought it. Blood, blue blood. Platelets. The stomach. The food tube. The food goes all through your body. The rib cage protect the little baggies and the heart. The skull. The ribs protect your heart and your little baggies. Where the baby grows. The stretchy place. I'm making a picture of inside my body."

Missy: "She's playing. She asked her mommy to get her a drink of water. And then she found a rabbit to play with. But she didn't want to play with the rabbit. Because she didn't like the color of it. She wanted the rabbit to be green, but the rabbit was yellow." Missy's portrait features green pants and a yellow shirt. "The heart. The heart pumps fresh air for the blood. Then the heart sends the brain and message. And then our lungs say something to the heart. And then the heart tells the brain tells the heart there's something hot that we're touching. Then the brain tells heart that we need to go peepees. And then the brain tells the blood to back up to get some more fresh air from the heart. And then the muscles tell the blood to get some more fresh air. The stomach takes all the food. The lungs take all the food and then everything takes all the food, cuz food helps us get energy. Cuz the fresh air helps us get energy and so does the blood. Then we eat more and then we get more energy. And then we drink and get more fresh air and more energy. Then it gets to our bum."

Well, they don't know everything there is to know. They've got some things mixed up. But they're only four and five years old. Hey, it's a start! The genitals no longer dominate the scene, but the children have the language and the practice and the permission, ready when they need it.

Elbow Tag and Mirroring

Outdoors I organize elbow tag. The children and grown-ups stand in a circle in pairs. Each pair links adjoining elbows, leaving a free elbow sticking out on each side. Around the circle, space is left between pairs. When the game starts, there are two people in the middle of the circle: a chaser and a runner. The runner becomes "safe" when she hooks an elbow onto a free elbow of one of the pairs. That forces the old partner out of that pair and she takes the role of the runner. When the chaser catches the runner, the old runner becomes the new chaser and the old chaser pops a new runner loose from a pair.

The children are ecstatic as we play, tracking the action with their eyes, swiftly exchanging roles, laughing and calling out as the scene continuously shifts. They are radiant in the sun and wind: bodies, minds, and spirits exultant.

And I am ecstatic watching them. No good guys or bad guys, no boys against girls, no winners and losers. We are all in it together, at home in our bodies, easy with each other. This game requires the children to take many perspectives in rapid sequence, to use peripheral vision, to work together, to be aware of themselves and each other in space. Before Bodyworks, it was too hard. Now it's an exhilarating challenge, and they are up to it!

Indoors at circle I demonstrate mirroring with Nita, then I direct the children to sit cross-legged, facing a partner. "Put your hands on your knees and close your eyes. Just breathe quietly for a minute, as if you were going to your Secret Place. Now open your eyes and look in your partner's eyes for a minute without saying a word. Think about "This Little Light of Mine," and let your eyes shine like a little candle for your partner. Keep looking in each others' eyes. Now, all the children I tapped on the shoulder will be the movers, and their partners will be the mirrors. Very, very slowly, when I say 'Begin,' the movers will start to lift both hands up with their palms out, the way I showed you, and the mirrors will follow exactly, but without any touching. Keep looking in each others' eyes the whole time. Begin. Keep it very slow, and move your hands a little up or down, a little side to side, maybe around a little."

There's not a sound except the wind in the trees. Smiles start creeping across children's faces. "Movers, finish up. Mirrors, you are the new movers. Start again with your hands on your knees and begin very, very slowly. . . ." This time the smiles come quickly. It's almost impossible to tell which child is the mover, which the mirror. They are deeply engaged, without exception.

When I bring the mirroring to a close, the hush remains for a long and blessed moment. *I know I can't really see the web of energy in this room, pulsing with our heartbeats, humming just under our breaths, shining in our eyes. I know I can't really see the web extending to the trees, the birds, the far horizon. I can't see it with my outside eyes, but I can feel it in this moment. It's real.*

Elbow tag and mirroring are my kind of assessment.

The Grand Finale

The one thing remaining is to attach the Outsides and the Insides. The Outsides have been tucked away since they were painted and cut out weeks ago. Nita and Terry and I arrive at school early and carefully slip the loop of each self-portrait over the child's completed body model. We space them all along the line from one end of the classroom to the other.

We've worked so hard and so long on each separate bit of this project. We step back to take a look. Suddenly we are out of the leaves and twigs and underbrush. The whole enchanted forest of children is there before our eyes. All the color, all the variety, all the personalities radiating from the array of bodyworks.

Oh!

We give each other hugs. There are tears in Nita's eyes as she says, "I can't believe what this semester has meant to me. It's like I got a chance to go back and be a kid again. And this time we did it right!"

In the background I put on a tape of hammered dulcimer music. The breeze is coming in through the windows, and the paper bodies are dancing. The children begin arriving for the day. Most of them run immediately to their own bodyworks, laughing and marveling to see it whole. Their parents are dazzled. I photograph each child holding the hand of her model body. The room begins to fill with people oohing and ahhing. They weave around the dancing bodies, admiring each in turn.

Inside my head the old Shaker song is ringing,

> *'Tis the gift to be simple, 'tis the gift to be free*
> *'Tis the gift to come down where we ought to be,*
> *And when we find ourselves in the place just right,*
> *It will be in the valley of love and delight.*
> *When true simplicity is gained,*
> *To bow and to bend we will not be ashamed.*
> *To turn, turn, will be our delight*
> *'Til by turning, turning we come round right.*

III. The Growing Edge

I've told the story of The Bodyworks. Now what?

What comes next is even harder to follow than the story that unfolded in my classroom. Although this part of the book may sound like a long monologue, I hope as you read you'll make it a dialogue. Interrupt me with your own thoughts. Argue with me. Get fed up. But please stick with me. As you'll see, we may have exciting work to do together.

I expected at this point to set forth the theoretical framework of the curriculum, and to offer step-by-step guidance for re-creating it. Perhaps you expected that too.

So here I am, surrounded by stacks of books, files of notes. I've had a wonderful time reviewing theories of child development, updating myself on current variations. I've indulged in long musings about educational philosophy and sniffed the prevailing winds.

The next step is simply to superimpose the theory on top of the story.

I feel tremendous resistance to doing this. Where is this resistance coming from?

For one thing, I'm a storyteller. I can't stomach the idea of ending, "And the point of my story is . . ." Either the point's embedded, or it isn't. If it is embedded, you got it. There's nothing that makes a storyteller feel more foolish than explanations.

My integrity as a storyteller aside, am I just lazy? It's hard to fuse theory to practice with such artistry that the joints don't show and the theory sprouts wings! Or am I afraid? Will my philosophy, my pedagogical principles seem naive, inconsistent, or defective? Maybe they won't hold up to scrutiny.

Yes, I'm afraid. If I remind myself that I'm a teacher writing for other teachers and parents, therapists and students—not for the powers-that-be—perhaps I can relax. My concern here is insight, not oversight. Take what you can use, and dump the rest!

I still feel some gut-level resistance to our expectations that my story must legitimize itself by reference to The Authorities. Some of my resistance comes, simply, from a sense of proportion. To attach Dewey or Piaget or Vygotsky or Bruner or Kamii to the story of The Bodyworks would be a little bit like grafting an elephant's head onto a field mouse's body!

And there's this to confess: In the three-ring circus of the classroom I don't think much about the elephants. As ringmaster I'm much more concerned about the trapeze artists, the lions and tigers, and the clowns. The elephants are there, essential, in the background. I count on their keepers to parade the elephants around on time.

I'm leery of mixing it up with the elephant keepers. Where there's theory there's power, and where there's power there's politics: those who propose, interpret, and extend the prevailing paradigm versus those who oppose, challenge, and seek to overthrow it. Whole careers are made and shattered over theories.

Whose careers? The careers of the powers-that-be: professors, publishers, administrators. These people are charged with oversight and they need yardsticks. So theory begets research that demands "objectivity." Unfortunately, in our effort to make education more rational and less whimsical, complex processes of learning and teaching are often reduced to the investigation of "objects" (ironically called "subjects.") In this culture, the bias is toward quantifying and standardizing the education biz.

Prevailing theories posit: 5 senses; 4 domains of development (perceptual motor, cognitive, affective, social); 3 kinds of knowledge (physical, logical-mathematical, social-arbitrary), 7 frames of mind . . . (and a partridge in a pear tree?). These parts don't add up to any child I've ever met. There's a whole child greater than the sum of these parts and she eludes us.

At Gorse Child Study Center I help to oversee student and professional research. I take much of this research, especially the quantitative, with a grain of salt. The "whole child" escapes quickly from the research frame. The "data" can be confusing, even misleading, because a child's behavior is often best explained by some ephemeral factor (what she ate for breakfast, the cold rain, whose birthday it is, the experimenter's purple shirt).

Theories about human development (and the educational philosophies that spawn them) boil down to one question: Nature or Nurture? On the Nature side, we have the child as seed, programmed to grow predictably in a sequence of stages. In its purest form, this theory relegates the teacher to the role of witness. On the Nurture side, the child is a blank slate to be written upon, cogs and wheels to be assembled. As agent for the culture, the teacher forms the child according to its specifications and values.

Like many theorists and most teachers, I straddle these extremes, struggling to find solid ground somewhere between them. There's no simple icon like "seed" or "blank slate" to represent this middle position. The middle is a muddle, or, in the clean, contemporary term, "process." Education is a process of mutual transformation. Nature *and* Nurture. Heredity *and* Environment.

I know The Bodyworks works as an educational process, but it doesn't seem at first to fit stage theory.

Much educational theory and research, seeking legitimacy as science, has focused on "subjects," "objects," and "behaviors" we can isolate for our experiments. If, like modern physicists, we assume we are looking at particles, we learn about mass and position. We lose the ability to see the waves of energy, the motion and direction, which are at the core of the process of education. The experimenter's own position determines her results.

Stage theory tells us that early childhood education is essentially an immersion in the concrete world, a pooling of many sensory experiences. This is the raw material from which the child's maturing brain gradually "constructs" an inner representation of reality. The child has everything to gain from direct manipulation of sand, water, pulleys, pendulums, shadows, ramps, and other "objects" which in and of themselves lead the child to "physical knowledge." Only at a much later stage can the child "operate" on more abstract levels. In early childhood education, the teacher's role is primarily to stock the environment with appropriate objects, and to intervene at appropriate moments with provocative questions or labels which may serve the young investigator. (How *do* we know which moments are appropriate?)

Stage theory implies that The Bodyworks could not work with young children. Theoretically, a teacher-directed model-building project is futile because children must themselves initiate and invent, construct their own versions of reality. Theoretically, model-making bores or confuses them, since they cannot distinguish levels of abstraction. At best, a teacher-directed model sucks off children's time and energy, short-circuits their creativity. At worst, it gives them the message that the teacher is the architect of cognition and the children only day laborers piling bricks according to the plan.

But The Bodyworks works! It's true that my perception is fogged by my investment in the project. My "participant/observer research" is crude, to say the least. My "sample" is highly skewed, my "documentation" biased and spotty. However, the responses of children, parents, teaching assistants, and observant visitors have been highly consistent over a period of eight years. There's even a fair amount of informal "longitudinal data" suggesting that individual children have retained and built upon the learnings triggered by The Bodyworks.

So how *does* the curriculum work? Is it due to "the Hawthorne effect?" Surely the excitement of being part of an experimental curriculum creates its own momentum. In my oversimplification I've neglected the subtleties of stage theory. Maybe there's a missing piece. Or is there an exception to the rule? Could it be that a child's learning about the human body differs in quality, quantity, and timing from other kinds of learning?

There's a common factor in these possible explanations for why The Bodyworks works—in apparent contradiction to stage theory. Let's call that factor "interest." (I'm a teacher writing for teachers. I use this word colloquially. Many words I use—"interest," "attention," "energy," "perception," and so on—may have a different meaning for cognitive psychologists.)

Young children are uniquely motivated and equipped to learn about their own bodies. They've spent four or five years amassing raw data about these bodies. This data is largely inaccessible: unconscious, preverbal, private. The children are eager to make meaning from their experience. The Bodyworks helps them gain access to their data, bringing it into consciousness where they can begin to articulate and to communicate what they know, pursue what they want to find out.

Most young children wake up for dinosaurs, and many learn a great deal about these prehistoric creatures—indirectly, of course. Even very young children do all kinds of defining, labeling, comparing, relating, classifying, and inferring . . . having a wonderful time throughout. Their interest in dinosaurs leads them to related fields. This is all secondhand stuff. Can we call it "science," if it's secondhand? And if the stage-theory is correct, how do we account for the children's leaps into abstract thought?

I suggest the answer lies in "interest." Interest in power, interest in the invisible, interest in the unanswered. (Why did dinosaurs die? Even the grown-ups don't know for sure!) Interest is a strong magnetic force. If significant people—a parent, a sibling, a librarian, a neighbor—share a child's interest, it may expand geometrically. Dinosaurs are powerful, invisible, and inaccessible, like the inside of the human body, and far less immediate. If dinosaurs can cause such a cognitive surge in the young child, why not the human body?

Children learn when they are interested. I note the root of the word "interest." I note the roots of the word "interest"—between, among (from "inter"), being (from "est"). To the Romans, "interest" meant "it concerns," "it is to the advantage of." That takes us right to mutuality, interdependence.

In The Bodyworks curriculum, the interest moves in loops. There's the fun of blowing on straws and squeezing balloons. There's the intrinsic interest of "the content" which relates immediately to the child's own experience. The individual child's interest is reinforced by "the context," the powerful collective interest of the peer community. Moreover, the children soon recognize that the construction and investigation of the human body "counts." The pursuit of this interest rewards them with adult attention and new standing in the real, grown-up world.

Organic energy moves along the lines of least resistance. How does this relate to "interest"?

When children are "not interested," it's because they feel somehow shut out. Then they're apt to resist, actively or passively. They fidget, they fuss, they go limp. They oppose. Many subjects seem irrelevant to them, or overdone. Or the opposite: some material may be too close to home, too hot to handle. Some children's lives have already singed them.

Barry Wadsworth, an authority on Piaget[10] and a constructivist, attributes some of the success of The Bodyworks to its powerful linking of the affective and cognitive domains. He suggests that my anecdotal reports present strong evidence of the kinds of activity Piaget sees as crucial: wheels are turning, concepts are being stimulated and modified, children are constructing knowledge about the self and the body. Despite the teacher-directed goal of the model-making, The Bodyworks in the larger sense is a process-oriented curriculum.

In other words, the curriculum actually moves in two directions: from the inside out and from the outside in. "The whole child" is the center of experience, reflection, evaluation, and extension. The whole child is interested.

Incredible as it may seem, *every* child is interested in The Bodyworks. This holds true for the children I've been unable to reach otherwise (like Jogger and Shirelle) as well as the hard-to-reach (Cara, Missy, Paul) and the easily-reached (Kahlil, Ani, Clint). From their first glimpse of the models, they each want their own. During the long haul of construction, that desire does not evaporate or even wobble.

It seems, in fact, that each child's bodyworks develops a life of its own. The personal model becomes a kind of beloved doll, an extension of the self. At school all the children engage in symbolic play with this crude mirror of their own making. Before, during, and after construction the children invest their models with the intensity of their imaginations.

Parents report the process continues after the bodyworks go home. As the years pass, many children keep their tattered models accessible on the back of a door or hanging in a closet. The bodyworks has become a transitional object, an intricate, intimate companion for leaps into consciousness. Long after the glue has dried, the mental constructing goes on.

Do the children lie in their beds at night, in the company of the familiar old bodyworks on the door, minding their bodies, and bodying their minds? Perhaps it's then they hear their own unvoiced questions. Who am I? Where did I come from? What do I know? What can I do? What am I becoming? How?

I found support for my concept of the bodyworks as a transitional object in an unexpected place. Seymour Papert, the developer of LOGO, worked for five years with Piaget. He left Geneva in the early 1960s convinced of Piaget's contribution to our understanding of the origins of knowledge. As an educator, however, Papert felt Piaget had barely investigated the powerful role emotions play in cognitive development, probably because of the inherent difficulties of research.

In *Mindstorms*[11] Papert looks back to his own early fascination with gears. It was this rich experience with gears (beginning at age two) which led him to formal mathematics. He describes his own body-knowledge of "turning" as a gear turns. "It is this double relationship—both abstract and sensory—that gave the gear the power to carry powerful mathematics into the mind. . . . [T]he gear acts here as a transitional object." He goes on to say, "*I fell in love with gears.* This is something that cannot be reduced to purely 'cognitive' terms. Something very personal happened. . . ."[12]

Papert notes that not every child has easy access to gears and adults who share that interest. He feels Piaget insufficiently appreciated the role of the environment, since a child can only structure knowledge from the "building materials" the culture provides. At M.I.T. Papert developed the LOGO Turtle as an "object for children to think with," in a culture he saw as rich in number but poor in the representation of "systematic procedures."

There are significant differences between the bodyworks model and The Turtle, most obviously the degree of interactivity. Nonetheless, the likenesses are striking. Both "transitional objects" powerfully link cognitive and affective learning. Both lead children to discovery. Both enable young children to function at "higher" levels of abstraction than stage theory allows. Both offer "building blocks" the culture fails to provide. (In the United States today, most children do not participate consciously in the natural cycles of plant and animal life and cannot construct knowledge based on that experience.) Papert and I share the hope that our "instruments of explanation" may become also the "instruments of change" in the way children understand and act in their world.

However, I'm wary of having young children spend much time with computers. Like television, the computer is a powerful and seductive tool, which may further unbalance early childhood in our visually-biased culture. I'm concerned that many children are getting hooked on this "transitional object," and may never make the transition. In contrast, her own handmade bodyworks refers the child back to sensori-motor experience, to the living bodymind. In The Bodyworks curriculum, the child—not the hyperstimulating "microworld" of the computer—is the primary source of intelligence, information, and vitality.

A child may learn from her own experience that water runs downhill. What if we toss the word "gravity" her way? The concept may rise into consciousness, linking storm-sewers and sandcastles and snowmen and the bagels the baby keeps dropping from the highchair: a new neuronal network.

The young child is eager, able to learn some scientific concepts now. Why make her wait until Newton's apple hits her over the head in Physics 101? That's too late, especially if the phenomenon is the child's own bodymind.

Papert stresses the triadic quality of his formative experience with mathematics: the two-year-old, the gears, the adults who loved the little boy and also loved the gears. Relationship is the heart of the muddle in the middle. There we find an intimate, indivisible trio: learner, content, context.

Many contemporary thinkers focus on the child as the center of the educational process, but they cast the teacher in a crucial role. Lucy Calkins, in *Lessons from a Child,* states "Teaching . . . interacts with development and changes it. Teaching can be the cutting edge for learning. . . ."[13]

Donald Graves, the dean of the whole-language movement, underlines the importance of the teacher-child interaction. He refers to Jerome Bruner's notion of scaffolding. "As the child grows, the scaffold changes, but the principles of change, of temporary structures, do not."[14]

Lev Vygotsky states unequivocally, "The only good kind of instruction is that which marches ahead of development and leads it; it must be aimed not so much at the ripe as at the ripening function."[15] He goes on to declare that instruction is especially crucial in science, because "scientific concepts . . . supply structures for the upward development of the children's spontaneous concepts toward conscious and deliberate use. Scientific concepts grow down through spontaneous concepts; spontaneous concepts grow upward through scientific concepts. The strength of scientific concepts lies in their conscious and deliberate character."[16]

I was thrilled to find Jean Harlan giving warm flesh to these abstractions in her superb *Science As It Happens! (Family Activities with Children Ages 4 to 8).*[17] Few children are born into Seymour Papert's gear-rich environment, but most spend many hours with adults in natural laboratories:

kitchen, bathroom, dining room table, car, playground, and supermarket. Harlan's guidebook offers parents the chance to develop as relaxed collaborators and mentors, sharing their children's curiosity and delight in daily encounters with the laws of physics.

She invites families to discover "science as it happens" at ordinary mealtimes, for instance—amid the crackers floating on the soup, the ice cubes melting, the glimpse of fingers magnified through a drinking glass, the salad dressing separating as it settles. These are the moments in which scientific concepts (absorption, displacement, the bending and refraction of light, and viscosity) may be constructed.

Harlan tells us young children's "discoveries circle back and weave through everyday experiences, enlarging and gaining meaning with each encounter."[18]

What if the everyday experiences are occurring in the child's internal environment, invisibly, inaccessibly, unconsciously? It's hard to know when and how to intervene appropriately in the child's bodymind. Of course, there may be outward signs, as any toilet trainer can testify! From time immemorial, toilet trainers have nudged children at moments ripe for learning. "Hey, notice what's happening," we say.

The bodyworks model stands in for us at subtler, unpredictable moments. It signals the child to pay attention to ephemeral personal sensations. "Hey," it says, "Feel that! What do you think's happening?" The bodyworks is more than a transitional object. It's also a scaffold, a three-dimensional nudge.

Of course young children are "ready" to learn about their bodies, and capable of making cognitive leaps to do so. It should come as no surprise to us that in building models of their own bodies young children may function at a "higher level" of abstraction than in many other activities. Her own body is the very center of the young child's universe. All learning proceeds from and loops back to this core. The surprise is that it's taken us so long to create The Bodyworks.

Why has it taken so long? Perhaps because it's so obvious. Perhaps because the theoretical compartments—"domains," "stages," and "kinds of knowledge"—have blinded us to "the whole child." Perhaps because we adults, in our technologically advanced society, are ill at ease, ignorant, and often ashamed of our own bodies. We have come a long way from the classical pursuit of a sound mind in a sound body.

There's more to consider. If we and our children are to come home fully to ourselves, our bodyminds, we must let go of some cherished notions central to our world view. Just as other generations had to relinquish their belief in a flat planet or an earth-centered universe, we have to break free of our assumptions that Earth is ours to dominate and control.

We're just beginning to grasp the fact that we're not separate from Earth's body, we're intelligent "cells" within it. We're only starting to experience interdependence as the fundamental truth of human life, to recognize the extremes of "individuality" and "autonomy" as cultural dead-ends. The study of the human bodymind will throw us hard against the inadequacy of our old beliefs and behaviors. Can we begin courageously to embrace the wisdom of a personal ecology in which the essential relationship is the continuous recycling of matter and energy?

For so long, we've concentrated our attention on matter. It's no wonder that our philosophies and theories of education have focused on observable and quantifiable interactions. We've been preoccupied with the "structures" and "stages" of development. Yet, whether or not we can accurately measure an individual child's ability to conserve number, we apparently cannot "teach" conservation. Where does that leave us?

The stage theory helps us to see differences in state. The eggs of the monarch butterfly, waiting—vulnerable—on the underside of a leaf. The inching, gobbling, bulging, black and yellow stripes of the very hungry caterpillar. The dramatic J-ing of the caterpillar and its metamorphosis into chrysalis. The waiting. The wriggling, squirming, splitting, soggy emergence. The waiting. The drying, unfolding butterfly, rehearsing flight.

So much waiting! At least, that's how it feels from the outside. What's going on during all that waiting? As a teacher, filled with my own importance in the child's development, I may try to speed things up. I may communicate anxiety; I will certainly miss the living itself.

Human stages are less dramatic than the metamorphoses of a butterfly. From infant to toddler is a relatively dramatic shift, occurring over a period of days, weeks, months. We know "what happens next." We may intervene or not: children are genetically programmed to learn to walk. But where do they learn? Who cheers them on? What do they walk toward? The answers to these questions make all the difference.

No one knows for sure what portion of a child's learning is simple maturation. We do know that the "how" of learning affects all that follows, especially when a skill is not hardwired.

What we contribute, as teachers, is "attention." We attend. The root means "bend toward." Ours is not a passive waiting state but an energetic, open expectancy. The energy of our "attention" helps to strengthen the pull of the child's "interest."

We pull together. Toward what? In a general way, toward the next "stage." But given the chaotic, fractal quality of much human development, we won't really know where the child is going until years later. At some level, we have to attend . . . and trust. We trust that the pull of the child's interest and the pull of the teacher's attention will cooperate to move the child along.

At its best, stage theory counsels me to be patient and helps me to enjoy the ride. It does leave me feeling sometimes that the child and I are up a creek without a paddle, waiting for the tide to turn—but as long as things seem to be evolving smoothly, we can share a hamper of sandwiches and lemonade while we wait.

There are moments, however, when I perceive that the child and the species are stuck. Evolution is spinning its wheels. I'm not good at dancing on the deck while the Titanic goes down. ("It was sad, it was sad, it was sad when that great ship went down. . . .") What can I do then? I need another theory.

Stage theory may be stretched to explain why The Bodyworks works, but "the overlap of cognitive and affective domains" does not seem adequate to describe my experience with the curriculum, nor does it offer me a lifeboat when I need it. What I want is a theory with some juice in it.

Years ago, a woman rose to speak in Quaker Meeting. She began, "I'm an archeologist. Periodically I'm faced with a heap of potsherds on my desk. I can't do anything constructive with them until I form a hypothesis. I ask myself, 'What if these were bits of, say, a water jar? Then this piece would have to go near the base and this one might fit at the lip.'

"I keep inventing, experimenting, modifying, sometimes discarding and replacing my original hypothesis. The jar may not turn out to be a water jar after all. It may turn out to be an amphora instead. In the meanwhile, the hypothesis centers my search and makes it possible to proceed."

She paused and then was moved to continue. "This experimental approach is true of my inner life as well. No one has ever proved to me the existence of God. It's basically a matter of choosing a hypothesis and proceeding. I approach the whole thing experimentally. If I assume there's a source of meaning and love and vision in my life, where does that hypothesis take me? So far, this is a much more productive assumption than the reverse."

What the archeologist said has stayed with me. It fits my life as a teacher (and as a seeker). There's no knowing, no certainty, in the muddle between

Nature and Nurture. What's my appropriate role? When do I intervene? I need a hypothesis.

Where do I find a hypothesis? Piaget started small, meticulously observing his own three children. My own thirty years of teaching and parenting must count for something.

Back to the beginning! In 1966 I enrolled at the Harvard Graduate School of Education, and started working my way through some of the great philosophers and early psychologists. During that semester in Israel Scheffler's class in the philosophy of education it became clear to me that "free will or determinism?" and "nature or nurture?" were essentially the same question. What was the point of teaching?

I had to assume some kind of middle-ground answer, even though I found no Authority who would state it for me. It seemed to me that Nature and Nurture must intersect. I imagined an opening at this intersection, and something happening there below the threshold of consciousness. I began to call this event "the leap." (A leap of interest? A leap of attention? A leap of will? A leap of faith?) I assumed a critical gathering of energy could overcome the drag of determinism, boost the learner out of the muddle. Imagining "the leap" gave me the vision and the strength to teach.

Thirty years later—after teaching adults and children in colleges, high schools, junior highs, elementary schools, nursery schools, Headstart, conference centers, and day care centers—I still don't understand what "the leap" is. I *know* that something does happen (or at least it can!) and my job is to make it likelier. It's time to develop my hypothesis. By now there must be some Authorities who can help.

Where we look often determines what we find. If we keep poking under the bed, we'll keep pulling out old socks and dust bunnies.

That's where stage theory leaves me: holding a lot of old socks and dust bunnies.

What if I look elsewhere? There's a lot of excitement in other fields. For years the ideas of physicists, physicians, biologists, anthropologists, linguists, philosophers, poets, storytellers, musicians, sculptors, and systems theorists have seemed more relevant to my classroom than the work of educational psychologists. (It's easy to take biologist E. O. Wilson's term "biophilia" and relate it to The Bodyworks. It makes perfect sense that "love of life" functions physiologically as well as psychologically in the successful individual and in the whole species.)

I have only the dimmest glimmer of what is meant by "the uncertainty principle," "black holes," "chaos theory," or "fractals," but phrases like these resonate for me. The concept of "sensitive dependence upon original conditions" certainly explains my classroom the morning after Halloween!

I imagine an enormous football stadium, empty except for a gnat hovering somewhere above center field. Now I try to see the girders and bleachers, the whole external shell of the stadium, as nothing more than electrons in motion, so quick that they leave traces, like jet streams that *seem* substantial. This is the actual nature of the atoms that constitute our "solid" physical bodies: mostly empty space.

Despite my sense of continuity, my physical body (its atoms, molecules, cells, organs) is constantly changing. Last year's Sandy is dead, having been replaced bit by imperceptible bit by a new Sandy. Where's the continuity? In the informing process through which waves of energy pattern themselves into "new" matter.

Many of us begin to understand body and mind are inseparable, like a two-sided coin. We recognize the tendency of the human bodymind to repeat and reinforce culturally-conditioned perceptions and thoughts. However, experience insists that within the continuous looping there are openings for change at the quantum level. ("Quantum" is the physicists' term for the smallest unit of information/energy. A "quantum jump" describes a space-time event which may give rise to a particle, a perceptible difference from what was there before.) In quantum jumps we have the capacity to become conscious of consciousness.

Aha, there's my "leap"! I can now identify the leap with the transformation of energy at the quantum level. The pull of the teacher's attention and the pull of the child's interest create an opening through which energy may flow along the path of least resistance. I sense there's a doubling going on, a mirror effect. Now I'm getting somewhere.

Piaget may be the Newton of psychology, but I'm looking for the Einstein who can take us into a paradigm shift. I can learn a great deal from contemporary scientists who see the whole. It was Einstein who offered wise counsel: If we really want to understand the nature of a thing, we have to stop worrying so much about its location in space and time.

I want to understand the leap, the growing edge at the heart of the process of education. For the time being, I have to try to learn about something I can't see or measure. Attitude is all. Gertrude Stein, on her deathbed, was asked "What is the answer?" "No," she's reported to have said, "what's the question?"

Teaching—like Life—is not a problem to be solved, but a mystery to be lived. I know I'll never understand "the leap" in any rational way.

Meanwhile, I need a scent to chase! Not only will the chase get my juices flowing, it may interest and attract you. That's another primary function of a hypothesis: to engage colleagues, to broaden and deepen the search.

To be sure, my "hypothesis" is blurry, embryonic. It's a mouse-sized head to stick on my mouse-sized story about The Bodyworks. In its simplest terms, my notion is that The Bodyworks works because it focuses on the waves instead of the particles in the process of education.

Let's assume that there's a rough pattern and sequence of "stages" in child development, but these proceed in a highly individual manner. The environment is crucial in determining the when, how, and whither of what emerges along the way. There are many branchings and turnings where intervention is crucial.

I suggest that there's a characteristic patterning of intelligent energy flowing within each child. There are moments when the energy can be sensed as a "growing edge," gathering into a "leap." "Generative form" may play a critical role, supporting intelligence at the growing edge. (For the moment, think of "generative form" as a simple structure, like a sandwich, that leads to endless variations.)

An attentive teacher, offering a generative form, may mirror the child's growing edge. The teacher's mirroring presence may focus the child's awareness, allow the child to experience herself as one-who-knows, one who knows she knows, one whose knowing can be expressed, named, shared.

Based on my experience, I suggest that The Bodyworks is a generative form. Because it attracts and stimulates such varied growth in so many different children, I suspect there's a fit between The Bodyworks and the developing bodymind of the young child. Perhaps this is a cultural fit at an evolutionary moment when our primary tasks are minding the body and bodying the mind.

I know, whether or not my hypothesis is "true," that The Bodyworks evokes among children and teachers the spirit of individual discovery within community, the joy of interdependence which is the heart of education.

Before I go further with "the growing edge" and "the generative form," let me go back, way back. I'm very big on "context"! Here are some deep assumptions underlying my nascent "hypothesis." You may not need to read these, but I now realize I need to own up to them here.

I assume that:

- The universe is made of matter/energy, structured by pulling and pushing (attraction and repulsion). We are in it and of it, like fish in the sea or a child in the womb. As individuals (and as a species) we begin unaware of our potential: to participate consciously in the ecosystem.
- Using our five senses, we learn gradually to perceive ourselves as individual creatures. However, our senses work by perceiving "differences" that arise in the status quo. We begin to conceive of ourselves as subjects, separate from the environment, and all else as objects to manipulate.
- We are "deconstructing" the unified field of the universe in order to construct an inner representation of it, composed of "thoughts." Our thoughts become gatekeepers, conditioning our reality, perpetuating our sense of separateness.
- The essence of our psychological development to this point has been "pushing." Increasingly, we feel isolated, lonely. We realize that, despite our manipulations, we can't control much. Some of us, individuals and cultures alike, push harder at this stage, trying to lose ourselves in destructive behavior.
- We dimly remember that there's more to life than this pushing. We begin to feel a pull, a yearning for the original oneness. If we're fortunate, we begin to notice the subtle guidance of a "sixth sense," supplementing the obvious five. It may seem strangely familiar, a perceptual mode we "outgrew" in childhood only to rediscover it in maturity. Some of us name this sense "intuition."
- As we pay more attention to intuition, we experience it as an integrative, generative faculty, the "pull toward" balancing the differentiating "push away" of the other five senses. Using this sixth sense, we discover a new fit, a way to cooperate rather than to control.
- Our task as mature individuals and as a species is to travel this looping path "home," retaining the consciousness created by our perceptions and thoughts, and expanding it through "intuition." The home we seek is not the original unconscious union of the fish in the sea. It's the web of life we're looking for, and our unique place and purpose within it.

Whew! Are you still with me? It's no wonder I was afraid to write this section. Deep down, I must have known I would have to put all my marbles right there on the table. They may be utterly irrelevant to you—just a few paragraphs from someone else's midlife metanoia. For me, those assumptions are the bedrock of my teaching, as well as the center of my being. I can't—or won't—compartmentalize.

What does all this have to do with learning, with teaching, with The Bodyworks? To explore "the growing edge," "the leap," and the role of "generative form," we have to look at the "energy" side of the bodymind coin.

What's "energy" anyway? As teachers we can't tell you what it is, but we know it when we're in the middle of it. We feel energy (or its lack!) in ourselves, sense it in the individual child, react to it in the group, detect it in the potency of certain activities, materials, and topics in the environment.

Webster's defines energy as "activity," linking it to "force" or capability, and "vigor" or health. I see energy not as the wind nor as the leaves, but in the relationship between them: the moving, blowing, trembling.

We can imagine energy as light or sound. I can most fully sense it moving through water.

It's August. I'm on Cape Cod, standing at the edge of a sandbar just after the turning of the tide. Shallow waves of water lick the furrows and feathers of sand formed by the receding ocean six hours before. Waves of light move through the water over the waves of sand, revealing the water-sand relationship as a fluid pulsing interaction.

It's a constantly changing but recognizable pattern—a living web, a honeycomb. The energy of the water builds as it gets deeper, dissolving the sandforms and absorbing the light, sucking up pebbles and flinging them down. The wind freshens. The waves of water approach from different directions, interpenetrating, augmenting, interfering with each other. I merge with the sea's sound, smell, taste, touch, sight, my meta-sensing bodymind at one, totally in the present, aware. Thc water and sand seek and find my feet, while my mind seeks and finds the sea. We are in relationship, in process.

A peak experience.

A lovely vacation.

What does the sandbar have to do with those fourteen wriggling children who will be cast up on my beach in September?

Everything!

The Chinese call it *wu li:* the patterns of organic energy. If these occur at the intersection of land and sea, do they not occur as well—below the threshold of ordinary perception—wherever energy moves? Everywhere, including my classroom!

I was taught to see the world in the pure forms of Euclid's geometry: circles, squares, triangles. These forms, like other mental constructs, do not exist in nature. I'm learning to see the natural world anew, as a ceaseless patterning of energy. Nature moves by spiraling, branching, exploding, cracking, meandering. So do children. So do I. So do you.

Think moonsnail: a child like Tanya spiraling outward from a central interest. Think dandelion: a child like Ani exploding in many directions at once, thrusting many rays into the surrounding space. Think river: a child like Jogger bouncing off his containing banks, cutting through in some spring flood. Think mudpuddle: a child like Shirelle or Paul evaporating in the sun without a sign, the dry ground suddenly cracking into irregular polyhedrons like a turtle's shell, cracks where seeds sprout. Think maple tree: a child like Clint branching purposefully from choice to choice.

What we recognize in all these patterns of learning is that the energy has a growing edge, and follows the path of least resistance. Our task as teachers is to recognize and trust the child's growing edge, encourage it to move into form. "Energy" is as real in our classrooms as tables and chairs, paper and pencils, blocks and books, and a lot more significant!

Clearly, we must learn to work in this other dimension.

Out on the sandbar I can't accurately predict which wave will carry off the pretty pebble, or knock me off my feet. I can, however, sense the "ripening" of those events, and perhaps intervene appropriately. In the classroom I can develop greater sensitivity to the movement of energy, the approach of the learning/teaching moment.

Massive movements of energy determine the weather. We use every tool we have to predict it: satellites, computers, TV meteorologists, the *Farmer's Almanac,* the colors of the sunset, the textures of the night sky, the number of wooly-bear caterpillars, our own aching joints. No tool is infallible. Even all together they can't give us certainty.

The same is true of the early childhood classroom. The movement of children's energy is as unpredictable, uncontrollable as the weather. Unanticipated and irregular fluctuations may change the whole "pattern," and we just don't have the perspective to see how they fit. We keep our umbrellas handy.

It's helpful, however, to try to perceive the whorls of energy swirling through the classroom. There may be teachers who get halo effects before migraines, or can read auras. Not I. The best I can do is "scan." Scanning the room or an individual child within it is a lot like scanning a book. Little quanta of information jump out of the soup. It's not only the scanning that releases the information. It's my focused attention, my intent, my interest.

We don't have to start from scratch in our effort to "see" energy. From the ancient Chinese to the Native American, many cultures teach us to recognize the energetic dimension as "real" and relevant to daily life. In these cultures, children learn to perceive and cooperate with intelligent energy as they learn to speak. The presence of words in other languages—and the absence of these words in our own—reminds us that language is a powerful determinant of reality. Semantics and anthropology demonstrate that it's not only that we believe what we see. We also see what we believe.

Names are useful. They allow us to isolate one bunching of waves from another. Naming is necessary, up to a point, or we literally lose sight of the patterning we experience, and it falls back into the stew of undifferentiated perceptions.

Centuries ago, the Hopi created the word *koyaanisqatsi* to describe a problem Anglos have only begun to grasp: "nature out of balance." (For much of the information that follows, I am indebted to Howard Rheingold.[19])

Germans conceptualized "the space between things" *(Zwischenraum),* certainly a useful complement to American clutter, and probably a necessary precondition for my "leap."

Many of us have heard that the Inuit have seventeen different words for "snow." One name is not adequate to communicate all the relevant information. Slushy snow, grainy snow, sticky snow, crusty snow—these are important distinctions in the Arctic, where weather conditions may determine survival. Our minds really boggle at the 170 words the Inuit have invented for "ice." Could we as teachers begin to describe and name the various kinds of "energy" we see moving in the individual child? in the group? This energy is as familiar to us as "ice" to the Inuit, and as crucial to our lives together.

Buddhi is a Sanskrit noun for "intuitive direct knowledge." Edgar Mitchell, the Apollo astronaut, has written about the intuitive understanding of Earth he received during his spacewalk. "It was not a matter of discursive reasoning or logical abstraction. It was an experiential cognition. It was knowledge gained through private subjective awareness, but it was—and still is—every bit as real as the objective data upon which, say, the navigational program or the communications system were based."[20] Sounds to me like a leap. Real knowing, but wavelike knowing, in the energetic dimension. Experience with metaphors and analogies may help to nurture this kind of knowing. Children are natural metaphor-makers.

"Alam-al-mithral" is an Arabic phrase for "the world where images are real." From oncologists to sports psychologists, many adults are learning the power of visualization. This is another skill children and teachers can practice together which will help us all learn to "see energy."

In some cultures a person's name changes several times during a lifetime, marking significant passages or shifts in state. Which is more important, the sameness or the changing? The task is to see continuity within fluidity, the ongoing process. There's the whole river, from spring to sea, the pools and rapids and bends that characterize it. There's the unique, chaotic journey of a single drop of water. How can we see both?

I live near a small river and I walk beside it each day. It seems continuous, unless I go out after a big storm to find a downed tree stuck in a bend, watch daily as the tree collects other flotsam and jetsam. Finally the mesh of material becomes dense enough to trap particles of soil. At which moment can I say for certain that an "island" has begun to form? Perhaps the river, swollen and quick, overflows its banks upstream of the log. Perhaps this cut becomes the primary new channel. As the water recedes, the meander remaining becomes a little oxbow lake, and finally that evaporates. When did the river change its course?

When I label children—the hurried child, the hearing-disabled child, the middle child, the abused child, the hyperactive child, the asthmatic child, the gifted child, the preoperational child—I tend to lose my focus on the energetic dimension. I may get stuck looking at a single factor in the child's development (birth order, family structure, metabolism), often a factor resistant to change. It's far more useful to try to see children as rivers, ceaseless and complex patternings of energy.

What happens if I see the child as a flow of energy? Here she pulls, here she is pulled. Here she pushes, here she is pushed. I begin to see her interdependent with her environment, inseparable from it but recognizable as a unique clustering of energies leaving their trace. Her bag of skin is in truth a very permeable membrane, a porous container which itself grows and changes.

Our common senses tell us the world is flat, not round, and fixed, not whirling through space. Matter, not energy.

Suppose we're like the experimental kittens reared in a room painted with horizontal stripes? As adults, those kittens could function only in a horizontal plane. They kept bumping into chair legs.

Similarly, our culture's bias toward materialism may have blinded us to the energetic dimension. But our young children may still have the capacity for sensing energy. How can we—already blind—develop their potential?

Surely we can "attend" to them, encourage them to become aware of what they know and to share their experience with each other. We can expect their perceptions to be different from our own, fresh. We can help keep the doors open longer. We can give them time to "play," to experiment and explore, to encounter the world through their own unique predispositions.

If we force the children too early into our culturally determined perceptions, we will never know what they know. If we wait too long to offer them generative forms for expressing and extending their own experiences, they will never know what they know.

If our relationship to the bodymind is indeed the growing edge of Earth's evolution and our children are our adaptive potential, then it's urgent that we find a way to help them make the leap, even if we can't follow.

And *they* can teach *us*. We can really try to see the world from a child's point of view, instead of rushing to convert her to our own. We can begin to attend to the "intimations" we remember from our own early childhood.

As I write, the children I learn with are present in me: Ani drawing Ani drawing Ani. Kahlil crooning his love song to the brain. Rosa whirling with all she intuits but cannot explain. Zack reminding me I said his Little Red Superhero was interesting and *important*. Clint speaking out for compassion and justice in front of his whole family. Daisy and Pip struggling to fit maleness and femaleness together. Jogger painting his spiked hair brown, fleeing his own vulnerability. Shane seizing every opportunity to "construct" a protective adult male. Paul waking up as a child among children, standing on his own two feet. Shirelle enchanted by the hidden human sameness. Cara wrapping herself in her own warm skin at last. Tanya persevering in her lonely struggle to represent what she loves most. Maggie flushing with the knowledge of her own ongoingness. Bo rejoicing in the new life that grows out of death. We are all companions at the growing edge. Our mutual interest and attention pull us forward in the spiral of the dance.

As a child I habitually perceived "the whole of things." Soon I learned to break my knowing down into concepts. But the concepts never fully matched the percepts. I was aware of trading the perfume and savor of my own experience for an easier "fit" into the community. It was a bittersweet deal. Maybe there are many children like me. Maybe *all* children are like me to some degree. The whole culture loses when we allow children's bodymind perceptions to slip away for lack of the language or the generative forms that will allow them to surface and to be contained.

We can help children value all kinds of "seeing," support them in learning to use and to integrate right and left hemispheres. What of the dream circles widely recommended by humanistic educators in the '70s? We all dream, whether or not we remember or value our dreams. To make time for dreams to be shared is to honor individual ways of knowing. It's not necessary or even advisable to interpret and guide these dreams as the "halak" does among the Senoi of Malaysia. It's enough to give them a place.

How can we see the children more fully as processes, complex interweavings of continuous change, with a history of emergent capabilities?

How can we help the children see themselves as processes, with the built-in potential for growing their own answers?

Perhaps we begin by learning to see the Earth as process.

The Chinese have a tradition of geomancy called Feng-Shui, literally "wind-water." It's a system for aligning cultural forms (such as houses, temples, gardens, farms, bridges, roads) with the lines of energy within the Earth. Westerners don't understand the system but notice its results: the unusual harmony of between natural and human forms in the traditional Chinese landscape; the healthy relationship between the people and the land.

We don't have to go to China to learn about the Earth's lines-of-force. All over Great Britain are the remnants of a system of ley lines marked by stones and mounds, dating from pre-historic times. This system too is based on wind-water, and it reminds us of ancient wisdom we can recover, if we're willing to learn. Modern scientists are just beginning to discover comparable forms in the American Southwest. Investigators appreciate the sophisticated relationship of these power grids to Earth's electromagnetic fields. Some have conceptualized these lines of force as the veins, arteries, and nervous system of Earth. It's been suggested that the underlying concept of "the breath of Nature" may lead us toward the unified field we hope will reconcile Newtonian and quantum physics.

Geologists tell us that there are essentially two forces which shape the earth, those that "build up" and those that "break down." In our machine-made culture, the trace of human energy is seldom glimpsed as an agent of change. Our young children at play with clay, paper, blocks, stones, sticks, sand, and water can learn many subtle distinctions in the processes through which their own forces build up forms and break them down.

They "build up" through piling, bundling, weaving, joining, tying, leaning, grasping, wrapping, enclosing, gathering. . . . They "break down" by tearing, splashing, crumpling, scattering, cutting, chipping, splitting. . . . They "change" and "transform" by swirling, rotating, smearing, pouring, rolling, creasing, folding, bending. . . . As the children become more aware of "processes," they also construct logical-mathematical "conservation!"

The children can become more conscious of the inside feel of their own energy at work. Now and then we can ask them to "Notice your arms, hands, fingers as you twist a chunk of clay. Which parts are doing most of the work? Can you do it with one arm? What does the clay look like when you start? When you finish?"

"How does tearing feel different from twisting? Which parts of your hands feel the work of tearing? Does torn paper look like torn clay? Does it feel the same? Does twisting clay feel the same as twisting paper? Do your arms and hands feel the difference? Your fingers?"

We can invite the children to become "energy detectives." "Can you look at this clay and tell how it got that shape? By twisting or by cutting? Could you do something different to it that would make it look the same at the end?"

In learning to feel and name the energetic processes that visibly affect forms and structures, children can begin to recognize and name what they know of interpersonal energy. Which gestures, words, tones of voice, facial expressions pull people together? Which push people apart?

Technology has extended our vision. We enter hidden dimensions through X-rays, time-lapse photography, infrared sensors, microscopic cameras, CAT scans, and MRI. Perhaps in time, innovations will allow us to "see" the waves of energy cohering, pulling a child into "a leap." In the meanwhile, we will have to imagine the emergent patterns and name what we intuit about the learning/teaching moment.

Neurologists tell us that the human brain is wired to perceive "difference," whether a qualitative or quantitative shift. I wonder about Rosa. Perhaps Rosa's gift is perceiving a shift in the energetic dimension. Let's assume the existence of the sixth sense, a potential present in us all but underdeveloped in our culture. We loosely call it "intuition." Is intuition the ability to access the subconscious, to use subliminal cues? Is it the capacity to "read" energy? Is it available to us all along, hovering in the shadows of our other senses? What if we could hold onto it throughout childhood, develop it along with our other senses?

This is precisely the capacity we need to develop at this evolutionary moment. We need to learn to sense the "growing edge"—in ourselves, in each other, in the Earth—in order to cooperate consciously with it.

In *Seeing Voices,*[21] Oliver Sachs has reported on the cultural experience of the profoundly deaf. In much of the Western world, the deaf were for centuries regarded as less than fully human. They were shunned, classified as retarded, not allowed to hold property or to vote.

In recent times we've begun to understand that the development of "thought" is highly correlated with the development of language. A signed visual language like American Sign Language is a true language with its own inherent structure. If a child deaf from birth is exposed early enough to a visual language, the brain is able to shift its structural potential for language processing from the auditory to the visual cortex, and from the analytic, time-oriented left hemisphere to the synthesizing, space-oriented right hemisphere.

Sachs describes how a deaf child may develop an extraordinary sensitivity to visual cues (like facial expressions and gestures) and a much more complex sense of space. Signing deaf children often outrank their hearing peers in tests of visual intelligence. On the other hand, if deaf children are denied access to visual language, they may fail to realize the potential for certain kinds of thought. Our plasticity depends on developing early and maintaining rich networks of neuronal connections.

Perhaps Rosa is like a deaf child born into a hearing world. How can we facilitate the development of an "energetic language" which will allow her fullest expression, for her own sake and for us all?

We urgently need to develop sensitivity to the subtle movements of energy. Often toxins work subtly, doing massive but imperceptible harm to the environment. There may be a long lag before we get feedback through our other five senses, and by then it may be very difficult to intervene. What if Rosa and other children like her are the shamans who can guide us into a new evolutionary stage? If we invite them to communicate about bodymind events, they may be able to validate each other's experiences. Surely these children can learn from each other. In the learning community, perhaps they can retain the perceptions that would otherwise slip back through the cracks of individual consciousness for lack of naming.

What would happen if all children were encouraged early to mind the body and body the mind? Where would those rich networks of experiences with names (neuronal connections) lead us all?

It's interesting to note that in life-or-death matters, we often respect intuition. Deepsea divers have a rule: If any member of the team feels uneasy during the dive, the signal to surface is to be given immediately—with no questions asked. We can begin to name and honor our own adult experiences with "energy," the perceptions we usually shrug off as bad vibes, good vibes, ambiance, "déjà vu," "premonition," ESP, and the like. It's time to pay attention when we "feel" a tingle and turn around to see a stranger's eyes pulling at us from across the room. What is happening?

Women in some tribal communities carry their naked infants in slings across their backs. These mothers are so sensitive to energy shifts they anticipate their babies' needs to urinate or defecate in time to hold them out at arm's length from their own bodies. As teachers we can't expect to match this bond, but surely we can develop greater sensitivity to children's wave lengths, their shifting mental, physical, emotional, spiritual energies. I'm not suggesting our society adopt the efficient low-tech tribal alternative to plastic diapers. I am suggesting that as we learn to read organic energy we may find simple solutions to many problems.

Our commitment to our own growth is an important element in the energy field we share with children. We can't be fully present to the children as teachers unless we are present to ourselves as learners. Much of the success of The Bodyworks can be attributed to the contagious excitement of adults actively assimilating and sharing new insights and information. If you teach The Bodyworks, plan to set aside time at home to explore something new to the body (rollerblading? Tai Chi?) as well as something new to the mind (reading *A Celebration of Neurons*[22]?). Children sense it when we're personally, actively, currently in touch with the risks and joys of learning—and they sense it when we're on the sidelines. What we model and practice is a great deal more powerful than what we preach.

The Bodyworks compels adults to be present to the children as teachers and as learners. There's no way to know what questions will come up, how to answer them. We're acutely aware of all we do not know. We're curious, tentative, stimulated, vulnerable. Like it or not, we're walking in the children's shoes, and they know it. We're mirrors and models, intensifying their interest. We can all feel the pull of the growing edge.

As teachers we can learn from past experiences with energy. We can give ourselves time to look backwards, trying to reconstruct the preliminary movement of growing edges which have already broken through. We can develop special sensitivity to transitions. We can name the processes and patterns we recognize, share our insights with colleagues. We can learn also by attending to the energy of the present, becoming more effective participant/observers by making time to "scan" and to mirror children's growing edges as we perceive them. We can learn to notice and trust the working of the sixth sense, to act in harmony with it. We can move into the future by committing ourselves to new learning, gathering energy for our own leaps as well as the children's.

What else can we do to support children's learning?
We can offer them an array of what I call "generative forms." A generative form is an open-ended structure. It's the catalyst which initiates a creative, expansive process. The end-result of the process is unpredictable. The process is the point.

Children love to play—to be "wild," spontaneous, surprising. They also love to be in control, to feel secure in structures based on pattern and predictability. For true power to develop, spontaneity and control must work together. Generative forms help to harmonize the two.

Generative forms function to some degree like mirrors, isolating and reflecting bits of the child's experience, inviting her to reconstruct it. They often channel group energy as well as individual energies, making learning contagious, collective, synergistic.

In the art area of some early childhood classrooms, children are offered a rich array of materials—paper, crayons, paints, markers, scissors, glue, scraps for collage—and are left largely alone. Some creative messing-about occurs, especially among the children already disposed toward "art." Other children stay away from the area entirely, far more attracted to puzzles or trucks or dramatic play and increasingly intimidated by the masterpieces their peers are cranking out.

In other early childhood classrooms, the teacher's plan book specifies: "Wednesday: Halloween Cats. Precut 2 black paper circles, 2 triangles, and 5" black yarn per child. Ditto-master lowercase c-a-t."

Between the art area slushpile and the copycats lies the huge territory of "generative form," where many children can discover and enjoy their growing edges. Early in the school year, I announce at circle, "Everyone, please spend a little time today with crayons. Make some up-and-down lines. Just lots of different lines on one piece of paper." Some children need to be reminded, but everyone can do it and everyone does do it. It's painless. A few children enjoy it—experimenting with colors and heights and thicknesses of line, filling a second, a third, a fourth page.

A few days later I make a second announcement. "Today's the day for side-to-side lines. . . ." And so on, through slanting lines, "corners," dots, curving lines, closed curves, filled-in curves.[23] By now, more and more children are trying the art area on their own, combining forms, calling me excitedly to "Come see!" No one has told them that with these few strokes they can construct every human alphabet, every abstract or representational drawing. The children's growing edges have simply begun to twine around paper and pencil. Generative form has led them down the path of least resistance.

Familiar generative forms support much learning in early childhood. The "house corner," now expanded to stimulate more varied dramatic play, is a classic example of generative form in the classroom. So is "Show and Tell." Math manipulatives like pattern blocks often spur insight and invention. Zipper songs like "Old MacDonald" and "She'll be Comin' Round the Mountain" invite the child to move from private extemporaneous "hums" into the public domain where songs can be shared and remembered. *Songs to Grow*[24] offers many simple open-ended compositions. Outdoors, the minimal reciprocal structures of run and chase, hide and seek, throw and catch give rise to innumerable variations.

Building on the ancient tradition of storytelling, the "whole language" movement has created a new generative form which is radically changing early schooling: the child-written, child-illustrated, child-published book.

The sand tray is a generative form developed by therapists. I find it particularly suitable for use with young children, whose expressive skills may not do justice to their capacity for symbol-making. In my classroom, we call the tray with its array of unique objects "The World," and children grow in joy and wisdom as they take turns for solitary play at Making a World. Their great-grandparents on farms did not need a sand tray—they had sticks and stones, acorn caps and apple dolls to play with beside the little brook out behind the house.

Children don't wait for us to offer generative forms. Browsing through the culture, they find something of "interest," chew that down to its bones, and use those to build something new. Games, questions, concepts, traditions, songs, stories, crafts, routines, rhymes—children seize upon these and use them to support their growing edges.

Silly examples from my own family come to mind. When Cricket was two, she began to make "lists." On scraps of paper she crayoned columns of horizontal lines, varying their lengths. She put these lists into the pocketbook she carried around. When she was three, she added small slants and squiggles to her horizontal lines. By the time she was four, her lists displayed recognizable letters. Before kindergarten, she was posting them on the refrigerator, reminding me to get BBFD (babyfood), DGFD (dogfood), MLK (milk), and whatever else she felt we needed. She moved quickly into pedagogy: "FROOT IS GOOOD TO EET," the refrigerator proclaimed.

When Duncan was two, his big sister was full of Knock-Knock jokes. Soon he could combine the basic elements. "Knock, knock," he would launch. "Who's there?" we responded on command. "Barbara," he would offer, already grinning. "Barbara Who?" we dutifully queried. "Barbara Bjorklund!" he would shout, capping it off with the name of his favorite baby-sitter and bursting into hoots of delight at his own wit. Of course his laughter was contagious. Having tasted the pleasure of rolling us in the aisles, he soon mastered real jokes with real punchlines, launching his career as family comic.

Young children take to rhythms, dance, creative movement, conscious breathing, yoga, and meditation like ducks to water. These too are generative forms, a kind of "energy technology" almost lost in the rubble of our materialistic culture. They may be routes to the roots of consciousness, a legacy we have lost in the "developed" world. They help take us together, adults and children, to the sound mind in the sound body we seek.

The body-mind synthesis, even though we don't understand it fully, urges us as teachers to expand our ways of working. We know children "have to move." We're likely to discover that the way they move profoundly affects the way they learn.

Creating movement opportunities for children is more than a pragmatic approach to classroom management. Traditionally shamans used rhythmic movement to open the door between the worlds. Perhaps the childhood chants and rhythmic games found in all cultures are the species' effort to preserve, share, extend the "patterning" of the bodymind. The simple pulse of these archetypal activities may help keep alive our earliest experience of interdependence within the mother's womb: her steady heartbeat, the expansion and contraction of her lungs, the tides of physiology. Rhythms may help us hold on to the sixth sense. They definitely help us ground ourselves and connect to each other.

Rhythm entrains. Throughout history, the makers of war have used the drum to march us toward death. We will be less susceptible to illusions of empire and glory if we teach our children to honor the power of rhythm and use it consciously to dance us toward life.

The chants and games of childhood strengthen the links around the circle. "Ring Around the Rosy" seems to be the quintessential game of earliest childhood. Young ones never tire of this game: coming together, holding hands, circling, falling down and breaking apart, re-forming. At some preverbal level, those simple patternings of rhythm and form can re-mind them of the dance of waves and particles at the root of our individual and collective beings.

Given world and time enough, would many children re-invent the wheel, the alphabet? How many would drown before they discovered the dogpaddle?

Our evolution as a species demands that we pass on to the children what can be learned from our collective experience, *and* that we free them to explore new territory, develop new skills, invent new tools. There's tension between these ends of the educational continuum, but it can be a creative tension.

Generative forms transmit the culture, but they invite transformation, pull toward expansions, spiral into change. The "dress-up area" of an early childhood classroom offers a place, a time, some props for children to "construct" social knowledge. There they think about things by acting them out, alone and together. The action may be verbal, nonverbal, or both. They puzzle over many of the complexities of family life as they create roles for themselves and each other.

I call the "house corner" a generative form because it generates learning. It offers easy access and intrinsic rewards, which help to renew the energy expended. It arouses, focuses, and supports children's need to know about a specific area of interest. It's a path of least resistance where energy can travel.

The Bodyworks curriculum is a suggestive, minimal kind of structure—a raft, not a shore. The making of the bodyworks model is like setting up a base camp for a push into new territory. Imagine helping the children create a "house" in the classroom—painting a cardboard box to make a "stove," building a simple doll bed from scrap lumber, making shelves from bricks and boards and filling these with boots and high-heeled shoes scrounged from home. The bodyworks model is like that "house," a very personal prop. It becomes the nucleus for a curriculum that evolves daily in response to the children's questions, investigations, needs. The model is the "object to think with," the visible tip that leads the child's growing edge. The Bodyworks curriculum is what emerges from the children in the context of the generative form (space, time, personal props) we provide.

I've suggested how The Bodyworks fits (awkwardly) into stage theory, and I've suggested that stage theory alone doesn't explain much of what goes on in my classroom. I've shared my hunch there's a hidden dimension that is very significant in the process of education. I've identified the leap of energy that is at the heart of learning, and explored the way interest, attention, and generative form help to engage and support the learner's growing edge. It's time now to look at the story of The Bodyworks.

What we have is a work-in-progress, a progress report on a process. It's about children, teachers, learning, energy, and power moving into the twenty-first century.

It's a hybrid: story, journal, curriculum without lesson plans. It asks a great deal of the reader because it does not demystify the process of learning and teaching. If anything, it revels in the mysteriousness of that process.

It seems to stretch, if not actually contradict, some prevailing assumptions about "science education" in early childhood. Perhaps it's best seen as "education for wholeness," helping to empower the child as a conscious center of thinking, feeling, sensing, and doing.

It actively engages the whole teacher as well as the whole child.

And it's a muddle. It's juicy and provocative, but it's jerky, hard to follow, repetitive, too long. The anecdotes don't even line up with the stages of the model making. Some children keep intruding.

Yes, like some school days, some school years! I've tried to make the children and the context "real." In the midst of things, I struggle for perspective. The children don't respond on cue, neatly dovetailing their issues with my construction schedule. Some topics keep coming up. Some entries go on and on, while others are so minimal as to lack a point. It's important to keep seeing the little things, scanning the energy, as well as wallowing in the big moments.

There's an awful lot about "fanciness" in the story.

It's possible that the concept of "fanciness" skews children's interest toward sexuality. I doubt it. Gender and birth order together profoundly affect the distribution of power among siblings, framing and defining many young children's search for self-esteem. Jogger, for instance, feels excluded from his home's power center: the big bedroom where his three older sisters share secrets, plans, friends, late bedtimes, ritual grooming, the regalia of beauty-power. He probably attributes his sisters' power not to circumstance (maturity, sameness of gender) but to the material attributes so compelling to a physical thinker: size, number, complexity of detail. Ironically, his sisters may see Jogger as the crown prince—heir to his father's own name, privileged occupant of a private room, sole owner of new boy clothes and boy toys, spoiled brat.

In Daisy's very different family, her first-born brother dominates the conversation, belittles her efforts to catch up. Daisy and Jogger (and many other young children) are trapped in their perceptions: the "difference" determines; I am lacking; how can I redistribute the wealth?

Who can separate sibling politics from the culture in which families are embedded? It's fair to say, however, that our children live in a sex-saturated society. They learn very early that gender is crucial, and that gender divides. Gender is inextricably wound up with power, a major theme for young children. I think "fanciness" provides most children with an age-appropriate context for these concerns, and allows them to move on to the rest of the human body. I'm still dissatisfied with the way I handle the male role in procreation, but haven't come up with a solution more respectful of children's and families' differences.

Some years, some groups of children seem more interested in sexuality than others. Group chemistry as well as individual history probably account for this. It seems important in sharing The Bodyworks with others to err on the side of over- rather than underrepresenting children's curiosity about sex, stressing that some of the interest in "sex" stems from perceived inequity.

Our Gorse population is fairly homogeneous. Maybe The Bodyworks won't work anywhere else.

The lack of diversity is out of my control, alas; however, teachers have grabbed the idea and run with it in their own very different settings. One teacher[25] used my article about The Bodyworks to create her own version of the curriculum with a class of 5–8-year-olds in a public school in rural Kentucky. She divided the class into several mixed-age groups. Within each group, the older children did "research" and read to the younger ones. Together the children decided how to represent the brain, circulatory system, respiratory system, and digestive tract in their collective "person," building on suggestions from the article.

This wise teacher waited for sexuality to come up, rather than structuring it into the model making—hoping in this way to sidestep potential disapproval from parents. Sexuality came up immediately in most groups, as the children decided whether to name their "person" with a boy's name or a girl's name. Some groups pursued the subject as far as pregnancy. After one model became "pregnant," another model added "twins." The teacher reported that the project was a huge success, and went on for weeks. In a school where parent involvement is rare, many parents visited her classroom to see the models. The parents expressed tremendous enthusiasm, amazed that their children were capable of such sophisticated learning.

The teacher would like to do The Bodyworks every year, allowing each child to experience the curriculum four times, deepening and broadening with his maturing skills and interests. However, she knows parents and powers-that-be would protest that the children had already "had" The Bodyworks. Realistically, she's resigning herself to wait until her youngest student has moved on before she can do it again.

Lots of organs are missing from the model. What about the liver and the endocrine system? Those are very important to children who live in an increasingly toxic environment and must make intelligent choices about mood-altering substances.

This is a real frustration for me. I've been thinking for a long time about how to incorporate the liver: a piece of sponge to represent its absorbing and storing functions; however, I'm not content with that oversimplification. I haven't come near the solution for the endocrine system. In fact, I think the current form of the model is as elaborate as a prototype should be. What I want to do now is experiment with individual extensions. How to help these young children move beyond the basic structure to create "eyeballs," fingernails, or anything else that pulls their interest?

The ecological links are provocative but underdeveloped.

That's another project that pulls me: "Earthworks" as the context for "Bodyworks." In the meanwhile, I continue to feel that the concept of growpower is key. There's an irreducible mystery at the heart of life. We've shied away from talking about that mystery for many reasons—because we don't understand it, because we fear we may stray into the region of "spirituality." We can't keep compartmentalizing the "stages" of the "whole child," nor the "processes" of the "whole earth." It's time to find our proper place in the wholeness we don't understand and can't control.

There are so many flaws in the curriculum, and in the book about it.

Yes, and these flaws are not going to go away. I've made a decision to let my bare face hang out. I'm less concerned here with looking good than I am with getting help. Children need help. Teachers need help. We're going to hang together or hang separately. It's time to get this book out there, to reach others on the same wavelength.

People have suggested that, despite its flaws, The Bodyworks is the work of a "gifted teacher," fun to read about but way out of reach for most teachers.

That makes me want to stand up and scream! There are many teachers aross this country and around the world who are responding with creativity and courage to the challenge of educating young children in a troubled time. The news of their remarkable innovations rarely gets past the thresholds of their own classrooms. Many great teachers are too modest to trumpet their successes, too sensitive to all that's left undone and too busy doing it. Others are reluctant to risk a high profile, lest they get their heads shot off. They're unwilling or unable to document and justify their work according to the current canon of "professionalism." So many gifted teachers stay anonymous.

I began this book thinking I was writing for my peers. Now I know I was writing for myself, to find out what I know and what I want to learn. I claim my place right in the muddle of the middle. And I'm calling out to you, asking you to join me. Let's share our insights about the energetic dimension of the educational process as we know it. Let's create a network called The Growing Edge.

We don't each have to do it all. Some of us can continue to develop The Bodyworks. Some of us can move toward The Earthworks. Some of us can concentrate on improving our ability to perceive energy. Some of us can help to name the patterns of energy as they're identified. Some of us can translate, interpret, and apply current brain research. Some of us can invent new generative forms, or extend old ones. Some of us can collect and edit the contributions of others. The Growing Edge Network can be an umbrella for all of us who are interested in making our classrooms centers for "whole knowing."

We're already used to borrowing from and building on each other. We all stand on the shoulders of anonymous colleagues like the one whose life-sized outline paintings inspired me to develop The Bodyworks.

Why wait for our Einstein to appear and effect the paradigm shift? Perhaps we, collectively, are the Einstein. Nothing would seem more fitting than a network replacing the solitary thinker on the growing edge of education. Indeed, we can take as our model that remarkable network of networks: the human brain, with its unimaginable capacity for evolutionary leaps.

Even if we don't have an Einstein, we could use a mentor.

You may have mentors to suggest. I've just found Bess-Gene Holt in the pages of the third edition of her *Science with Young Children*.[26] Her book stands out for its wisdom, its theoretical soundness, and its practicality. As I return to my classroom focused on learning from children as well as teaching them, she will be my guide.

Holt's elaboration of the concept of personal ecology integrates philosophy and psychology with a deep appreciation for the real teachers and real children growing together in early childhood classrooms. She respects the interplay of levels of experience and understanding, the many modes of being-doing-feeling-sensing-knowing that are inseparable in the young child. Her book offers many suggestions for engaging what I call the "growing edge."

Her simple statements resonate. "I think children need to know more, and I feel strongly that they need to know some things differently. The attitudes toward the world and one's place in it form in the early years. . . . Children who appreciate and celebrate life have a strong sense of their own worth without the need to feel superior."[27]

I cherish Holt's understanding of the complementary weaving of first-hand sensory encounters and "vicarious" experience. Conversation, books, folklore, and other resources have a place beside sand, water, animals, soil, and other natural phenomena. "Concepts of balance, harmony, cooperation and interdependence . . . are ways in which all forms of life coexist and support each other naturally. It is an emphasis long overdue."[28]

Holt quotes researchers who emphasize that naive misconceptions are inevitable in the child's construction of knowledge and suggest that these can be most easily revealed and modified through early exposure to scientific concepts in the early childhood curriculum. This is certainly my experience with The Bodyworks.

I repeat Holt's charge, "It is the early childhood teacher's challenge to fit the truth of the world into the child's system of knowing it."[29] Through the human bodymind we experience directly the self-organizing complexity of the universe. Our truth and our system of knowing it are one and the same, a continuous cycling of matter, energy, and intelligence dancing at the growing edge where child and teacher meet.

Periodically I ask myself some leading questions. Who am I? Who are these children? What will they need to thrive in the world they'll inherit? What do they and their parents expect of me? What resources are available to us? What limits are built in? Where is our growing edge?

I can never answer all these questions, but the exercise is always useful. Here's my most recent version of "The World They'll Inherit":

- *As far as we know, Earth is the only habitable planet.*
- *Pull and push (attraction and repulsion) are fundamental to Earth's structure and to our ways of knowing it.*
- *Interdependence is the core reality of life on earth.*
- *We have no choice except to share the elements in our spaceship, to recycle mindfully what we know is not "mine" or "yours" but "ours."*
- *Where interdependence is the primary relationship, communication is a need as basic as food and water.*
- *Through communication we can set priorities, develop cooperative strategies, and resolve conflicts without violence to the whole.*
- *To live mindfully within the complex, changing Earth organism, we must be able to continuously encode, store, retrieve, and decode massive amounts of information.*
- *We already know how to do this: the human bodymind is a microcosm. We need to learn to integrate our five common senses with our sense of intuition.*
- *Ongoing change necessitates ongoing evolution, experimentation, improvisation.*
- *The crucial skill is learning how to learn.*
- *Life itself remains a mystery, unknown and unknowable to reason alone.*
- *Within the mystery, we have a profound need for emergent meaning and guidance.*
- *We seek pattern, purpose, order, beauty, love, joy, the sense of belonging.*
- *Through minding the body, we can enter the learning spiral ultimately*

leading us to maturity: conscious participation in the co-creative process.

- *"Interest" and "attention" are primary cues to the growing edge being pulled by generative form.*

It's time to test The Bodyworks with this group. If Outside-In *turns these children on, we'll proceed with "Outsides." And if those are a big hit, we'll go for "Insides." If I've engaged the growing edge of this group, I should expect things to start happening.*

It's plain that whole science belongs at the core of our classrooms. The root of "science" is the Latin verb "to know." A new sense of knowing is what we need.

I imagine being part of a network of teachers learning to see the children and ourselves as *wu li,* patterns of organic energy as dazzling as butterflies, thunderstorms, light dappling water.

I imagine us helping each other to become more aware of awareness. More conscious of the role of generative form and practiced in its use. More sensitive to the gathering of energy into the mysterious "leap." More able to support the growing edge when we recognize it.

I imagine us blessing and celebrating breakthrough moments.

I imagine us refining "participant/observer" methodology so we can carry out research that respects the "whole child" and adds to our understanding of how the domains overlap.

I imagine us contributing to the understanding of different learning styles and rhythms. I imagine us learning to channel our own energies, avoiding burnout.

I imagine us collaborating with children in exploring the interplay of sensation/perception/information/action/reflection. I imagine learning from them about the latent sixth sense we can cultivate.

What can you imagine? What do you want to know?

Recently a mother asked me, "What do I tell my son when he asks me questions I can't answer? The big ones, I mean, like 'Where did I come from?' and 'What happens when people die?' I've tried telling him, 'Some people think this . . . and some people think that . . .' but it's not good enough for him. He wants to know what *I* think. Like about God. I was brought up in a strict church, but in college I became an atheist. Now I'm not so sure! So what do I tell him?"

I gave her my only answer. "It sounds like you're on the right track, trying to match the depth of your responses to the depth of his questions. It's tricky, because children believe we're the authorities and they want straight simple answers we don't have. Above all, they need to trust us. After you explain that different people believe different things, but no one knows the answer for sure, the most trustworthy response you can give your son is something like this:

"I used to think one thing and then I thought something different, and now I'm not sure. It feels to me like I'm still growing my answer. Some questions are like that. The important thing is to keep asking, and to notice how the answer grows and changes. We keep learning all the time but we still never know everything. I'm so glad you're already starting to grow your own answers to the big important questions. What do *you* think?'"

We gave each other a hug.

I finished up, "Inviting your son to grow his own answers will serve him well in the long run. Even when your answers are clear and firm and easy to articulate, it's important for your child to know that you grew into them, and he will grow into his own."

I've come this far, trying to grow my own answers. It's hard work. I think about the wise old teacher who lit four candles at her supper table each evening. "For faith, hope, love, and mystery," she said.

I turn that over in my mind. What do I have faith in? The growing edges of children seeking fullest expression.

What do I hope for? That I may attend, serve children, and in the process be myself transformed. That our mutual learning may serve the Earth's evolving.

What do I love? The aliveness, the juice! Being immersed with the children in the flow of energy, our sense of belonging together in this moment of the journey into the unknown.

What of the mystery? There's an essential oneness (unknown and unknowable but mirrored and resonant) guiding us. I'm a part of it somehow. I know more than I know. I'm part of the intelligent energy. I help to create the meaning that emerges. I help to birth what I don't understand.

A pregnant mother cannot consciously construct the developing baby, yet she profoundly influences its bodymind through what she chooses to eat and drink, how she prepares herself for birth, the rhythms of her living.

The energy I bring to the classroom, my very "being" may make all the difference. My smile or frown may be the butterfly wing that alters the course of a child's development. What happens if I see children as bundles of domains and stages and frames of mind? What if I see them as mysterious patterns in the dance of energy I can barely visualize?

The mystery is that the hypothesis matters. It shapes the reality. So I choose to imagine a growing edge green and shimmering in myself, in each child I teach, in our species. The story of The Bodyworks is my invitation to you to join me in exploring the growing edge.

Epilogue

After weeks of very long days, writing at white heat to finish "The Growing Edge" section of this manuscript, I turned off the computer exhausted. I was discouraged. I could hear my inner Critic carping that the insights were half-baked and the writing was too loose. My Critic warned me that no one would want to read through all I had written. I had no trouble believing that! I asked for help, and I went to bed.

I woke up in the web of a strong dream.

The Bodyworks began as a dream that woke me in the middle of the night. The new dream brought me full circle. I offer it to you. Take from it whatever you can.

(The first part of the dream wasn't like a dream at all, more like an experience.)

I am being and seeing at the same time. I'm suspended but floating in what I see. What I'm in is empty but not dark. It's translucent all around me and it feels full, alive. Little bursts of light rise, curve, and disappear like shooting stars, in some huge complex pattern. There's no beginning or end to this. It's all here and now. I'm not separate from it, but aware of being in the midst of it—myself in my own body, but weightless and buoyant as an astronaut. There's no "action." There's just this quality of being and seeing at the same time. This is simply happening, ongoing, and I know it is more real than anything else. Unimaginably real.

(There was a shift, and I moved into the second part of the dream—still strange, but much more like a usual dream.)

I'm leaving the awareness, moving into some other kind of moment. A word is forming inside me and emerging, surrounding me. The word is CONSCIOUSNESS. *I have to pick three letters from the word, to take with me.*

One letter begins to vibrate. It's silver, like a small slim cylinder. I pick it. It's the "I." A kind of voice, deep and gentle and clear—like a big bell inside my chest—tells me: "You made a good choice. The 'I' stands for Air."

I feel my own voice saying back, "But 'I' isn't even the first letter of the word Air. I'll never remember it stands for Air."

The other voice assures me I'll remember the experience I've just had, being the "I" in the middle of the aIr, part of it but surrounded by it all at the same time.

Now I have to pick another letter. The "O" begins to shine silver and vibrate like the "I" did. I pick it. The voice lets me know that's another good choice. It tells me, "O is for Motion, like in the ocean. O is for the waves of Motion you felt but couldn't see."

I wonder how there can be such a thing as a wave without water or air for it to move in. I don't say this out loud, but I think it. The voice answers that I know waves of Motion even though I can't explain Motion without referring to something that moves.

I have to pick my last letter. The "S" comes forth and the rest of the letters fade away.

"Another good choice," the voice tells me. "And here's a "T" to go with it. Your last word is Sunlight—"S" at the beginning and "T" at the end."

"But," I can hear myself protesting a little, "there wasn't any 'T.'"

"Oh, well! You know the limits of words!" The voice is laughing a wonderful laugh. "Words are never quite complete. But CONSCIOUSNESS was a good one. It covered most of the territory you have to remember when you go back. 'Sunlight' really isn't a perfect word either, but it's a good handle to hold on to your experience of the bursts of light like shooting stars. The 'S' is the sparks—that's easy. Think of 'S' completing itself by making a figure 8, like a Möbius strip curving back into itself forever. The 'T' is to remind you of the crossing points, the junctures where the sparks push through and fall back in. Remember the light as pulsing in a pattern, not burning out but visible at the intersections—that's why you've got the 'T.'"

I've turned into a silver Pac-man, and I'm swallowing the letters one at a time. I'm really swallowing the meaning behind the words. "Air" is the unified field. "Motion" is the waving energy. "Sunlight" is the small visible tip of a huge spectrum.

Now I am a pack, like a knapsack, and I'm enclosing the experience so I can carry out the insights when I go back.

2 September 1995
Amherst, Massachusetts

IV. The Bodyworks

Tips for Teachers

Now that you've read the book, you can understand why each teacher has to recreate the curriculum each year. The bodyworks model is only the generative form, and the curriculum emerges at the growing edges of the children and the teacher alike.

I can, however, offer some suggestions. I'll reiterate a few thoughts from the Orientation section (which may have more meaning now that you've read the rest of the book), and toss out a few new ideas. Following these tips, you'll find Bodyworks Bogglers, a brief annotated bibliography of books for The Bodyworks, blueprints and diagrams for the bodyworks model, and photographs.

- The curriculum begins as a teacher initiative, but it takes shape in response to the children. Not everything comes up every year, but most things surface sooner or later in some form, especially The Biggies.
- Much of the time you'll be improvising from a strong center of sensitivity, self-knowledge, and information. The information is the least crucial—you can't know everything, but you can look things up as needed.
- The Bodyworks demands a certain level of maturity in the teacher, as a human being and as an educator. It's challenging to handle so many live wires at once. And to have all your buttons pressed repeatedly. (What are *your* buttons?)
- Consider my journal "notes from the field." Use it as a workbook, a private role play to help you discover in advance some of your own strengths, anxieties, information gaps, and growing edges.
- Do you have a support system at school? at home? Who'll help you find perspective? Who'll help you locate resources in response to the children?
- Beyond maturity and the willingness to take risks, The Bodyworks asks the teacher to reawaken in herself the sense of wonder. Play—exploration, not competition—is the surest route to new awareness. Play enables us to listen deeply. It's the deep listening that prepares you to "teach" this curriculum and invites the children to bring you their discoveries and their fears, their questions and the answers they're beginning to grow.
- Think of yourself as the "lead learner" opening a channel that eases the flight of those who follow. Your curiosity and enthusiasm create an energy stream.

- Try asking yourself, family, and friends some simple questions to set your minds wondering. The Bogglers might get you started. Why do we have fingernails? ear lobes? arches between our heels and toes? Why are our elbows bony? Imagine, hypothesize, *then* look it up.
- Take your questions to the children's section of a good library. Scan, browse, get hooked. Follow up your curiosity about some specific aspect of the human body. Don't worry how you're going to use your new information. You're priming the pump so you'll brim with insights, metaphors, demonstrations, and improvisations at the teachable moment.
- Be aware of your own attitudes, especially your response to decay and death. If you were taught to view certain aspects of the body as "dirty," think long and hard. How can you gently and firmly reeducate yourself before beginning to teach this curriculum? You may be able to enlist the children as allies in helping you change. ("When I was a little girl, lots of people didn't know the correct names for some parts of their bodies. We didn't know how to ask questions about ourselves. Sometimes I still get embarrassed talking about my body, but I don't want *you* to be shy about your bodies. Please be patient with me if I act uncomfortable. I'm still learning. You can help me.")
- Before you commit yourself, consider the mechanics of teaching the curriculum. How will you store the materials and bodyworks-in-progress? Will you sequence the construction process? How will you encourage and support the curriculum as it emerges from *your* children? What record-keeping system will help you track each child's progress on the model, as well as the individual learnings that emerge? Will you make a special effort to communicate with parents before, during, and after The Bodyworks?
- Why are you attracted to this curriculum at this time? Where does it fit in your scale of priorities for the children's growth? How does it mesh with other classroom offerings?
- Think of The Bodyworks curriculum as the visible tip of a meta-curriculum emerging over the course of a school year, an ongoing exploration of personal ecology: Who am I and how do I fit in the world? Then think of bodyworks models as the visible tip of The Bodyworks curriculum that will emerge from you and the children. Now think about all you and the children already know and do that fits under the general topic of "minding the body, bodying the mind." Have you done bar graphs of children's eye colors? A photo album of

children's baby pictures? Rhythms and movement games? A multicultural food festival? Consider how you can extend tried-and-true activities, linking these to the broad general theme.

- As you and the children develop extensions of the bodyworks model, try to match material and function. How to represent the eye? The child's first thought might be to find something that looks like an eyeball, perhaps a Ping-Pong ball. Frame questions to help the child go deeper. What's the eye's job? What could we use to show that eyes see? Ultimately, the child might decide to split the Ping-Pong ball in half and glue in a bit of mirror. A very sophisticated child might appreciate your suggestion of straight pins as "rods" and colored pushpins as "cones." You might remind the child to attach string for nerves and yarn for blood vessels, connecting the eye to the brain and heart. You may want to work with small groups of children to develop models of organs not included in the basic bodyworks. This skin is an important and complex organ we often overlook. What jobs does it do? Using a nylon stocking for the external layer of epidermis (with Elmer's glue thickly spread so it can be "flaked off" like dead skin?), how could you represent blood vessels? sensors (for pain, cold, heat, pressure)? hairs? sweat glands? oil glands? nerves?
- What are your own sources of strength? Build on these as you develop the curriculum. We try to broaden our interests and skills enough to make a strong connection to each child's learning style, life experience, growing edge. But ultimately we teach what we are. Be sure the children have to opportunity to catch your fire. They won't all follow in your footsteps, but they'll be warmed and lit by your glow. As you probably noticed, I often use music and movement to help the children experience concepts. Perhaps your delight is mathematics, or games.

  If you are a mathematician, this would be a perfect time to do some work with topology. Try measuring each child's height with lengths of strong thread or fine twine. Have the child loop the string into a small container, like a thimble. This is one way the body fits long parts into short spaces, like the lining of the small intestine.

  Or take two long lengths of yarn. Leave one whole. Have the child cut the other length into small bits, using these to glue a branching pattern. This is how the body sends blood to every nook and cranny.

  Cut lengths of string for each child's and each teacher's height (and add a little extra for knots). Have the children lie down in a long line, their strings parallel to their bodies. Tie all the ends together, making one long "class measuring string." How many school buses long is it? How far across the playground does it reach? How small a ball can you make by rolling up that string? Will it fit into a paper cup?

Try translating big body statistics into child-based quantities. (Physical thinkers that they are, children love being associated with bigness!)

Cheerio facts: 1 cup = approximately 350 Cheerios. Family-size box = 14 cups, approximately 5,000 Cheerios. Family-size box weighs 15 oz. It is 12" high, 8-1/4" wide, 2-3/4" deep. Family-size box is approximately 270 cubic inches.

Truck facts: Longest U-Haul trailer is 24 ft. It contains 1,167 cubic feet. (One cubic foot is 1,728 cubic inches.)

Dinosaur facts: Ankylosaurus: 15–25 feet long, 6 feet wide, 4 feet tall; 5 tons. Brontosaurus: 70–75 feet long, 15 feet high at shoulders, 30 tons. Dimetrodon: 10–13 feet long. Pteranodon: 27-foot wingspan, 33 pounds. Stegosaurus: 11 feet tall, 25 feet long. Triceratops: 25–35 feet long, 9–10 feet high at shoulders, 8 tons. Tyrannosaurus: 50 feet long, 18 feet high at shoulders, 6 tons; 60 teeth, each 3–5" long and serrated.

The classroom: Ours is about 30 feet long, 25 feet wide, 10 feet high.

Gather some body facts that excite you. (You can start with some of the Bogglers. Remember, there's no way to know "exactly" how many neurons we have, or how far our capillaries would reach if stretched end to end. Scientists disagree. They guesstimate, rounding off by millions and billions. Feel free to adjust numbers to fit your ballpark.)

For instance, the body manufactures (among many other things) approximately 2 million red blood cells every second. If you imagine every one of these is the size of a Cheerio, your body is making the equivalent of 45 boxes of Cheerios every second. That would make a stack of boxes about 7 feet tall in the corner of your classroom.

Are activities and facts like these wasted on children who cannot yet "conserve?" How might the children benefit?

Maybe you're not intrigued with math, but you love to play games. Try making up a game based on the fact that different parts of the brain report different kinds of information, all of which have to be coordinated:

One child can be the blindfolded Brain. Tuck four long strings into her blindfold. Give the far end of each string to one of four children stationed around the classroom. Assign each of these four children one quality to observe and report to the Brain. Child A reports only color. Child B reports only shape. Child C reports only movement. Child D reports only location.

You perform a simple action everyone can see except the blindfolded Brain. Each child walks (or crawls) quickly to the Brain and whispers her bit of information. The Brain's job is to put the bits together and announce what happened. (A Yellow Paperclip Fell on the Rug. A Red Ball Bounced on the Table.) Of course you *could* do this with competing Brain teams, but please don't. See how much fun it is simply to play it, when *everyone* wins.

- Enlist the strengths of families in the class community. *Everyone* is an expert on the human body and can contribute something to the emerging curriculum. Perhaps there's a big brother who enjoys photography. Could he do close-up shots of each child's eyes, nose, mouth? Can the children guess who's who? Can children work with the photographs or with mirrors, trying to draw their own eyes? Their mouths, smiling? Their mouths, frowning? Whatever their representational skills, the process will help them "see"—not only form but also "energy."
- Offer key concepts repeatedly—in many modes—but don't force-feed. "Interest" is the criterion, not "mastery." What kinds of learning do you expect? What evidence will convince you (or your principal) that learning is happening?
- Help the children begin to pay attention to what we know and *how* we know it. I say "My heart beats," but I've never seen my own heart. What do I know firsthand? What have other people told me? How do *they* know? These are questions that will open the world to children, and empower them to move in it more joyfully and safely.
- Be prepared to deflect some questions without squelching the questioner. You might post a list or keep a log just for questions. Encourage the children to bring their questions to you anytime "because questions are important," but let them know that "There are so many interesting questions we won't get to answer them all in this class. Every day I'll pick a few questions from our list and we'll all think about those and try to find the answers."
- Anticipate special sensitivities related to obvious or subtle differences among children and their families. How can you use the curriculum to make the class community more inclusive and comfortable for all?
- Experiment. Start small and don't commit yourself to the whole

bodyworks. Just do "Outsides" and then introduce a stripped-down model that includes, say, the lungs only (a nice safe bit of physiology). See how it goes.

- As the curriculum emerges, keep in mind the four basic principles of ecology Barry Commoner outlined in his *The Closing Circle*.[30]

    1. Everything is connected.
    2. Everything goes somewhere.
    3. Nature knows best.
    4. There's no such thing as a free lunch.

  See how you can incorporate these four important concepts, so that they take root in the children as they begin to mind their bodies, their own personal ecosystems.

- **Have fun!**

Bodyworks Bogglers

The Bogglers are here to engage you. Perhaps they'll pique your curiosity about some aspect of the body, send you to the library to "look it up." As you absorb a critical mass of information, you'll became more and more aware of your own body, your complex and mysterious workings. Your learning process will develop the sensitivity and the mastery of resources you'll need for The Bodyworks. It will prepare you to guide children as they discover their own questions and grow their own answers.

Should you try the Bogglers with children? Body facts can amaze children—or overwhelm and distress them. A good teacher must be ready to help children translate and, perhaps, tame some facts in order to assimilate them. Remember: everything depends on the context, the climate of trust and openness in the learning community.

Questions

1. What's the real shape and size of my eyes?
2. How many muscles do I use to smile?
3. What's my odorprint?
4. How fast is a sneeze?
5. Which muscle can twist and turn the most?
6. What's the purpose of an eyebrow?
7. Would I get a good night's sleep in my friend's greenhouse?
8. How strong is a hair?
9. How much saliva does my mouth make?
10. Why do I always think of my grandmother when I smell vanilla?
11. How hard does my heart work?
12. How long does a cell live?
13. Where do all those dead cells go?
14. Can I swallow standing on my head?
15. What's my smallest bone?
16. How big is my brain?
17. Is skin mainly a bag for flesh?
18. Why do I need 8 hours of sleep?
19. What part of my body is the most important?
20. Why do I need a layer of fat?

Answers

1. Each eye is the size and shape of a pingpong ball.
2. It takes 14 muscles to smile, more to frown. We use 100 muscles to make faces.
3. Your scent is as unique as your fingerprint (ask any dog). By smell, a mother can pick her own newborn's shirt from others' in the nursery. Even strangers can smell-match T-shirts worn by a mother and her young children. There's a huge industry devoted to suppressing natural scents. What are we missing? Napoleon wrote Josephine from battle: "Don't wash. I'm coming home."
4. A sneeze was clocked at 103 mph! Sneezes hold about 20,000 droplets of air. The largest fly 15 ft. before falling. The smallest stay in the air up to an hour. Millions of viruses fit into a drop the size of the period at the end of this sentence.
5. Your tongue! It's the only muscle that's free at one end.
6. It protects your eye from dripping sweat, and also deflects some glare.
7. Probably not. You'd be competing for fresh air with the plants. Plants respire carbon dioxide in daylight, but at night they respire oxygen like you.
8. Stronger than a steel wire the same diameter! Try taping one end of a hair to a clothes pole. You can suspend up to 2 oz. from the other end.
9. Your salivary glands secrete 1–2 quarts a day.
10. Smell and long-term memory centers are neighbors in the brain. A lot of neurons must have crisscrossed in your grandmother's kitchen.
11. Clasp your hands together and put them in a basin of water. Squeeze. Relax. Do that 70 times in one minute. Tired? Your heart pumps 1-1/2 gallons a minute, 8,000 gallons a day. It beats well over 2 billion times in a life of 75 years. If your blood vessels were stretched end to end, they'd reach around the world several times, or almost halfway to the moon. They hold 25 trillion red blood cells, each of which lives 3–4 months. Your body makes 2 million red blood cells every second.
12. A scavenging white cell: 30 hours; a gut cell: 3-5 days; skin: 19 days; sperm: 2-1/2 months; eyelash: 3–4 months; liver cell: 8 months; hair: 2–4 years; bone cell: 15–25 years. Your body replaces 98% of its atoms every year.
13. About 1/3 dry feces is dead cells; 1/3 is bacteria; 1/3 is indigestible fiber.

14. If you can stand on your head, yes! Put your fingers on your Adam's apple. Feel it move—closing off your windpipe by pushing it against your epiglottis, so you won't choke. Waves of contractions—muscles, not gravity—do the rest of the job.

15. The stirrup bone in your middle ear is the size of a grain of rice.

16. If you could order up a brain at your local deli, it would fill 3 pint containers, about a pound each. It contains tens of billions of neurons, with ten times that number of glial cells. It would take about 30,000 neurons to fill the head of a pin, but a neuron's nucleus contains a molecule of DNA which—if it could be stretched out—is a meter long! Take a cubic centimeter of brain tissue and splice together all its little pathways—end to end they'd reach about 400 miles (Boston to Washington? Los Angeles to San Francisco?).

17. Some baggie! Your skin weighs in at about 6 pounds, covering 20 square feet of body, and it does a lot of important work for you. Put a quarter on your forearm. The skin under that quarter contains about 3 million cells, 3 feet of blood vessels, 100 sweat glands, 250 sensory receptors, and 50 nerve endings.

18. You probably know about REM sleep (usually about 2 hours a night), and the psychological disruptions that occur when we are deprived of dreamtime. The bodymind uses the other six hours for complex tasks, for instance: the organization of neuronal networks; the increased secretion of growth hormone needed to replace all those cells you're sloughing off every second.

19. The brain devotes widely different amounts of tissue to different body parts. Your hands and face may not be "the most important," but from the brain's perspective, they are perhaps the most labor-intensive. Your thumb and tongue take up the most space in the brain. It's no coincidence that our human species is noted for tool use and complex language.

20. That fat of yours holds your skin on, insulates you, serves as an emergency pantry to keep you going when food runs out, and does the work of springs and shock absorbers.

Books for The Bodyworks

Many of the books I found most useful won't be available to you. Some of the best are out-of-print. (Due to changes in our tax laws, many new books are quickly remaindered.) Your library probably has a core of good books about the human body at every reading level. I list only a few.

Allison, Linda. *Blood and Guts.* Boston: Little, Brown, and Co., 1976. For older children, and to inspire teachers. Good experiments and exercises in that "do-it-yourself" spirit.

Buxbaum, Susan and Rita Gelman. *Body Noises.* NY: Alfred Knopf, 1983. The how and why of sneezes, snores, yawns, hiccups, burps, gas, stomach growls, cracking bones, etc.

Bruun, R.D. and Bertel Bruun. *The Human Body.* NY: Random House, 1982. Excellent reference for adults. Anatomy and physiology, tissues and cells by system.

Eyewitness Books. *Visual Dictionary of the Human Body.* London: Dorling Kindersley, 1991. Like others in this series: wonderful illustrations from models and photographs.

Glaser, Linda. *Wonderful Worms.* Brookfield, CT.:The Millbrook Press, 1992. The perfect picture book on the subject.

Harlan, Jean D. *Science Experiences for the Early Childhood Years* (6th ed.). Englewood Cliffs, NJ: Prentice-Hall, 1996. An indispensable resource for teachers. Few of us feel well-prepared to guide "discovery science." This book empowers us to learn as we teach.

Holt, Bess-Gene. *Science with Young Children* (rev. ed.). Washington, DC: NAEYC, 1989. Her concept of "personal ecology" provides firm footing for the teacher reinventing The Bodyworks.

Ingoglia, Gina. *Look Inside Your Body.* NY: Grosset and Dunlap, 1989. A board book, somewhat less enticing than *Outside-In*, but very sturdy and well-conceived.

Kaufman, Joe. *How We Are Born, How We Grow, How Our Bodies Work, and How We Learn.* NY: Golden Press, 1975. Aimed at children 6–12, an excellent family or classroom reference book to help children understand and adults explain.

Plaut, Thomas F., M.D.*Children with Asthma: A Manual for Parents.* Amherst, MA: Pedi Press, 1988, 1995. As environmental pollution increases, so does the incidence of asthma. Dr. Plaut's work empowers children, their parents, and physicians to form an effective partnership for the management of symptoms, with minimum danger and disruption. This book will help teachers understand and support children who have asthma, and also help their peers develop an appropriate attitude toward chronic illness.

Quinsey, Mary Beth. *Why Does That Man Have Such a Big Nose?* Seattle: Parenting Press, 1986. Some "embarassing questions" and their answers. How to respect children's curiosity while developing their sensitivity to others' feelings.

Rockwell, Robert, Robert Williams, Elizabeth Sherwood. *Everybody Has a Body.* Mt. Rainier, MD: Gryphon House, 1992. A compendium of one-page body activities for early childhood teachers, with a useful overview of information for adults at the beginning of each section.

Samuels, Mike and Nancy Samuels. *The Well Child Book*. NY: Summit Books, 1982. Three big sections: Preventive Medicine (for parents), How the Body Works (for children), Common Illnesses and Accidents. A good source of ideas for games and demonstrations, as well as an excellent reference for teachers.

Settel, Joanne and Nancy Bagget. *Why Does My Nose Run?* NY: Atheneum, 1985. The why of wrinkles, ear wax, dead skin, laryngitis, yawns, shivers, goose bumps, hair falling out, etc. All the questions and answers, concise and clear. For older children, but relevant sections can be read aloud as is.

Smallman, Clare and Edwina Riddell. *Outside-In.* Woodbury, NY: Barron's, n.d. The best of the best, but plan to supervise its use due to the flaps (I hinged these in clear plastic, and added color tabs, greatly adding to the classroom life of the book).

Stein, Sara.*The Body Book.* NY: Workman, 1992. This one was in the children's section at the library, but it's as sophisticated as I will ever need. Up-to-date comprehensive view of biochemistry as well as anatomy, physiology, embryology, etc. In a vigorous and poetic style, Stein does justice to the wonder and the complexity of her topic. She does a terrific job relating the human body to the larger world and throws in amazing and memorable facts that will change the way you think.

Stinson, Kathy. *The Bare Naked Book*. Toronto: Annick Press, 1986. Another of Annick Press' warm, droll, down-to-earth offerings. Very few words. Lots of pictures of people of different ages and sizes and colors and genders being at home in their bodies in a variety of familiar ways.

Watson, Jane Werner. *My Body—How It Works*. NY: Golden Press, 1972. Part of a series done in cooperation with the Menninger Foundation. Low-key, no-nonsense, exactly what young children want to know.

Blueprints for The Bodyworks

The Self-Portrait ("Outsides")

Materials

large sheet of sturdy paper (brown wrapping paper), approximately 36" x 48"
indelible marker, brushes, and tempera paints
scissors, hole punch, gummed reinforcement hole
8" length of string
coat hanger
large role of cellophane tape (for repairs)
full-length mirror, if possible

Method

The child lies down on wrapping paper, arms/hands/fingers slightly spread out. The teacher outlines the child's body with marker. The child looks in mirror, notes hair/eye/skin color, placement of features, other distinguishing characteristics (birthmarks, freckles, missing teeth, etc.). The teacher and child mix paints to match. The child paints her head. The child plans colors and patterns for clothes, to match today's or a favorite outfit at home. The teacher helps mix paints. The child paints the remainder of her body, moving gradually from the head down to the feet.

When the painting is dry, the child cuts out the outline, punches a hole at the top of the head, and glues a reinforcement hole to each side. The teacher and child tie a length of string and loop it through the hole, then suspend the finished portrait from a coat hanger, ready to be enjoyed. (If there's a group of children, it's helpful to write each child's name on the back side of the right foot, easy to identify when there's a whole rack of bodies being assembled.) A large roll of tape is handy for repairs—some enthusiastic scissor-wielders are apt to make dismaying slashes.

Concepts

This is the time for relaxed, affirming conversation about what makes the child special. It will take skill and sensitivity to help the child navigate realistically between her own desires for detailed representation and her mastery of the paintbrush. (Some children set impossible standards for themselves. Others try to avoid the issue by, say, intentionally painting their faces "green like the Joker.")

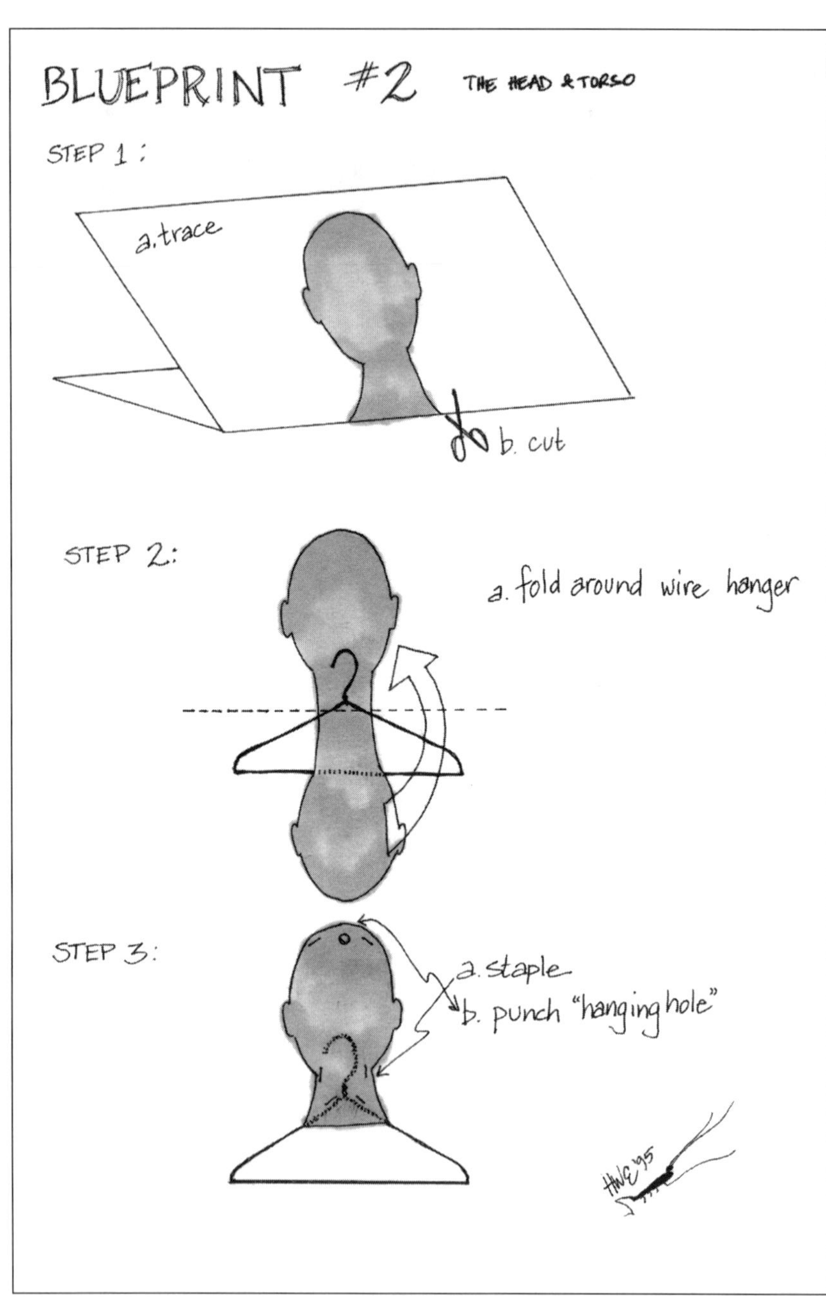
BLUEPRINT #2
THE HEAD & TORSO
STEP 1:
a. trace
b. cut
STEP 2:
a. fold around wire hanger
STEP 3:
a. staple
b. punch "hanging hole"
HWE '95

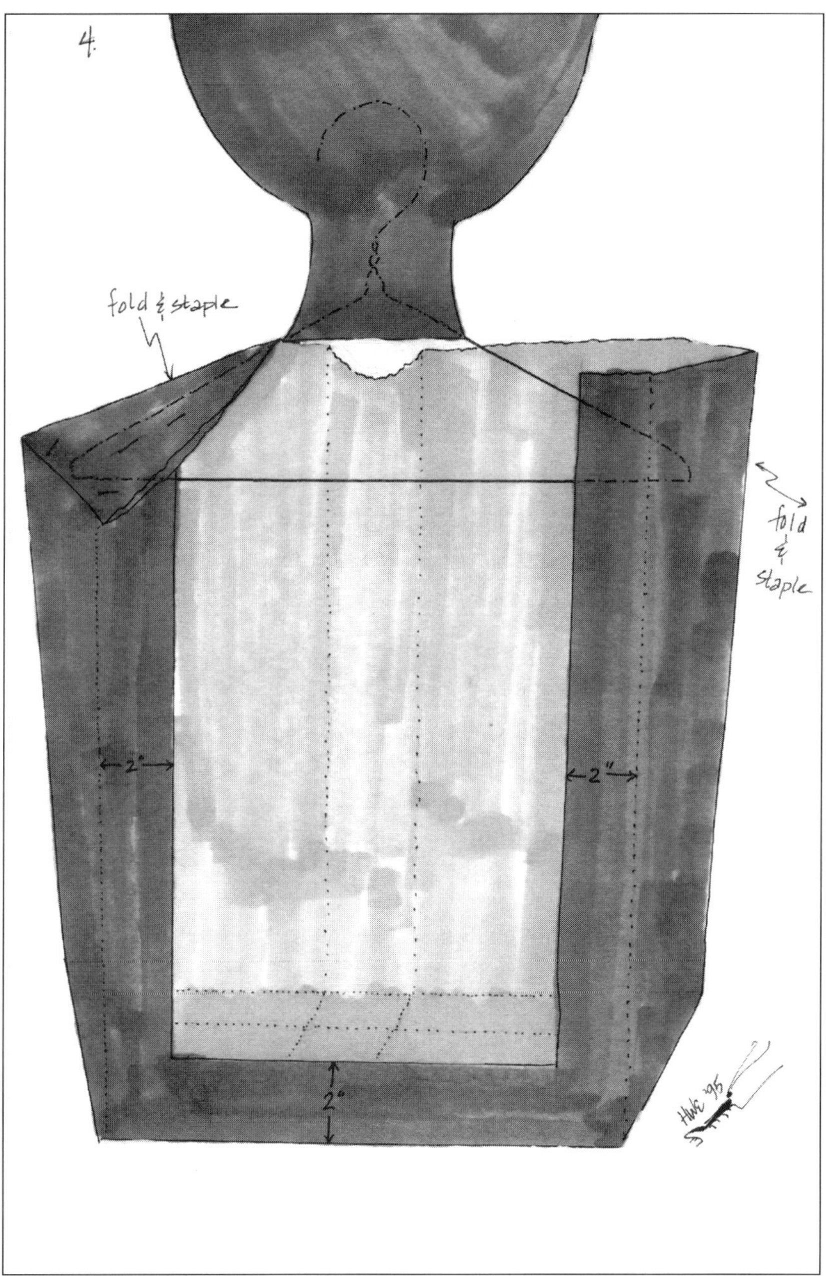
4.
fold & staple
fold & staple
2"
2"
2"
HWE '95

The Head and Torso ("Insides")

Materials

poster board/oak tag approximately 8" x 20"
large standard brown paper grocery bag
coat hanger
8" length string
gummed reinforcement holes
hole punch, stapler, scissors, pencil

Method

Fold the cardboard lengthwise. Have the child lie down on the floor with the folded cardboard as a "pillow." Place the fold where the neck meets the shoulders. Beginning at the fold, trace up one side of the neck, around the ear, across the top of the head and down to the other shoulder (or have the child trace a pattern you've made). Cut around the outline, taking care not to cut through the neck.

Open this double "head" piece and lay it flat. Then place the hook of a coat hanger on the fold. Enclose the hook by joining the two "heads" at the top. Help the child staple them firmly together. You now have a poster board "head" and "neck" attached to coat hanger "shoulders."

Take the paper bag and spread it open as if to fill it. Cut away most of the front panel, leaving a margin of 2" around the side and bottom creases of the bag. Slip the coat hanger head-and-shoulders into the top of the bag. Hold the front and back edges of the bag together and fold them as one thickness over the "shoulders" of the coat hanger. Help the child staple the bag securely in place.

Now you have the basic head-and-torso of the "Insides." Punch a hole at the top of the head, reinforce it, and loop a string through it as you did with the self-portrait. It can be suspended from the same coat hanger as the child's "Outsides," although you may find it easier to store them separately during the construction process.

Concepts

There's not much a young child can do to help at this stage, since the cutting requires adult scissors and skills. You may prefer to prepare the torso in advance. However, if you have time, the child may enjoy the planning, laying out materials and tools, and finishing touches.

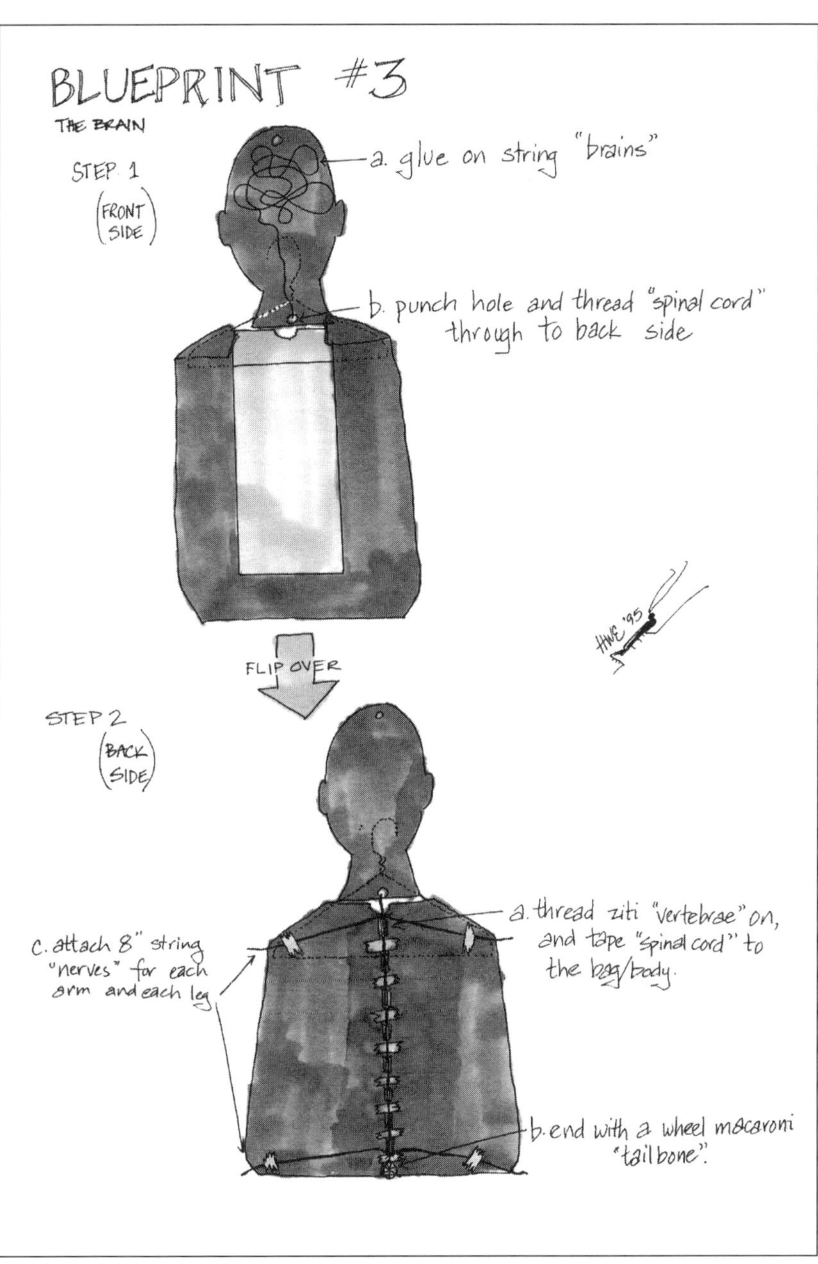
BLUEPRINT #3
THE BRAIN
STEP 1
(FRONT SIDE)
a. glue on string "brains"
b. punch hole and thread "spinal cord" through to back side
FLIP OVER
STEP 2
(BACK SIDE)
a. thread ziti "vertebrae" on, and tape "spinal cord" to the bag/body.
c. attach 8" string "nerves" for each arm and each leg
b. end with a wheel macaroni "tailbone".
HWE '95

The Brain

Materials

ball of gray yarn or heavy white twine
approximately 12 large "rigatoni" or "ziti" macaroni, uncooked
one "wheel" macaroni, uncooked
glue, cellophane tape, scissors, hole punch

Method

The child cuts a length of yarn or twine, approximately 48". The child applies glue to the top of the front of the head, then loops and coils twine randomly in the glue to represent brain mass, leaving a loose end approximately 24" long. This will become the spinal cord. The child punches hole at base of neck and passes the end of the twine through the hole to the back of the head, gently pulling it straight down the middle of the outside of the "torso" bag. With a piece of tape, the child anchors the twine to the top of the bag.

The child threads one piece of ziti onto the twine and pushes it up to the base of the neck, then secures it by taping the twine to the bag directly below the piece of ziti. This represents the top vertebra. The child repeats the process, vertebra by vertebra, until the spinal column runs the length of the bag. At the end of the twine, the child attaches the wheel "tailbone," and tapes that in place.

The child cuts 4 lengths of twine , each approximately 8". She tapes one length of twine to the spinal cord somewhere near the top, and extends it out to one side of the bag, as if it were to connect to an arm. She pairs this "nerve" with another length of twine extending from the same place to the opposite side of the bag. This process is repeated with the remaining lengths of twine, which are attached somewhere near the bottom of the spinal cord, as if to connect to each leg.

Concepts

- The brain is inside the head, protected by the skull bones.
- The brain tells other parts of the body what to do.
- Messages travel back and forth from the brain, on nerves.
- The nerves are like streets that connect all the parts of the body to the brain.
- If you put your finger on a hot stove, a message travels fast along the

nerve to the brain, saying "HOT!" Then the brain sends a message back to your finger muscle, saying "GET OFF!"

- Many nerves are bundled together in a big highway down your back so messages can go fast from your brain all the way to the tips of your fingers and toes; this highway is called the spinal cord.
- The spinal cord is protected by lots of little bones called vertebrae—you can feel the bony bumps down the middle of your back.
- Your back needs to be able to bend and twist around—that's why there are many small bones instead of one big bone. (Feel the difference between your back and your shin bone, which can't bend at all.)

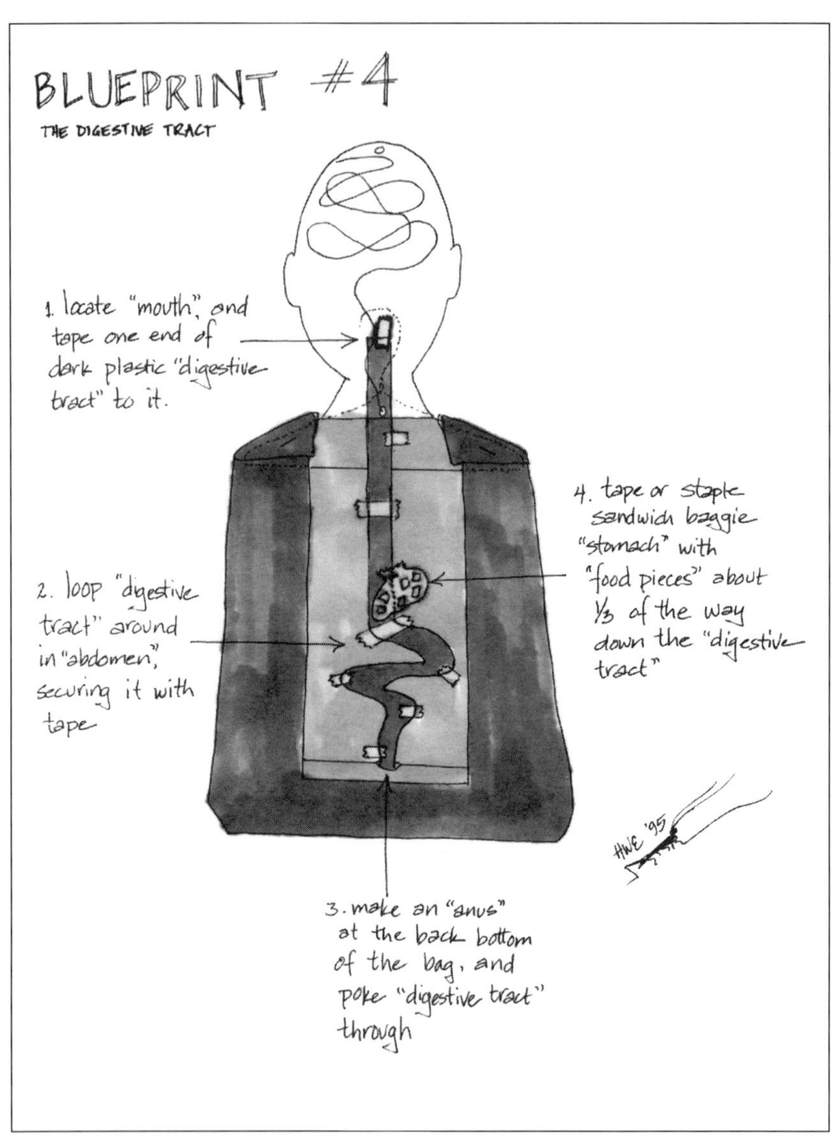
BLUEPRINT #4
THE DIGESTIVE TRACT
1. locate "mouth," and tape one end of dark plastic "digestive tract" to it.
4. tape or staple sandwich baggie "stomach" with "food pieces" about 1/3 of the way down the "digestive tract"
2. loop "digestive tract" around in "abdomen," securing it with tape
HWE '95
3. make an "anus" at the back bottom of the bag, and poke "digestive tract" through

The Digestive Tract

Materials

1 1/2" x 30" strip cut from large dark-colored baggie (garbage can liner)
small sandwich baggie
assorted colors of construction paper (Scraps are fine.)
transparent tape, hole punch, scissors

Method

Preparation for the digestive tract easily overlaps with the construction of the brain. Each child lists what she ate at dinner the previous evening and matches each item to an appropriate color of construction paper. The teacher records the menu. Children use scissors to "chew" small bites of paper, which they collect into a sandwich baggie "stomach."

"Stomachs" can be made with minimal supervision. As the children work, they may enjoy chatting about foods they like and don't like. It is a natural moment for "nutrition education." You may prefer to allow the children to develop and direct the conversation themselves, and to give yourself the opportunity to be more active as observer than as participant, or to oversee other areas of the classroom.

Use circle time to introduce the digestive tract, so you can set the tone for straightforward discussion of a subject area you know will be "loaded" for children (and many adults). The entire group can offer suggestions as you trace a bite of dinner from the table to the toilet.

The addition of the digestive system to the bodyworks does not take much time. It is represented simply by a long strip cut from a giant "garbage baggie." The child tries to determine approximately where the "mouth" would be on the "head" of the bodyworks. She tapes one end of the strip at the location of the "mouth," and tapes the "esophagus" portion down to the point where the "stomach" will be attached.

Then she loops "the intestine" portion of the "food tube" back and forth inside the torso, taping the coils in place on the inside surface of the bag.

She leaves the end free, and uses scissors or a hole punch to poke a small hole in the base of the bag near the back wall. She inserts the free end into the hole now named the "rectum" (or "anus").

She staples or tapes the "stomach" baggie full of her construction paper "dinner" about 1/3 of the way down the digestive tract.

Concepts

- Food gives our bodies energy to live and grow and do things. (We need food for energy, like a car needs gas to go.)
- Our bodies have to change the food to get the vitamins and minerals out of it. (We call these changes "digestion.")
- The changes start in our mouths, when we chew the food into little pieces and our saliva/spit helps make it juicy and soupy so we can swallow it easily.
- Food goes down a tube/pipe into our stomachs. (The "esophagus" is the part of the tube that goes from our mouths to our stomachs.)
- Our stomachs are like blenders where all the food is broken up into little tiny parts that can travel in our blood to all the other parts of our bodies.
- Our bodies can't use everything—some of what we eat is left over inside us. This is "garbage" we have to get rid of.
- The "garbage" is squeezed through another part of our food tube called the "intestine" (or the "guts"). The intestine is 30 ft. long ("as long as . . ." our classroom?), all curled up in the middle of our bodies. The muscles in the intestine move the food down the tube the way our hands squeeze a tube of toothpaste.
- At the end of the tube is an opening to the outside, called the "rectum" (or "anus").
- We can feel when our bodies are ready to throw the "garbage" away, so we go sit on the toilet. Our muscles open up the hole and squeeze the "garbage" out.
- There are many different names for this "garbage" we flush down the toilet: bowel movement, stool, poo, poopees, kaka, etc.
- We don't touch the "garbage" from the bodies of people and other animals, because it contains bacteria that may make us sick. However, worms and other small creatures that live in the earth use our garbage for food. When our "garbage" passes through their bodies, it goes back into the earth, making food for plants. The plants suck up the vitamins and minerals from the earth. The plants put this energy into fruits and nuts and seeds and leaves, which feed people and other animals.
- Everything people eat comes directly from plants, or through other animals that eat plants. People, the soil (full of little creatures like earthworms), and plants are food partners. The food goes around in a big circle.

• Sometimes we swallow air with our food. Some food is hard to change into energy inside our bodies. It makes little bubbles of gas. When gas in our stomachs bubbles back up and comes out our mouths, we call it a "burp." When gas in our intestines bubbles out our rectums, we call it a "fart" or "gas."

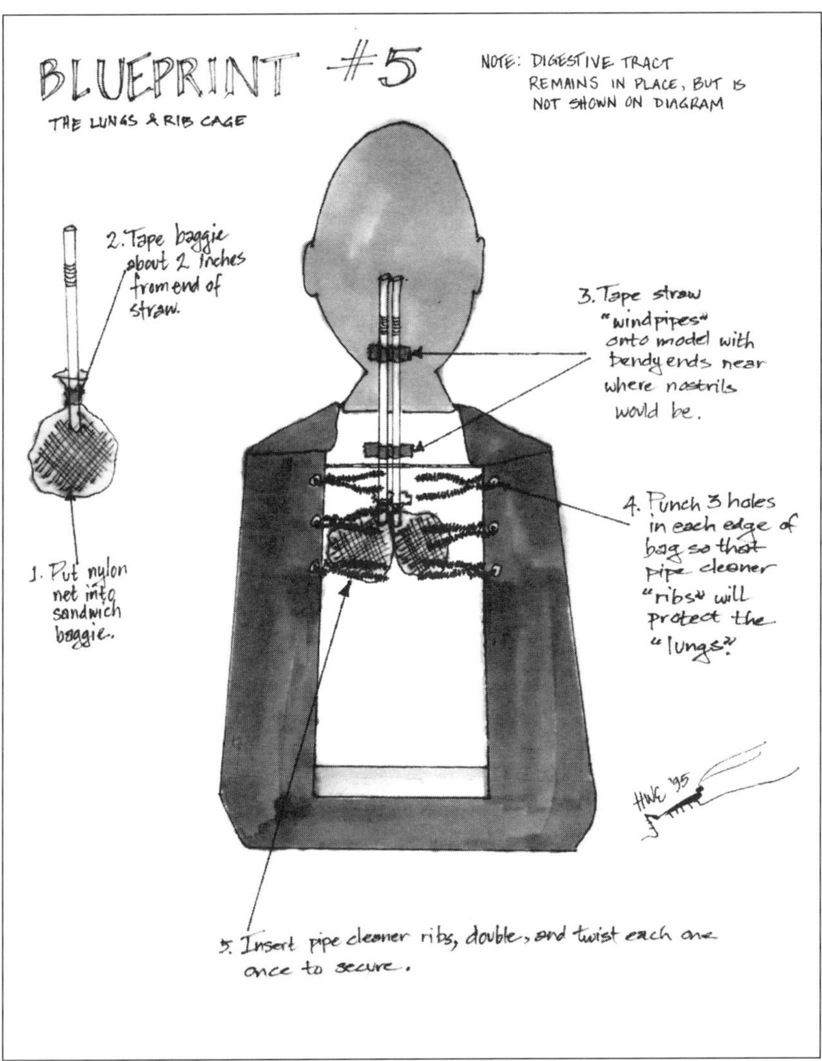

The Lungs and Rib Cage

Materials

2 bendy straws
2 2" x 12" pieces of pink nylon net
6 12" pipe cleaners (all one color, if possible, but not yellow)
2 sandwich baggies
transparent tape, hole punch
(*Optional:* 2 small branching twigs without leaves, collected when shrubs are pruned, etc.*)

Method

The child puts one piece of nylon net in each small baggie.

The child inserts the straight end of a bendy drinking straw into each baggie, and tapes the baggie shut about two inches from the base of the straw. She tapes the two straws together in the middle, with a baggie hanging from each straw. She positions the bendy ends of the straws on the head of the bodyworks, at the approximate location of the "nostrils," and tapes the "windpipe," in place at several points. She leaves the ends of the straws free to bend so she can blow through them to inflate the baggie "lungs," which extend down into the "chest."

To make the ribs, the child punches three holes along each edge of the big grocery bag "torso" at chest height, about 1/2" from the edge. She inserts a pipe cleaner into each hole, bends it in half, and twists it twice at the hole to secure it. These "ribs" extend across the "chest" cavity, partly enclosing the lungs. (*Optional:* At the end of the project, after all other organs are in place, the ends of the pipe cleaners may be joined to those opposite, in order to close the rib cage.)

Concepts

- We can't see air, but we know it's there—we can blow it out to fill a balloon, or see it make a cloud on a mirror.
- When we breathe, air goes in and out our nostrils and sometimes our mouths.
- The air goes down a breathing tube next to the food tube. We call this the "windpipe."

*To underscore the relationship between animal and plant life, wrap the nylon net around the branching end of a small twig. Put the net-wrapped twig into the baggie with the branches at the bottom and the stem-end up, to look like an upside-down tree.

- There's a flap on top of the windpipe, to cover it up when we swallow food. When we choke, it's because the flap didn't close in time and food starts to go down the wrong tube by mistake.
- The lungs are like air bags full of little tubes and tiny pockets for air.
- The rib bones are curved. They move in and out as the lungs fill and empty.
- The blood carries the fresh air from the lungs to all the other parts of the body.
- The used-up air goes back out the nostrils when we breathe out.
- The used-up air isn't good for people and other animals after we breathe it out, but it's healthy for plants and trees. They use the air and change it, so when the plants and trees breathe out the air, it's good for people and animals again. Plants and animals are breathing partners. Air goes around in another circle like the circle of food.
- Our lungs full of little tubes look like upside-down trees full of branches.
- When you have a bad cold, your breathing tubes may fill up with mucus, which is the thick gluey stuff your body makes to trap germs. There is always a little mucus, but when there's a lot, it may be hard to breathe.
- Many children have asthma, which makes it hard for them to breathe if they get near certain things like animals or plants or dust. They learn to pay careful attention, so they know when to take medicine to help clear out their breathing tubes.[31]

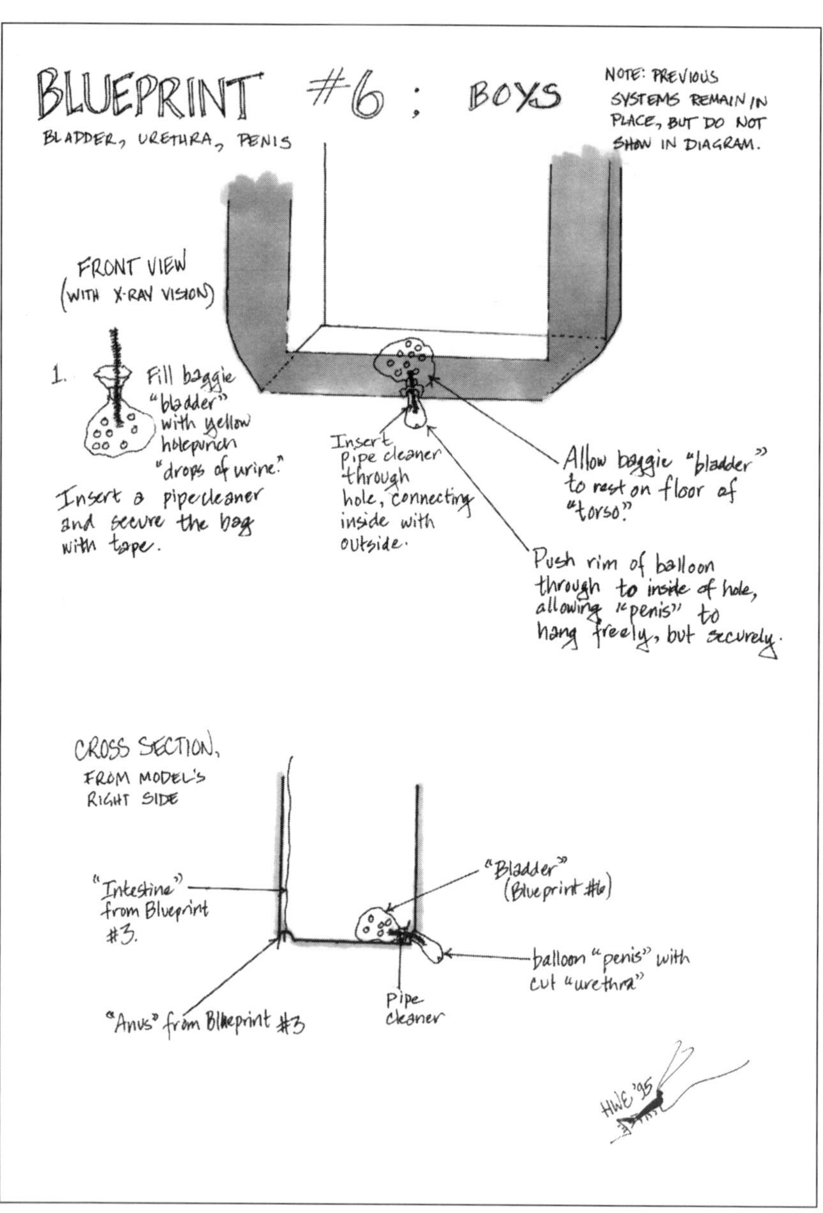
BLUEPRINT #6 : BOYS
BLADDER, URETHRA, PENIS
NOTE: PREVIOUS SYSTEMS REMAIN IN PLACE, BUT DO NOT SHOW IN DIAGRAM.
FRONT VIEW (WITH X-RAY VISION)
1. Fill baggie "bladder" with yellow holepunch "drops of urine."
Insert a pipecleaner and secure the bag with tape.
Insert pipe cleaner through hole, connecting inside with outside.
Allow baggie "bladder" to rest on floor of "torso."
Push rim of balloon through to inside of hole, allowing "penis" to hang freely, but securely.
CROSS SECTION, FROM MODEL'S RIGHT SIDE
"Intestine" from Blueprint #3.
"Bladder" (Blueprint #6)
balloon "penis" with cut "urethra"
Pipe cleaner
"Anus" from Blueprint #3
HWE '95

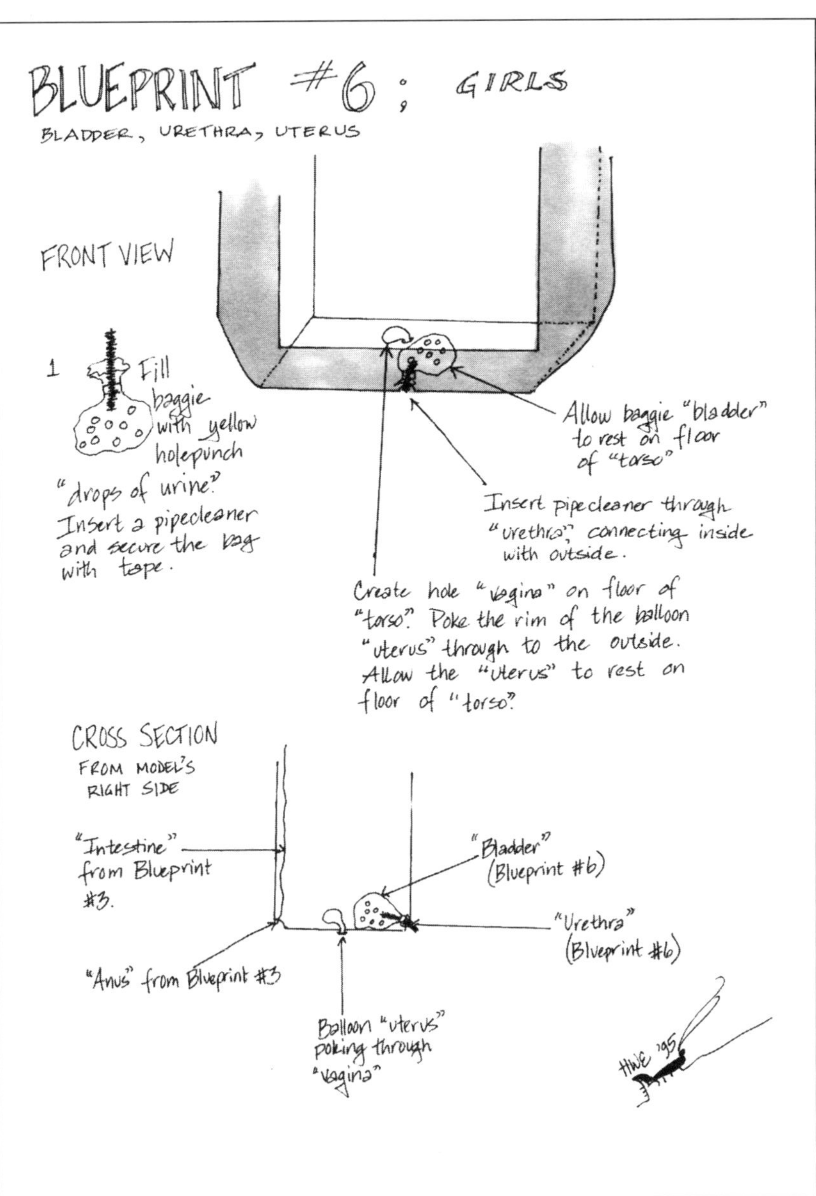
BLUEPRINT #6: GIRLS
BLADDER, URETHRA, UTERUS
FRONT VIEW
1 Fill baggie with yellow holepunch "drops of urine." Insert a pipecleaner and secure the bag with tape.
Allow baggie "bladder" to rest on floor of "torso"
Insert pipecleaner through "urethra," connecting inside with outside.
Create hole "vagina" on floor of "torso." Poke the rim of the balloon "uterus" through to the outside. Allow the "uterus" to rest on floor of "torso."
CROSS SECTION
FROM MODEL'S RIGHT SIDE
"Intestine" from Blueprint #3.
"Bladder" (Blueprint #6)
"Urethra" (Blueprint #6)
"Anus" from Blueprint #3
Balloon "uterus" poking through "vagina"
HWE '95

Bladder, Urethra, Penis, Uterus

Materials

2 1/2" balloons in various colors (not inflated)
small baggie
yellow construction paper
12" pipe cleaner (yellow, if possible)
transparent tape, hole punch, scissors

Method

Discuss the urinary tract at circle time, reinforcing concepts already introduced in work on the digestive tract. These subjects clearly stir deep feelings. Some children may "forget" the words they use for "urine" and "urinate." Some may giggle when others volunteer family vocabulary. Some may fidget and squirm during the discussion.

Introduce or reinforce the notion that in most ways girls' and boys' bodies are alike. However, boys have a penis on the outside, while girls have a uterus (womb) on the inside, where a baby can grow if the girl decides to be a mother when she grows up). Sing "Everybody's Fancy" with the children.

The week before construction of the bladder, have the children punch many small circles from the yellow construction paper. (The small circles represent drops of urine.) This activity can be a sociable time for a tableful of children, without adult help.

The following week, each child—working with a teacher— collects a small handful of yellow circles (10–20) in a sandwich baggie, and inserts a yellow pipe cleaner partway into the baggie. The child gathers up the open edges of the baggie and tapes it shut around the pipe cleaner. The teacher helps the child use pointed scissors to poke a small hole in the base of the brown paper bag torso, near the front.

Each boy chooses a balloon to represent the penis, and works from the outside of the torso to push the rim of the penis balloon through the hole in the base of the paper bag. The rim of the balloon remains inside the bag. To link bladder and urethra, the boy inserts the end of the pipe cleaner into the neck of the penis balloon. He cuts a tiny hole (urethra) in the tip of the penis balloon.

To link bladder and urethra, each girl inserts the end of the pipe cleaner into the hole (urethra) at the front of the base of the paper bag. Each girl chooses a balloon to represent the uterus. She uses the pointed scissors to poke another hole (the vagina) in the base of the paper bag torso, midway between the urethra and the rectum. Working from the inside of the torso, she inserts the rim of the balloon through the vagina hole, leaving the body of the balloon inside the base of the torso.

Each boy's and each girl's bladder will lie loosely inside the torso until a later stage of construction. Then, the tying-on of veins and arteries will suspend the bladder inside the torso.

Concepts

- The bladder is a kind of bag that fills up with wet garbage, liquid your body needs to throw away.
- You can feel when your bladder is getting full, and your brain sends a message: "Time to go to the toilet."
- When you get to the toilet, your brain tells your muscles to let go so all the urine/pee/tinkle/toto can come down a tube and out a little opening called the urethra.
- A boy's urethra is at the end of his penis; a girl's urethra is at the front of her body, between her legs.
- Boys' bodies look fancy on the outside because of the penis. Girls' bodies look fancy on the inside because they have a special place called a uterus where a baby can grow if the girl decides to be a mother when she grows up. The stretchy opening of the uterus is called the vagina.

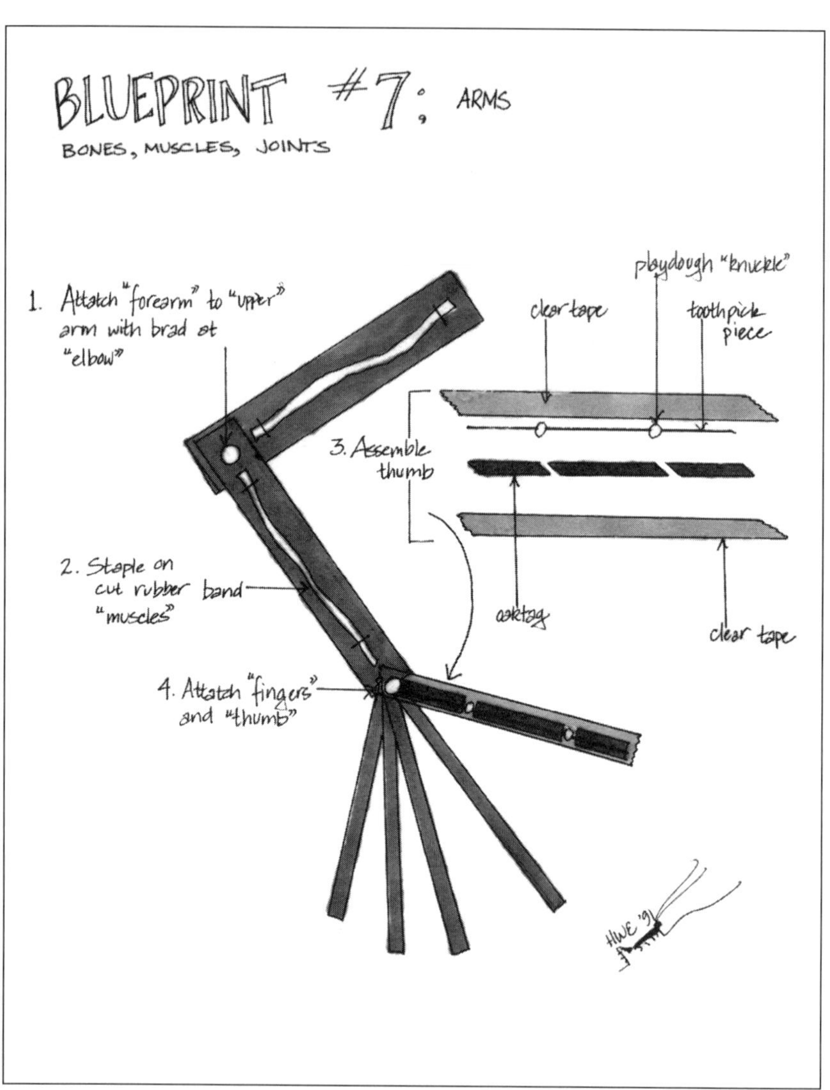
BLUEPRINT #7: ARMS
BONES, MUSCLES, JOINTS
1. Attatch "forearm" to "upper" arm with brad at "elbow"
2. Staple on cut rubber band "muscles"
3. Assemble thumb
4. Attatch "fingers" and "thumb"
playdough "knuckle"
clear tape
toothpick piece
oaktag
clear tape
HWE '91

Bones, Muscles, Joints

Materials

poster board/oak tag strips (Use scrap from heads.)

approximate measurements:

- 2 thighs, 3" x 8"
- 2 shins, 2 1/4" x 9"
- 2 upper arms, 2" x 8"
- 2 forearms, 1-1/2" x 7"
- 10 foot/toe pieces, 1/4" x 8"
- 10 hand/finger pieces, 1/4" x 6"

2 toothpicks

4 small balls of playdough (1/4" diameter)

8 brass brads (paper fasteners, 1" long)

4 wide rubber bands (approximately 3" diameter, 9" long when cut)

wide transparent tape, hole punch, scissors, pencil, stapler

Method

The child punches a hole at the end of each precut oak tag arm and leg segment. She joins arm segments with a brad representing the elbow. She joins leg segments with a brad representing the knee. She punches a hole at each "shoulder" of the paper bag torso, and attaches the arm segments with a brad joint. She punches a hole at each lower front corner of the paper bag torso, and attaches the leg segment with a brad representing the hip joint.

She cuts the rubber bands in half, then staples one end of a rubber band "muscle" onto the oak tag "upper arm" near the "shoulder" and staples the other end of the muscle to the oak tag near the elbow. Another rubber band muscle is stapled to the oak tag "forearm" from elbow to "wrist." She attaches muscles to the leg segments, from "hip" to "knee", and "knee" to "ankle."

This is probably enough work for one day.

Another day, the child marks with a pencil and then snips off long narrow strips of oak tag to match the length of each one of her own toes from tip to ankle, and each finger from tip to wrist. She punches a hole in one end of each strip, and inserts a brad through five toe strips, then through the "ankle" hole on the "shin" segment.

For each "thumb," the child cuts the measured oak tag strip into three segments, and lays these on a broad piece of transparent tape, leaving small spaces between. She rolls tiny playdough balls for "knuckles" and places these in the spaces on the tape. Then she inserts bits of toothpick between the "knuckles" and lays another piece of broad transparent tape over the top, effectively enclosing the "skin, bones, and joints" of the thumb. She punches a hole through the base of the "thumb" and inserts a brad through the hole, followed by the four other finger lengths in sequence. She attaches the brad full of fingers to the hole at the "wrist" of the forearm segment, and spreads the fingers apart, with the thumb nearest the body.

The fingers and toes are a lot of work, and a child may need more than one "turn" to finish. It may be necessary to find shortcuts. (For example: The teacher may mass produce finger and toe segments. The children may only do one arm and one leg. Additional parts may be sent home to finish with parents.)

It's important to remind children that each finger and toe has small joints and bones, although only the thumb is fully constructed on the bodyworks. Similarly, there are muscles all over the body, although only the arm and leg muscles appear on the bodyworks.

This is the time to make full use of props: animal bones, skeleton, X-rays. Play the "Skelly" game. Sing "Bones, Muscles, and Joints." Experiment with stiff fingers or immobile thumbs. Try thumb prints and thumb print pictures.

Concepts

- Bones are hard, and they give the body a shape, "the skeleton."
- Muscles are the stretchy parts that move the bones when the brain tells them to move.
- Joints connect the bones, and allow parts of the body to bend.
- Some joints are like hinges on a door. Hinge joints let the bones move back and forth or up and down, like the jaw. Some joints are like balls. Ball joints let the bones move all around in a circle, like the shoulder, the neck, and the hip.
- Fingers have many joints, called knuckles, so hands can do all kinds of moving.
- Thumbs are connected to the side of the hand and this lets human hands pick up and hold things in special ways. Most other animals cannot use tools.
- The skin on the tips of fingers and toes has a pattern of lines and ridges. Even though the patterns look a lot alike, no one's pattern is exactly the same as anyone else's.

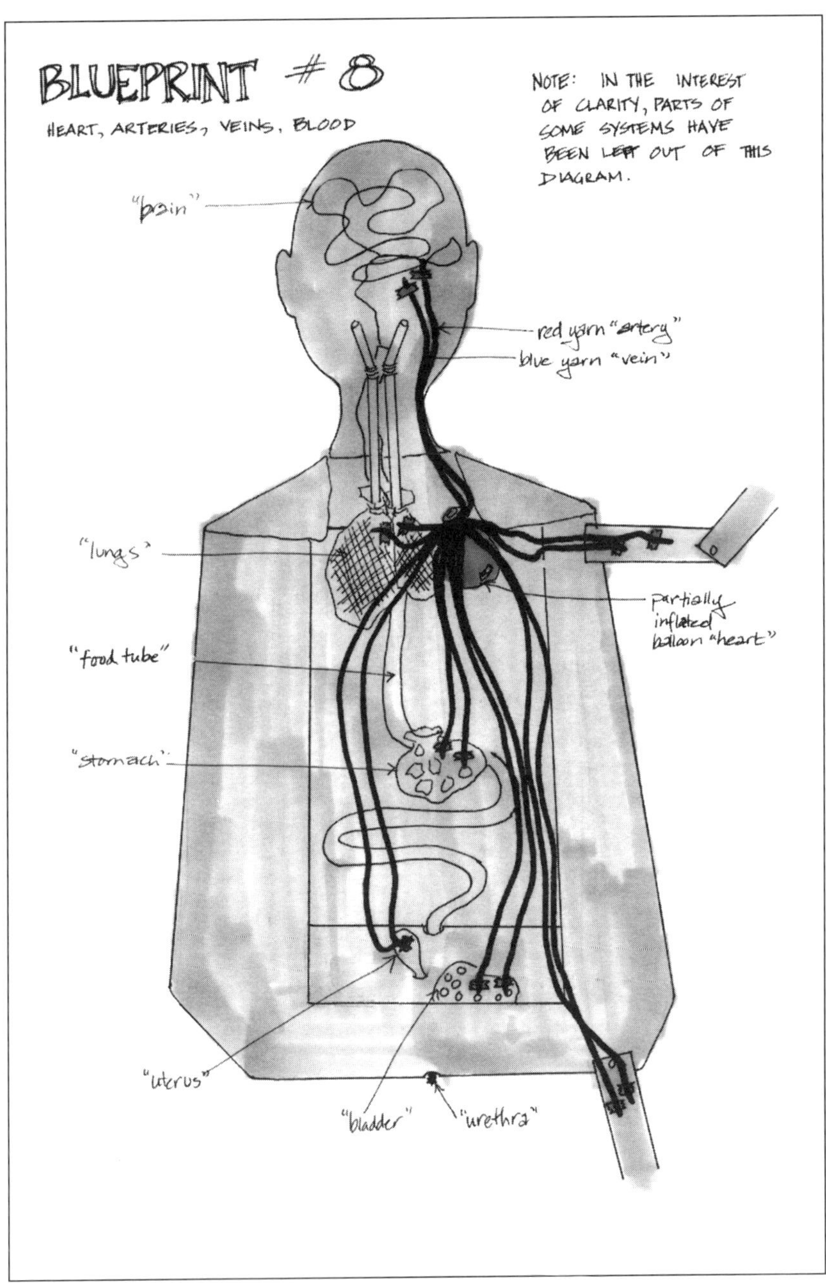
BLUEPRINT # 8
HEART, ARTERIES, VEINS, BLOOD
NOTE: IN THE INTEREST OF CLARITY, PARTS OF SOME SYSTEMS HAVE BEEN LEFT OUT OF THIS DIAGRAM.
"brain"
red yarn "artery"
blue yarn "vein"
"lungs"
partially inflated balloon "heart"
"food tube"
"stomach"
"uterus"
"bladder"
"urethra"

Heart, Arteries, Veins, Blood

Materials

4" red balloon (heavy-duty, not inflated)
9 16" lengths of red yarn
9 16" lengths of blue yarn
transparent tape

Method

After some stretching of the heavy-duty balloons, many children may be able to partially inflate them—a source of considerable satisfaction. (Beware of fully-inflated balloons, which tend to pop, crowd the torso, and cannot be "pumped.")

The teacher knots the neck of the balloon, and helps the child tie nine paired lengths of red and blue yarns around the neck of the balloon. (This can be done with one large knot, or pair by pair.) Next, teacher and child place the heart balloon inside the chest cavity of the bodyworks, tying the veins and arteries in one large knot to the clothes hanger.

Using transparent tape, the child attaches the free ends of one red and one blue yarn pair (artery and vein) to each organ: brain, lungs, stomach, bladder, penis or uterus, and also to each arm and each leg.

The heart has been saved for last. The big red balloon has been a prime attraction from the very beginning, helping to keep motivation high through some tedious moments. The veins and arteries serve to connect the different parts of the bodyworks.

Concepts

- The heart is a very strong muscle that pumps blood all through the body. A child's heart pumps almost 100 times a minute. It pumps many millions of times in a lifetime.
- Using long lengths of clear tubing, a bulb aspirator, and a bucket of red-colored water, each child can explore the pumping mechanism and develop a healthy respect for the strength of the heart.
- With a stethoscope, children can listen to the heart.
- To show the pulse, insert a toothpick into a small ball of playdough, then balance the playdough on the inside of a child's wrist. The toothpick moves slightly with each heartbeat.
- The blood is like a river that travels in pipes all over the body. It carries food to all the different parts, and it takes the garbage away.

- The blood also carries other things around the body. Red blood cells are like boats full of air going all over the body. White blood cells fight germs that make you sick. (To illustrate the blood as a distribution system: From an assortment of sequins and glitter, the children choose particular shapes and colors to represent red blood cells, white blood cells, platelets, food particles, oxygen, etc. Put these into a clear soda bottle containing water and red food coloring. Or try a Bodyworks snack: Dissolve gelatin into cranberry juice, and chill. When the gelatin is partially set, stir in raisins, cheerios, celery, nuts, etc. to represent red blood cells, white blood cells, platelets, food particles, oxygen, etc.)
- If you cut yourself, platelets make the blood get thick (or "clot"). The thick blood plugs up the hole, and then makes a hard scab to keep the rest of your blood inside your body. New skin grows under the scab.
- The heart pumps the blood full of fresh air all around your body in tubes called arteries. The blood full of fresh air looks red. You can see some of the little red arteries if you gently pull down your lower eyelid. (Wash your hands first.)
- When your body has used up the fresh air, your heart pumps the blood back to the heart in little tubes called veins. If your skin is light, the veins underneath look blue. You can see the veins on the back of your wrist, carrying the blood back to the heart for some more fresh air.

Bodyworking

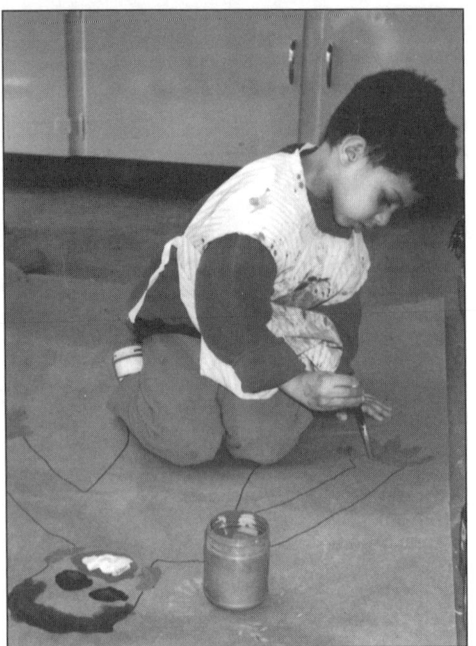

I'm painting me.

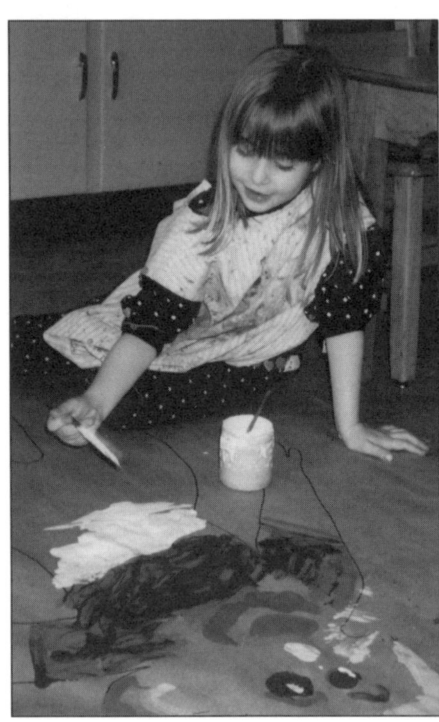

I matched my colors!

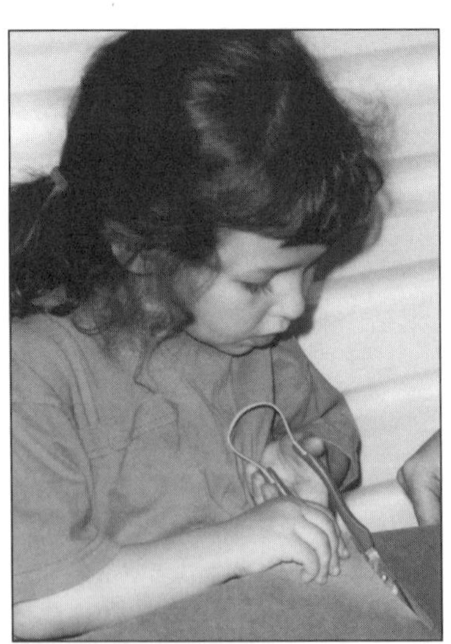

Cutting takes a long time.

THE WONDERFUL EGG
The little
RED
SEEDS AND MORE SEEDS
Draw Me a Star
Germs

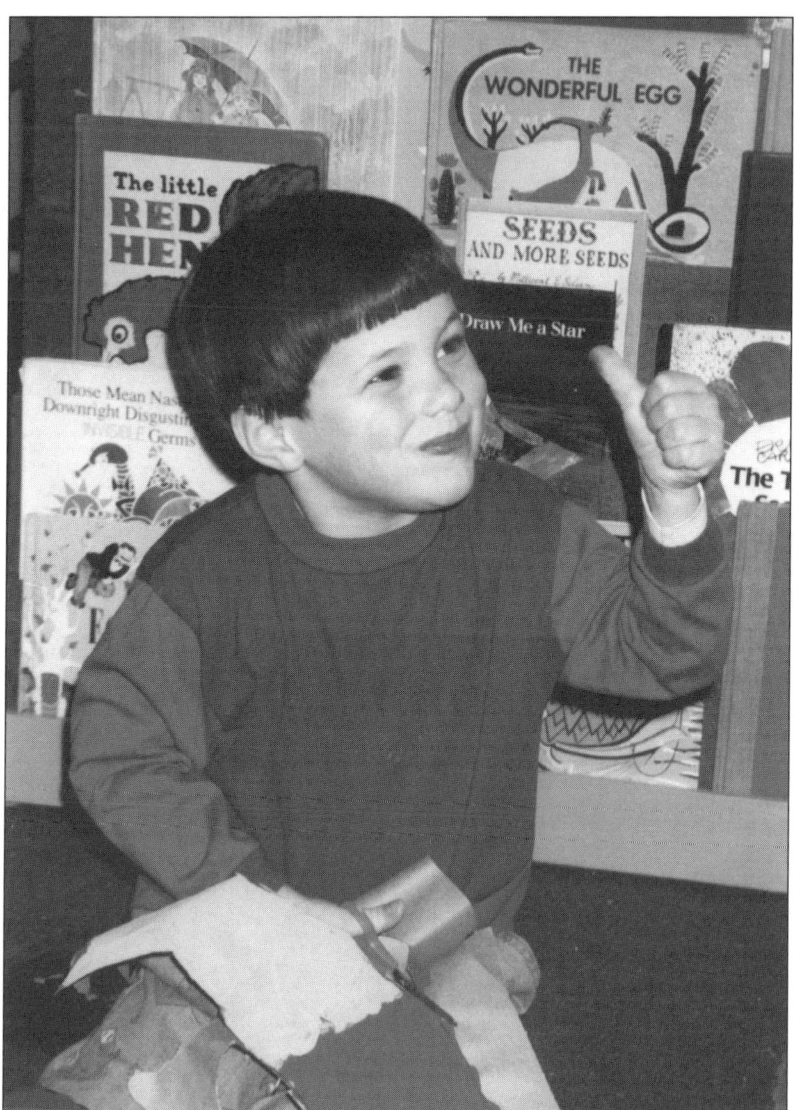

It's worth it.

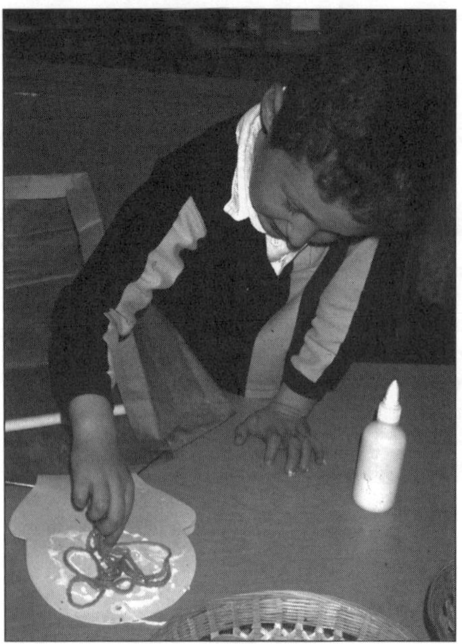

The brain sends messages.

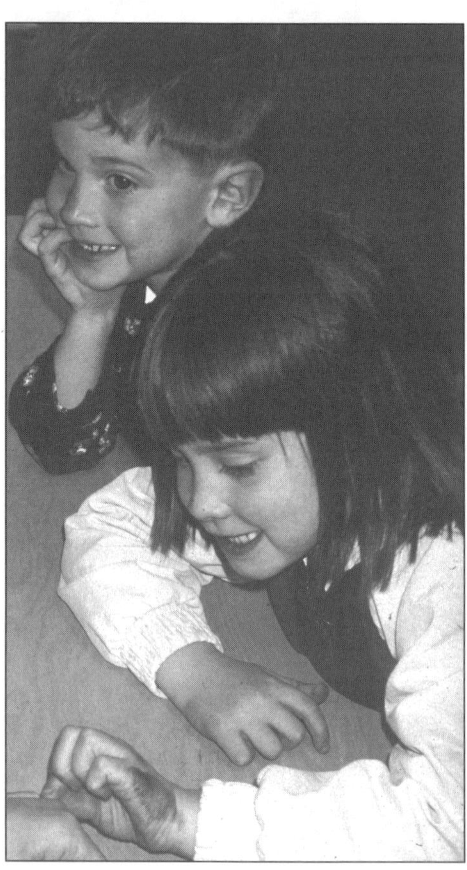

People have a thumb.

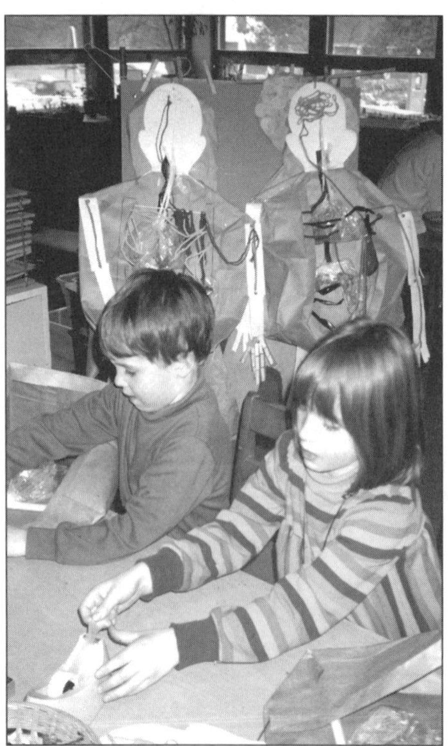

Taping the food tube.

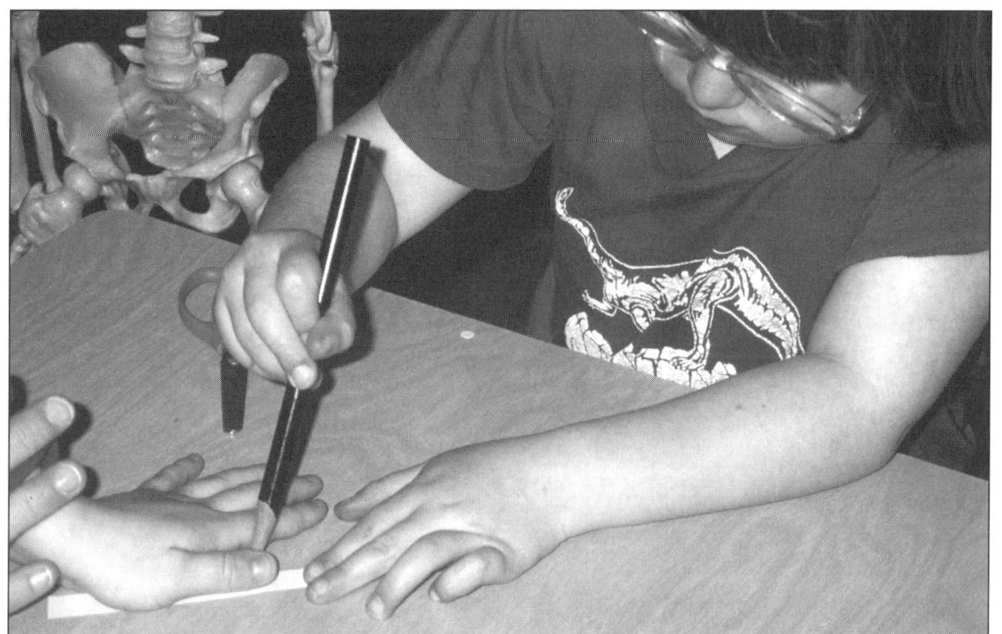

Working in pairs.

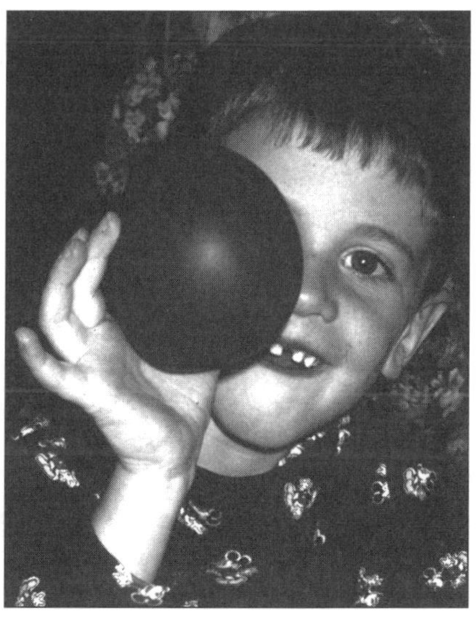

I blew up my heart myself.

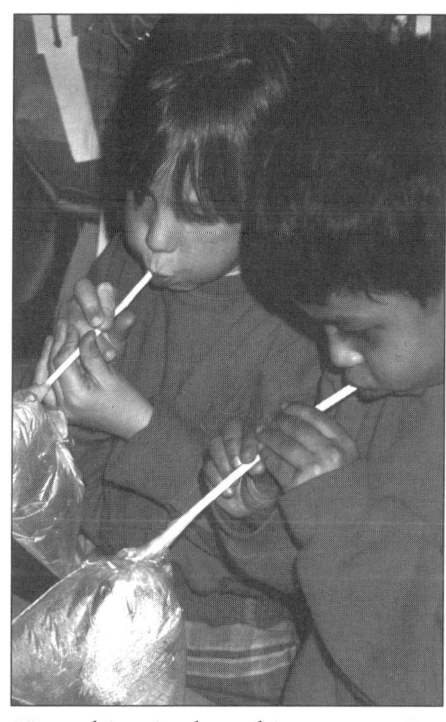

"Breathing in, breathing out . . ."

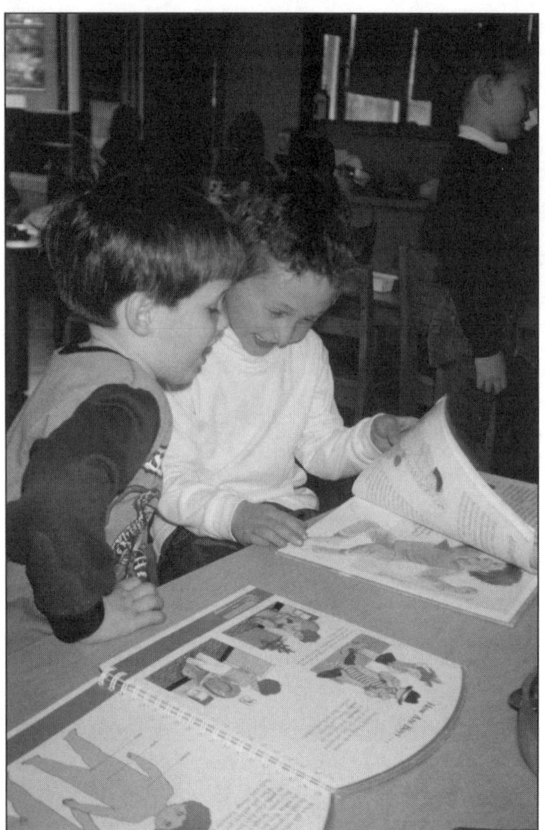

Research in *Outside-In*.

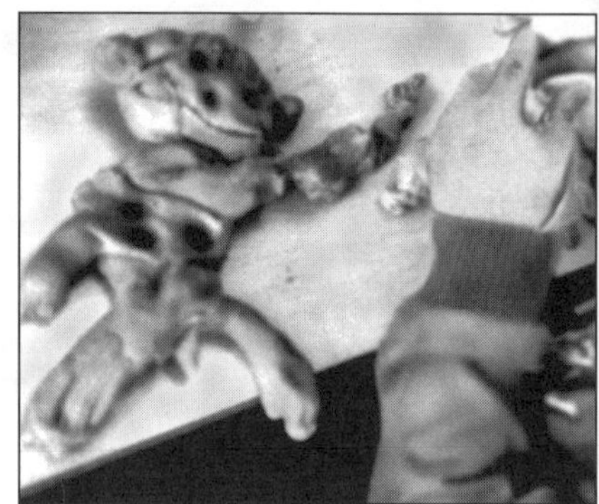

He has milkies and a peepee.

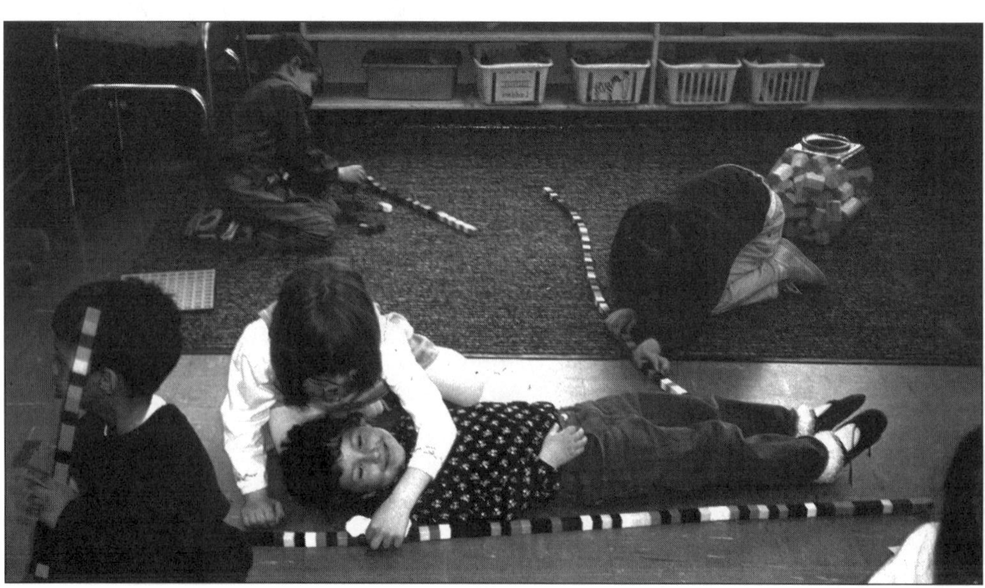

Measuring bodies in Unifix cubes.

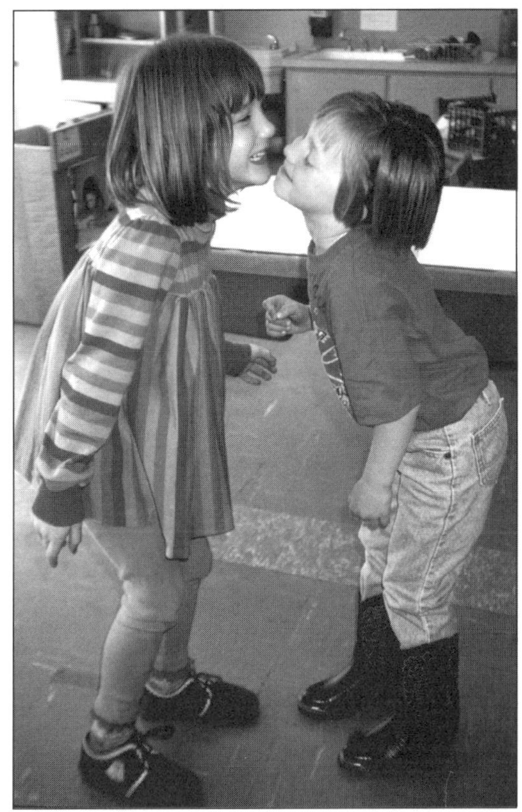

Chin to chin,
partner to partner.

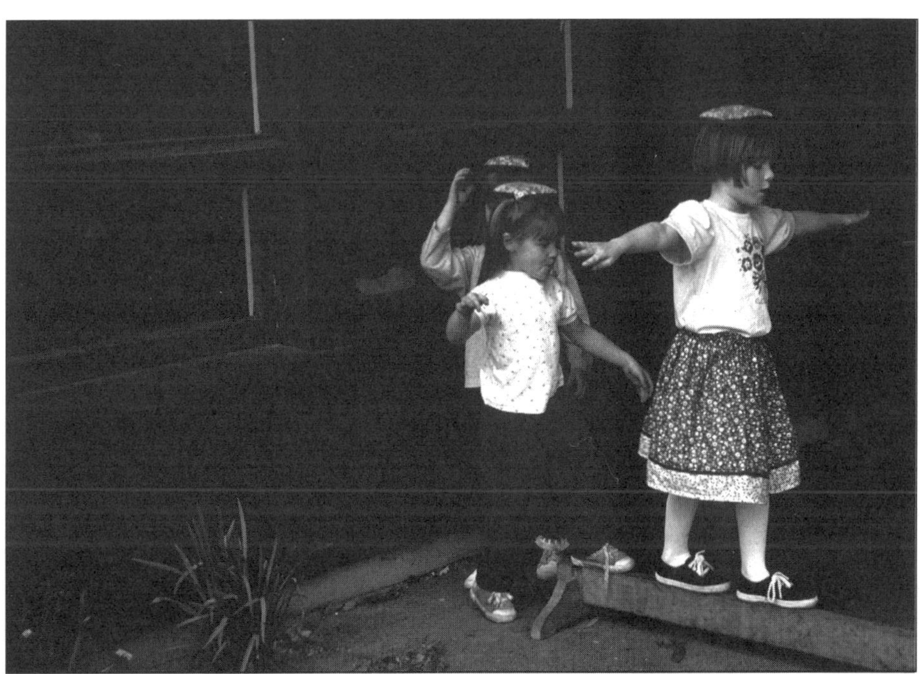

The growing edge–balancing beanbags on the beam.

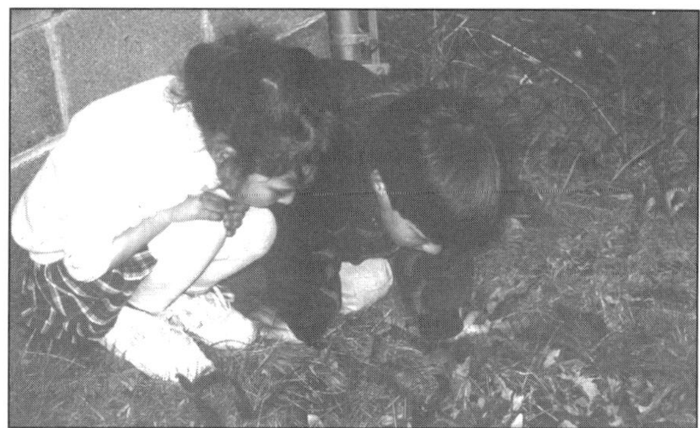

The dead squirrel makes some flowers

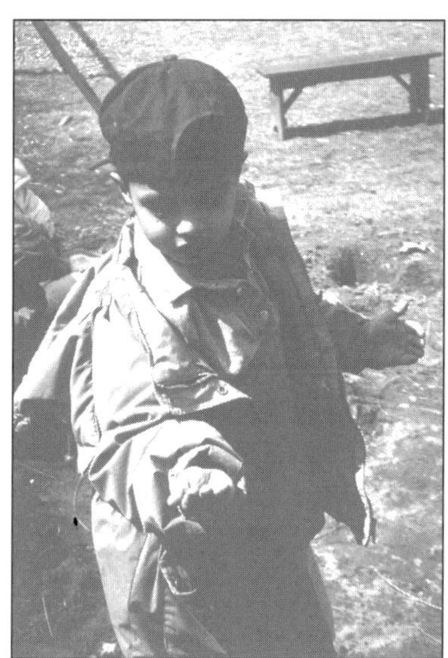

Worms are our partners.

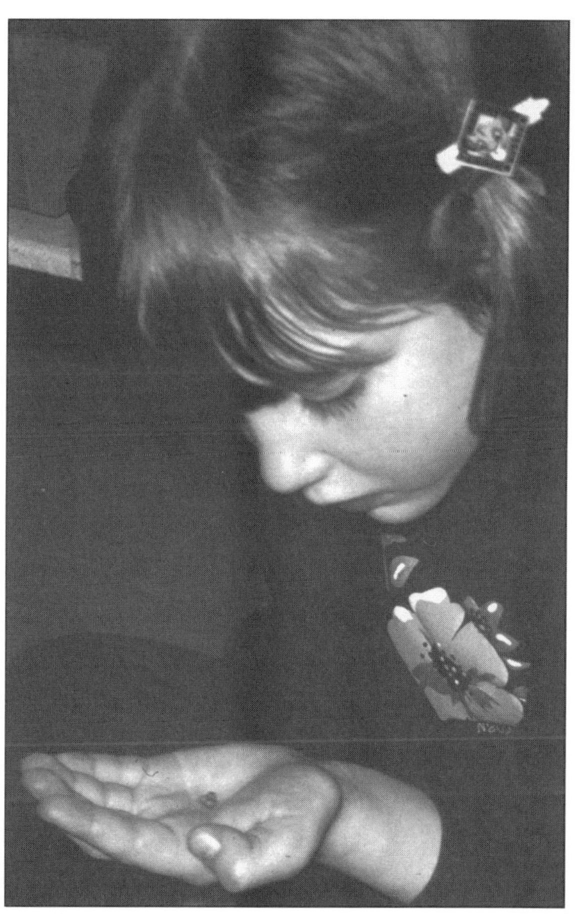

Seeds have grow power.

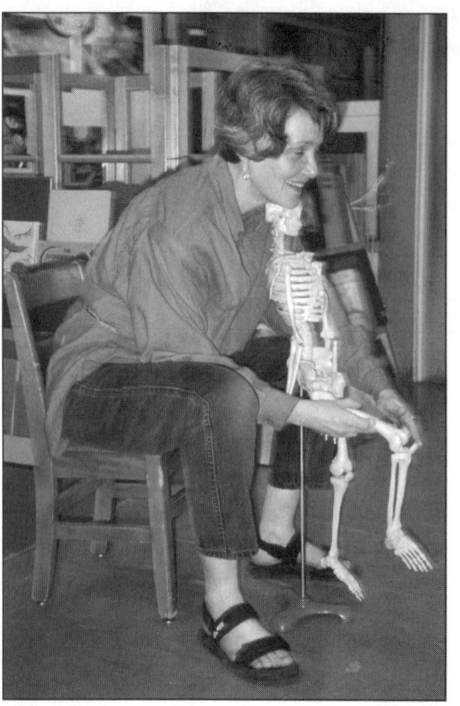

The knee bone's connected . . .

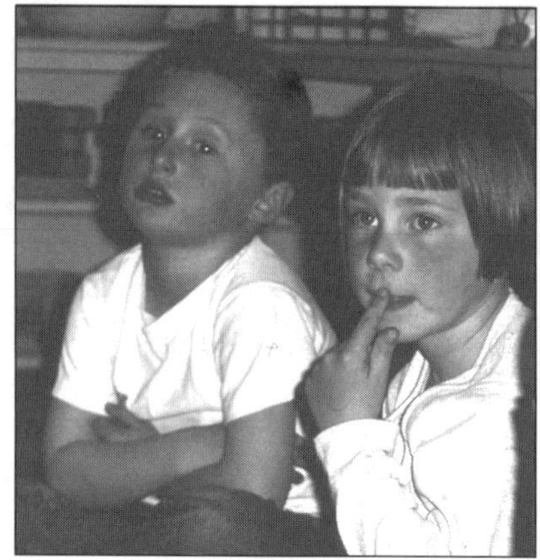

What if the babysitter . . . ?

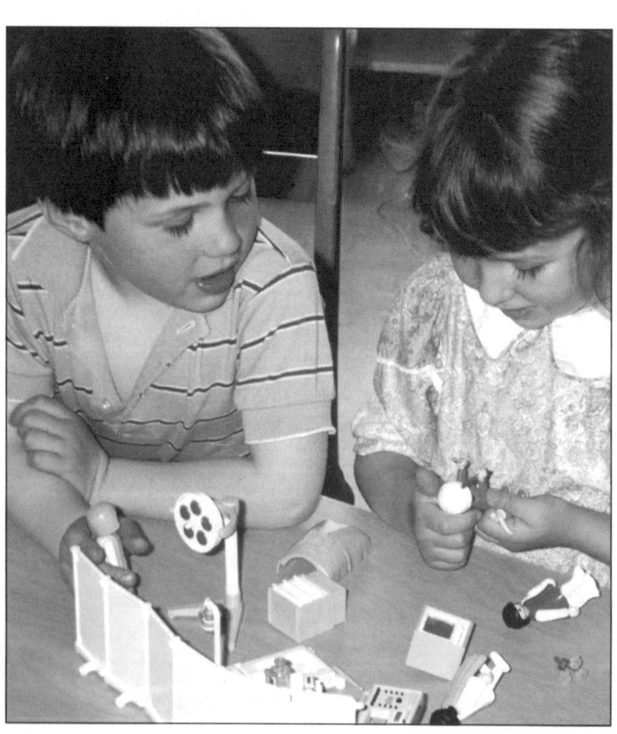

They call 911.

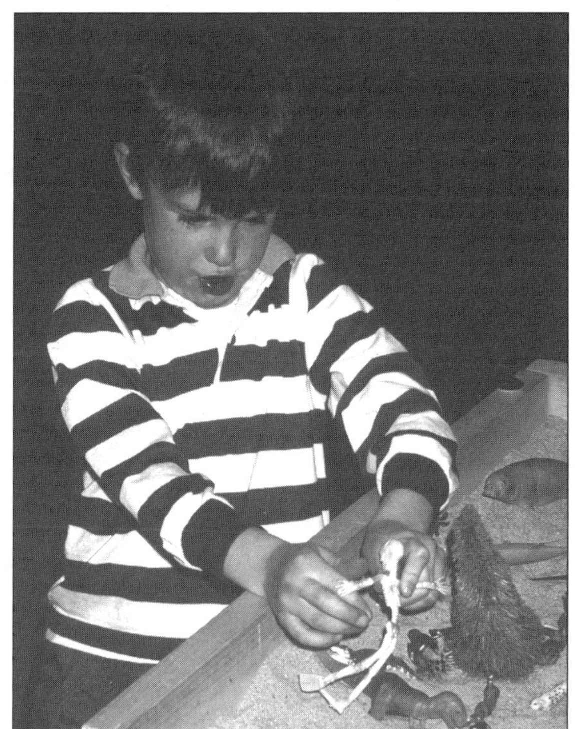
He had super powers, so . . .

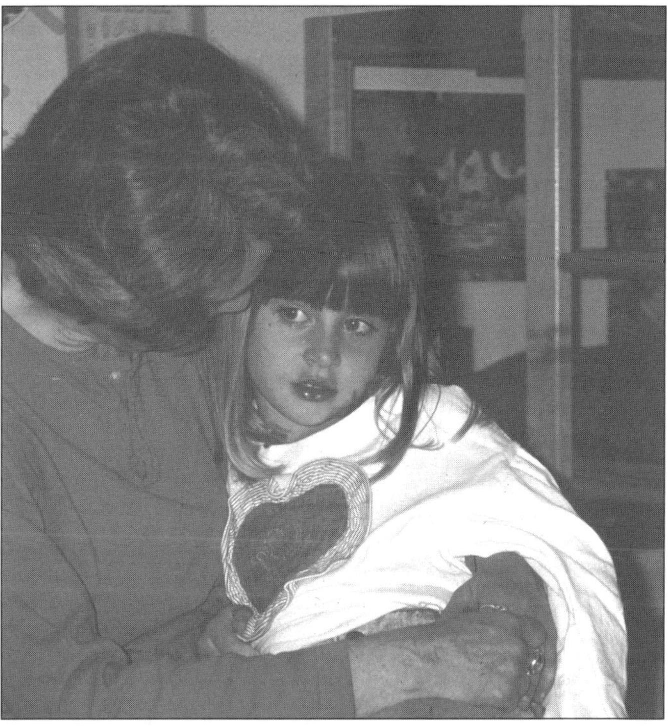
Everyone needs a hug sometimes.

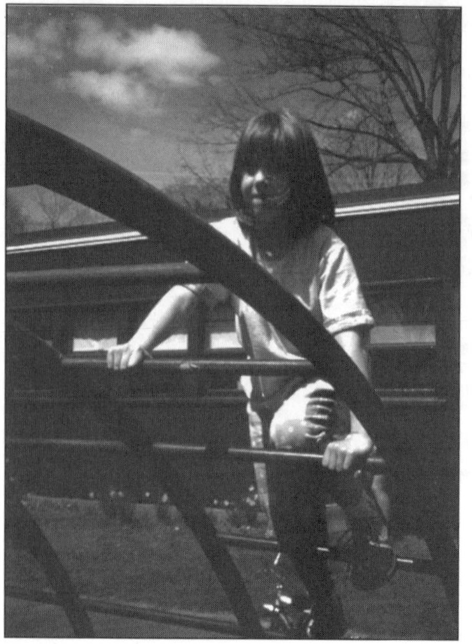

Trying one more time . . .

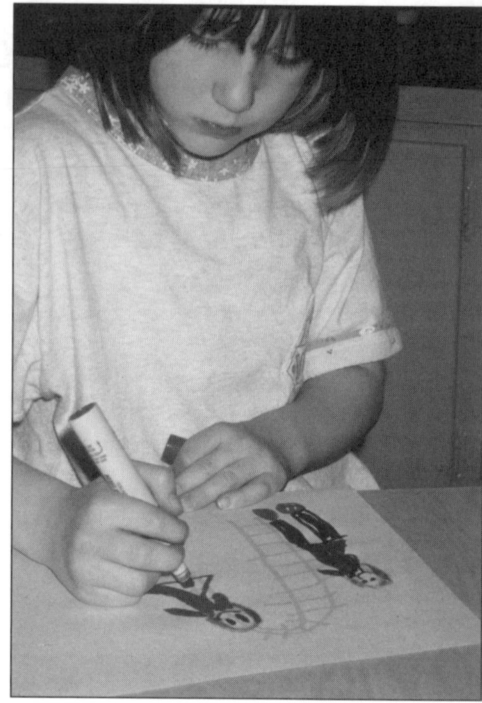

I went Over the Mountain.

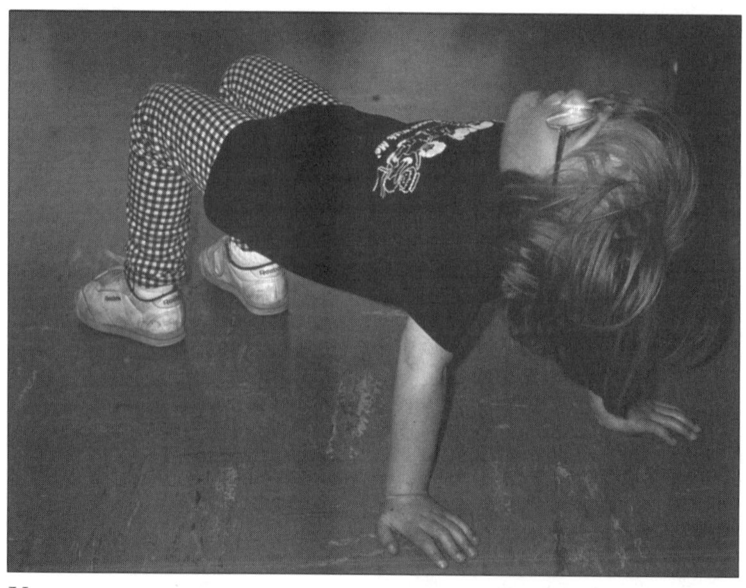

Yoga

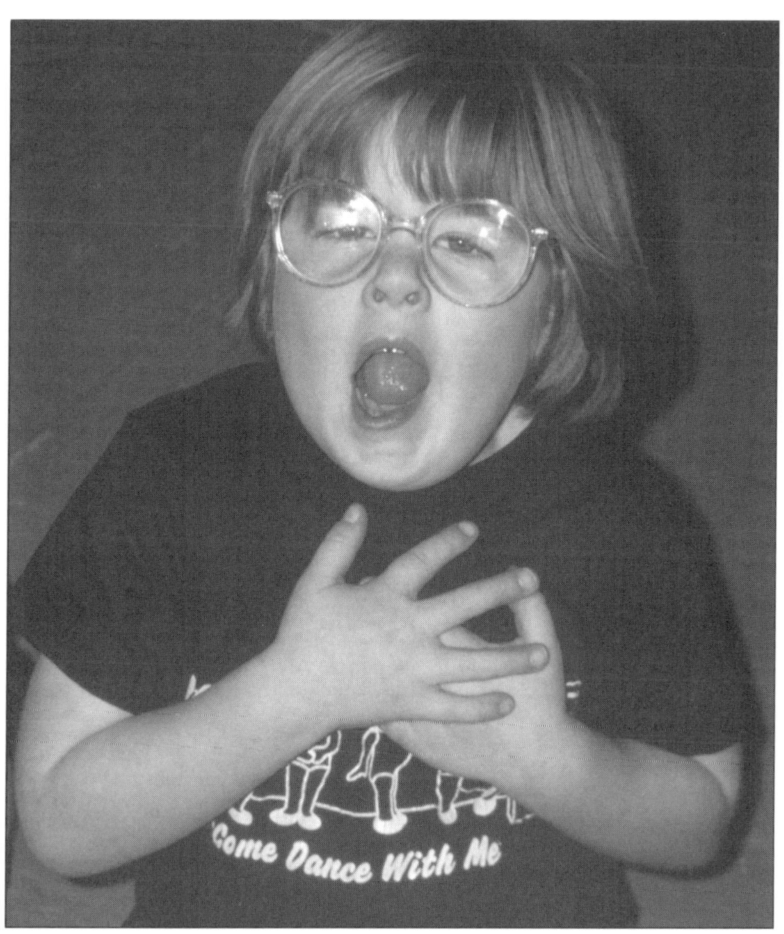

This little light of mine . . .

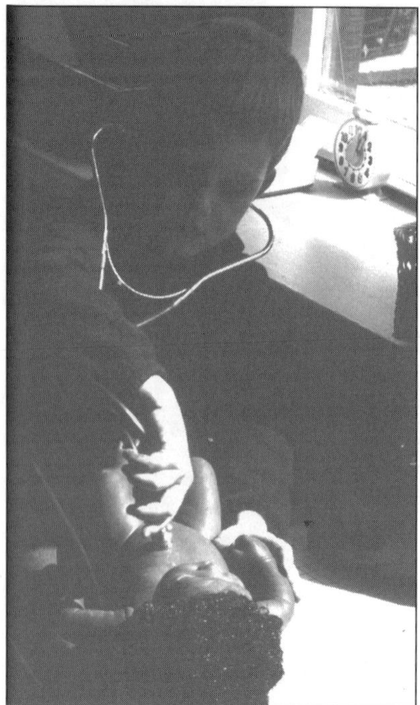

Doctors can help.

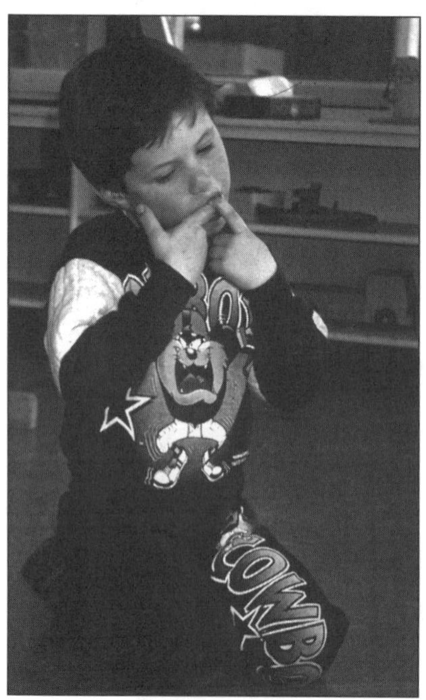

Feeling sad-mad.

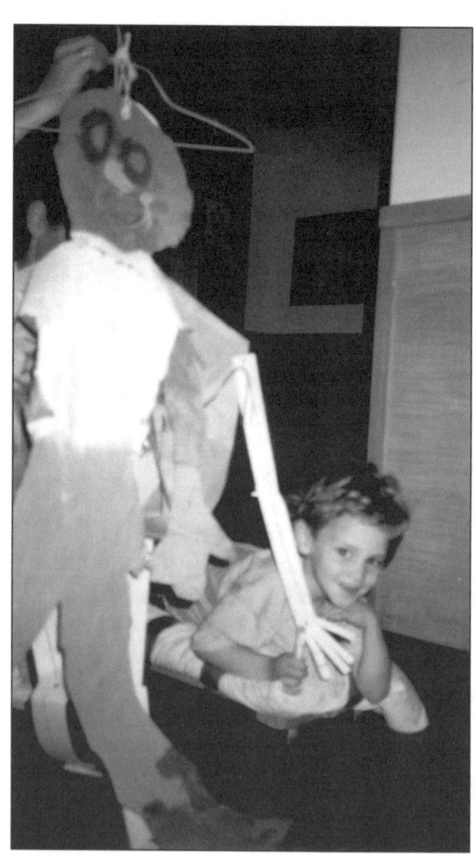

After traction, a belly board.

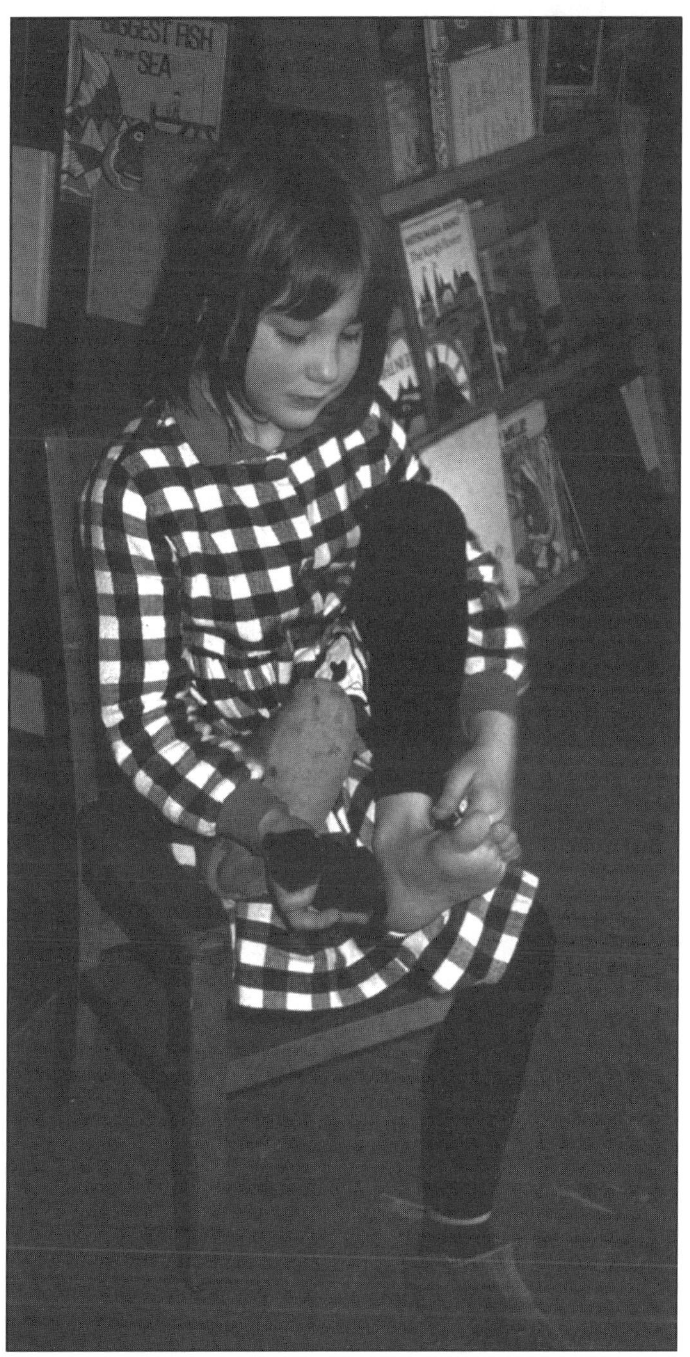

Health bulletin.

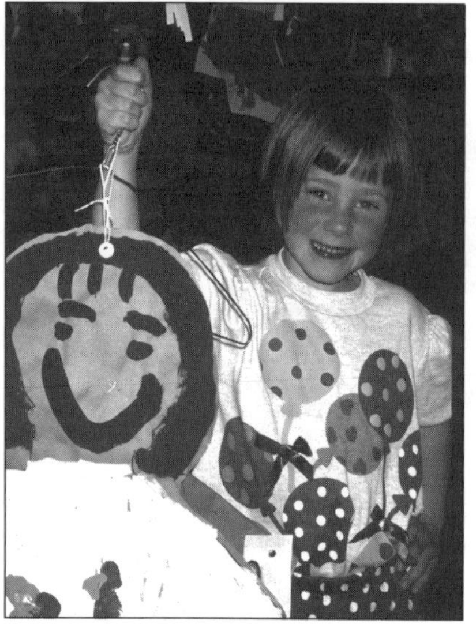

My grandpa wants to borrow it.

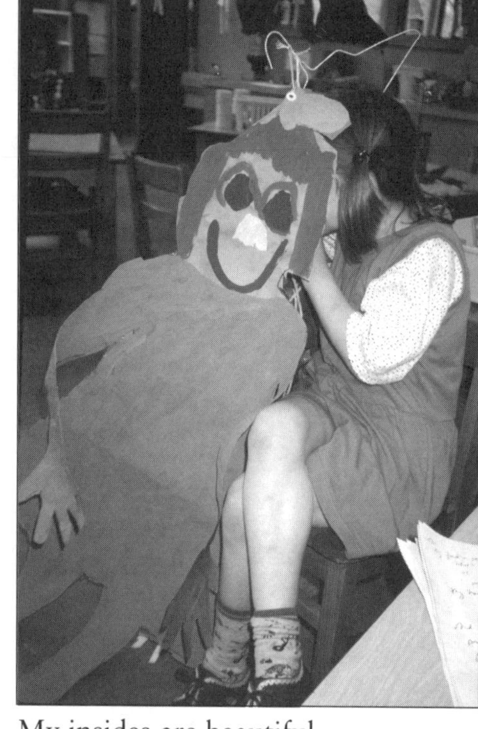

My insides are beautiful.

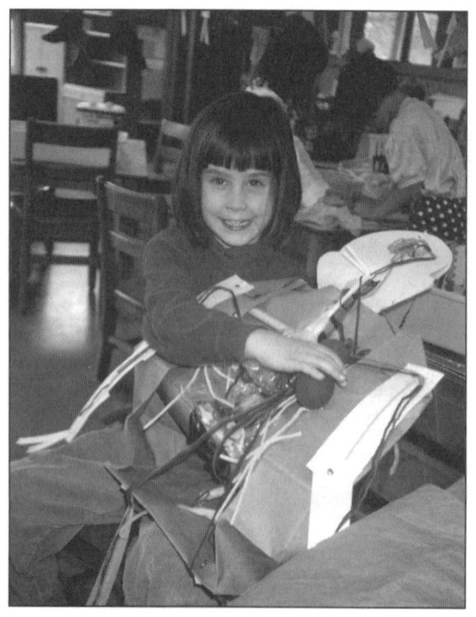

It pumps fast when I run.

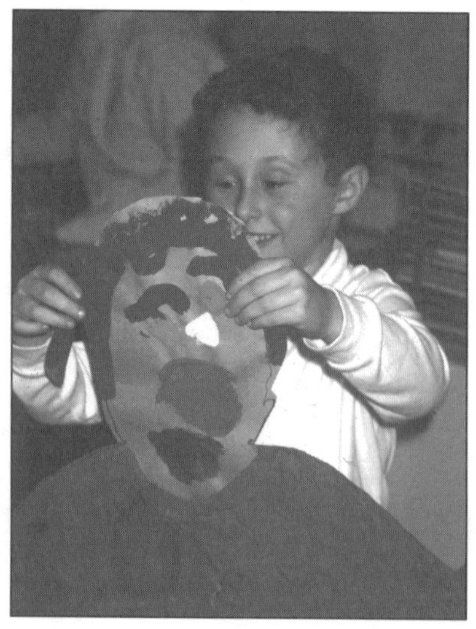

He's got curly hair, just like me.

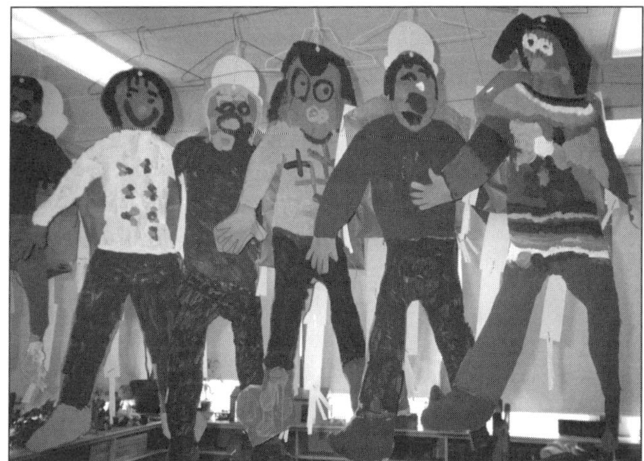

’Tis the gift to be simple . . .

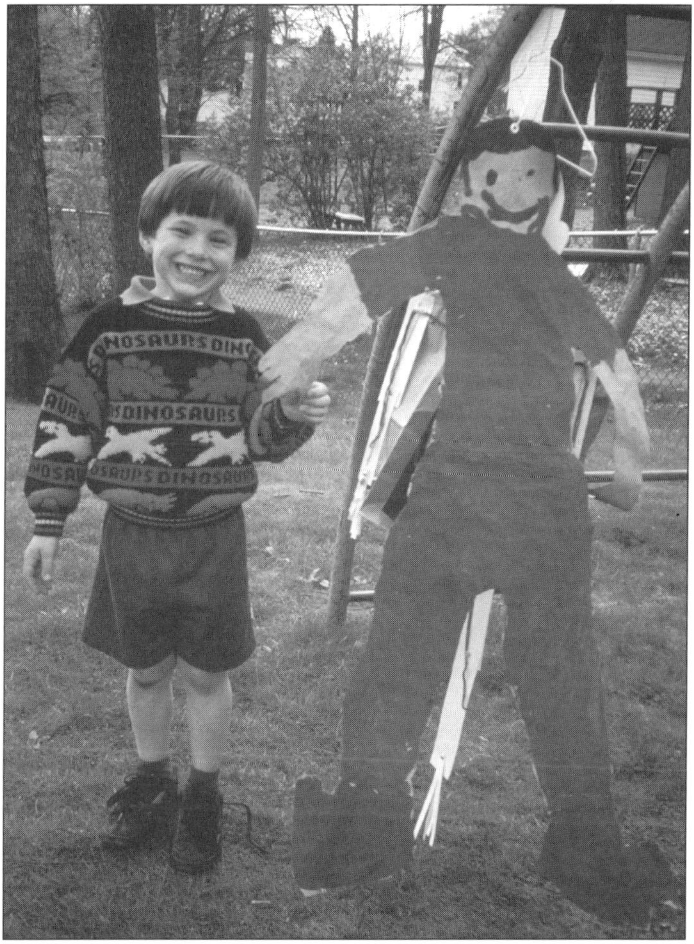

I’m going to keep him forever.

Notes

1 Claire Smallwood and Edwina Riddell, *Outside-In* (Happauge, NY: Barron's, n.d.).
2 Bess-Gene Holt, *Science with Young Children*, rev. ed. (Washington, D.C.: NAEYC, 1989), p. 3.
3 Sarah Pirtle learned this song from Gil Rodriguez. She included it on her cassette "The Wind is Telling Secrets" (see note 8).
4 Song copyright © 1990 by Fred Rogers, Family Communications, Inc. Used by permission.
5 For her naming of the three kinds of power, I am indebted to Starhawk in her book, *Truth or Dare* (San Francisco: Harper and Row, 1987).
6 "Can't Kill the Spirit," copyright © Naomi Littlebear Morena in her Hermanas songbook, available from the author, c/o Quiet Thunder, 11046 Silver Run, Morena Valley CA 92388.
7 In *Songs for Our Small World* (n.d. Presumed to be in the public domain).
8 "My Roots Go Down," copyright © 1984, words and music by Sarah Pirtle, Discovery Music. Used by permission. You will find this song and many others in Sarah's wonderful recording, "Two Hands Hold the Earth." To receive a flyer about her three national award-winning cassettes, her book on self-esteem and music (entitled *Linking Up*), or her school residencies, send a postcard to Sarah Pirtle, The Discovery Center, 63 Main Street, Shelburne Falls MA 01270.
9 "Lots of Worms," words and music by Patty Zeitlin, copyright © 1963, Bullfrog Ballades, ASCAP, used by permission. You will find this song and other irresistible songs to inspire healthy attitudes toward nature on Patty's wonderful recording "Spin, Spider, Spin." To order Patty's cassettes and songbooks, write her at 12233 Ashworth Ave. N, #40, Seattle WA 98133. You can contact Patty about her seminars and workshops at (206) 367-3840.
10 Barry Wadsworth, *Piaget's Theory of Cognitive and Affective Development: Foundations of Constructionism* (New York: Longmans, 1985).
11 Seymour Papert, *Mindstorms* (New York: Basic Books, 1980).
12 Ibid., p. vii.
13 Lucy Calkins, *Lessons from a Child* (Portsmouth, NH: Heineman, 1983), p. 60.
14 Donald Graves, *Writing: Teachers and Children at Work* (Portsmouth, NH: Heineman, 1983), p. 271.

15 Lev Vygotsky, *Thought and Language* (Cambridge, MA: M.I.T. Press, 1986), p. 188.

16 Ibid., p. 191.

17 Jean Harlan, Ph.D., *Science As It Happens! Family Activities with Children Ages 4 to 8* (New York: Henry Holt, 1994).

18 Ibid., p. 16.

19 Howard Rheingold, *They Have a Word for It* (Los Angeles: Jeremy P. Tarcher, Inc., 1988).

20 Ibid., p. 129.

21 Oliver Sachs, *Seeing Voices* (Berkeley: University of California Press, 1989).

22 For brain food, try Robert Sylwester, *A Celebration of Neurons: An Educator's Guide to the Human Brain* (Alexandria, VA: Association for Super-vision and Curriculum Development, 1995).

23 I am indebted to Mona Brookes for isolating these elements, although our respective agendas and methods of using them with children are very different. Mona Brookes, *Drawing with Children* (Los Angeles: Jeremy P. Tarcher, Inc., 1986).

24 Helen Eccleston, *Songs to Grow* (Boston: UUA Press, 1974).

25 Personal communication with Barbara Yarbrough.

26 Bess-Gene Holt, *Science with Young Children.*

27 Ibid., p. 7.

28 Ibid., p. 10.

29 Ibid., p. 3.

30 As suggested by Robert Sylwester in *A Celebration of Neurons.*

31 Thomas F. Plaut, M.D., *Children with Asthma: A Manual for Parents* (Amherst MA: PediPress, 1988, updated 1995).

Index

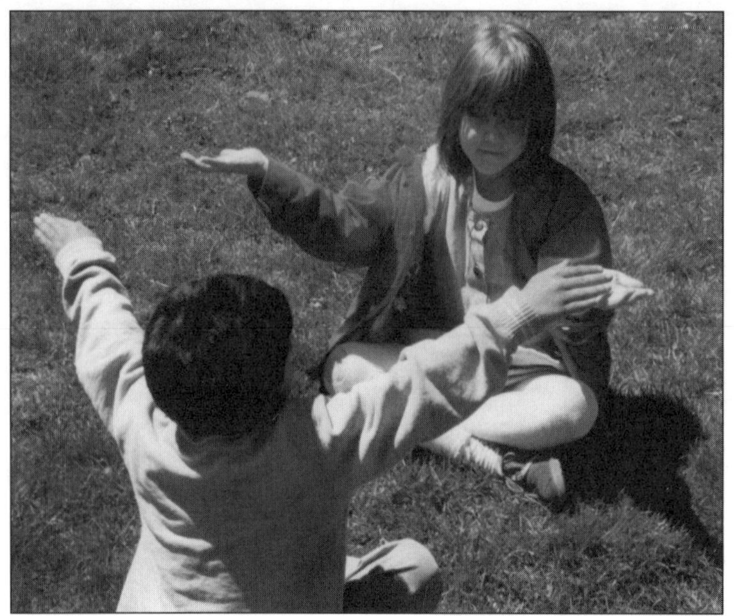

Mirroring.

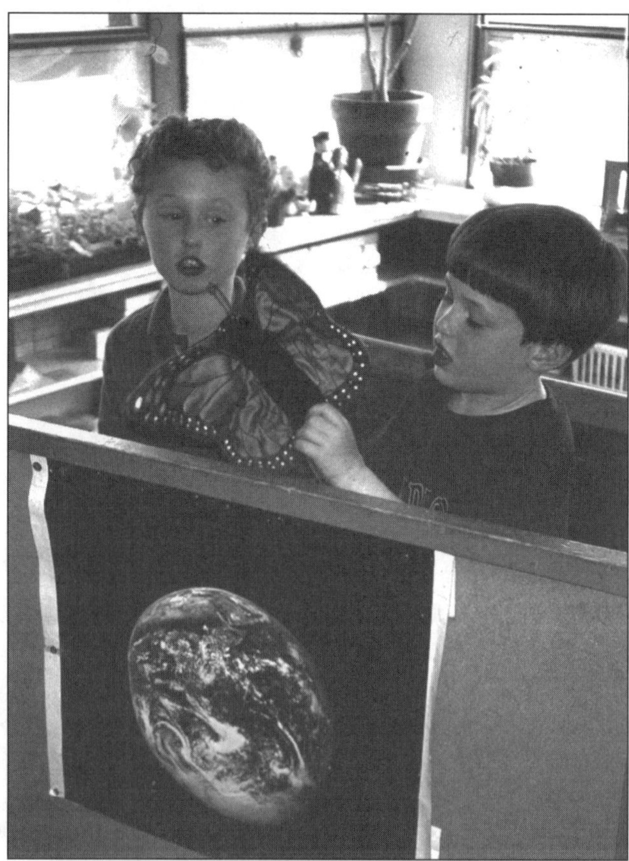

Butterflies practice before they fly.

Dear Reader,

If you wish to deepen and expand your commitment to children by linking with others who share your interest in *The Growing Edge,* please write to me. I may not answer personally, but I will collect and coordinate reader response. If there's a critical mass of us, I'll get back to you with networking suggestions. Please complete the questionnaire that follows.

To encourage and inspire you, I print with permission the personal statements of two prepublication readers.

Sandy Johnson confirms my sense that the development of self-awareness has far-reaching implications for environmental stewardship. Self-esteem is critical to our psychological well-being. When we value ourselves, we become less judgmental and more willing to take risks. Our potential expands enormously. Understanding that our bodies are sacred, we recognize the same sacredness in the world around us.

A sustainable future depends on our relationship to nature and to each other. Sound earth education is rooted in the notion of interdependence, the place of humanity in the mosaic of vast, complex and dynamic ecosystems that sustain planet earth. Becoming aware of those systems and responsive to them is half the challenge.

The other half of the challenge is advocacy. Children, as Sandy Johnson points out, thrive when they feel successful, part of a solution. The human body is the perfect model for long-term stability through interdependence and cooperation. Learning about their bodies empowers children. They can see and communicate the inextricable connection between earth stewardship and human well-being. Positive self-image flowers naturally into effective advocacy.

The Growing Edge *demonstrates that adults can learn to observe children as mirrors to nature, always in motion, in a state of change, striving for balance. We can cultivate the awareness, the patience and the skills to guide ourselves as we guide children toward more fulfilling lives. Here is the foundation for a sustainable future.*

Robert Olney, elementary science and health teacher; trustee, Maine Audubon Society

(continued)

I am quite beside myself at the fullness of The Growing Edge, the courage it evidences, the at-homedness it grants me. I thank Sandy Johnson for thinking, watching, trying, knowing, trusting, risking, hearing, seeing, telling, sharing, linking, opening, bothering, waiting, writing, writing, writing.

Reading this book is such a relief. It makes such sense and feels so true. It puts words to ideas which feel so good to hold, then allows these to join other ideas. While reading The Growing Edge, *I felt dearly and nearly connected to others near and far, not yet born and long ago, and the physical earth itself as well as energy and power—all kinds!*

Sandy's thoughts are so useful to me as a therapist. I think my work, like teaching, dwells constantly in the sixth sense and I share with her the impossibility of naming it. As I get older I find myself granting it more space and authority than ever before, except perhaps as I welcomed each of my sons into this world.

It would be a mistake to be beguiled into thinking this book is about little kids and a razzle-dazzle curriculum. The Growing Edge *is really an invitation to a revolution.*

Jenifer McKenna, psychotherapist

QUESTIONNAIRE FOR READERS

Name ____

Address ____

Telephone ____

E-mail ____

Workplace ____

Workplace, address/phone ________________________________

Your title/job ____

Please describe the population you serve.

When/how did you first learn of *The Growing Edge?* The Bodyworks curriculum?

Please consider each part of *The Growing Edge.* I. Orientation, II. Journal (1) anecdotes (2) reflections, Theory, Tips for Teachers, Bibliography, Blueprints, Diagrams, Photos. Which were most valuable to you? Why?

Which parts were least valuable to you? Why?

Please rank your interest (High 3 to Low 1). ☐ **Explore/extend The Bodyworks?** ☐ **The Earthworks?** ☐ **Concepts about the process of education (e.g., the leap of energy, the growing edge, the generative form)?**

What other books about learning and teaching have influenced you?

Please attach any responses, anecdotes you've collected from children, parents, colleagues, students. Attach additional sheets, if needed.

Thank you so much for participating. Please return to:

Helen Johnson, c/o GEMINI PRESS, 506 Pine Street, Amherst MA 01002

ORDER FORM

Please send The Growing Edge to:

Name ______________________ Daytime phone ( ) ____________

Address ____

City ______________________ State ____ Zip ____________

Books: ___ copies @ $22.00 each $ ______

Sales Tax 5% if shipped to MA address $ ______

Postage & handling $2.25 ($1.00 each additional book) $ ______

Air Mail @ $3.25 each book $ ______

Total payment enclosed $ ______

Enclosed is my check or money order $ ______

Please charge my MasterCard ☐ or VISA ☐

Account # ____

Expiration date ________ Signature ______________________

Please direct mail orders, remittance, and correspondance to:

Gemini Press, c/o Odyssey BookShop
Village Commons, South Hadley MA 01075
Phone (413) 534-7307 or 1-800-540-7307
FAX (413) 540-3564

ORDER FORM

Please send The Growing Edge to:

Name ______________________ Daytime phone (   ) __________

Address ____

City ______________________ State ____ Zip __________

Books: copies @ $22.00 each $______

Sales Tax 5% if shipped to MA address $______

Postage & handling $2.25 ($1.00 each additional book) $______

Air Mail @ $3.25 each book $______

Total payment enclosed $______

Enclosed is my check or money order $______

Please charge my MasterCard ☐ or VISA ☐

Account # ____

Expiration date ________ Signature ______________________

Please direct mail orders, remittance, and correspondance to:

Gemini Press, c/o Odyssey BookShop
Village Commons, South Hadley MA 01075
Phone (413) 534-7307 or 1-800-540-7307
FAX (413) 540-3564